Fortran Programming for the Behavioral Sciences

Donald J. Veldman
The University of Texas

HOLT, RINEHART AND WINSTON
New York   Chicago   San Francisco   Toronto   London

Copyright © 1967 by
Holt, Rinehart and Winston, Inc.
All rights reserved
Library of Congress Catalog Card Number: 67-11808
ISBN 0-03-065940-X
Printed in the United States of America
456   090   9876

PREFACE

Why should a behavioral scientist learn how to program a computer? The answer is that ability to use a computer vastly increases the efficiency and scope of one's research. A common rejoinder to this argument is that computer programming is a highly technical specialty which is best left in the hands of mathematicians and engineers. Many psychologists, sociologists, and educational researchers believe that they can always find an expert to aid them in a consultative capacity when and if they ever attempt any quantitative studies on a large enough scale to require the use of a computer. There are a variety of these common misconceptions about computers and their use which we hope this book will help to correct.

Consider the notion that computers are only practical in large-scale quantitative research. The advantages of using a computer are certainly more obvious in large-scale investigations; a large proportion of the studies that are considered ordinary today would never have been attempted ten years ago because of the inordinate costs of gathering and analyzing so much data. Although most of us had plenty of experience mashing the keys of a desk calculator during our research training, those who have learned to use computer programs — even if they have not yet learned how to write them — seldom use a desk calculator for routine calculations, even with small samples. The advantages of speed and errorless computation more than compensate for the trouble of putting the raw data into punched-card form. As we will see in Chapter 2, even this disadvantage evaporates when one has access to a remote time-shared terminal in the latest computer systems.

Another major misconception is that programming is an esoteric specialty of mathematicians. In the early days of computer development this did tend to be true. Modern programming languages, however, are remarkably close to algebraic notation and require no training in higher mathematics or special knowledge of electronics. You can become a competent computer programmer in much less time than it took you to learn the techniques of statistical analysis.

Many research workers have had rather disillusioning experiences with consultants in the field of computer programming. It has been the author's observation that some researchers actually have spent more time explaining a single data-processing problem to a consultant than they would have spent in learning the Fortran programming language. Of course, if you are fortunate enough to have access to the services of a behavioral scientist who programs, the difficulties of communication will be greatly lessened. For some time to come, though, there will not be enough of these people to meet the need. In any event, no consultant — no matter how skilled — can be familiar with all of the subtleties and possibilities involved in the research of everyone who comes to him for assistance. In fact, the probability is small that any consultant knows as much about your area of investigation as you do, and even smaller that he is as interested in it as you are. Ability to program a computer frees you of dependence upon consultants, enabling you to formulate procedures in computer-oriented terms and to carry out these procedures without expensive and often unsatisfactory help.

There are other benefits that accrue from knowledge of computer programming. All too often, a standard statistical routine from a computer-center library must be modified slightly to handle a particular problem. You can do this yourself without soliciting the help of a specialist. You can make use of a computer almost immediately with a newly published methodological innovation or test out a new technique of your own invention without having to convince some programmer that a sufficient need exists to warrant his time. Most computer programs are written for particular data-processing jobs that are relatively simple, but tremendously valuable in terms of the time, effort, and money saved. If you can program, you can write such routines whenever they are needed.

This is the type of book I needed when I began trying to use a computer for statistical analysis back in 1960. It represents an attempt to systematize the most essential aspects of what I have learned since then. Like any other book which does not attempt an encyclopedic coverage of a field, it is inevitably biased toward the kind of research in which I have been engaged and those aspects of computer applications which I think I understand best.

If there is an underlying theme here, it is the notion that Fortran is a language, and that the basic principles of language learning hold for it as well as for any language. The most important of these principles is that the ability to use the language effectively can be acquired only through actual experience in its use. Exercise problems have been included with each chapter, but the serious student of the language cannot be content with the small amount of practice they provide. To achieve real facility of expression, a kind of "divergent thinking" about problem-solving is indispensable. As in the use of any language, there are always alternative ways of expressing the same idea; in computer programming the same results can always be obtained by more than one procedure. Some methods are more efficient than others, just as some ways of expressing an idea in natural language are more elegant than others. The skilled writer can express the same idea in many ways; the skilled programmer is able to select the most elegant procedure from among many possible alternatives. We learn elegance of expression by paying close attention to the effects our verbalizations have on others, experimenting with various ways of conveying our ideas. The programmer, too, will try out various methods of communicating with the computer. The criterion is unambiguous; the machine either yields the right answers or it fails to understand the programmer's intent. The programmer's skill, then, is a direct function of the amount of experience he has in communicating with computers. A book such as this can present the vocabulary and grammar of the language, and can give examples of fluent use of the language, but these are only the raw materials. How well you learn to use them is up to you.

The subroutines and programs described in Chapters 8 through 12 constitute a comprehensive library of statistical routines. Although the investment of time and effort is considerable, it may be worthwhile to have the complete set of routines punched at your installation — particularly if this book is to be used as the text for a course in computer applications. The author has found that a student can learn a great deal about statistical analysis, and can build a strong base for learning Fortran, simply by running each program in a library such as this. The best experience, of course, is to apply the programs to data obtained by the student in his own research, but a set of artificial data such as that provided here may simplify discussions of the methods in class.

Many individuals and organizations have contributed to this book either directly or indirectly. The graduate students who have taken the author's course in computer methods in the Department of Educational Psychology at The University of Texas during the last three years have been of enormous assistance with their suggestions as well as their willingness to point out weak areas in the Fortran chapters.

Among my colleagues, Dr. Earl Jennings deserves special thanks for his continued interest and for his generous assistance in the development of the chapters on multivariate techniques. Richard Purnell, Hugh Poynor, and John Sheffield contributed many valuable critical reviews of particular chapters, as well as assistance in the preparation and check-out of the programs included here. My data-processing specialist staff — Peggy Hampton, Janie Opheim, Susan Sullivan, and Kay Sullivan — provided superb technical support and took care of many of my myriad mistakes without complaint. Most of the three major mauscript revisions were typed by Peggy Hampton with the help of Jane Portis.

This book could not have been completed without the financial support of the U. S. Public Health Service grant titled "Computer Analysis of Personality" (Grant No. MH06823). For their continuing support and encouragement, the author wishes especially to thank Doctors Robert F. Peck and Carson McGuire, who are largely responsible for the development of facilities and research programs which provided much of the background for this book. The University of Texas Computation Center and Linguistics Research Center provided the hardware and systems used to test the programs, and their staffs were unfailingly cooperative in providing the specialized assistance needed from time to time.

My wife and children have shown remarkable patience with me during the writing of this book, for which I am grateful.

D.J.V.

Austin, Texas
February 1967

CONTENTS

Preface   iii

1. Introduction to Computer Systems   1

    General description   1
    A brief history of computers   3
    Input media   5
    Output media   7
    Storage media   7
    Processing control   9
    Time-shared remote consoles   11

2. Programming Languages and Applications   14

    Stages of processing   16
    Levels of computer language   17
    List-processing languages   20
    Program libraries and systems   22
    Behavioral science applications   24

3. Punch-Card Processing   30

    Organization and coding of data   34
    Data-card fields and formats   35
    Card-sorting techniques   38

viii   CONTENTS

4. Fortran: Vocabulary and Grammar   43

    Fortran compiler programs   44
    Fortran program card format   46
    Constants and variables   47
    Array variables and subscripts   49
    Reservation of storage areas   51
    Format statements   52
    Input and output statements   58
    Magnetic tape statements   61
    Input/output of array variables   63
    Variable format   68
    Replacement statements   68
    Decision statements   72
    The DO statement   76
    Functions   80
    Frequently used library functions   81
    Terminating a program   82
    Summary of Fortran statements   82

5. Fortran: Program Organization   86

    Flow charts   87
    Program ONE   89
    Program TWO   90
    Program THREE   92
    Program FOUR   93
    Program FIVE   95
    Program SIX   96
    Program SEVEN   97
    Program EIGHT   99
    Program NINE   101
    Program TEN   104
    Program ELEVEN   107
    Program TWELVE   110

6. Fortran: Functions and Subroutines   115

    Formulas as functions   115
    Subprogram organization   116
    Dimensioned arrays   118
    Mode agreement   119
    Variable dimension specifications   119
    Subroutine subprograms   120
    Function subprograms   121
    Statistical functions and subroutines   123

Contents   **ix**

      Input deck arrangement   132
      Array output subroutines   134

7. Fortran: Matrix Algebra   142

      Definitions and notation   142
      Equality of matrices   144
      Transpose of a matrix   144
      Square and symmetric matrices   145
      Diagonal, scalar, and identity matrices   145
      Matrix addition and subtraction   147
      Matrix multiplication   148
      Matrix multiplication by a scalar   153
      Vector multiplication by scalars   153
      Matrix multiplication by vectors   154
      Matrix multiplication by diagonal matrices   155
      Matrix inversion   156
      Square roots and powers of diagonal matrices   159
      Normalization   160
      Standardization   161

8. Test Scoring and Distribution Statistics   164

      Multiple-choice tests   164
      Questionnaires   165
      Rating scales   165
      Data recording   166
      Program TESTAT   170
      Arrangement of the input deck for Program TESTAT   171
      Output listings   177
      Program DISTAT   181
      Computer systems without tape units   185

9. Intercorrelation and Factor Analysis   190

      Intercorrelation subroutines   191
      Program LAGCOR: Auto- and cross-lag intercorrelation   200
      Factor analysis   206
      Roots and vectors of a matrix   207
      Principal axis factor scores   213
      Rotation of factor axes   213
      Varimax rotated factor scores   215
      Image analysis   218
      Program FACTOR   219
      Comparison of factors   236
      Program RELATE   238

10. Analysis of Variance 246

    Program ANOVAR   247
    Input deck organization   247
    Program organization   249
    Program AVAR23   257
    Input deck arrangement   258
    Program organization   259
    Multiple discriminant analysis   268
    Program DSCRIM   273

11. Regression Analysis 281

    Canonical correlation analysis   282
    Program CANONA   286
    Multiple regression analysis   294
    Program REGRAN   295

12. Miscellaneous Statistical Methods 308

    Hierarchical grouping analysis   308
    Program HGROUP   311
    Successive intervals scaling   318
    Program TSCALE   319
    Contingency table construction   326
    Program CONTAB   327
    Chi-square analysis   332
    Program CHICHI   332

13. Compilation and Analysis of Verbal Data 338

    Some recent research with verbal data   339
    Number systems and alphameric data   340
    Compilation of a response list   347
    Stage one: List compilation   348
    Stage two: Frequency ordering   352
    Stage three: Alphabetic content ordering   353
    Compilation by sublisting   355
    Program LISTB   360
    Response grouping   366
    Program SCORE   370
    Function LGTH   374
    Subroutine ROOT   376

Answers to Review Exercises   380
References   392
Index   397

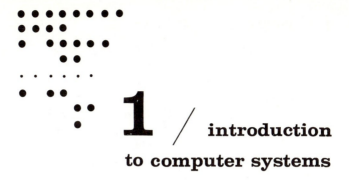

1 / introduction to computer systems

Few words in current use arouse more interest than "computer." Thanks to the cartoonists and science-fiction dramatists, the word evokes a complex image emotionally loaded with both anxiety and wry humor. One imagines a room full of complex machinery, whirring reels of tape, enigmatic boxes emitting eerie sounds, huge consoles full of blinking lights—and a dedicated man in a white coat who seems almost a servant to the machine.

In some ways the image is valid. Most computers do occupy a large area, although they typically consist of a number of small machines connected by cables, and the cabinets are seldom more than six feet high. Some of the input and output units do make noise, but the central computational unit is completely silent. Blinking lights are not uncommon, but they seem to be going out of fashion as the sophistication of the hardware increases. Regarding the dedicated servant in the white coat, the image has little basis in reality. Some of these "servants" have been known to kick a balky unit to get it started, and most of them speak of computers with about as much reverence as they do of their lawnmowers.

GENERAL DESCRIPTION

The term "computer" may be considered an abbreviation of *stored-program digital computer system*. There are two basically different types of computers in use today: *analog* and *digital*. The procedures in this book were developed exclusively for digital computers, but we will discuss the differences between the two types in order to emphasize certain important characteristics of digital machines. The term "system" implies the fact that modern computers consist of a number of semiautonomous machines interconnected and centrally controlled. Another important characteristic of modern digital computer systems is that the programs of instructions that control their operations are stored in the same memory units which hold the data processed by these programs. Until 1950, the few computers in existence carried out a fixed sequence of operations which were hand-wired into an external plug board for every problem. Internal storage of the program not only increases the speed of operation, but also permits the machine to modify its own instruction sequence automatically during the processing.

Analog versus Digital. The terms "analog" and "digital" refer to different ways of representing quantitative information. Analog devices register quantities as the physical status of some medium that can vary *continuously* over a range of values. A *thermometer* is an analog device; the level of liquid in its stem can assume an infinite number of possible positions. A *slide rule* is a simple analog calculator. Highly sophisticated analog computers—some of them entirely electronic—are used today primarily in the fields of engineering.

Digital devices are exemplified by the ordinary *light switch* with its two possible states, *on* and *off*. The representation of information is a *discrete* variable; only a few specific values can be represented by a digital unit. An *abacus* is a digital calculating device, using a series of wires strung with movable beads to indicate numerical values. Each bead on its wire must be considered at one end or the other; in-between values are not allowed. The *adding machine* or desk calculator is also a digital device. Each geared number wheel has ten possible positions, and only ten. Most of the computers in use today are digital machines, which employ a series of binary (two-state) units to represent numerical values and to code qualitative data.

A very important difference between analog and digital calculation may be noted with regard to the problem of accuracy. For example, the fraction $\frac{1}{3}$ can be represented exactly by an analog device, within the limits of the physical device itself. The nature of the physical unit is an absolute limit, however. With a digital device, the fraction $\frac{1}{3}$ cannot be represented exactly by physical units which have a number of states not divisible by three. The interesting thing here is that the value of the fraction *can be approximated* to any desired degree of accuracy, including accuracy beyond the practical limits of analog devices, simply by increasing the number of physical units (such as counter wheels) in the device. This essential difference between analog and digital machines can become critically important in calculations involving long series of mathematical operations, since device errors tend to accumulate.

Computer System Components. A stored-program digital computer system consists of a variety of electronic and mechanical devices which may be grouped functionally into four major subsystems: (1) input, (2) output, (3) storage, and (4) processing control. Figure 1-1 illustrates the relationships among these components in terms of the flow of data through the system.

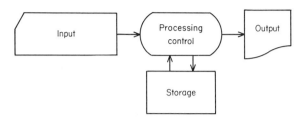

FIGURE 1-1. Functional components of a computer system.

The *input* section includes machines that convert information from external media such as punched cards into signals which can be recorded in central storage and processed according to a program of instructions. The computer also receives its own instructions through these devices.

The *output* devices convert information from central storage into some kind of display or hard copy, such as printed pages. With the input devices, these machines are the slowest part of the computer system, often forcing the central processing unit to operate far below maximum efficiency.

The *storage* unit in most modern computer systems is an intricate matrix of wires strung through as many as 16 million tiny iron rings. Each ring may be in one of two magnetic states, and constitutes the basic information-recording unit of the computer system. Computer memory units are sometimes called "core storage" after these little metal cores. This and other types of storage devices will be discussed in more detail later in this chapter.

The *processing control* section is the heart of the system. It interprets the instructions and sequences their execution, whether they concern operation of the input and output devices, retrieval of data from storage, or the calculation of new data from old. This part of the computer system has advanced greatly in its capabilities compared to the early machines as more and more of the routine functions are wired permanently into the hardware instead of being performed under control of programmed instructions (software).

A BRIEF HISTORY OF COMPUTERS[1]

Although the computer revolution in this country is only about fifteen years old, with almost all of the explosive development since 1953, the use of machines for numerical calculation has been traced as far back as the

---

[1] The material in this section was abstracted from a number of sources (Borko, 1962; Green, 1963; Schmidt and Meyers, 1965). Borko's treatment of the topic is especially thorough and well-illustrated.

time of the ancient Greeks. The use of mechanical devices as an aid in calculation can be traced back to 3000 B.C., when the Babylonians began to use marks on a dust-covered tablet instead of their fingers for counting. The invention of the abacus by the Chinese has also been traced this far back in man's history. This device is still widely used in the Orient as an aid in calculation; a well-publicized race in 1946 between a skilled abacus user and an electric desk calculator operator resulted in a clear victory for the abacus.

Although remnants of an ancient Greek calculator strongly suggest that such machinery was in use around 100 A.D., the first "modern" mechanical calculating aid was constructed in 1617 by John Napier, the Scot who invented logarithms. This device consisted of a set of numbered rods which were used to assist multiplication, and was called "Napier's Bones." In 1642 Blaise Pascal constructed a mechanical adding machine, and in 1694 Gottfried Leibnitz completed a model of a multiplying calculator. The true forerunner of the modern computer was Charles Babbage's "Difference Engine," constructed in 1822. This machine calculated and printed mathematical tables.

Meanwhile, another line of development had begun which was to have far-reaching effects on the future of data-processing techniques. As early as 1728 French weavers employed cards with holes in them as a means of automatically controlling the operation of their looms. Joseph Jacquard in 1801 demonstrated a loom which used a punched-card system for controlling the patterns and colors of the woven material. Certainly the most significant first in the history of data processing, however, was Herman Hollerith's use of punched cards for the 1890 census of the United States population.

The first automatic calculator was the work of Howard Aiken of Harvard University, aided by the International Business Machines Corporation. This machine, first operational in 1944, was constructed from thousands of mechanical counter wheels and electrical relays.

The first electronic computer was called Eniac. It was built by J. P. Eckert and J. W. Mauchly at the Moore School of Engineering, University of Pennsylvania, in 1946. This machine contained 18,000 vacuum tubes, and was externally programmed by means of plug boards which had to be changed for every problem. Edvac was the next machine built by Eckert and Mauchly in 1950, and was particularly important for its use of the binary number system and an internally stored program. The British also developed a similar machine called Edsac which was first operated in 1949 at the Cambridge University Mathematical Laboratory. A machine called Whirlwind I, built at the Massachusetts Institute of Technology, was fitted with the first core memory unit in 1953, and the computer revolution had begun. The introduction of transistors in 1958 to replace vacuum tubes further increased the rate of technological improvement.

Input Media   5

Development of commercial computers began with the production of Univac-I by Sperry Rand for delivery to the Census Bureau in 1951. Later in the 1950s IBM brought out their 704 and 650 models and began to acquire a larger and larger share of the commercial computer market. Today this company sells or rents roughly three-quarters of all the computers manufactured.

The rate of technical advance in the capabilities of computing machinery has been truly phenomenal. The speed of internal operations has increased from 3/10 of a second per addition in 1944 to 1.5 *ten-millionths* of a second (1.5 nanoseconds) today. The size of the central storage has grown from 72 locations in 1944 to more than 262,000 locations of core memory in the largest current machines. The number of machines has grown from 100 in 1951 to an estimated 30,000 in 1965. In the year 1964, a total of 21 companies made 250 different computer models ranging in price from $8800 to $4,300,000. The federal government spent a billion dollars for computing machinery in that year, but commerce and banking in this country have also come to depend on computers to a rather startling degree. It has been estimated that by 1970, without computers, all of the women in the United States between the ages of 21 and 45 would be needed by the banks just to process checks.

INPUT MEDIA

By far the most common means of entering information into a computer is the *punched card*. Almost all computers have card-reading devices attached to them, and both instructions to the computer and data to be processed are commonly entered in this manner. Chapter 3 will treat this topic in considerable detail.

Another widely used input medium is *punched paper tape*. The pattern of round holes in the tape represents information in much the same manner as do the holes in tab cards. One might even consider a paper tape as one long tab card, although the coding pattern is considerably different. These tapes vary around one inch in width, and may be hundreds of feet long. Paper tape is read into a computer more slowly than are punched cards, but the machines used to prepare the tape are cheaper than those used to prepare punched cards. Its most serious disadvantage is with regard to error detection and correction. The independence of individual tab cards provides much greater flexibility in this respect.

Magnetic tape is another widely used input medium. The most common type is one-half inch wide, and is physically like the magnetic tapes used in sound recording, although the quality is higher and the recording technique is not the same. Information is stored on a magnetic computer tape as the pattern in which a series of "spots" are magnetized. Just as each punch position in a tab card or paper tape may be in one of two states—punched or not punched—so also each spot on a magnetic tape may be magnetized in one *direction* or the other. A common tape system uses seven such spots across the tape for each character of information.

Magnetic tape has the primary advantage of speed. As many as 50,000 characters per second may be transferred into the computer—a rate 100 times that of the fastest paper tape input. Even faster speeds are possible with some of the most recently developed tape units. Magnetic tape is also reusable, unlike punched cards or paper tape. Just as audio tape may be rerecorded, so also may computer tapes be rewritten with new information in place of the old. Although machines have been developed for entering information from a keyboard directly onto magnetic tape, this medium is used mostly for permanent storage of data output by a computer. Some computer systems input and output all information via magnetic tapes, which are prepared or decoded into other media by a smaller computer which is used specifically for these purposes.

Keyboard Stations. Most computers have a modified electric typewriter built into the central console to allow the machine operator to communicate directly with the processing control section. Although such keyboards are normally used only for monitoring the computer's operations, they also can be used to enter data directly into the machine. Because this means of information transmission is so slow, it is seldom used on the larger standard computer systems. Recent developments in the organization of computer systems are bringing these devices back into the picture, however, as time-sharing systems permit a single computer to service hundreds of users simultaneously.

Optical Scanning Devices. Probably the most active field in computer technology today is that which concerns methods of encoding information directly from source documents. Banks, for instance, now routinely process checks with automatic machines which "read" symbols printed with magnetic ink. Other devices, some of them still expensively experimental, are able to recognize printed characters in a wide variety of type fonts. The state of the art is still far from the human ability to read handwriting, however. Even the development of a reasonably priced and reliable machine which could read typewritten pages would constitute a tremendous advance, since the cost of entering information to a computer system is currently one of the factors most inhibiting utilization of computers for information processing.

Input from Other Computers. As the development of computer systems proceeds, and the machines are used to monitor and control more and more of the routine functions of business and government, it has become increasingly feasible and worthwhile to link the computers directly over various communication media such as telephone, teletype, and microwave channels. Such transmissions of information do not depend on the limitations of mechanical equipment and can proceed at fantastic speeds.

OUTPUT MEDIA

The most common form of output from a computer system is the printed page. Reproductions of such output will be found throughout later chapters to illustrate the operation of various computer programs. The *typewriter* is the slowest of the machines in this group—up to 15 characters per second. A common printer is a modified *accounting machine* which achieves about 150 lines (120 characters maximum) per minute. Most current computers utilize a faster type of *line printer* which operates at speeds between 500 and 1000 lines of print per minute. Even faster electrostatic printers are currently in the experimental stages of development.

Another common form of computer output is *punched cards*. Data output in this form can be easily manipulated by unit-record machines such as those described in Chapter 3, and can be re-entered to the computer for further processing with a minimum of handling. In later chapters you will encounter listings of such computer-punched output decks, which in some cases have been used as input to other programs.

An increasingly common technique for representing the results of computer processing is the use of *cathode-ray display* units, which resemble ordinary television screens. Although such output is not permanent, it may be completely adequate for many purposes—particularly in the context of time-shared systems such as those to be described later in this chapter. Some of these displays are two-way devices, in that their screens are sensitive to a "light pen" which can be used to send signals back to the computer to direct further processing. Development of hardware such as this which permits close man-machine interaction is one of the most fascinating aspects of current computer technology.

Magnetic tape is a widely used output medium; its advantages were described earlier. This particular mode of recording data might be included logically among storage media as well. There are a number of semipermanent storage techniques of this kind, most of which have as their primary function the storage of data during and between processing runs.

Most large computer systems in university settings provide special devices called *plotters* which will produce graphs from computer output of point coordinates. This hard-copy output is being supplanted to some extent by the photographing of cathode-ray displays, but is still widely used as an output medium.

STORAGE MEDIA

Almost all modern digital computers use a *magnetic core memory* as the central storage device, although supplementary devices with slower access and more permanence are normally included in the system also. (Access time is that required to bring the content of a memory location from central storage to the processing unit.) These memory units are constructed from hundreds of thousands of tiny iron "cores" through which are strung wires that carry electrical impulses to directionalize the magnetic states of the cores. Each core carries a *bit* (binary digit) of information, and these bits are grouped to form "words" of storage. We also use the terms "storage location" and "memory cell" to describe such a series of bits which together are used to represent numeric quantities or strings of symbols. Most of the computers in use today employ 36 bits per word of storage, although other computers may be organized with as many as 60 bits per storage location. A few of the smaller machines, such as the IBM 1620, do not have fixed word lengths, but permit the programmer to set this parameter at will.

Most of the large machines in use today have a basic 32,768-word core memory, although the newest large-scale systems may have more than 262,000 locations of core. A point is reached in the expansion of this type of memory beyond which further increases become uneconomical in comparison with less expensive mass storage devices with slower access time. Access time in the most recently announced computer systems is measured in ten-millionths of a second.

Magnetic tape may be considered a storage medium since it is commonly employed to hold data temporarily during processing runs, freeing the central memory for other purposes. A number of the programs presented in later chapters use magnetic tape in this way to hold raw data from a sample of subjects while the program carries out an analysis of the data. Some analyses result in sets of weights which can be applied to the raw scores of the original sample by reading the data tape back into memory one subject at a time under control of the same program that carried out the analysis.

Magnetic drums and disk files are part of many large-scale computer systems. Magnetic drums were the most common central storage device before the development of core memories. As the name implies, the device is basically a large cylinder with a magnetically coated surface which rotates rapidly under a set of read-record heads. Drum storage devices have been improved tremendously during the last decade, but access time, although much faster than magnetic tape, does not begin to approach that of the core memory.

Magnetic disk files look somewhat like stacks of phonograph records. The disks are coated with magnetic material upon which "tracks" of data are recorded. These devices are something of a compromise between the fast access and small capacity of drum storage, and the slow access but large capacity of magnetic tape. Some disk storage devices allow the use of disk "packs" which may be removed from the unit and stored much like magnetic tapes.

Many other types of central storage have been developed and used with various data-processing systems, but magnetic core memory, drums, disks, and tape are the most widely used. The selection of storage devices involves consideration of a variety of factors, including speed of access, permanence of recording, cost per unit of storage, and convenience in demounting units of storage from the device itself. With regard to this factor, magnetic tapes and disk packs are separate storage units which can be filed and mounted as needed. Core memory and magnetic drums, however, do not permit detachment of independent storage units. Most large installations do not rely upon a single storage medium, but include a mix of devices most suited to the particular needs of its users. From the viewpoint of the programmer, most Fortran systems do not distinguish among the various types of auxiliary storage devices except by unit numbers. Even so, it is worthwhile to become familiar with the available devices at your installation in order to capitalize on their particular capabilities.

We mentioned earlier that central storage is used to hold the program of instructions to the computer as well as the data to be processed and the intermediate and final results of the processing. Auxiliary storage devices such as tapes and disks are often used as repositories for such programs, which can be brought into the central memory under the control of "driver" programs as needed. We will describe the organization of such programming systems in more detail in Chapter 2.

PROCESSING CONTROL

A computer is nothing more than an automatic tool. It follows faithfully a predetermined set of instructions concerning the processing of information. It makes no decisions "on its own," although the instructions given to it may be *open ended* in that they require the machine to select further instructions on the basis of values it has computed previously. The important point is that the machine cannot do anything that has not been explicitly planned for it as a sequence of specific instructions.

The control-processing unit (CPU) of the computer system executes the program of specific instructions supplied to it by the system operator. Before a program can be executed, it must be stored in the central memory of the machine. Instructions are then called out of memory by the CPU in a predetermined order and executed one at a time. Because these instructions are stored in the central memory as numbers, they can be modified by the CPU during execution of the program. For instance, the execution of a particular instruction may send the CPU back to an earlier instruction in the program sequence. Thus, it is possible for the programmer to write an instruction series which unintentionally becomes an interminable loop during execution.

The processing unit of the computer operates on the contents of only one or two memory cells at a time in executing each instruction. It carries out these minute steps, however, at a fantastic rate of speed, since all operations are electronic in nature, and all of the instructions to be executed are already in core storage before the execution of the program begins. Because the CPU in most digital computers operates much faster than the other devices in the system, it may spend as much as 70 percent of the time necessary to execute a program just waiting on other parts of the system. A number of hardware improvements have been aimed at freeing the CPU from waiting and from routine operations.

Buffered input-output systems employ special memory areas and hardware control to transfer blocks of data to and from memory without involving the CPU directly in the transfer process. While a tape is being read into one memory area, for instance, the CPU may be busy computing results using data from another memory area. In some systems this concept is carried to the point of using a series of specialized preprocessing CPU's to take care of some of the routine data-transfer functions while the main CPU handles the primary computational burden.

Multiprocessing and multiprogramming systems have become the focus of considerable developmental effort in recent years. These methods of organizing a computer system attempt to keep the CPU as busy as possible by permitting a number of independent problems to be solved simultaneously rather than sequentially. In contrast, ordinary processing is serial, since only one program at a time occupies the entire machine until it is completed. The terms "multiprocessing" and "multiprogramming" have been used in a variety of ways; both terms might be subsumed under the more general heading "timesharing," since the purpose of these techniques is to maximize the amount of problem solving per unit of time. (The term "throughput" is sometimes used in this connection.)

A *multiprocessing* system has multiple arithmetic and logical units which give the effect of multiple CPU's when operating simultaneously under the control of a system monitor program. The term "multiprogramming" refers to the simultaneous execution of two or more programs by a system monitor which switches the CPU back and forth among the jobs in memory, giving each a time slice, or changing programs whenever an input/output operation is begun.

Although time sharing might appear to impose a serious restriction on the programmer's freedom to use large memory areas and peripheral equipment, in actual practice this is not the case. Demands upon the core memory are anticipated by the system for each program so as to maximize utilization of storage as well as CPU time.

From the programmer's viewpoint, the particular features of the computer system at his installation are relatively unimportant. He need not be concerned with *how* the system executes his program, and can assume that he has the whole machine to himself while his program is being run. This is the tremendous advantage of programming languages such as Fortran; they free the programmer from concern about the hardware, letting him concentrate on the conceptual aspects of the problems to be solved.

TIME-SHARED REMOTE CONSOLES

Quite similar in nature to multiprocessing systems is another recent development which very much affects the programmer and the way he approaches the solving of problems. Although only operational at a few installations, these systems almost certainly represent the "wave of the future" in computer organization.

Imagine a very large computer in the center of a university campus, connected over cables, phone wires, or microwave links to hundreds of terminals located in faculty offices, laboratories, dormitories, libraries, and even professors' homes. These terminals in most cases are tabletop devices, consisting of a keyboard, a television-like screen, and perhaps an audio speaker. Some terminals may also include a card reader and a printer.

All of these terminals are serviced *simultaneously* by the central computer with its massive files of permanently recorded information. A student seated at one of these consoles may work his way through a course in sociology with the computer acting as his personal tutor, asking questions, providing hints, evaluating his performance. The same student might later use the same console to search the literature for references he needs for a term paper in another course. Meanwhile Professor X has instructed the machine to use a factor analytic program and a file of data to test a notion that came to him while shaving that morning. While this analysis is being conducted by the computer, he types in a request for salary information and other data on his research project, and begins to make out a budget proposal for the following year.

Such an *information utility* is entirely within the limits of present technology. Time-shared systems which service hundreds of remote consoles have been built. Extensive bibliographies in many fields have been compiled for computer access. Central personnel records are being used in many business concerns and institutions. Computer-assisted instruction research is expanding rapidly, and many students of all ages are familiar with terminals such as those described earlier.

The first large scale time-shared computer system was installed at the Massachusetts Institute of Technology as an experimental program called MAC, or Machine-Aided Cognition (Corbato, 1962). It services over 400 users whose terminals are located in offices, labs, and at least one professor's bedroom. The central computer system supplies answers to questions and solves problems under direct control from the remote terminals.

A more recent development by **IBM** is the Quiktran Remote Terminal System (Morrissey, 1965) which consists of 40 IBM typewriter terminals connected over ordinary phone lines to a medium-size digital computer. A restricted version of the Fortran programming language is used to communicate with the machine, which responds with no more than a 10 second delay to each message. The terminal can serve as a powerful calculator, as a stored-program computer (using the central machine's storage devices), or simply as an initiator of central processing and a receiver of final results.

Another aspect of remote terminal systems is their usefulness for document retrieval and bibliographic search. One can easily visualize a system by which a researcher at a remote terminal with a display screen could examine a series of topic indexes, quickly zeroing in on the small number of specific references he needs, and finally signaling the machine to produce a copy of the complete text of each of the two or three articles that are of most importance to him.

Medlars (Medical Literature Analysis and Retrieval System) (Austin, 1964) is one prototype of such systems. It was developed by the National Library of Medicine, a federally supported institution in Bethesda, Maryland, and indexes roughly 200,000 papers in the fields of medicine and biology each year. The system serves three functions: (1) *Index Medicus* is a list of references published monthly with an average of 14,000 per issue; (2) recurring bibliographies are produced regularly for certain special fields such as cancer research; and (3) demand bibliographies are produced for particular topics on request by searching the files of titles using key-word techniques.

Remote consoles connected to a time-shared computer system do not in any way reduce the need for computer programming. If they have any effect, it will probably be to expand the amount to computer-based problem solving by making data more accessible for analysis. Judging from past experience, the number of questions and their scope almost immediately expands to exploit the potential created by each technological advance in the computer industry. The *manner* in which a programmer goes about his work using a remote console may be quite different, since the program can be entered line by line as it is conceived, and can be automatically checked for consistency with the rules of the language. Short tests of program segments can be conducted immediately, thus avoiding the common problem of locating a subtle error in a very long program. In many situations the user may be satisfied to get back his answer on the display screen, and then erase both program and results from central storage. Since every user will have to "talk" to the machine in some language which they both understand, skill in the use of computer languages will quite likely become an indispensable part of the training of behavioral scientists—much as ability to understand and carry out statistical analyses is now considered to be a fundamental part of research training.

Review Exercises

1. Reconstruct from memory Figure 1-1, which shows the relationships among the four major functional sections of a computer system.
2. Define the terms *analog* and *digital* as they apply to computers. Which kind of device is each of the following?
   - a. thermometer
   - b. light switch
   - c. adding machine
   - d. abacus
   - e. slide rule
   - f. speedometer
   - g. thermostat
   - h. telegraph
3. If someone asked you when the first computer was built, what would your answer be?
4. Which of the following media and devices are used for input? Output? Storage?
   - a. punched cards
   - b. punched paper tape
   - c. magnetic tape
   - d. magnetic drum
   - e. magnetic disk
   - f. magnetic cores
   - g. typewriter
   - h. optical scanner
   - i. line printer
   - j. cathode-ray display
   - k. coordinate plotter
   - l. light pen
5. Explain the concept of an *information utility* in terms of remote time-shared computer terminals. What effects might such systems be expected to have on the organization of universities and the conduct of research in the future?

2 / programming languages and applications

Hardware is useless without software; a digital computer system is only as effective as the programs it executes. While some hardware systems offer the programmer more speed and flexibility, such differences among modern digital computers are far less important than the quality of the software—programs—which are available for them. It is also true that highly sophisticated programming languages are of no value to research workers who cannot "speak" them fluently. The computer language called Fortran is closer to the status of a "universal" computer language than any other. There are a number of computer languages that are quite similar to Fortran and which have certain superior characteristics, but none of these other languages is as widely used and generally available in the United States as is Fortran.

Programming languages may be classified into two major levels which we will call *assemblers* and *compilers*. Another major distinction will be made between *object* and *source* programs. Very few programs are written in a form which can be directly executed by a computer without some degree of translation. Because computer instructions are stored in the central core memory unit before being executed, they must be expressed in the form of binary numbers before they can be used by the machine. Assembler and compiler languages are symbolic languages in which the instructions are expressed as alphameric symbols or as algebraic expressions according to particular highly restricted sets of rules. *Source* programs written in these higher-order languages must be translated into *object* programs in the numerical notation that the control-processing unit of the computer can understand—sometimes called "machine" language.

The necessary translation from source program to object program is accomplished by the computer itself in a pre-execution stage of the processing. The complexity of this translation process is much greater and the time required is hence much longer for compilers than it is for assemblers. Some computer systems actually translate first from the compiler language to the assembly language, and then convert the assembly-language commands to machine-instruction codes.

Assembly languages are relatively machine-specific, although some "families" of computers such as the IBM System/360 series or the CDC 6000 series utilize common assembly languages. At this level, programs are sometimes said to be coded in "symbolics," since the commands are usually designated explicitly as alphabetic and numeric codes. Assembler translation programs convert almost on a one-to-one basis (that is, one source statement is translated into a single machine-language instruction), since the instruction codes of these languages correspond almost exactly with the machine-command repertoire. This close correspondence accounts for the fact that assemblers tend to be machine-specific.

Compiler languages are relatively machine-independent. Fortran,[1] for instance, is entirely so, since the language can be compiled on any of the larger modern computers. Other compilers such as Cobol[1] and Algol[1] are also widely available, and approach the status of universal languages. Still other compilers such as PL/I, IPL–V, and Jovial[1] are not available for many machines. When we say that a language is "available" on a given machine, we mean that there exists a machine-language program for that particular computer model which is capable of translating statements written in the source language into machine-language commands. Obviously, there are as many Fortran compiler programs as there are computer models. In fact there are many more than one per machine, since Fortran as a general language has gone through two major revisions—as well as countless minor variations undertaken by one or another manufacturer or user. We will discuss these "dialects" more fully in Chapter 4.

[1] Fortran: *FOR*mula *TRAN*slation, an algebraic language developed by IBM.
 Cobol: *CO*mmon *B*usiness *O*riented *L*anguage, especially suited to nonscientific data processing.
 Algol: *ALGO*rithmic *L*anguage, similar to Cobol and used primarily in Europe.
 PL/I: A general-purpose compiler developed by IBM, which claims for it the best features of Fortran, Cobol, and IPL–V.
 IPL–V: Information Processing Language, Version 5. The most well-known of the list-processing languages.
 Jovial: Jules Own Version of the International Algorithmic Language, named by and for Jules I. Schwartz who developed it.

STAGES OF PROCESSING

Figure 2-1 illustrates the stages of processing in a typical computer installation. This complete sequence is sometimes called a "load-and-go" operation. The computer automatically carries out the separate stages as a continuous procedure, from initial input of the program and data decks, through translation from source language to object program, to the execution of the instructions utilizing the data which produces the output.

The diagram indicates that the source program enters the system as a punched-card deck, which is translated by the computer, utilizing a translator program — an assembler or compiler — which is brought into the machine automatically from one of its magnetic tape units. We have shown the resulting object program as a magnetic tape, but in some systems the object program remains in core storage ready for execution. Whether or not it is written onto a temporary tape, it may also be punched into tab cards in machine-language form. Such *binary* object program decks may be used in later processing runs, obviating the necessity of recompiling or assembling from the source program.

The object program is *loaded* into the central memory in the next stage of the sequence, unless it is already there. Control of the computer is turned over to the object program at this point, and it goes ahead with the processing of the data which may be waiting in the form of cards or a mag-

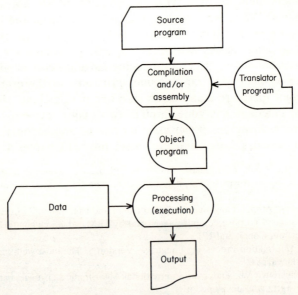

FIGURE 2-1. Stages of computer processing.

netic tape. The program produces output from the machine as printed pages, punched cards, or stores results in other media such as magnetic tape.

Error Diagnosis. Most computer systems provide two types of diagnostic procedures for handling program or processing faults. One set of diagnostic checks is built into the compiler or assembly program which translates the source program. Most systems will not execute programs containing such *syntax* errors. The other diagnostic system goes to work whenever the program's instruction sequence leads to a recognizable error condition. Such a *logical* error would be present if the user had supplied fewer data cards than were called for by the program. These diagnostic systems are often quite sophisticated, but of course they cannot anticipate every possible kind of error. This results, as often as not, in a diagnostic which does not really fit the error—although an error is actually there. Also, some errors simply lead to erroneous results or to no results at all—and no diagnostics either. The important thing to remember is that a lack of diagnostics is no guarantee of a correct program. If the fault lies with the *method* used to solve the problem, the computer will turn out nonsense at the same amazing rate at which it correctly answers questions. One of the major advantages of remote-console time-shared computer systems is that they permit line-by-line error diagnosis as the programmer composes his routine at the terminal.

LEVELS OF COMPUTER LANGUAGE

Digital computers operate on binary numbers, although any symbol may be assigned a unique numerical code for processing purposes. The instructions that control the computer's operation are also represented by particular numeric codes which are recognized by the hardware as commands to set particular circuits to send or receive signals from other parts of the system.

To illustrate the different conceptual levels of computer programming we will use in following paragraphs a subtask which might form a part of a much larger statistical program. This example is intentionally quite superficial, since we wish to convey here only an intuitive notion of the nature of programming languages without becoming ensnarled in the intricacies of any one language or the wide variations among the lower-level languages peculiar to particular machines.

Let us assume that earlier instructions in this hypothetical program had obtained three numeric values from a data card, and had placed them in memory cells 301, 302, and 303. We now want to add these three values and place their sum in location 304. Later instructions will print this result.

Machine Language. At the most basic machine-language level all operation codes, addresses, and data are coded as binary numbers. Without attempting very strenuously to duplicate any actual machine-language system, let us suppose that every instruction consists of two parts: a two-digit operation code and a three-digit operand. Depending on the nature of the operation code, the operand in our simplified programming language will be the address in memory of the source or destination of the data concerned.

Almost all computers have in their processing sections a special register which serves as the focal point for all operations; this cell is sometimes called the *accumulator*. All three of the following operation codes concern this cell.

22 = replace the current value in the accumulator with the value stored in the location specified by the address
23 = replace the current value in the location specified by the address with the value now in the accumulator
56 = add to the current value in the accumulator the value stored in the location specified by the address

In all three of these instructions, the content of only one cell is changed — either the accumulator or the memory location concerned. These three instructions may be used in the following sequence to achieve the addition of the three values and the storage of their sum in location 304.

22 301
56 302
56 303
23 304

Each of these instructions would occupy a cell in the same memory unit that contains the data.[2] Thus it is entirely within the programmer's power to use instructions and addresses which will result in modification of the program itself during its operation.

Symbolic Language. The next step upward in the hierarchy of computer languages permits the use of alphameric symbols (numbers and letters) instead of numeric operation codes and memory addresses. The computer's operating system automatically translates these symbols through the use of a symbol equivalence table in order to obtain the numeric codes it needs to execute the program. Let us assume that a permanent symbol table is available in the computer to equate the operation codes as follows:

---

[2] Although the numerals used here are from the decimal number system, it should be understood that their equivalents in the binary number system actually occupy the memory locations. We will not need to concern ourselves with nondecimal number systems as such until Chapter 13.

22 = LDA = load the accumulator
23 = STA = store the accumulator
56 = ADA = add to the accumulator

Let us further assume that the assembly program has previously assigned the symbols KA, KB, KC, and KT to the four memory locations 301, 302, 303, and 304, respectively, which are "open" in that they are not needed for program instructions. We may then code our earlier machine-language instruction sequence as symbols which have considerably more mnemonic value than did the numerics previously used.

    LDA KA
    ADA KB
    ADA KC
    STA KT

Because the correspondence is one-to-one between the symbolic and numeric operation codes, this language level retains a maximum amount of flexibility for the programmer. Higher-order languages such as Fortran inevitably sacrifice some of this flexibility because of the necessity of relatively rigid rules by which their statements are translated to the symbolic machine-language instruction level.

Algebraic Compilers. The Fortran programming language is by far the most widely used of the algebraic compilers. The term "compiler" signifies the fact that statements in this language must be translated down to the machine-language level, where a series of basic instructions is established which will carry out the necessary operations. This translation typically results in a considerable expansion of the program. As shown here, a single algebraic statement usually implies many machine-language operations.

Machine Language	Symbolic Language	Algebraic Compiler
22 301	LDA KA	
56 302	ADA KB	KT = KA + KB + KC
56 303	ADA KC	
23 304	STA KT	

Natural Language Translators. The next logical step in the development of computer programming languages would appear to be a system which would translate from verbal expressions of the solution technique which do not require the use of a fixed system of symbolic notation. For instance, we would like the machine to be able to translate, "Define KT as the sum of KA, KB, and KC." A moment of thought suggests that we also would like it to be able to understand, "KT *is* the sum of KA, KB, and

KC," or "Add KA, KB, and KC to form KT," to mean the same set of operations. The problem with computer languages at this level is obviously that of the flexibility of expression in natural languages; the rules of English permit so many variant ways of saying the same thing. The restrictions of an algebraic language reduce the possible variations sufficiently to permit a reasonably uncomplicated set of translation rules. Because of the character of natural language itself, little progress has been made toward construction of a genuine natural language compiler. Some of the more recent algebraic compilers such as Algol and PL/I permit expressions which are somewhat closer to natural language than are the equivalent Fortran statements, but such improvements are quite minor in terms of the ideal characteristics of a language at the next level.

LIST-PROCESSING LANGUAGES

Although most of the applications of computers by behavioral scientists have been in statistical analysis of quantitative data, a computer is basically a symbol manipulator, and many of the most interesting problems in behavioral research are most adequately expressed in terms of *lists* of symbols. List-processing languages have been developed to deal with such problems in ways which make maximum use of the limited storage space in the computer memory. These languages also use a concise notation for specifying complex list-manipulation processes. The most well-known list-processing language is IPL–V, which was developed by Newell, Shaw, and Simon (Newell, 1961) and serves as the vehicle for their *General Problem Solver* program which will be discussed later in more detail. Other list-processing languages are Lisp (McCarthy, 1960), FLPL (Gelernter, et al., 1960) which is built out of a Fortran compiler, and Comit (Yngve, 1958) which is intended to handle linguistic material.

List-processing languages are used to implement *heuristic* problem-solving procedures, which require dynamic memory organization because of the continual restructuring of the problem that takes place during its solution. The contrast between *algorithmic* and *heuristic* problem solving is exemplified by the solving of an algebraic equation with a given set of values as opposed to winning a game of checkers. The solution to the equation is a straightforward computation using a completely specified sequence of rules. This is not the case with game-playing problems, which change with every move the opponent makes. Human problem solving is characterized by the use of heuristic techniques; thus, list-processing languages are well suited to experiments in computer simulation of cognitive processes.

The most important distinction between algebraic compilers and list processors is in the way they organize the open memory areas which hold data during processing. Algebraic compilers reserve blocks of memory under specific symbolic labels and employ subscripts to designate particular elements within these tables. The problems to which list processors are most appropriately applied are marked by the need for designating many lists of varying lengths which must be changed frequently in arrangement and length during the processing sequence. Furthermore, these lists are often arranged in a *nested* or *hierarchical* structure, so that an element in a particular list at one level designates an independent list at a lower level. This list-of-lists organization of data is extremely awkward within the notational conventions of algebraic compilers.

In the list processors the addresses of all uncommitted memory locations form a single list which may be drawn upon by the program as necessary to form new lists. Locations which held deleted list elements are returned to this pool as they are released by the program. No fixed blocks of consecutively addressed locations are used to hold lists of elements. Rather, each list element carries with it the address of the next element in the list of which it is a part. This address is called the "link." If it is some special symbol — perhaps zero — the element is recognized as the last in its list.

In addition to maximizing utilization of available memory by evading the necessity of reserving blocks of locations, the list processors permit insertion and deletion of particular elements in a list with a minimum of disturbance. Instead of shifting the locations of all list elements to make room for the element to be inserted, only the link of the immediately preceding element need be changed. The link for the insert is then set as the address of the list element which follows it logically.

Figure 2-2 illustrates the organization of 12 memory cells in a very much simplified example of the insertion of a four-element sublist into an eight-element primary list. This insertion was accomplished by changing only the link for cell 4(A),* and link for cell 9(AD).** The latter cell's link was changed from zero, which formerly signified that it was the end of an independent list, to the address of the next location in the primary list:

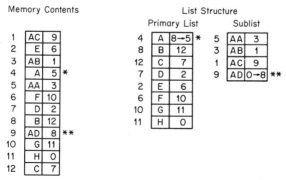

FIGURE 2-2. Simplified example of list-processor memory organization.

8(B). Once this insertion has been completed, the sublist is an integral part of the primary list.

List structures are built by using the starting locations of lower-order lists as the symbol portions of elements in a single list at the next higher level of the structure. A special prefix is used to indicate that the symbols in this list represent other lists. A variation of this superordinate list concept may be found in Chapter 13.

The use of list hierarchies is necessary for most problems in the field of applications for which list-processing languages were developed. For instance, consider the analysis of natural-language data such as Thematic Apperception Technique (TAT) stories. The story could be the unit or element in the primary list. Each of these elements could designate a second level of lists designating particular paragraphs. Each paragraph element could be a list of sentences, each of which in turn might be organized in terms of parts-of-speech lists.

Although list-processing languages facilitate the programming of many analytic procedures of interest to behavioral scientists, some of the concepts can often be used within the restrictions of algebraic compilers to handle specialized tasks. In fact, one of the list-processing "languages" mentioned earlier (FLPL) consists only of a series of subroutines written in the Fortran language. Chapter 13 in this book also illustrates in detail the use of the Fortran language to implement a list-processing technique.

PROGRAM LIBRARIES AND SYSTEMS

Most large computer installations maintain their own libraries of computer programs for the procedures most in demand. These libraries are more or less adequate in scope, and the programs are more or less well documented from one installation to another. Some installations depend almost entirely on the computer manufacturer to supply their software, while other organizations—particularly university computing centers—often take the lead in developing software systems to suit their own purposes. Flores (1965) provides an excellent general introduction to the field of systems programming.

In the last few years a number of computer manufacturers have announced software "packages" of statistical routines for some of their larger machines. Some of these program libraries are more comprehensive than others, and the routines included in them vary considerably in quality. In addition, many university research groups have built similar software packages and a few recent books have included Fortran programs for various types of statistical analysis (Cooley and Lohnes, 1962; Horst, 1965).

Another form of program library development is implicit in user organizations such as Share (Society to Help Avoid Repetitive Effort), which consists mostly of IBM installations. A central file and documentation system is made available to a group of cooperating users who contribute their own routines to the common pool of tested programs.

Although all of these sources have been of some help to research workers in the behavioral sciences, no single program library can ever satisfy all of those who want to use a computer for statistical analysis. This book contains a rather comprehensive group of statistical programs, but our intent is not simply to offer another program library to workers in the field. Our primary purpose is to provide the reader with the basic language and the examples he needs to develop his own skill in writing programs, which eventually he may wish to work together into his own program library.

There are two distinctly different ways of approaching the organization of a general-purpose program system. We will call these the *program library* and the *subprogram system* methods. Each has its own advantages, depending primarily on the sophistication in computer techniques of those for whom the system is intended. In general, the program library method is more often suited to use by research workers in the behavioral sciences, most of whom employ a limited set of statistical methods with standardized research designs. However, a few installations have succeeded in combining both approaches into a single system which provides easily used standard programs as well as the flexibility of a comprehensive library of specific routines which the specialist can combine effectively to carry out unusual procedures.

The *program library* concept is based on the notion that statistical methodology consists mainly in selecting an appropriate standard analytic procedure, such as factor analysis, from among a limited array of clearly differentiated techniques. Each procedure is programmed separately and will carry out the analysis from raw data to final results in an entirely automatic sequence. A few options may be provided, but these may be considered only as choices among alternative standard paths. The statistical programs in this book exemplify such routines. The control-card system permits the user a maximum of flexibility in applying the program to various sets of data, but the procedure options are minimized. Such a system can be quickly learned by a statistically sophisticated, but computer-naive behavioral researcher. If the user wishes to carry out standard analytic procedures, the required investment of time to learn the system is minimized.

The *subprogram system* concept assumes that users are not only sophisticated in statistical theory, but also that they have a rather thorough understanding of a particular programming language. Programs as such are not a part of a system of this type. Rather, a wide variety of subprograms called *subroutines* and *functions* are provided to the user. We will present a number of such subprograms in later chapters. The user must write a *driver* program which usually does little more than call into operation a particular series of these subprograms. Because a pure subprogram system does not include complete programs, a user must build his own routine for each research problem from the pieces provided by the system. The advantage of such a system is the greater flexibility it affords the user in designing his own analytic techniques to suit individual research problems. Its disadvantage is the need to write a special driver program for every research problem. For an example of these systems, see Jennings (1964).

The obvious compromise between these two extremes is a system of subprograms which also contains a variety of general-purpose driver programs that are written so as to accomplish standard analytic procedures. To some extent, the programs in this book employ this sort of compromise, in that most of them rely upon a relatively small number of specialized subprograms to carry out particular parts of their operations. However, the separate programs cannot be linked together without considerable revision. For examples of linked-program systems, see Jones (1964) and Tryon and Bailey (1966).

Program libraries and subprogram systems are quite often stored in translated form (as object programs) on a magnetic tape which is left mounted on the computer system. This avoids the awkwardness and opportunities for error that accompany the use of card decks. To use a subprogram system which is stored on tape, one would still need to use card decks for the driver programs, but these normally are quite small.

BEHAVIORAL SCIENCE APPLICATIONS

A number of books and papers have been published in recent years which survey the surprising variety of uses to which behavioral scientists have put computers (Borko, 1962; Green, 1963; Sterling and Pollack, 1965; Tomkins and Messick, 1963). In this section we will describe the more significant types of applications and cite some examples of each type. The interested reader will also find many relevant articles in two professional journals, *Behavioral Science* and *Educational and Psychological Measurement,* which devote a part of each issue to developments in computer techniques.

Statistical Analysis. The first use to which behavioral scientists put computers was in statistical analysis, since it followed the obvious capability of the machine to carry out routine mathematical calculations. It is still the most common use made of computers in behavioral research, and the proportion of quantitative research has increased rather than diminished with the advent of computing machinery. The data faced by behavioral researchers is necessarily voluminous because of the extreme variability of the phenomena they seek to understand, and computers are especially suited to routine analytic reduction of data. Because computational burden is no longer a consideration in decisions regarding the choice of analytic procedures, a rapid growth in the use of complex multiple-variable techniques has taken place in recent years (Cattell, 1965). These techniques, such as factor analysis, discriminant analysis, and canonical correlation, have been available for some time, but were seldom employed with the necessarily large samples of data they required simply because of the immense cost of data processing and analysis.

Analysis of Verbal Data. As understanding of the nature of computers deepened, it gradually became apparent to more and more behavioral scientists that these machines were more than high-speed calculators. A computer is a lightning-fast *symbol manipulator;* the symbols and conventions of mathematics are only a special case of the general power of a computer to process information.

Much of the research on human behavior concerns *verbal* behavior. Reduction of verbal data to quantitative indexes which can be subjected to analysis has always been an expensive and somewhat subjectively colored part of the study of personality and social behavior. Computers have been used in a variety of ways to speed and objectify procedures in this type of research. Chapter 13 in this book reviews some of the most interesting applications, and describes some of the basic techniques.

Personality Assessment. A continuing debate over the question of idiographic-clinical versus normative-actuarial approaches to the description of personality and the prediction of behavior has occupied many psychologists for more than a decade (Allport, 1966; Meehl, 1954; Sarbin, et al., 1960), although the history of this difference in approach to the study of human behavior can be traced back to the beginnings of scientific psychology.

Without doubt, the *normative* approach to the study of personality is ideally suited to implementation with computer techniques. Gathering together the data necessary to establish normative expectations for responses to standard stimuli has been enormously facilitated by machine techniques which in some studies have been extended all the way back to the presentation of stimuli and recording of responses by automatic devices.

Less obvious, but perhaps more significant, is the recent development of computer-based interpretive systems for standard psychological questionnaires such as the *Minnesota Multiphasic Personality Inventory* (Swenson, et al., 1965). Scoring systems have also been developed for the two most widely used ink-blot perception methods, the *Holtzman Ink-blot Technique* (Moseley, et al., 1963) and the *Rorschach* (Piotrowski, 1964). The importance of these interpretive systems derives from the way in which their creation forces the unambiguous specification of interpretive rules. A programmed interpretive system for a particular instrument actually amounts to an operational definition of an assessment theory (Helm, 1965). Because the theory is expressed in completely operational terms, its validity can be systematically tested by applying the program to selected sets of data. The inferential moves which are part of the more complex systems can be traced backward to isolate weak spots in the network of assumptions.

The *idiographic* approach to personality description may be seen primarily in the simulation studies of the behavior of individual subjects. The work of Kleinmuntz (1963) and of Cogswell and Estavan (1965) exemplify one form of this approach, in which the actual test-interpreting behavior of a specific expert is studied and translated into computer programs which are then used to interpret scores from new samples of subjects. Cogswell and Estavan carried this procedure to the next logical stage of programming a time-shared computer to conduct vocational counseling interviews with students, utilizing the data provided by the interpretive routine. Starkweather (1965) has extended this kind of application still further into the realm of psychiatric screening interviews, with mixed success. The closer such applications move toward the need for detecting subtle emotional-symbolic cues in the use of natural language, the harder it is for the behavioral scientists to specify the necessary unambiguous interpretive rules.

It would appear that the most promising applications of computer techniques in the field of assessment and prediction of individual behavior are those which aim at a combination of normative machine analysis with the sensitivity of clinical specialists to subtle aspects of face-to-face interviews. As remote-terminal time-shared systems become more widely available, some exciting advances in the art/science of personality assessment may be expected.

Simulation. The essential idea in simulation is to use a computer system as the raw material for constructing a *process model* of that which one wishes to study. The computer program thus embodies a theory which can be compared to the behavior of that which is modeled, modified, or extended as indicated by these comparisons, and subjected to conditions which may be impossible in the real world.

For instance, the flow of traffic over highway systems has been the subject of a great deal of computer modeling that has contributed substantially to the design of freeway systems. It is quite feasible to determine what would happen under conditions of a threatened atomic attack; we hope that we will never have to observe the real thing, but a computer model can suggest the result just as easily as it can the expectations for the highway system on a normal July weekend.

The same kind of extreme-condition modeling can be carried out with various aspects of human behavior which can be represented with reasonable accuracy by computer programs. We can derive data which may suggest answers to questions about the effects of stress too extreme to impose ethically upon human subjects. As yet, our computer models of human behavior are too crude to yield more than some entertaining and thought-provoking demonstrations, but this field of applications is certain to grow rapidly.

Some of the best-known simulation research is that of Newell and Simon (1961) concerning cognitive processes. With J. C. Shaw, these authors developed the *General Problem Solver* (1959), a computer program employing heuristic principles which has been applied to a variety of tasks such as solving problems in symbolic logic. Many game-playing programs, such as the one developed by Shannon (1956) which plays a respectable game of chess, and Samuel's (1959) checker-playing program, are organized so as to apply human problem-solving techniques.

As far back as 1952, A. C. Oettinger demonstrated that computer programs could learn, in the sense of simple conditioning. The computer (Edsac) gradually became able to respond selectively to a varying stimulus as a function of previous trials which had been "rewarded" or "punished." The later work of Feigenbaum (1961) with verbal learning (nonsense syllables) and that of Feldman (1962) with binary choice behavior exemplify simulations of more complex thought processes. These authors have also edited a collection of papers on this topic (Feigenbaum and Feldman, 1963). Their procedures were derived from careful analysis of the verbal descriptions of the problem-solving experiences produced by human subjects. Computer programs were constructed to match the human behavior, and the output was then compared with the behavior of human subjects confronted with new tasks of similar nature.

A different level of simulation research is described by John Loehlin (1963) in a delightful description of the behavior of Aldous ("His Is a Brave New World"). Aldous is a computer program of about 750 instructions which consists of three simple subsystems called *recognition, emotional reaction,* and *action preparation,* plus a "memory" system for past interactions with his "environment." The three action systems are simply numerical generators controlled by parameters set by the experimenter and/or modified by "experience." The simulated personality responds to a series of stimuli in the form of numeric inputs. The behavior of Aldous is remarkably human, particularly when it interacts with other personalities programmed with different characteristics.

Extension of this more broadly conceived type of computer simulation of human behavior to the study of large organizational structures (Rome and Rome, 1962) has received some attention, but relatively little work has appeared concerning the interactive behavior of small groups. This would seem to be a particularly promising field for the application of simulation techniques.

Computer-Assisted Instruction. Time-shared computer systems are ideal vehicles for presenting "programmed learning" materials to individual students. Note that the term "programmed learning" in this context does not necessarily signify the use of a computer, but rather describes the fact that the materials to be learned are presented in a carefully preplanned and controlled sequence. When a computer is used to present such materials, it becomes possible to provide alternate paths through the material, under the control of the *computer* program which examines student responses to each part of the presentation. The rate of presentation, the need for drill or review, and testing can be automatically handled by the machine during the learning process and subsequent presentations can be selected to best suit the students' needs. In an ordinary schoolroom the teacher carries out these functions, but she must of necessity adapt her later presentations to the class average, for the most part. Some teachers make heroic efforts to provide individual students with special instruction, but generally classes are taught as units, and at the level of the class average. Time-shared systems with computing facility also permit the design of programs which allow the student to learn through "discovery" of underlying principles by actually testing out hypotheses as part of the programmed-learning process (McCracken, 1966).

A number of research organizations, such as System Development Corporation (Silberman and Coulson, 1962), have conducted experiments with this application of computers, in some cases organizing an entire classroom around a central computer with a console for each child. Many universities are now engaged in extensive research programs to learn more about the capabilities of this approach to general education. Some computer manufacturers have also invested sizable amounts of equipment and staff time into the development of CAI systems. IBM, for instance, has developed a special programming language for this field called Coursewriter.

The teacher in a CAI environment is freed to do what her training and abilities enable her to do best: to give individualized attention to the learning difficulties and special talents of individual students. The use of a computer also allows the curriculum planner to range far beyond the limits of printed programmed-learning materials. He can employ audio and graphic devices as well as printed text, and can use a variety of techniques to adapt the presentation of the material to the needs of the particular child at the console through use of specialized review and remedial tracks.

Programmed learning, which individualizes the routine part of classroom learning, along with team-teaching, which permits each teacher to contribute from her individual strengths, constitutes a genuine breakthrough in education, and will be the center of an increasing amount of research activity by behavioral scientists in the future.

Review Exercises

1. Distinguish by defining
    a. compiler, assembler, and machine languages
    b. source and object programs

c. algorithmic and heuristic problem solving
   d. algebraic and list-processing languages
   e. program libraries and subroutine systems
   f. personality measurement and simulation
2. Reconstruct from memory the diagram in Figure 2-1, which describes stages in the computer processing sequence.
3. Project the effects of the use of computer-assisted instruction upon the future organization and operation of elementary, secondary, and higher education.

3 / punch-card processing

Punch cards, sometimes called "tab" cards or "IBM" cards (after the giant of the industry), were first used for information processing by Herman Hollerith at the Census Bureau in 1886. Today the punch card has become a symbol of automation in our culture, and the familiar admonition, "Do not fold, spindle, or mutilate" has been the topic of many jokes—as well as some serious questions about the implications of machines for the future of man.

Although other forms are still in use, by far the most common type of punch card is illustrated in Figure 3-1. Punch cards are available in a wide variety of colors and with virtually any conceivable printing. A popular variation is a buff card with a pastel stripe along the top edge. Cards with numbers printed in the numeric punching positions simplify visual interpretation of the punched information. Tab cards often have one or the other corner clipped to aid in aligning the top edges, and some suppliers offer cards with all four corners rounded to decrease damage during handling.

As you can see from the card pictured in Figure 3-1, there are 960 positions in a card which can be punched: 12 rows and 80 columns. *Only the holes punched in tab cards are significant for machine processing.* The color, corner clipping, and printing are all irrelevant, since the machines can only sense each position with regard to whether or not it is punched out. Beginning at the top of the card, the *rows* represent + (plus), − (minus), and the numerals 0, 1, 2, 3, 4, 5, 6, 7, 8, 9. The +, −, and 0 are sometimes called "zone punches." Also, the minus and plus are called an *11* or *low* and a *12* or *high punch,* respectively. The bottom of the card is sometimes called the *9 edge* and the top is called the *12 edge.*

Except in the special applications described later, each card column is used to represent *one character,* which may be a numeral, a letter of the alphabet, or one of a certain set of special characters, all of which are shown in Figure 3-1. This character set is currently the most widely used in business and scientific applications in the United States, although other more extensive character sets have been developed—particularly for systems which involve the use of cathode-ray display screens. The +, −, and numeral symbols are each represented by a single punch in a card column, while alphabetic characters are represented by double punches in a column, and most of the special characters require three punches per column. Thus, each character occupies a single card column; the code is based on the configuration of punches in its 12 possible positions.

The Key-Punch Machine. Data are recorded in a punch card by a machine which is operated very much like a typewriter. A keyboard resembling that of a typewriter—even to the space bar—is used to enter the symbols into sequential card columns. A "shift" key is incorporated into the design of the console, but unlike a typewriter, only capital letters are available; the upper register is used for numeric and special characters. The most important difference between key punching and typing is with regard to errors—which cannot be corrected in the same card.

Blank cards are stacked on the right side of the machine, and feed into the *punching station* one at a time under the control of the keyboard or an automatic feeding mechanism. The card leaves the punching station and passes through a *reading station* before being automatically stacked on the left side of the machine. The reading station is important in that the punch-

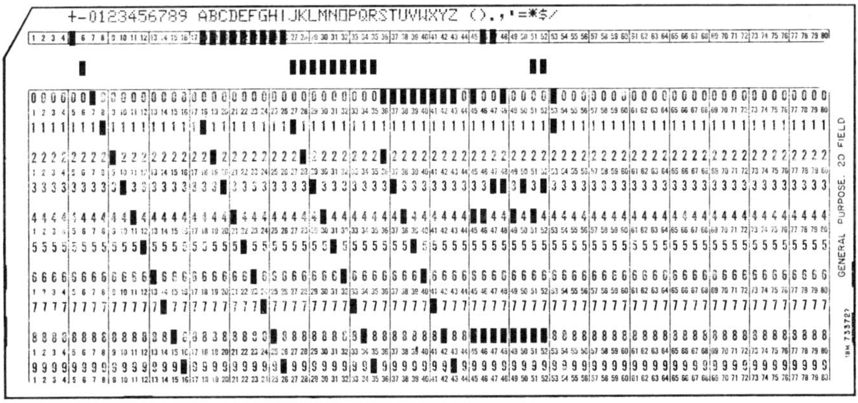

FIGURE 3-1. A typical punch card.

ing in a card there can be automatically duplicated into corresponding columns in another card at the punching station. The operator can switch from duplicating to entry of new information at any column, thus simplifying the repunching of cards containing errors. Another device called the "program drum" permits the operator to prespecify the duplication or skipping of particular card columns automatically. The instructions for each column are punched with a special code in an ordinary tab card which is wrapped around the drum and inserted in the key-punch machine.

The most widely used model of the key-punch machine is an IBM 026 Printing Card Punch. The printing along the top edge of the card in Figure 3-1 was done by this machine at the same time that the card was originally punched. Such printing vastly simplifies sorting and identification of cards after they have been key punched. There is a wide variety of special features available on various models of key-punch machines in addition to those described here, but most of these special features are important only to those whose responsibilities center upon the preparation rather than the processing of data cards.

The Reproducer. This machine will be found in almost all data-processing installations. Tab cards wear out through repeated handling, and repunching the data card by card would be prohibitively expensive in time, effort, and errors. The reproducer has two hoppers—one for blank cards, and one for the deck which is to be duplicated. The input rate of this machine is sufficiently slow (100 cards per minute) for the mechanism to tolerate imperfections that would jam other faster card-processing machines.

The reproducer has a control panel which can be wired column by column to completely reorder (or eliminate) information between input and output. Particular columns of the output cards can also be punched with identical predetermined symbols; this is called *gang punching*. Other special features are available on various models of this machine, one of which is a great asset to users who gather data from individual persons. A reproducer equipped with a *mark-sensing* attachment will interpret information recorded on one section of the card with an electrographic pencil and will punch the information in designated columns of the same card. A maximum of 27 mark-sense columns may be included on a single tab card; the interpreted information may be punched in any desired columns of the same card. This data-recording system is particularly valuable in situations involving the gathering of information from many subjects by means of a standard questionnaire. Although usually employed for short forms, this technique has been successfully used to gather data from patients at the Mayo Clinic on the 550-item *Minnesota Multiphasic Personality Inventory* (MMPI) (Swenson, 1965): The obvious advantage of this system is that it completely bypasses the cost and error opportunities of manual key punching.

Cards punched by the reproducer do not have content printing along their top edges. Such printing can be accomplished with a special machine called an Alphabetic Interpreter, or by a special model (21) of the 026 Card Punch machine which will automatically interpret and print the content of already punched cards.

Card Handling and Storage. Learning how to operate each of the card-processing machines is largely a matter of actually using them, since the skills involved are motor skills for the most part. The information presented in this chapter is only intended as a survey of the most common machines and their uses. Detailed manuals are available that describe the features of the particular machines at your installation, and we believe that the time spent studying such manuals, combined with actual practice in card handling, will be worthwhile even for the reader who has a staff of technicians to carry out his routine data-processing work. Actually manipulating decks of cards affords a certain concrete familiarity with the basic units of information storage that seems to facilitate acquisition of the more abstract skills at a later time. For those who wish to go further into the topic of card-processing techniques, two books may be of special interest: Salmon (1962) considers machine operation in considerable detail, while Gregory and Van Horn (1960) provide a comprehensive survey of business and scientific data-processing machines and procedures.

Tab cards are supplied in cardboard boxes containing 2000 cards each. Although punched cards can be stored in these same boxes, metal trays with pressure plates are much better. If the cardboard boxes are stacked, they soon begin to sag—bending and crushing the edges of cards in the lower boxes. The edges of the cards are crucial, since the mechanisms which feed cards into the various machines apply force against one or the other of these edges. For this reason also, rubber bands should be used sparingly to bind decks of cards, since even a mild tension will cut the card edge over a period of time. Paper clips also should only be used for short periods, and never to hold together more than two or three cards.

Other Card-Punching Devices. IBM has developed a system known as *Porta-Punch,* which is useful for individual-subject data gathering as an alternative to the electrographic mark-sense system. Special preperforated cards are used, which will hold up to 40 columns of information. Holes are punched out by the subject himself with a special platen and stylus. The cards can then be processed by any of the machines previously mentioned.

Another device, the *IBM 1230 Optical Mark Scoring Reader,* uses answer sheets that can be marked with an ordinary lead pencil, and a special attachment permits direct output of item data or summary scores on tab cards. This machine will be discussed in more detail in Chapter 8.

Punched cards also may be output by computers. Some of the smaller computers, in fact, can *only* produce output on punch cards, although most current machines also employ a typewriter. Larger computers, of course, can produce any kind of output from graphs on paper to visual displays on cathode-ray screens.

ORGANIZATION AND CODING OF DATA

The importance of planning the organization and recording of data *before* it is gathered cannot be overstressed. More than one large research project has ended with an indecipherable mountain of paper instead of the concise answers to well-defined questions which are always presented in the textbooks on research methods. Of course, no researcher can foresee all of the problems and possibilities implicit in a program at its inception, despite the implications of omniscience that almost universally pervade the writing of research reports. Still, a lack of planning for data recording can only reduce the likelihood of meaningful compilation, analysis, and hypothesis generation or testing.

Personnel. There is no adequate substitute for a capable data-processing specialist whose skills include those of a secretary, file clerk, and machine operator. To trust the central recording and filing of data (original forms and punched cards) to a group of research assistants, or worse yet, to a series of research assistants, is to invite eventual disaster. Code books and well-labeled files are very important, but having one staff member who knows where and what everything is can save a great deal of time, effort, and confusion.

The need for accuracy on the part of key-punch operators and others involved in coding and recording data is obvious. Much less obvious is the value of a perceptual-temperament "trait" that seems to defy detection by the usual employee-selection procedures: the ability to notice an incongruity while actually working with the data for some other purpose—a kind of serendipity that can be extremely valuable when it occurs.

Code Books and Locator Files. Any research project that involves the use of more than two instruments and/or more than two testings of the same subjects should develop a central system of tracking the data available for each subject in each sample. In some cases the use of handwritten lists is most practical, but with larger data-acquisition programs a special card deck may be prepared solely for the purpose of recording basic information about each subject and his available data. In conjunction with a machine called a *collator,* such card decks allow rapid selection of subsamples for particular processing runs.

Subjects should be code numbered, although alphabetic identifying information can be retained in the locator file. It is crucially important to use identical subject-code numbers to label all original forms as well as the data cards punched from those forms. A particular card field (set of consecutive card columns) should be reserved for the subject's basic number.

When multiple instruments or multiple administrations are used with the same people, *other* card fields should be defined to hold such information.

A basic identification block of fields should be defined which will be written on or punched in every form or data card for every subject from whom data are gathered. For example, suppose that we wish to initiate a program of research which will involve the testing of 100 college students of each sex from each of three different colleges at the ends of each of their four years of college education. The test battery will consist of a personality inventory, a multiple-choice biographical information form, and a questionnaire which asks for characterization of the school they are attending.

The basic ID code block might consist of these fields:

    col. 1: school code number (1 – 3)
    cols. 2 – 4: subject code number (1 – 100)
    col. 5: subject sex (1 = male, 0 = female)
    col. 6: year of testing (1 – 4)
    col. 7: instrument concerned (1 – 3)
    col. 8: card number (blank, if only one card is needed for the instrument concerned)

This eight-digit number would be written on every instrument as soon after collection as possible, except for column 8, which only pertains to punch-card records. The subject's sex was included in the basic code block because we had decided to consider this as an independent variable throughout the research design, and its presence on every record will simplify later sorting of data cards. The same reasoning holds for the inclusion of a school-code digit. We need not code the 600 subjects serially, since the school and sex-code digits will differentiate the six persons given the same subject code number (max = 100).

Although handwritten lists of subject codes, names, and checklists of available data might be sufficient for this project, a locator card deck could be punched to hold this information. The advantages of such a card deck are: (1) it can be updated easily by additional punching or correction of single cards, (2) printed listings of the card contents can be obtained quickly and easily with an accounting machine such as the IBM 407 or 402, which are available at most machine installations, and (3) the card deck can be duplicated, sorted, and collated with data decks through the use of card-processing machines—vastly speeding the selection of subsamples for particular analyses.

DATA-CARD FIELDS AND FORMATS

Every data card originated by a key-punch operator from a printed form, or punched automatically by a machine, should contain an identification block such as that just described. We prefer to use the *first* eight to ten card columns for this ID field, although some researchers use the end of the card for this purpose. The data-analysis programs presented later which involve the use of subject-ID codes, all assume that these codes are punched at the beginning of the data cards, before any of the data which are to be analyzed. The remaining card columns may be arranged in any way that suits the designer of the data-recording system, within certain constraints which are discussed in the following paragraphs.

Each kind of information to be recorded on a data card should be initially analyzed to determine the maximum number of consecutive card columns that might be required. Every number, letter, or special character requires a separate card column. If the data from a single source, such as a questionnaire item, are known to consist only of numerals between one and nine, then only one card column will be required for this information. However, suppose that the responses to the item could be negative as well as positive numbers. In this case two card columns would be necessary for the item, since the minus sign requires a separate card column when it occurs. We need not punch a plus sign in this column for positive numbers, since this will be assumed automatically for numbers not preceded by minus signs; the "sign" column may be left blank or punched with the numeral zero. If all scores are positive, no sign column is necessary.

A series of consecutive card columns assigned together to a single purpose is called a *field*. Theoretically, a field may consist of from 1 to 80 card columns. Within each field, numeric values are assumed to be "right-justified," which means that the contents of the fields are arranged so that corresponding decimal places are always in the same card columns on every card punched according to the same format.

What about noninteger values? As long as the numbers are aligned by decimal place, we need not punch the decimal point in the data cards. It is permissible to punch the decimal point (a period symbol), but a separate card column is required for it, and it serves no significant purpose in most data-processing applications in the behavioral sciences. At this point you may wonder how the computer can distinguish a four-digit integer from a four-place decimal fraction. The fact is that it cannot, except through the use of special instructions which are submitted to it along with the data deck when a processing run is initiated.

To continue the earlier example, suppose that we wished to punch data cards with item scores from a personality inventory, using as many cards as necessary for each subject to hold these scores. The first eight columns of each card would be set aside for the subject's identification block. Suppose that the questionnaire consists of 60 items, each of which requires a choice from among seven alternatives. Since no negative numbers are involved, each item's field will consist of one card column. We do not have to jam everything together in this case, so let us begin with item one in card-column eleven and continue punching the 60 item scores through column 70.

Leaving the two blank columns (9-10) between the ID block and the data was not necessary, but aids in visual checking of the card contents.

Unanswered Items. Almost inevitably in large-scale questionnaire studies, some subjects fail to answer some items. What do we punch in the corresponding card columns? We could instruct the key-punch operator (or a precoding clerk) to insert some middle-of-the-scale value in such cases, if the items contained ordered alternatives. We could use another digit for the no-answer response; zero is usually reserved for this purpose. We could simply leave the card column blank. There are some not-too-obvious traps involved here, because a computer cannot distinguish between zero and a blank column when it has been instructed to read a card field as a numeric value. The use of zero or blank for no answer when the field holds an ordinal-scale score would yield a numeric value smaller than the lowest scale point. Computer programs can be written to replace zero scores with a predetermined number (as exemplified by Program TESTAT), but they cannot distinguish between blanks and zeros. We will discuss this problem further in Chapter 8.

Field Lengths. When the data to be punched in a card vary in decimal placement or field length, it is usually worthwhile to waste a few card columns in order to obtain consistency of field type across successive fields. The reasons for this have to do with the instructions to the computer program regarding the data-card format mentioned earlier. For instance, suppose the data to be punched in a card led to these *minimum* data descriptions:

(1) a two-digit integer
(2) a two-digit integer (possible negatives)
(3) a one-digit integer
(4) a three-digit integer
(5) a five-digit number with two decimal places
(6) a four-digit integer (possible negatives)
(7) a four-digit number with three decimal places

To expand all of these fields to the same field type would require 56 card columns, aligning each value in its field to permit a sign column, four integer columns, and three decimal-place columns. Of course, the minimum necessary number of columns would be 23, but every field would be arranged differently. By using 36 columns, we can get away with only two different field types: (1) a three-digit integer for items 1-4, and (2) an eight-digit number with three decimal places for items 5-7. Note that the minus sign may occupy any column preceding the first significant digit, but must not itself be preceded by anything within the field except blank columns.

Repeated Measurements. When the same instruments are administered to the same subjects on different occasions, it is very important to see that the card format used to punch each administration's scores is the same as that for other administrations. If this rule is followed, data-processing procedures will be considerably simplified. A separate card column within the ID block should be reserved for a digit designating the testing session from which the data were obtained. There are, however, some circumstances in which it may be advisable to punch repeated measurements across a single data card in consecutive fields, using one card per subject. This is especially true when the number of tests is few and/or there are many repeated measures to be analyzed.

Nonnumeric Data. For most data-processing purposes the use of numeric codes should be preferred over letter codes. The primary reason for this is the fact that a computer can read data-card fields in either of two ways: as numeric values *or* as symbols. Numerals may be read in this second mode, but their significance as numbers cannot be utilized. Letters and special characters, on the other hand, cannot be read in the first mode. A less significant, but important, consideration will be discussed in the next section when we describe techniques for sorting data cards: letters require twice as much machine work as do numerals.

There are exceptional situations where letter coding is worthwhile, particularly when the data represent unordered categories and a wide variety of such categories are potentially codable for a particular card field. We will also describe techniques for handling alphabetic data which consists of words rather than letter codes in Chapter 13.

CARD-SORTING TECHNIQUES

Probably the second most common card-processing machine after the key punch is the sorter, available in many models. This machine will interpret the holes punched in a single card column and will distribute the cards into particular "pockets" accordingly. Some sorters are supplied with a bank of counters to automatically record the number of cards accumulated in each pocket. The cards are fed into the mechanism one at a time from the bottom of a stack, which is inserted into the feed hopper face down, so that the first card in the deck goes into the machine first. The card passes across a reading station that senses the location of a hole in the column being sorted, and the card is then automatically routed to the appropriate pocket.

There are 13 pockets into which cards may be sent; these correspond to the 12 rows of punch positions (+, −, 0, 1, 2, 3, 4, 5, 6, 7, 8, 9) plus a *reject* pocket which normally receives cards that do not contain any holes in the column being sorted. A set of switches may be used to suppress sorting on any of the 12 rows; instead of going to the appropriate pocket, the card will be sent to the reject pocket if the hole appears in the row designated. By setting these switches to suppress sorting on all rows except one, cards with the punch *not* designated may be picked out of a deck without disturbing the original order of the other cards, since they will stack up in the reject pocket as they were entered. Another switch has the effect of suppressing sorting on all rows from 1–9; this is used in alphabetical sorting.

Numeric Sorting. Suppose we have a deck of cards containing three-digit scores in columns 11–13 which we wish to arrange in rank order. The problem would be the same, of course, if we simply wished to put a deck into the serial order of the subjects' code numbers. The key to all sorting procedures involving multiple columns is to work from the lower-order column to the highest-order column consecutively; in other words, work from right to left within the field. Therefore, we would first sort the deck on column 13. We would then retrieve the cards from the sorter pockets in a systematic fashion so as to stack the smallest column-13 digits at the front and the largest at the end of the reassembled deck. We would then insert the deck again into the feed hopper and reset the column designator to column 12 to get a second distribution of the cards. Again we would assemble the deck so that the smallest column-*12* digits were at the front of the deck. (The smallest column-13 digits will still be at the front also.) After inserting the deck into the feed hopper and resetting the locator to column 11, we obtain a third sorting. When the deck is assembled now we will find that the cards are arranged so that the first in the deck contains the smallest score, while the last contains the largest. If we had wanted the deck arranged from largest in front to smallest at the end, we would simply reverse the order of retrieval of the cards from the pockets on each of the three sorts, but we would still sort column 13 first. If the scores had included some negative numbers it would have been necessary to first separate the negative scores from the positives and then order each subdeck separately. The table shown here illustrates the results of each step in a simple numeric sorting problem.

Deck at Start	Deck After First Sort	Deck After Second Sort	Deck After Third Sort
009	041	001	001
041	321	002	002
321	001	003	003
002	002	306	009
077	052	009	041
306	003	321	052
001	306	041	077
376	376	052	306
052	077	376	321
003	009	077	376

The top of each list represents the beginning of the deck, and therefore the first card to be sorted, since the deck is inserted upside down into the feed hopper. Underlines in each column indicate which groupings of cards would be sorted into separate pockets on the sort concerned. If these cards had not been punched with leading zeros, the reject pocket would be retrieved in such a way that the blanks preceded the zeros in the reassembled deck.

It is always wise to *sight check* each set of cards as it is retrieved from a pocket, especially at the beginning of a large sorting operation, to be sure that the machine is operating correctly. Sight checking is simply looking *through* the entire card deck to be sure that all cards in the pocket actually do contain identical punches.

Although it may not be immediately obvious, a series of nonconsecutive card columns can be treated as a single multiple-digit number, even reordering the actual card columns to achieve a desired sequence in the final reassembled deck. For instance, suppose we wished to obtain a deck with all males in serial code-number order followed by a subdeck of all females in serial code-number order. Suppose further that the sex-code digit was in card column 6, while the code numbers were in columns 1-2. We would first sort on column 2 and then on column 1 to achieve serial code-number order without regard to sex. *Then,* we would sort on column 6, stacking the males in front of the females. Since the sorting on column 6 was done last, the serial code-number ordering *within* each subdeck would be maintained.

Alphabetic Sorting. As you will find by inspection of Figure 3-1, each alphabetic character is represented by two punches in a single column—a numeric punch (1-9) and a zone punch (0, −, +). The alphabet is divided into three subsets: A-I, J-R, and S-Z. Your first notion of an alphabetic sorting method might be to sort the deck into three subdecks on the zone punch, and then sort each subdeck on the numeric punches. Although this procedure will work, the following method is more efficient.

As in sorting a sequence of numeric columns, a set of alphabetic columns should be sorted from the lowest-order character first to the highest-order character last. Beginning with the lowest-order column, sort the deck in the usual way with numeric switch settings. Since the cards are read 9-edge first, and only a single punch can be interpreted, the cards will be distributed into pockets on the basis of the numeric-punch portion of the alphabetic character code. Without changing the column locator, set the alphabetic sort switch on, which effectively suppresses sorting on the digits 1-9. Run the deck through again, yielding three subdecks for the zone punches. After reassembly, the deck will be alphabetically ordered on the single column concerned. If blank columns are present, these cards will fall into the reject pocket on the first sort. They may be held out or picked up and placed in front of the deck; if they are included in the second sort, they will again fall into the reject pocket.

Sorting a series of alphabetic columns proceeds from column to column as in numeric sorting, except that two sorts per column are required. When simple numeric punches are included among the alphabetic characters, the sorting procedure described here will place them in order at the beginning of the final deck, *except* for simple zero, which is one of the zone punches. All zero cards will be together in the final deck, ahead of the cards containing an "S" punch, and can be replaced in their ordinal position ahead of the 1-punched cards. The following table illustrates the steps in an alphabetic sorting problem involving two card columns.

Deck at Start	After First Numeric Sort	After First Zone Sort	After Second Numeric Sort	After Second Zone Sort
BA(+2,+1)	ZΔ(Δ)	ZΔ(Δ)	(1)AA	(+)AA
MA(−4,+1)	BA(1)	BA(+)	(1)AB	(+)AB
AB(+1,+2)	MA(1)	MA(+)	(1)AM	(+)AM
ZA(09,+1)	ZA(1)	ZA(+)	(2)BA	(+)BA
ND(−5,+4)	AA(1)	AA(+)	(2)BB	(+)BB
AA(+1,+1)	AB(2)	AB(+)	(4)MA	(−)MA
NB(−5,+2)	NB(2)	NB(+)	(5)NB	(−)NB
AM(+1,−4)	BB(2)	BB(+)	(5)ND	(−)ND
BB(+2,+2)	ND(4)	ND(+)	(9)ZΔ	(0)ZΔ
ZΔ(09,ΔΔ)	AM(4)	AM(−)	(9)ZA	(0)ZA

Sorters are available in many models, some of which use electromagnetic sensing while others use a photoelectric cell to detect the position of the hole in the card. Sorters vary in speed from 450 to 2000 cards per minute, and a wide variety of designs may be found in various installations. The manufacturer's manuals for the card-processing machines at your installation are well worth studying in order to make maximum use of the capabilities of the machines. The introduction offered here is only intended to be a starting point for developing your knowledge of card-processing techniques.

Card Counters. Some sorters are equipped with card-counting devices. The simplest version is a single counter that trips each time a card passes the reading station. This device can be used for determining sample sizes and for rough checks of data decks. Less common is the bank of pocket counters that is attached to the sorter in some installations. For obtaining frequency distributions or contingency tables for combinations of a few variables, the counter-sorter is quite efficient. Since each variable requires a separate pass of the card deck through the machine, however, this method quickly becomes impractical as the number of variables increases. Computer programs which compute frequency distributions, as well as a number of descriptive statistical measures, will be presented in later chapters. The use of a computer program for contingency tabling on a series of variables is even more necessary because of the number of sorts required for each variable involved. The number of sorts is important not only because of the time required, but also because of the wear on the card deck produced by repeated handling.

Preplanning of the steps in a complex sorting task is very much worth the "extra" time involved, and can often save hours of unnecessary effort. By considering all stages of the task together, one can arrange the sequence of operations to eliminate redundant steps. Quite often such preplanning also yields side benefits due to the more integrated understanding of the problem achieved in the process of planning the analytic operations. The same thing holds for computer programming; preplanning is crucially important, and usually results in a better understanding of the problem to be solved.

Review Exercises

1. Could this sentence be punched into a tab card?
2. What are "zone" punches? What is their significance in coding alphabetic characters?
3. What machine would you use to duplicate a deck of punched cards? Why not use a key-punch machine?
4. Devise a hypothetical example of a locator file.
5. How many columns long should the identification block be for subjects in a sample of 1000 which contains 500 boys and 500 girls, and which will be tested once with seven instruments?
6. If the following series of scores represent the largest fields required for six different variables, how should the data-card fields be arranged? Need the decimal points be punched?

   −22.3356   2.66   1.6
   654.975   9.99   −.42

7. In Chapter 8 of this book, a set of 16 data cards are output by a program called TESTAT (problem two). These cards are used as an example deck for programs in Chapters 9-12. For practice in the use of card-processing machines, punch these cards with a key-punch machine, make a duplicate copy of the deck with the reproducer, and then sort the 16 cards with the sorting machine so that the ninth (total) scores are in order from lowest to highest. Re-sort the cards from highest to lowest. Now punch a different *name* in the last few columns of each card and use the sorter to put the cards in alphabetic order. If there is a line printer at your installation, make a listing of the card deck.

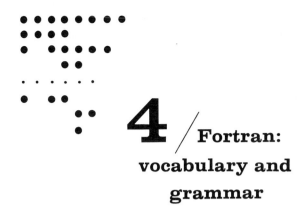

4 / Fortran: vocabulary and grammar

Fortran was created in 1954 by a group of 13 men at International Business Machines. The name of the language was derived from *FOR*mula *TRAN*slation, since its original purpose was to help scientists state mathematical problems for machine solution. It is by far the most widely used programming language today, particularly among those engaged in quantitative research.

Fortunately, the Fortran language has not remained static since 1954. Two major revisions have appeared, called Fortran II and IV. These improved versions of the language are due largely to the vastly increased capabilities of modern hardware, especially the development of large core memories. Some of the improvements can be traced to the independent development of Fortran-like languages by university computing centers and manufacturers wishing to extend the versatility of their own machines. Fortran is therefore a generic term for a number of different "dialects" which share a common vocabulary and grammar. Some versions of Fortran offer an extended vocabulary, while others may permit certain relaxations in rules of usage.

In this book we will present only the most central or commonly available aspects of the Fortran language. We will omit some of the features of the language which are relatively unimportant from the viewpoints of most behavioral scientists. Mastery of the basic language presented here will permit the coding of programs that will run at your installation with few, if any, changes. After learning the basics of the language and its use, determining the special conveniences and capabilities available at your installation should be relatively easy.

To supplement this book you should obtain a copy of the manufacturer's manual on the Fortran language for your machine. These manuals are intended for reference purposes, and may appear bewildering at this stage because no attempt is usually made to organize the presentation in terms of essentials and less significant features. In addition to manufacturer's manuals, a number of excellent general texts on the Fortran language are available, such as those by Golden (1965), McCracken (1965), Organick (1963), and Plumb (1964). Recent texts by Dimitry and Mott (1966) and Sprowls (1966) provide excellent introductions to Fortran and other compiler languages. These books are all oriented toward the fields of engineering and mathematics, however, and the examples are drawn from these fields. Topics of relatively minor interest to behavioral scientists are often emphasized at the expense of certain aspects of programming which are crucially important in the field with which the present volume is concerned.

FORTRAN COMPILER PROGRAMS

In Chapter 2 we pointed out that compiler languages such as Fortran, Algol, and Cobol cannot be understood directly by any computer. The statements in these source languages must be translated into instructions which the machine can execute. Many machine-language instructions may be required to express the operations implied by a single Fortran statement; the ratio may go as high as 20 to 1 for some mathematical programs.

This translation from source language to object language is carried out automatically by the computer, thus saving the programmer tremendous amounts of time and effort. Even more significant is the fact that one need not learn machine language in order to use the computer effectively.

Another advantage of machine translation from source to object language is that the compiler program which does the translation can include checks for various kinds of clearly invalid statements or sequences. During the compilation of a Fortran program, questionable statements may result in printed messages to the programmer, although the processing is allowed to continue. Some kinds of errors, however, would inevitably result in useless output or prevent completion of the translation process, and so the compiler program prints an error message and begins to compile the next program. These error messages are commonly called *diagnostics*. Fortran compilers vary considerably in the amount of such checking that they include. Although experienced programmers are sometimes annoyed by the zealousness of some compilers, which prevent certain short-cuts and subtle algorithms, the overall savings in programmer time and erroneous output are unarguable. As you learn the language and submit small problems for processing, it is well worth the effort to be sure you understand the reasons for every diagnostic the machine prints for your programs. In some cases you will find that diagnostics come in groups, with one major error resulting in a rash of other error messages which can be traced to the earlier mistake. Generally speaking, you will learn far more from a program which does not run the first time—if you take the trouble to fully understand the reasons for its failure. There is almost always a logical explanation for every action the computer takes, since random machine malfunctions are very rare.

The object program produced by the Fortran compiler may be saved in the form of a card deck, or may be stored for later use on some other medium such as magnetic tape. Most computer systems provide a compile-and-execute procedure which permits the programmer to submit a single deck of cards including both his Fortran source program and data. The machine automatically compiles the object program, stores it in memory, and executes the program using the data as input, all in a continuous operation. Obviously, the constant use of such a procedure with programs which are thoroughly "de-bugged" and frequently employed would be unnecessarily wasteful of machine time. At most installations, once a routine has been checked out, the object program can be retained in the form of a card deck or in some other external medium, such as magnetic tape, and need not be recompiled every time it is used to process data. Retention of object programs in a program library is a natural step in the development of any computer installation and it is not uncommon for users in a particular field such as the behavioral sciences to develop their own common library of programs.

The major differences among Fortran compilers are a function of the machines' memory capacities. Although variations will be observed in diagnostics, in the restrictiveness of the rules for coding such things as array subscripts, and in the availability of such conveniences as statement separators, the Fortran compilers for machines with the same amount of memory will have roughly equivalent capabilities. The Fortran language presented in this book is intended for use with machines such as the IBM 7040 or the CDC 1604, which have at least 32,768 locations of core storage (a standard memory size). Machines with 16,384 words of storage will be able to handle the Fortran statements to be described in this chapter, but the programs presented in later chapters will have to be modified to restrict the sizes of the largest problems they can accept. Machines such as the IBM 1400 series or the CDC 160, which have considerably smaller core memories, will be unable to compile some of the statements described here. While these smaller machines are far from useless to the behavioral scientist, they are quite limited with regard to ease of programming and the size of the problems which they can efficiently process. On the other hand, if you have access to one of the extremely large systems such as an IBM System/360 Model 75 or a CDC 6600, you may wish to expand the programs described later to handle larger problems.

FORTRAN PROGRAM CARD FORMAT

The basic unit of the language is the *statement*, which is roughly equivalent to a natural-language sentence, or an algebraic equation. Unlike sentences in the natural language, however, no redundancy is possible, since the rules for coding instructions to a computer in Fortran are both restrictive and precise. Each Fortran statement begins on a separate tab card, although a statement may be continued onto additional cards if necessary. Unlike data cards, in which all 80 columns may be utilized as needed, Fortran program cards are arranged with certain definite fields reserved for particular kinds of information. Figure 4-1 illustrates these fields. Note, however, that cards printed like this are not necessary for Fortran statements; a computer can only read the holes punched in a tab card.

Column one is used only to hold the letter "C" if the card is for *comments,* and is not meant to be a part of the operating program.[1] Comment cards are ignored by the Fortran compiler, but will be printed whenever the program is listed. Such cards will be used liberally in the programs in later chapters to assist tracing of the operational sequences and to note the contents of various storage areas. Any of the remaining columns in a comment card may contain any legal key-punch symbol. Comments may be continued to other cards only if a "C" is punched in column one of each card.

Columns two through five in Fortran statement cards are used for *statement numbers.* Only certain Fortran statements are normally given such numbers, which may be any positive (unsigned) integer value. Although statement numbers must be integer constants, they are interpreted only as symbols by the Fortran compiler; that is, the numeric values of the statement numbers do *not* determine the sequence in which the statements are

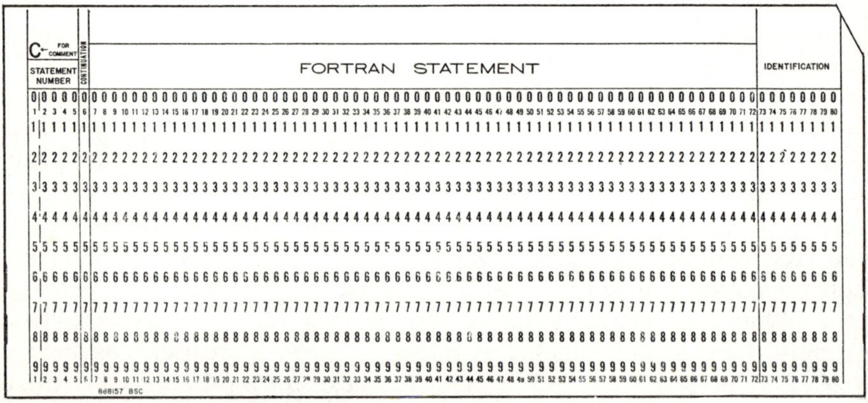

FIGURE 4-1. Arrangement of fields on a Fortran program card.

[1] In most Fortran systems column one may also be used for the first digit of a statement number.

excuted. No two statement numbers within a single routine may be the same, but the values may be assigned without regard to serial order. In writing programs you should assign statement numbers in order, however, just to make it easier to trace the program's operational flow. It is also a good idea to skip numbers regularly (5, 10, 15, . . .) so that you can maintain the sequence if you find it necessary later to insert additional statements requiring numbers.

Column six is normally blank. If any legal key-punch character other than a blank or a zero appears in this column, the statement on the card will be interpreted as a *continuation* of the statement begun on the previous card in the program deck. To aid in checking the program card deck, it is advisable to punch a zero in column six of the first card of a multiple-card statement, and to punch serial numbers 1, 2, 3, . . ., in this column of the second, third, fourth, and so on, continuation cards. Up to five continuation cards per statement will be accepted by any Fortran compiler. (Most compilers allow more.)

Columns 7 through 72 contain the *text* of the Fortran statement. If continuation cards are used, column 7 of each continuation card is assumed to follow immediately after column 72 of the preceding card. Blanks are not significant in this text field of the Fortran statement, and may be inserted anywhere to increase readability. When the Fortran compiler reads the statement, it squeezes them out, since they are irrelevant to the translation process. There is an exception to this rule in the case of Hollerith fields, which will be discussed later in this chapter.

Columns 72 through 80 in Fortran statement cards are ignored by the compiler. They may contain any legal key-punch characters, and are sometimes used to hold sequence numbers representing the proper order of the cards in the program deck. Such serial numbers can be very helpful if you accidentally drop the deck.

CONSTANTS AND VARIABLES

There are two types of operands in the Fortran language: constants and variables. *Constants* are specific values which appear in Fortran statements and remain unchanged during execution of the program.[2] *Variables,* on the other hand, are "open values" which may be changed during the program execution. The first time a variable name or a particular constant is encountered in a Fortran program, the compiler assigns it to some address in memory. Thereafter, the appearance of the same constant or variable name in another Fortran statement will automatically be referred to the correct location in the computer memory.

Variable names may conveniently be considered as names of memory

[2] Unintentional changes in such values can occur with faulty subroutines or subscript values. This will be discussed in Chapter 6.

locations. Actually, the values of constants also serve this purpose for the Fortran compiler. The fact that the Fortran compiler automatically keeps track of actual memory addresses is one of the major advantages of the language.

It is important to distinguish between the name of a variable and the specific value its location may contain at a given point in the program sequence; the name of the variable remains the same throughout the program, even though the contents of the memory cell to which it refers may change repeatedly. In contrast, the names and contents of memory cells holding constants are the same, and remain unchanged during program execution.

There are two types of number representation available to the Fortran programmer: *integer* and *real*. Because the internal storage and arithmetic manipulation of these two modes are entirely different, certain conventions must be followed with regard to variable names and the representation of constant values in Fortran statements. Alphabetic data are stored in the machine's memory in still another way, which will be discussed later.

Integer Mode. Integer constants are distinguished by the lack of a decimal point. As the name implies, only whole-number values can be represented in this mode, which for this reason is sometimes called "fixed point." Integer values may be positive or negative and include zero. The maximum (absolute) value of an integer constant or variable in Fortran depends on the word size of the computer concerned. In IBM computers of the 7040 and 7090 series, this maximum is $2^{35}-1$, while in the System/360 series it is $2^{31} - 1$ (single precision). In CDC machines such as the 1604 and 3600, the maximum is $2^{47} - 1$; in the CDC 6600 it is $2^{59} - 1$. Positive integer constants are normally written without a sign, but negative values must be preceded by a minus sign. Commas are *never* used to separate groups of three digits in large numbers in Fortran statements or in data to be processed by Fortran programs. Some examples of valid integer constants are:

0   1   −59   2040   −32768

Integer variable names are distinguished by the initial alphabetic character; if it is an I, J, K, L, M, or N, then the compiler assumes that an integer-mode value is stored in the memory location so named. Variable names may be one through six characters in length, any of which may be letters or numerals, as long as the first character is alphabetic. Examples of valid integer variable names are:

K   K23   I2J   MEAN   II

Real Mode. Real constants are distinguished from integer constants by the presence of a decimal point. These values are stored in the computer memory as a mantissa and exponent, much in the manner of logrithmic notation. For this reason, real mode is sometimes called "floating point." The maximum magnitude of such values is extremely large, but the number of significant digits is quite restricted, varying between 7 and 16, depending on the computer concerned and whether or not the programmer has specified "double precision," which is possible in most versions of Fortran. For most practical applications in the behavioral sciences double precision is unnecessary, and for this reason we will place the topic in the category of "advanced" programming.

Any number may be represented as a real-mode constant. These numbers may be positive or negative, and include zero, whole numbers, and any decimal fraction or mixed number. Most Fortran compilers permit a variety of forms for writing real-mode constants, but we will consider only the most frequently used: simply a number containing a decimal point. As with integer constants, positive values are normally unsigned, and embedded commas must not be used. Extra leading or following zeros are permitted but unnecessary, as illustrated in these examples.

0.	or	0.0
1.	or	1.00
−2.607	or	−02.6070
.025	or	0.025

Real-mode variable names are distinguished from integer-mode names by the initial alphabetic character; if it is a letter *other than* I, J, K, L, M, or N, the location so named is assumed to hold a real-mode number. In other respects, integer- and real-mode variable names follow the same rules: up to six characters (letters or numerals), the first of which must be a letter. The following are valid examples of real-mode variable names:

    X X23 X2K AMEAN ZZ

Alphameric Data. This mode is sometimes called "Hollerith" after the pioneer in the use of punched cards for data processing. Such constants are most commonly used in Fortran programming to output titling information. We will discuss this technique when we consider FORMAT statements.

Alphabetic data may also be stored in the computer memory in variable-named locations. Either integer- or real-mode names may be used for this purpose, but it is advisable to choose one or the other mode for a given program to avoid unintentional "mode conversion." Chapter 13 will be concerned with some important applications of this mode of data storage and manipulation.

ARRAY VARIABLES AND SUBSCRIPTS

Variable names in either mode may signify single memory locations, or they may designate sets of memory locations. The Fortran compiler refers to the DIMENSION statement of the program to decide whether a variable name applies to one or more memory cells. Any variable name which does *not* appear in the DIMENSION statement is assumed to be a *simple* or single-location variable.

We will use the term *array* for any multiple-location (dimensioned) variable. Two particular types of arrays are *vectors* (lists) and *matrices* (tables). These are illustrated in Figure 4-2. Note that three-dimensional arrays also may be designated by a single variable name.

In ordinary mathematical notation a particular cell in an array is designated by lower-case subscripts attached to the symbol for the array. Since the Fortran character set includes only capital letters, subscripts are indicated by integer values enclosed in a pair of parentheses immediately following the array-variable name. For example, X_{ij} in ordinary notation designates the element at the intersection of row i and column j of the table X. In Fortran this single memory location would be specified by X(I, J). Note that a comma is used to separate the row and column subscripts. Of course, the integer variables I and J themselves refer to particular memory locations. If the values 2 and 3 were stored in these memory cells, respectively, then X(I, J) would be interpreted as indicating the cell located at the intersection of row 2 and column 3 of the array named X. The *contents* of X(2, 3) would be a *real* number, such as 471.975.

It is convenient to adopt a consistent way of conceptualizing the dimensions of arrays. Consider the first subscript to mean *rows*, the second *columns*, and the third *slices*, as illustrated in Figure 4-2.

Remember, if a variable name appears in the DIMENSION statement of a program, and is therefore intended to designate an array rather than a simple (unsubscripted) variable, the variable name should be followed by the appropriate number of subscripts in parentheses wherever it appears in operational program statements. Exceptions to this rule will be explained later.

Subscripts in Fortran must be integer-mode constants or simple integer variables. Either real or integer array-variable names may be subscripted. Certain forms of integer-mode expressions are also permitted, as shown in the following examples which illustrate the seven possible subscript forms.

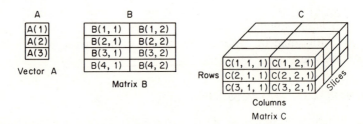

FIGURE 4-2. Conceptual arrangement of arrays.

X(I)
X(2)
X(I+ 2)
X(I − 2)
X(2*I)
X(2*I + 2)
X(2*I − 2)

Note that constants must follow + or − operators, but they must precede the multiplication operator (*). Multiplication will precede addition or subtraction when the subscript is evaluated. Division is not permitted, nor is the use of more than one variable name within the subscript expression.

These restrictions apply only to each single subscript. Therefore, the following examples are permissible.

X(I, I+ 1, I+ 2)   ALPHA(K+ 2, 2*KK, KAPPA)
KA(23, I+ 17, 2*J)   MOUSE(KUE, K+ 5, 2*II − 1)
BETA(40, 1, 2*K+ 3)   MIX(MIN+ 1, MAX − 1)

Although these restrictions may be annoying, they do not really hamper programming flexibility to any extent.

RESERVATION OF STORAGE AREAS (DIMENSION)

The DIMENSION statement reserves series of memory locations for array variables, and appears as the first statement in the program. If the program uses no array variables, no DIMENSION statement is required. This statement is not operational, but serves only as a reference for the Fortran compiler as it translates the source program.

The key word is followed by one or more array reservations separated by commas. Each array name to be used in subsequent program statements is followed by its dimensions enclosed in parentheses. The dimensions must be indicated by integer-constant subscripts. In the DIMENSION statement, however, these integers represent the lengths of the lists or sizes of the tables of memory locations to be reserved for the variables named. The DIMENSION statement for the arrays in Figure 4-2 is as follows:

DIMENSION   A(3), B(4, 2), C(3, 2, 4)

As can be seen in Figure 4-2, three memory locations are needed for vector A, eight for matrix B, and 24 for matrix C. Note that commas are used only between array reservations and between dimension integers within parentheses. Integer variable names may appear within these parentheses *only* in the special case of variable dimensioning for subroutines that will be discussed in Chapter 6. In program DIMENSION statements only integer constants may appear in these parentheses. Examples follow.

DIMENSION ALPHA (20000)
DIMENSION A(2), B(100), C(2, 5), KK(6), XD(3, 3, 3)
DIMENSION R(100, 100), V(100, 100), B(100, 20), X(100), Y(100)

In the first example, most of the available portion of a 32,768-word computer memory has been asigned to the array named ALPHA. The sum of all locations reserved in the DIMENSION statement must not exceed the available memory, which varies somewhat for machines of the same size, depending on the length of the program, the monitor system, and so forth. Note that in the preceding example the third DIMENSION statement reserves 22,200 locations, an amount that might not be accepted by some computer systems. If the available memory is exceeded, the Fortran compiler will reject the program with an error diagnostic indicating this reason.

FORMAT STATEMENTS

Format statements are not operational, but serve as references for input/output statements. They describe the modes and arrangement of data on an external medium, such as punched cards, printer paper, or magnetic tape. Every FORMAT statement must have a statement number. The key word FORMAT is followed by a left parenthesis, which is followed by a series of field specifications separated by commas, and a right parenthesis completes the statement. For example:

5 FORMAT (1X, A3, 6X, 7F4. 1, I3, 2HAB)

Each field specification indicates at least three things:

(1) the number of times the field is to be repeated sequentially
(2) the mode of data transfer (F, I, A, X, H)
(3) the length of the field (number of characters)

There is a wide variety of data-transfer modes available in most versions of Fortran, but we will mention only those which are most useful in behavioral science programming. Once you understand these thoroughly, you will have little trouble extending your knowledge by consulting the manufacturer's Fortran manual at your installation.

The storage modes of field specifications are indicated by single letters, which are *not* variable names but standard codes recognized by the Fortran system. These same letters (F, I, A, X, H) may be used as variable names in other program statements. The letters F, I, and A imply transfer of data to or from one memory location for every field specified. Numbers appearing before these letters indicate sequential repetition of the field specification. The letter X is used to skip character positions in the external medium; the number preceding the X indicates the number of positions to be skipped; no number follows the X, but a number must always precede it. The code letter H is used for Hollerith constants. Blank columns may be inserted anywhere in FORMAT statements; however, they have special significance in Hollerith fields.

FORMAT statements may be located physically anywhere in the program card deck, since they are not part of the operational sequence, but are only referenced by number by input/output statements. Usually FORMAT statements are placed immediately after the input or output statement that first references them in the program.

F Specifications. F stands for *floating point*. On input, this mode interprets the content of the field in the external medium as a real number and stores this real value in the memory location specified by the input statement that referenced the FORMAT. One real value is transferred to one memory cell from each field designated. On output, the content of each cell of memory is interpreted as a real number and is placed in a separate field of the external medium. Since decimal fractions are possible in real numbers, the field specification must include information about the number of decimal places as well as the length of the field. The general form for an F specification is: $a F b . c$ The a stands for an integer field-repetition factor; b is an integer giving the total number of character positions in the field; and c is the number of decimal places in the field. Note that a period must always appear between the integers b and c. If the integer a is the value one (no repetition), it may be omitted. Remember that the value b is *total* field length and thus will always equal or exceed the value c.

Decimal points need not be present on the *input* medium, but if they are present, their positions in the external fields will override the designations of decimal places contained in the FORMAT specifications of those fields. Decimal points will be placed on the *output* medium, however, and a character position must be allotted for this purpose in determining the appropriate output field length for real values. Negative signs occupy separate character positions preceding the first significant digits in both input and output fields. Positive signs are unnecessary on input and are omitted on output. Despite the omission of positive signs on output, a separate column must be reserved for the sign in the integer portion of every output field. Furthermore, provision must be made for at least one integer digit in every output field. This leads to the following rule for F-mode *output* fields: the total field length b must exceed the number of decimal places specified c by at least three columns.[3]

At least one digit will be printed in the integer portion of the output field, even if it is a zero. To the left of the first significant integer, however, blanks will be inserted to fill out the field. Digits will appear in all decimal positions specified. On input in most Fortran systems, blank columns will

---

[3]Many minor variations of the rules in this section appear in different Fortran compilers. The rules given here are conservative versions, which will be workable for all compilers.

be interpreted as zeros. On output, the value will be rounded automatically to the number of decimal places indicated by c.

In the following example, different FORMATS are used to read data into memory and to output the same values. The symbol Δ is used to represent a blank character position in this book; the key-punch symbol is a blank column. Note the decimal-point override for the last input field.

EXAMPLE OF F (REAL MODE) CONVERSION

0123Δ45-2.546	input medium (col 1-13)
(F3.2, 3F2.0, F4.0)	input FORMAT specifications
.12 | 30. | 45. | -2. | .546	values in 5 memory locations
(5F6.2)	output FORMAT specifications
ΔΔ0.12Δ30.00Δ45.00Δ-2.00ΔΔ0.55	output medium (col 1-30)

I Specifications. I stands for *integer*. Only whole-number values may be input or output. As with F specifications, a number preceding the letter I indicates sequential repetition of the field specification, and may be omitted when the value is one. Only a single number follows the letter I, indicating the length (number of character positions) in the field. As with F specifications, leading zeros are replaced with blanks on output (except in the case of a zero value, as in the next example), blank columns will be interpreted as zeros on input, and negative signs occupy separate positions preceding the first significant digits.

EXAMPLE OF I (INTEGER MODE) CONVERSION

Δ4506076-2	input medium (col 1-10)
(3I1, I3, 2I2)	input FORMAT specifications
0 | 4 | 5 | 60 | 76 | -2	values in 6 memory locations
(3I2, 2I3, I4)	output FORMAT specifications
Δ0Δ4Δ5Δ60Δ76ΔΔ-2	output medium (col 1-16)

A Specifications. A stands for *alphameric*. Data input with this mode of conversion may include any legal key-punch symbols: letters, numerals, and special characters. The manner in which these symbols are represented in the computer memory varies from one computer to another, as does the maximum number of characters that can be stored in a single memory location. IBM machines of the 7040 and 7090 series, as well as GE machines, utilize a six-bit character-coding system and store up to a maximum of six characters per memory cell. IBM System/360 machines use an eight-bit code, and store up to four characters per single word of storage. CDC machines such as the 1604 and 3600 use a six-bit code and allow up to eight characters per word, while the CDC 6600 permits a maximum of ten characters per cell of memory. We need not be concerned here with the particular coding system for alphameric conversion. Most Fortran compilers currently in use will accept programs written with six-character alphameric groups, and we will impose this limit for programs in this book. In System/360 Fortran a relatively simple program modification can be used to define variables as double length in order to meet this requirement; no changes will be necessary for CDC machines with larger word sizes.

The length of the field in characters is specified by an integer following the letter A. We will arbitrarily restrict this value to a maximum of six. As with F and I specifications, an integer preceding the letter A indicates sequential repetition of the field specification, and may be omitted if one. Each field is coded into one storage location, left justified, with any unused character positions coded as blanks. If the length specified for the field exceeds the character capacity of the words of storage in the computer being used, the right-most maximum number of characters will be stored, and the leading surplus characters in the field will be ignored on input. On output where the length exceeds computer word capacity, leading blanks will be inserted to fill out the field.

Numerals may be read in A mode, but because of the coding system these symbols cannot be used in arithmetic operations. This is not to say that data read by A mode specifications cannot be numerically manipulated; this is possible in all computer systems, and can be a very useful approach to certain problems. The techniques involved are rather complex, however, and they differ from one machine to another. We will discuss one such use in Chapter 13.

This mode of data transfer is used most frequently to hold subject identification, titling information, and so forth. It is also used in dealing with verbal behavior data, such as those examined in Chapter 13. Another special usage is for "variable FORMAT" statements.

EXAMPLE OF A (ALPHAMERIC) CONVERSION

ABC1.3*TΔ5G12				input medium (col 1-13)
(2A3, A1, A6)				input FORMAT specifications
ABCΔΔΔ	1.3ΔΔ	*ΔΔΔΔ	TΔ5G12	values in 4 memory locations
(A7, 2A3, A4)				output FORMAT specifications
ΔABCΔΔ1.3*ΔΔTΔ5G				output medium (col 1-17)

H Specifications. H stands for *Hollerith*. This mode is used primarily as a means of placing alphameric constants on an output medium without necessitating the reading and storing of such values by use of the A specification. The string of characters to be placed on the output medium is taken from the FORMAT statement itself, and no reference to memory locations appears in the input-output statement that is involved. FORMAT statements containing H-mode fields also can be referenced by input statements, in which case the constant is automatically replaced by whatever appears in the corresponding field of the input medium. However, most programmers prefer to use A mode for input of alphameric data.

The number preceding the letter H designates the length of the field, which starts immediately after H. Blanks in this field *are* significant, and are treated just like any other alphameric characters. The length of an H field is limited only by the nature of the output medium.

EXAMPLE OF H (HOLLERITH) OUTPUT

(2X, 13HMEANSΔFORΔG2.)   output FORMAT specifications
ΔΔMEANSΔFORΔG2.   output medium (cols. 1–15)

Repetition of Field Sequences. Parentheses may be used around a series of field specifications which is to be repeated. An integer precedes the left parenthesis to indicate the number of repetitions. For instance, (2(2X, I3, F10.4)) is equivalent to (2X, I3, F10.4, 2X, I3, F10.4). Such parenthesis sets may not be nested more than one level within a FORMAT statement. Repeated use of such sets at the same level is permitted, however.

Line Control. The maximum sum of field lengths must be appropriate to the external medium that the FORMAT is intended to describe. Punched cards have 80 columns, while printer lines and external (BCD) tape records hold 120 characters. More than one line (or card) of input/output may be described in a single FORMAT statement through the use of the slash (/) symbol, which means "end the present card, line, or record." If a slash appears at the start of a FORMAT, a single line will be skipped before output begins, or a single card will be skipped before input begins. Single slash marks are used within the list of FORMAT field specifications to instruct the external device to go to a new card, line, or tape record; carry-over of specifications from the end of one line or card to the beginning of the next is *not* automatic. If multiple slash marks are used within the list of FORMAT field specifications, the number of lines skipped will be one less than the number of slashes. Each time a FORMAT statement is begun, input or output automatically begins on a new line, card, or tape record.

Spacing of values within a line, card, or record on the external medium can be achieved by the use of X specifications in the FORMAT, or by artificially increasing field lengths, since leading blanks will be inserted in the latter case on output.

Automatic FORMAT Repetition. The amount of data—the total number of values—transferred by an input/output statement is not controlled by the

FORMAT, but by the variable list of the input/output statement. The FORMAT serves only to describe the arrangement of data on the external medium. If the variable list of the input/output statement specifies transfer of more values than are described within the FORMAT, the entire FORMAT will be repeated until the input/output list is satisfied, provided that no subset of the FORMAT is parenthesized. Each time control returns to the beginning of the FORMAT, a new card or line will be begun automatically.

It is possible to repeat only part of a FORMAT in this automatic way by parenthesizing the latter part of a FORMAT without putting a repetition factor in front of the left parenthesis. The general rule for automatic FORMAT repetition that reflects these specifics is that when the input/output list is not satisfied at the end of the FORMAT, control returns automatically to the *last left parenthesis not preceded by an integer,* and transfer continues, starting on a new card or line. The following example illustrates this principle, as well as the use of slash marks.

EXAMPLE OF FORMAT LINE CONTROL

| 2 | 3 | 5 | 4 | 9 |

values in 5 memory locations

(2(1X, I1), (2X, I1))   output FORMAT (alternative 1)

(2I2, I3 / I3 / I3)   output FORMAT (alternative 2)

ΔΔ2Δ3ΔΔ5
ΔΔ4   lines printed with either FORMAT
ΔΔ9

Printer Control Symbols. In FORMAT statements intended for use with PRINT output statements, the first character position of each output line is reserved to control the printer itself, and should not be used for data. Some variation among Fortran compilers exists with regard to the available printer control symbols, but all compilers provide the following:

Character in column one	Printer action before beginning the line
blank	single space
0	double space
1	eject page

If the first symbol to be printed on a line is in a Hollerith field, the printer-control symbol can be incorporated as follows:

5   FORMAT (7H0MEANS., 2F10.4)

Note that a skipped line would have also resulted from the use of a slash mark:

5   FORMAT (/7H MEANS., 2F10.4)

If the first field on the line is to be numeric output, and printer control other than single spacing is desired, a one-character Hollerith field can be used:

    5 FORMAT (1H1, 2F10.4)

This last example would begin the line on a new page. Note that it is important to leave sufficient field length to insure an initial blank character in column one if single spacing is desired. If the numeric values to be output do not exceed four digits in the integer portion (and are also positive), the following FORMAT will be only single spaced:

    5 FORMAT (2F10.4)

Single spacing will be guaranteed by the use of a separate X specification for column one:

    5 FORMAT (1X, 2F10.4)

Fortran compilers do not attempt to check mode consistency (real, integer, alphameric) between the variable names in the lists of input/output statements and the corresponding specifications in the FORMAT statements which are referenced. For this reason, errors in such matching of memory contents with FORMAT specifications will often result in no output whatsoever. The same kind of undiagnosed output can often result from faulty subscripting of array variables leading to storage references to unintended memory locations.

INPUT AND OUTPUT STATEMENTS

Input and output Fortran statements are operational; their placement in the statement sequence of the program is significant, unlike any of the other statement types so far considered. Input/output statements control transfer of data between the computer memory and external devices such as a card reader, card punch, or printer. Statements for input/output with magnetic tape will be discussed later in this chapter. The initial key word of one of these statements is always followed by a FORMAT statement number. After a comma, a list of variable names appears. The variable names are separated by commas. Although the words READ, PRINT, and PUNCH are intended as direct references to particular input or output devices, many installations use monitor systems which refer such commands to tape units. Thus, a READ statement may initiate the input of data cards from the programmer's viewpoint, and a PRINT statement may actuate the printer as far as he knows. In actual operation, however, the installation may transfer all submitted card decks to a magnetic tape, which will be actuated automatically by any programmed READ statements. Similarly, all programmed PRINT statements will automatically result in transfer of output data to another magnetic tape that can be dismounted at the end of a processing run and printed through a less expensive small computer while the main machine continues with other work. Still another magnetic tape may be reserved for other kinds of output such as punched cards resulting from PUNCH statements. Some of the newer Fortran systems are organized on this principle and permit use of general-purpose READ and WRITE statements, in which the specific external device is only indicated by a unit code number. All current Fortran systems will accept the specific-purpose statements described in this section.

Tab Card Input: READ f, v. The f stands for a FORMAT statement number, and v stands for a list of variable names which designate the destinations of the input data in the computer memory. Each time a READ statement is encountered in the program, a new data card is read and the FORMAT is referenced from its beginning. Reading of cards continues until the list of variables has been satisfied. The FORMAT will be repeated automatically as often as necessary if it specifies fewer fields than are demanded by the variable list. If the variable list is satisfied before the end of the FORMAT is reached, however, control will simply leave the READ statement in the normal manner, and go on to the next operational statement in the program. Without knowing the FORMAT referenced, it is impossible to tell how many *cards* will be input by a particular READ statement; the variable list only defines the number of *values* to be input.

The memory locations named by the variables appearing in the list of the READ statement will be filled with data from cards in the order that these cards were submitted, and in the order of the variable names in the list. It is important to realize that the computer cannot reread data cards, nor can it read them in any order other than that of the data deck as submitted. It is essential, therefore, that the sequence of data match the sequence of variable names in the READ list, just as the variable-name list must correspond to the order of field specifications in the FORMAT statement which is referenced. This is especially important when both integer and real values are to be input. The computer will follow the instructions given it by the programmer, whether or not they are appropriate for solving the problem.

EXAMPLES

> READ 5, A, B
> READ 42, I, AB2D, KK, TOTAL
> READ 10, Q

Tab Card Output: PUNCH f, v. This statement causes output of data from memory into punched cards until the list of variables is satisfied. The same rules regarding list satisfaction and order of output hold for this statement as for input of data with the READ statement. Although the FORMAT may not specify more than 80 characters per card, it may describe more than one card's arrangement by the use of slash marks.

Punched-card output is a means of holding intermediate results when the solution of a problem requires different programs for each of a series of stages. A magnetic tape can also be used in this manner, but many applications are facilitated by the flexibility of punched cards, which can be sorted, collated, and otherwise manipulated between processing runs on the computer. Punched-card output of composite or rescaled scores for samples of subjects is the primary use of this statement in behavioral sciences programming.

EXAMPLES

>   PUNCH 12, A, B, C
>   PUNCH 3, A, KA, B, KB, C, KC
>   PUNCH 105, I, J, K, D

Printed Output: PRINT f, v. Output from this statement follows the same general rules that govern card input and output. Instead of an 80-character maximum, however, up to 120 characters[4] may be designated for a single line of print. The first character position on each line is not available for data, but is reserved for the printer-control symbol. As is the case with all the statements in this section, the number of lines output by the execution of a particular PRINT statement can be determined only with knowledge of the FORMAT statement that is referenced, since multiple-line FORMATS are permitted, and automatic FORMAT repetition will occur as often as necessary to satisfy the list of variables. For example, the following pair of statements would produce four lines of printed output, including two skipped lines, since the entire FORMAT would begin a second time automatically in order to output the value of variable C.

>   PRINT 5, A, B, C
> 5 FORMAT (/2F10.4)

Other examples of PRINT statements are:

>   PRINT 42, K, KAPPA, L, LAMBDA
>   PRINT 10, AVG, SIG
>   PRINT 2, I

In this section we have used only simple-variable names as examples in the lists of input/output statements. We will continue this restriction in the next section on tape statements, and then discuss in detail the methods for transferring data to and from array variables.

Note that it is not necessary to have a variable list with any of the statements in this section. A FORMAT containing only a Hollerith field would be output using a PRINT statement such as:

>   PRINT 5
> 5 FORMAT (2X, 6HMEANS)

[4] Some printers allow 132 characters per line of print.

If the programmer wanted only to position the printer at the start of a new page, he might write:

    PRINT 15
15 FORMAT (1H1)

The uses of such variable-less statements will be more apparent later when we take up program construction.

MAGNETIC TAPE STATEMENTS

Magnetic tape operations on a computer are similar to those involved in the use of an audio tape recorder. In fact, the standard computer tape width (one-half inch) is exactly twice that of ordinary audio tape, and worn computer tapes are sometimes split lengthwise to be used for home recorders. Just as an audio tape must be rewound to its beginning before it can be played back (read) after sounds have been recorded (written) on it, so also must a computer tape be positioned at a specific starting point before it is used by an input/output statement. The beginning of a magnetic computer tape is known as its *load point,* and the following Fortran statement is used to position the tape initially and at other appropriate points in the program:

    REWIND u

The symbol u stands for some integer constant or variable which designates the unit number of an auxiliary storage device such as a magnetic tape drive. The unit numbers used in Fortran tape statements are called "logical" unit numbers, since they are automatically assigned to particular pieces of equipment by the Fortran systems used by particular installations. The number and nature of the devices available to the programmer varies among installations. Some of the programs presented later in this book require one such unit, although most programs do not require the use of auxiliary storage.

Two basically different types of magnetic tape statements are available in all Fortran systems. We will call these *external* (BCD)[5] and *internal* (binary) modes of data transfer. The external tape mode is like that used for READ, PRINT, and PUNCH, and involves references to FORMAT statements. In fact, tape records in this mode can be output to a printer or punch unit, or can be read into memory like cards, since the coding system is the same. The internal tape mode does not involve any reference to FORMAT statements and is somewhat more compact and rapid, since data are transferred to and from the tape records in the same form that they have in the computer memory. This mode is normally used only for high-speed transfer of

---

[5] BCD stands for *binary-coded decimal,* which is the generic name for input/output coding systems that employ six binary digits to represent each character transferred.

data to and from the memory as a temporary means of expanding the computer's storage capacity during processing. Permanent storage of data is normally in the form of external tape records.

EXTERNAL (BCD) TAPE STATEMENTS

>   READ (u, f) v
>   WRITE (u, f) v

The same rules govern the use of these statements as apply to the PRINT statement. Record length is 120 characters, as in the case of PRINT, but slashes among the FORMAT specifications may be used to designate multiple records.

The magnetic-tape unit number and the FORMAT statement number are separated by a comma and enclosed in parentheses. The list of variable names then begins. Different READ and/or WRITE statements in a program may reference the same tape unit and/or FORMAT whenever appropriate. It is important to remember that, as in audio tape recording, writing over a portion of a magnetic tape replaces whatever had been recorded there previously. The same thing is true of the computer memory cells, for that matter: input replaces the contents of memory locations, but output does not affect them. One other characteristic of tape use must be kept in mind: the programmer cannot (for reasons beyond the scope of this book) assume that any tape records *after* a newly written section of the tape will be unaffected by the writing process; he can only assume that records *before* the written portion will remain valid. For example, if you use three WRITE statements to output three sets of data, REWIND the tape, use a single READ statement to input the first set, and then decide to WRITE another set of data in place of the second set on the tape, you cannot assume that the *third* set will still be readable. It might be, but you cannot be certain of this in most computer systems.

EXAMPLES

>   READ (2, 20) A, B, C
>   WRITE (3, 42) XMEAN, SIGMA
>   REWIND 2
>   READ (4, 12) KA, A, KB, B
>   WRITE (2, 13) K

External tape mode is most used for economical permanent storage of data; a single tape will hold data from at least 25,000 cards. For temporary storage of data during execution of a program, or between executions of related programs, the internal tape mode is faster and simpler.

INTERNAL (BINARY) TAPE STATEMENTS

    READ (u) v
    WRITE (u) v

These are the only input/output statements that do not reference FORMAT statements. Through their use the effective size of the computer memory is tremendously increased, although the logistics of problem solution are complicated to some extent, and access time to data on tape is considerably slower than to that within the central memory. All of the previous points about positioning the tape apply to these statements as well.

Because no FORMAT is referenced in this tape mode, care must be exercised in organizing input and output of multiple records. The most straightforward way of dealing with this problem is simply to use the same variable lists in both the READ and WRITE statements that handle a particular set of data. The variable list may be of any practical length in these statements, and each time one of these statements is executed, the programmer may consider the entire list as a single record on the tape. Remember that two records (written with two internal WRITE statements) cannot be retrieved with a single internal READ statement. It is also wise to avoid the use of both internal and external tape statements with a single tape unit in the same program.

EXAMPLES

    READ (2) A, B, C
    WRITE (3) XMEAN, SIGMA
    REWIND 2
    READ (4) KA, A, KB, B
    WRITE (2) K

Before going on to the topic of array input and output, we will list the various input/output statements that have been discussed:

READ f, v	input from cards
PUNCH f, v	output to cards
PRINT f, v	output to printer
READ (u, f) v	external (BCD) tape input
WRITE (u, f) v	external (BCD) tape output
READ (u)	internal (binary) tape input
WRITE (u)	internal (binary) tape output
REWIND u	rewind tape to beginning

INPUT/OUTPUT OF ARRAY VARIABLES

Input/output of array variables is usually the most confusing aspect of the Fortran language, and therefore deserves careful study. So far, we have used examples of input/output lists containing only simple-variable names. Before we get into the methods for indicating transfer of series of values from arrays, we should point out that single locations within an array can be referenced by the use of subscripts. For instance, suppose that five values are stored in simple variables A, B, C, D, and E and we wish to print them. We could write:

  PRINT 3, A, B, C, D, E
 3 FORMAT (5F10.4)

Now, as an alternative, suppose we had stored these five values in an array called X, for which five locations had been reserved at the beginning of the program by:

  DIMENSION X(5)

We can print the five values out of this array by designating each of the locations separately with appropriate subscripts:

  PRINT 3, X(1), X(2), X(3), X(4), X(5)
 3 FORMAT (5F10.4)

Vector (List) Indexing. We stated a rule on page 50 to the effect that any array-variable name must be followed by the appropriate number of subscripts wherever it appears in the various statements of the program. There is one exception to this rule, which applies only to input/output statements.[6] If the programmer wishes to transfer *all* of the values in a dimensioned array, he can use the array name without any subscripts. The computer will automatically refer to the DIMENSION statement of the program to find out how many values are to be transferred. For example, here is another way to achieve output of five values from vector X:

  PRINT 3, X
 3 FORMAT (5F10.4)

This print statement will accomplish the transfer of all five values out of array X, since the array name appears in the list without subscripting. The values will be transferred in the order of their normal indexing.

If a number of variables appear in an input/output list, each array name will be considered in turn. For instance:

  DIMENSION X(10), Y(5)
  READ 4, X, W, Y(4), Y(2)
 4 FORMAT (13F1.0)

The 10 cells of vector X will be filled by the first 10 digits on the data card, then the eleventh value on the card will be stored for simple-variable W, then the twelfth value from the card will be stored in the fourth location

---

[6] Another exception is in the calling of functions and subroutines (Chapter 6).

of vector Y, and finally the thirteenth value will be stored in the second location of vector Y. Locations 1, 3, and 5 in vector Y will be unaffected.

Indexing Notation. The use of an array name without subscripts results in complete transfer of the values in an array. If we want to transfer all *or part* of an array, we can designate each array location to be transferred as shown earlier, or we can use a compact notation for indexing a series of single-location transfers. Each of the following PRINT statements results in complete transfer of the values in array X:

```
    DIMENSION X(5)
    PRINT 4, X(1), X(2), X(3), X(4), X(5)
    PRINT 4, X
    PRINT 4, (X(I), I = 1, 5)
  4 FORMAT (5F10.4)
```

The indexing notation in the third PRINT statement above uses a simple integer variable (I) to control the sequencing of the subscripts of vector X. Following the equals sign (=) are two limits for the values which the index variable will assume. The first of these two values (1) is the initial value, and the second (5) the final value for I, after which the transfer from X is complete. If we had wanted to print only the last three values from vector X, we could use the statement:

```
    PRINT 4, (X(I), I = 3, 5)
  4 FORMAT (5F10.4)
```

Note that the *number* of values transferred is controlled by the input/output statement and not by the FORMAT, which in this example designates five values.

Considerable flexibility is afforded by the use of this kind of indexing notation. In the next example we will use an integer variable as one of the limits on the index variable, and will also show how a single index variable can be used to alternate storage of values into two arrays.

```
     DIMENSION KODE(100), X(100)
     READ 5, K
   5 FORMAT (I5)
     READ 10, (KODE(I), X(I), I = 1, K)
  10 FORMAT (A6, F4.0)
```

This sequence might be used to read values from subject data cards in a program for which the number of subjects may vary from one problem to another. Vectors KODE and X are used to hold subject code numbers and their single scores in corresponding locations. Each data card is assumed to contain the code number and score for one subject. We read in a "control" card before the data cards; it contains only the number of data cards which follow. Therefore, if we had a sample of 20 subjects to input, the control card would be punched ΔΔΔ20 in columns 1–5. Columns 6–80 could

66 FORTRAN: VOCABULARY AND GRAMMAR

contain anything; they would be ignored. The twenty data cards following would then be input, reading a subject code number (columns 1–6) and a score (columns 7–10) from each card in turn, and alternately storing these values in the first 20 elements of vectors KODE and X. Note that a pair of parentheses always encloses the indexing instructions and the subscripted variable name(s) to which they apply.

Another variation of the indexing instructions is helpful where systematic, but nonsequential, transfer of values is desired. In the next example we will print values from vector X, but output only those whose index positions are even numbers (2, 4, 6, and so on).

```
      DIMENSION X(10)
      PRINT 4, (X(I), I = 2, 10, 2)
    4 FORMAT (5F10.4)
```

To accomplish this, we use a third indexing parameter, which is the *increment* for variable I on each successive step in the indexing. When the increment is 1, this parameter need not be specified. Locations in vector X from which values will be output are X(2), X(4), X(6), X(8), and X(10).

Before we discuss the more complicated indexing of matrices, let us consider one more example. In Figure 4-3 is a schematic diagram of the vectors KX and KY and the single location KZ with the values they will hold after reading a data card which holds the digits 1–9 in columns 1–9.

```
      DIMENSION KX(4), KY(10)
      READ 5, KX, KZ, (KY(I), I = 1, 8, 2)
    5 FORMAT (9I1)
```

Do not go any further with this chapter until you understand how the PRINT statement works in this example. Note that only four of the ten locations in vector KY are affected by the READ statement; the other locations will continue to hold whatever values they had. The skipping takes place in array KY and not in the data card.

Matrix (Table) Indexing. We can use a matrix-variable name without subscripts in an input/output statement list, just as we did in the case of vector variables. The entire array will be referenced in a particular order. With vectors, the order was simply the natural indexing sequence. With matrices, the order followed is indicated by the diagram in Figure 4-4, which illustrates a matrix dimensioned B(2, 3).

This order of indexing will be called the *natural array order*. The se-

```
         1  2  3  4
    KX [ 1| 2| 3| 4]
    KZ [ 5]
         1  2  3  4  5  6  7  8  9 10
    KY [ 6|  | 7|  | 8|  | 9|  |  |  ]
```

FIGURE 4-3. Memory cell contents after input of nine scores.

	Matrix B	Second Subscript		
		1	2	3
First	1	1	3	5
Subscript	2	2	4	6

FIGURE 4-4. Natural array order for a two-by-three matrix.

quence is down columns of the matrix continuously, completing each column in turn. This is the order that will be followed whenever a matrix variable name appears without subscripts in an input/output statement.

We can employ indexing instructions in the case of matrix variables also, but two index variables are required, with their own parenthesis sets. The index variable of the inner parenthesis set will be run through all of its values before the index variable of the outer parenthesis set is incremented. Consider carefully the following example, which illustrates three different but equivalent ways of entering values to fill matrix B.

    DIMENSION B(2, 3)
    READ 5, B
    READ 5, B(1, 1), B(2, 1), B(1, 2), B(2, 2), B(1, 3), B(2, 3)
    READ 5, ((B(I, J), I = 1, 2), J = 1, 3)
5 FORMAT (6F2.0)

The first of these alternatives automatically fills all cells of the array in the natural order shown in the previous diagram. The second statement specifies each cell as a simple variable. In the third statement, the indexing notation has been extended to two dimensions, employing different integer variables for the row and column subscripts. Note that two sets of parentheses are nested; the inside index variable will proceed through all the values implied by its parameters before the variable in the outer parenthesis set is incremented.

If the nonsubscripted array name is used, the programmer has no control over the order of storage or the number of values which will be input, except as he sets up the DIMENSION statement. In the second version, he has complete control over the order and number of values entered, but this method is impractical with large numbers of values. The third method permits considerable flexibility with relatively economical notation.

Suppose that the programmer now wished to punch these six values on two output cards, with one *row* of values on each card. This is not the natural array order, so the unsubscripted array name could not be used. Either of the following statements would achieve the desired results, however.

    PUNCH 10, B(1, 1), B(1, 2), B(1, 3), B(2, 1), B(2, 2), B(2, 3)
    PUNCH 10, ((B(I, J), J = 1, 3), I = 1, 2)
10 FORMAT (3F5.0)

In the second statement we have used the same integer-variable subscripts for the variable name B, but we have reversed the placement of the

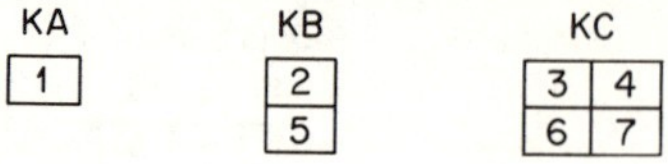

```
            KA      KB       KC
            ┌───┐   ┌───┐   ┌───┬───┐
            │ 1 │   │ 2 │   │ 3 │ 4 │
            └───┘   ├───┤   ├───┼───┤
                    │ 5 │   │ 6 │ 7 │
                    └───┘   └───┴───┘
```

FIGURE 4-5. Order of output from three variables.

indexing parameters within the two sets of parentheses. Remember that the inner index variable will be advanced through all of its values and reset before the outside index variable is incremented.

As a final example, suppose we wanted to output values from a single cell, a vector, and a matrix in the order indicated by the numbers shown in Figure 4-5. The following statements would accomplish this purpose.

>   DIMENSION KB(2), KC(2, 2)
>   PRINT 5, KA, (KB(I), (KC(I, J), J = 1, 2),I = 1, 2)
>   5 FORMAT (I3/(I3, 2X, 2I3))

Output lines, including control column 1:

> ΔΔ1
> ΔΔ2ΔΔΔΔ3ΔΔ4
> ΔΔ5ΔΔΔΔ6ΔΔ7

VARIABLE FORMAT

Although all FORMAT statements normally appear within the program deck, it is possible to define a vector of memory locations for the purpose of holding a FORMAT which is to be input from a data card when the program is executed. The input/output statements (usually for card reading) that reference this variable FORMAT vector contain the variable name of the vector instead of a FORMAT statement number. The variable name may be of either mode, and appears without any subscripts.

This technique requires the reading (A mode) of a data card containing the FORMAT specifications, including the parentheses that enclose them, prior to executing any input/output statements which reference the variable FORMAT vector. An example of such a sequence of statements is:

>   DIMENSION FMT(16), D(30)
>   READ 5, FMT
>   5 FORMAT (16A5)
>   READ FMT, D

In this sequence an ordinary READ statement is used to input an entire card (16A5 = 80 columns) in alphameric mode to the vector FMT. Once stored, this FORMAT may be referenced by the name of the vector (FMT) as shown in the last statement. The contents of the first card in the input deck might have been:

> (10X, 30F2.0)

This procedure is very convenient for multipurpose programs which must be run repeatedly with varying data-card arrangements.

REPLACEMENT STATEMENTS

The most common type of Fortran statement is the replacement statement, which is identified by an equals sign (=) following a variable name. This initial name and any others that appear in replacement statements must always be subscripted if they also appear in the DIMENSION statement, and are therefore array variables.

The replacement statement changes the contents of the single memory location designated to the left of the equals sign to the value designated by the constant, variable, or expression which appears after the equals sign. The term "replacement" is used for these statements because the statement is operational and directional; only one location is changed—that designated at the left of the equals sign. All memory locations referenced to the right of the equals sign remain unaffected by the statement.

The simplest form of a replacement statement causes transfer of data from one memory location to another. Examples are:

```
A = 1.0
KX = KY
BETA(I) = 25.47
ZZ = XX(42)
```

Expressions. The term "expression" refers to a combination of operators and operands, which yields a single value when numeric values are given to all variable operands and the expression is evaluated. (2 * K + 3) is an expression which was used earlier as an example of a subscript. When a specific numeric value is given to K, the expression can be evaluated and reduced to a single value. For example, if K is 5, then the expression reduces to the value 13. Note that the modes of constants and variables appearing in the same expression must be consistent, with one exception in the case of exponentiation. Examples of Fortran replacement statements containing expressions to the right of the equals signs are:

```
M = 2 * K + 3
KK = KK + 2 * I
A = B * C - D * E
```

The restrictions described earlier for subscript expressions do not hold for these replacement statements; order of constants and variables is unrestricted, as is the use of more than one variable name. In the second statement, the use of the same variable name on both sides of the equals sign is illustrated. The original value of KK would be used in evaluating the expression, *and then* the contents of KK would be changed to the value resulting from reduction of the expression.

It is important to distinguish clearly between expression subscripts and expressions which include subscripted variables. Note that in the following example, the expression evaluated for the replacement statement is the simple addition of the contents of two memory locations. The subscripts designating the particular locations in the matrices A and B, however, also include expressions.

$$C = A(K + 2, 3*I) + B(I + 1, K)$$

Arithmetic Operators. There are three classes of operations in the Fortran language: (1) exponentiation, (2) multiplication-division, and (3) addition-subtraction. Operators may appear only to the right of the equals signs in replacement statements, unless they are part of a subscript expression. Two arithmetic operators may not appear next to each other, nor may two variable names appear together without an intervening operator. This is not the case in ordinary algebraic notation where AB implies multiplication of A and B. In Fortran "AB" would be compiled as a single variable name.

Exponentiation. This operation is denoted by two asterisks (**), and the exponent follows this two-column symbol. The exponent may be an integer or real constant, variable, or expression in parentheses if the operand is real. An integer operand may only have an integer exponent. Whenever the exponent is a whole number, it should be represented as an integer constant or variable, if convenient, since the compiled object program will be more efficient. Examples of replacement statements with exponentiation are:

A = B**2	A = B**(X − 1.0)
A = B**3.5	A = B**K(6)
A = B**I	M = J**2
A = B**C	M = K**I

Multiplication and Division. Multiplication is indicated by a single asterisk(*). The operator symbol for division is a slash mark (/). Caution should be employed with regard to integer division, since the result will be truncated to a whole-number value, not rounded. K = 5 / 3 would be evaluated as the number 1 for storage in location K. Examples of replacement statements employing these operators are:

A = B * C	K = I * J
A = 4.0 / C	K = I / 2
A = 367.25 * B	K = KA * KB * KC * KD

Addition and Subtraction. These operators are the usual plus (+) and minus (−) signs. For example:

A = B + C	M = K − J
A = 4.5 − B	M = 3 + K − I

Order of Operations. The three classes of operations have a natural order of execution within the Fortran language. Exponentiations are executed first, followed by multiplications and divisions, and then additions and subtractions are performed. Within a particular class, the operations are executed from left to right as they appear in the Fortran statement after the equals sign. This order does not apply to subscript expressions; these are evaluated before the execution of the replacement statement is begun.

The programmer may override this natural order of operations to any degree necessary through the use of paired parentheses to separate sub-expressions. Such parentheses sets may be nested up to twelve deep. Operations designated within parentheses will be executed (parenthesis removal) before operations at the same level will be executed. For instance:

$$A = B + (A - 1.0) * 2.5$$

In this case, 1.0 will be subtracted from A, then the result will be multiplied by 2.5, and then B will be added to the product to form the final value for storage in A. A right parenthesis may *not* be followed by a left parenthesis to indicate multiplication, as is common in algebraic notation. The correct way of expressing this would be:

$$A = (B + 0.5) * (C | 0.5)$$

Removal of parentheses proceeds from the deepest (innermost) level outward. Redundant parentheses which duplicate the natural evaluation order are allowed, and when in doubt it is best to insure the evaluation order by their use. For example, these two statements are equivalent in function:

$$A = (B) + (C * 1.5)$$
$$A = B + C * 1.5$$

Within parentheses, the normal operator hierarchy and left-to-right order of execution will be followed. It is well worth the effort to count the numbers of left and right parentheses in complex expressions to be certain that they agree.

In the first of the following examples of complex expressions, note that the final value stored in K will be 22.

FORTRAN STATEMENT	MATHEMATICAL FORMULA
K = 4**2 + (6 / (5 - 2) * 3)	$K = 4^2 + \left(\dfrac{6}{5-2}\right)(3)$
A = B * C(K) / (R - 1.0)	$A = \dfrac{BC_k}{R-1}$
B = ((A + 1.0) / (A - 1.0))**S	$B = \left[\dfrac{A+1}{A-1}\right]^S$

Mode Consistency and Conversion. Some of the more recent Fortran compilers permit mixing real and integer mode constants and variables on the expression side of the equals sign in replacement statements. Since we wish to present the most widely applicable version of Fortran in this book, we will not discuss the rules regarding such mixing of modes, but will

72   FORTRAN: VOCABULARY AND GRAMMAR

simply note the possibility. You will be able to add this convenience to your command of the language very easily by consulting the manufacturer's manual at your installation once you have achieved facility with the simplified rules presented here. We have already noted that all Fortran compilers permit the use of integer exponents—constants or variables—with real or integer variables. Also, integer constants and/or variables are always used for subscripting purposes.

The restriction of mode consistency within expressions does not apply across the equals sign in a replacement statement. When the modes on the two sides are different, the mode of the value on the right will be converted automatically just before the final storage in the location specified on the left side of the equals sign. This mode conversion will take place no matter what the contents of the particular locations happen to be, and this is the primary reason for consistent use of one or the other mode for variables that are to hold alphameric values. A mode-converted alphameric string will no longer resemble meaningful character codes. Examples of automatic arithmetic mode conversion follow:

$A = K + 2$ (If $K = 4$, the value 6.0 is stored in A)
$K = 1.0$ (1.0 is converted to 1 and stored in K)

When a real value with a decimal fraction appears after the equals sign, it will be truncated as part of the conversion to an integer value, which means that the fractional part will be lost; no rounding will occur automatically as in output of real numbers. Rounding can be accomplished, however, by adding the constant 0.5 to the expression. Examples are:

$K = 1.2$ (1 is stored in K; the fraction .2 is lost)
$K = B$ (If B contains 2.6, the value 2 will be stored in K)
$K = B + .5$ (With $B = 2.6$, the value 3 will be stored in K)

To summarize the rules we will observe in this book:

(a) operands in expressions must be of the same mode, except for exponents of real values, and

(b) operands of different modes across the equals sign in a replacement statement will result in automatic conversion to the destination mode just before final storage.

DECISION STATEMENTS

The order of statement execution in a Fortran program proceeds according to the arrangement of the statements in the program deck unless a statement specifically transfers control to some statement other than the next in line. Such transfer of control is accomplished by statements to be described in this section. These transfers may be unconditional, or they may be dependent on the contents of designated storage locations or evaluated expressions.

Decision Statements

Unconditional Transfer: GO TO s. The key term, GO TO, is followed by the number of the statement to which control will immediately be transferred. The statement number, of course, must be a positive integer constant. For example: GO TO 15

Conditional Transfer: GO TO (s_1, s_2, . . . s_n), k. This form of the GO TO statement permits optional transfer to any one of a series of statements, depending on the current value of the integer variable k which is named. This integer variable name appears following a comma after the right parenthesis of the pair that encloses the series of statement numbers, which are themselves separated by commas. The value of k may not exceed the number of statement numbers provided as options, and may not be less than one. For example:

GO TO (23, 50, 14), KT

Three options are given. Control will be transferred to statement 23, 50, or 14, depending on whether the value of the variable KT is currently 1, 2, or 3, respectively. Any number of options may be included within the parentheses.

Conditional Transfer: Arithmetic IF. The key word IF is followed by a parenthesized expression, which in turn is followed by three statement numbers separated by two commas, which are the optional destinations of control transfer, depending on the evaluated expression. If the expression yields a negative value, control is transferred to the first option; if it is zero, control goes to the middle option; and if it is positive, control goes to the third option. The general form of the statement is:

IF (expression) s_-, s_0, s_+

For example, if A = 10.0 at the time the following statement was encountered, control would go to statement 12, since the value of the expression would be −30:

IF (A * 2.0 − 50.0) 12, 13, 27

Modes in the parenthesized expression must be consistent, according to the same rules that apply on the right side of the equals sign in a replacement statement. A single variable name may appear alone within the parentheses; this is equivalent to the expression which would be formed by subtracting zero from the variable:

IF (V) 5, 6, 7 is equivalent to IF (V − 0.0) 5, 6, 7

It is also permissible to compare two locations holding alphameric values. For instance, if both KA and KB held the contents ALPHAΔ, the middle option would be taken in the following statement, and control would be transferred to statement 15:

IF (KA − KB) 20, 15, 20

Note that the plus and minus options are the same, since both indicate nonidentity of the values KA and KB.

Logical/Relational IF Statements. All recent Fortran compilers provide logical/relational capability, although the form of the statement differs for some compilers.[7] The most common form, which is used by IBM, is shown here:

    IF (expression) statement *t*
    statement *f*

The expression is evaluated only as being *true* or *false* and control is transferred on this basis. If the expression is *true*, the Fortran statement appearing after the right parenthesis of the expression is executed, and then control passes to statement *f*, which is the next statement in sequence. If the expression is evaluated as *false*, control goes directly to statement *f*. Thus, this form really consists of three Fortran statements: the IF statement with its expression, the statement executed when the expression is *true*, and the statement executed when the expression is *false*. This is shown in Figure 4-6 as a simple flow chart.

The evaluation of an expression as *true* or *false* is accomplished through the use of *logical* and *relational* operators. These operators are distinguished by the appearance of a period before and after certain combinations of letters. The use of periods prevents confusion of the operators with variable names with the same letter combinations.

There are six relational operators available in Fortran. They are used between constants, variables, or arithmetic expressions to form relational expressions which can be evaluated as *true* or *false*.

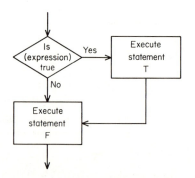

FIGURE 4-6. Flow chart for the logical/relational IF statement.

---

[7] CDC Fortran employs a form of the logical IF statement which is very much like the arithmetic IF. Only two statement numbers follow the parenthesized expression; the first of these is the option taken if the expression is evaluated as *true*, and the second option is taken if the expression is evaluated as *false*.

.GT. *means "greater than"*
.GE. *means "greater than or equal to"*
.EQ. *means "equal to"*
.NE. *means "not equal to"*
.LE. *means "less than or equal to"*
.LT. *means "less than"*

Consider the following examples, which are artificial since the use of constants on both sides of a relational operator would be pointless in a Fortran program.

Relational Expression	*Evaluation*
3 .GT. 2	true
3 .GE. 2	true
3 .EQ. 2	false
3 .NE. 2	true
3 .LE. 2	false
3 .LT. 2	false

Each such relational expression can be evaluated unequivocally as to its truth or falsity; either the specified relationship holds between the values of the operands, or it does not. Note that the operands may be constants, variables, or expressions of either mode, but that mode consistency must be maintained within the parentheses of the IF statement. Note also that parenthesized subexpressions may be used as needed.

Relational expressions that might appear in logical IF statements are:

(A .LE. B)
(A * 2.0 + B .GT. 5.0)
(KSA . EQ. KSB)
((A * B + C * D) / T .LT. 0.0)

A further facility in writing logical IF statements is afforded by the logical operators .AND. and .OR., which may be used to connect relational expressions within the IF statement. If two relational expressions r_1 and r_2 are connected by the logical operator .AND., the complete expression (r_1 .AND. r_2) will be evaluated as *true only when both r_1 and r_2 are true*. If r_1 and r_2 are connected by the logical operator .OR., the complete expression (r_1 .OR. r_2) will be evaluated as *true when either r_1 or r_2 or both are true*. The .OR. operator thus expresses a *disjunctive* relationship between the two relational-expression operands, while the .AND. operator expresses the more restrictive *conjunctive* relationship.

Once you have mastered the notation of logical/relational variables, you will probably want to use this form of the IF statement rather than the arithmetic IF, except in those few cases where the use of three branches is more economical than multiple logical IF statements. There are three restrictions on the use of the logical IF which make its use awkward under some conditions. The *true*-branch statement may not (a) have a statement number, (b) be another logical IF statement, although it may be an arithmetic IF statement, or (c) be a DO statement.

EXAMPLES OF LOGICAL/RELATIONAL IF STATEMENTS

    IF (A * 2.0 .EQ. B) K = 2
    IF (A .EQ. 0.0) GO TO 12
    IF (G .LT. 0.0 .OR. G .GT. 0.0) R = 1.0 / G
    IF (A .GT. B .AND. B .GT. C) K = 1

It is not necessary to put parentheses around arithmetic expressions linked by relational operators, nor need relational expressions be parenthesized when connected by logical operators. The arithmetic operators take precedence over the relational operators, which in turn take precedence over logical operators. Alternate ways of accomplishing the same end are often possible within the flexibility of this notation. For instance, the third IF statement above could have been written more economically as follows:

    IF (G .NE. 0.0) R = 1.0 / G

THE DO STATEMENT

The DO statement is the most powerful single feature of the Fortran language, because it permits concise specification of enormous amounts of repetitive work. The DO statement itself marks the entrance to a series of statements which constitute a *loop*. The DO statement specifies the statement number of the last statement in the loop and also contains information about the indexing and the number of times the loop is to be executed. The general form of the DO statement is:

    DO s k = n_1, n_2, n_3

s is a statement number, k is an integer variable name, n_1 is the initial value for k, n_2 is the final value for k, and n_3 is the increment for k after each pass through the loop. n_3 may be omitted if the value is one. Any or all of the values n_1, n_2, and n_3 may appear as integer constants or variables, but not expressions. Within the range of the DO loop, the integer variable k must not be changed by any statement. If may be referenced, however, whenever needed for use in a subscript, on the right side of the equals sign in a replacement statement, and so forth. When any of the parameters n_1, n_2, or n_3 are variables, they must not be changed by statements within the loop.

The following are legitimate DO statements:

    DO 5 I = 1, N, 2
    DO 12 KK = I, J
    DO 40 K = 1, 10

The Do Statement

Suppose we wished to accumulate the sum of 50 values from a vector called D, and store the sum in T. It would not be practical to specify them all as follows:

$$T = D(1) + D(2) + \ldots + D(50)$$

We can accomplish the same thing with the following set of statements:

```
       T = 0.0
       K = 1
   5   T = T + D(K)
       IF (K .EQ. 50) GO TO 10
       K = K + 1
       GO TO 5
  10   next statement
```

The DO loop provides a still more economical way of achieving this summation:

```
       T = 0.0
       DO 5 K = 1, 50
   5   T = T + D(K)
       next statement
```

Statement 5 is the terminal statement in this DO loop, and will be executed fifty times. The location T is set to zero before the loop begins so that the final value of T will be the sum of all elements in vector D. Each time statement 5 is executed, the contents of T are replaced by the sum of the previous value of T and a new element of D. After the fiftieth pass through this loop, control will be passed to the statement following statement 5 in the program deck.

The following sets of Fortran statements are equivalent to the accompanying common statistical formulas:

$$T = \sum_{1}^{N} X_i \qquad\qquad T = \sum_{1}^{N} X_i^2 \qquad\qquad T = \left(\sum_{1}^{N} X_i\right)^2$$

```
   T = 0.0              T = 0.0                  T = 0.0
   DO 5 I = 1, N        DO 5 I = 1, N            DO 5 I = 1, N
 5 T = T + X(I)       5 T = T + X(I)**2        5 T = T + X(I)
                                                 T = T**2
```

Nesting DO Loops. The sequence of statements from the one immediately following the DO statement through the terminal statement is known as the *range* of the DO loop. The ranges of DO loops may overlap if each is contained completely within another, or if they terminate on the same statement. This is equivalent to saying that control may not be transferred *into* the range of a DO loop. However, control may be transferred *out of* the range of a DO loop at any point. When DO loops are nested, the innermost DO statement is *satisfied*—indexed through all values specified by its parameters—before the next outer DO index variable is incremented. For example:

    DO 5 I = 1, 3
    DO 5 J = 1, 2

In this case, statement 5 will be executed six times. The sequence of combinations of I and J for these six passes will be as follows:

Pass:	*1*	*2*	*3*	*4*	*5*	*6*
I:	1	1	2	2	3	3
J:	1	2	1	2	1	2

Another example of *coterminous* DO loops is given below. Trace the execution of these statements using the data shown in Figure 4-7.

    A = 0.0
    DO 5 I = 1, 3
    A = A + X(I)
    B(I) = 0.0
    DO 5 J = 1, 2
  5 B(I) = B(I) + Y(I, J)

Nested DO loops are commonly used in statistical programming to obtain values described by double summation notation:

$$T = \sum_{i=1}^{M} \sum_{j=1}^{N} X_{ij}$$

    T = 0.0
    DO 5 I = 1, M
    DO 5 J = 1, N
  5 T = T + X(I, J)

$$T = \sum_{i=1}^{M} \sum_{j=1}^{N} X_{ij}^{2}$$

    T = 0.0
    DO 5 I = 1, M
    DO 5 J = 1, N
  5 T = T + X(I, J)**2

Nonserial Indexing. The notation for indexed input/output variable lists is a specialized form of the DO statement. You will recall that a third parameter may appear after the equals sign, to indicate an incrementing factor other than one. To illustrate this, the following example assumes the values shown for six elements of the vector KA.

23	12	19	4	20	10

    KT = 0
    DO 5 I = 1, 6, 2
  5 KT = KT + KA(I)

X	Y	A	B
3.0	1.0 2.0	9.0	3.0
2.0	0.0 3.0		3.0
4.0	5.0 5.0		10.0

FIGURE 4-7. Contents of memory locations after completing DO loops.

These three statements will produce summation of the first, third, and fifth elements of KA: 23 + 19 + 20 = 62, which will remain in KT after completion of the loop. Statement number 5 will be executed three times, with values for I of 1, 3, and 5. Since adding 2 to I when it is 5 would yield 7, which exceeds the terminal value 6, the loop is not executed again. An exception to this rule would occur on the *first* pass through the loop in most Fortran compilers, since the loop will be executed once even if the initial value exceeds the terminal value.[8]

Some other restrictions on the use of DO loops should be kept in mind. The index variable may not be zero or negative at any time. This means that the initial, terminal, and increment parameters may not be given zero or negative values. A DO loop may not terminate on a sequence-control statement such as GO TO, an arithmetic IF, or another DO statement, nor may it terminate on a nonoperational statement such as FORMAT. In order to avoid this, it is sometimes necessary to use a "do nothing" statement, which is simply the word CONTINUE with a statement number, to terminate the loop.

```
    DO 5 I = 1, 10
    IF (X(I) .LT. 0.0) X(I) = −X(I)
  5 CONTINUE
```

This example of the continue statement converts the elements of vector X to absolute values. We will describe another way of accomplishing this in the next section of this chapter.

Upon completion of a DO loop, control is automatically transferred to the statement immediately following the terminal statement of the loop. If the loop is satisfied in the normal manner, the value of the index variable will be indeterminate when the loop is completed. If control is transferred out of the range of the loop *before* the loop is satisfied, however, the programmer may assume that the index variable will continue to hold the value it had when control left the loop.

As with most Fortran statements, it is often helpful to verbalize the instructions implied by the DO-statement notation. For example, DO 5 I = 1, 15, 2 can be read as follows: "Do all statements from the one following this through statement number 5 as many times as are necessary to step the value of the index variable I through all the values beginning with 1 and

---

[8] This is not true in CDC Fortran; such a loop would be skipped completely.

ending with a value no greater than 15, incrementing I after each pass through the loop by a value of 2."

FUNCTIONS

A function in Fortran is a procedure defined by an independent set of statements, yielding a single value from one or more values sent as arguments to the routine. In Chapter 6 we will discuss the writing of function subprograms. A wide variety of functions are automatically available as part of the Fortran language, however. In this section we will be concerned with these "library" function routines, since function "calls" bear a sometimes confusing resemblance to ordinary subscripted variable names.

In the previous section we discussed converting the contents of ten cells in a vector to their absolute values, which can be done without an IF statement by using the absolute-value function ABS available in all Fortran systems:

    DO 5 I = 1, 10
  5 X(I) = ABS (X(I))

The function name is followed by a pair of parentheses containing the *arguments* to the function. These arguments may be constants, variables, or expressions of whatever mode is appropriate for the particular function concerned. The ABS function requires a real-mode argument, and the result is a real-mode value. An integer-mode version of this function, IABS, is also available in all Fortran systems.

The square-root function SQRT is probably the most frequently used of all library functions. Like ABS, it requires only one argument, but there is no integer-mode version. The following example illustrates the fact that function names may act as pseudo-variables when included in complex Fortran statements.

    A = B + SQRT(2.5 + ABS((C + 1.0) * 20.0)) / D

Also illustrated here is the fact that any legitimate arithmetic expression, including other functions, may be used as the argument to a function. A function may even be used as one of its own arguments. This statement would replace R4 with $X^{1/4}$:

    R4 = SQRT(SQRT(X))

If more than one argument is required for a function, they are separated by commas. The integer-remainder function MOD requires two arguments; the value of the function is the integer *remainder* when the first argument is divided by the second. For instance,

    K = MOD(5, 3)   would yield a value of 2 for K, while
    K = MOD(5, 2)   would return a value of 1

The arguments of a function are said to be "sent" to the routine, which "returns" a value for the function name. The arguments are unchanged by the function routine in all cases.

The important distinction here is between function names followed by arguments in parentheses, and array-variable names followed by subscripts. This may be quite confusing when tracing someone else's program, unless you are familiar with the various library function names. Also, array variable names always appear in the DIMENSION statement, while function names never do. We will describe only those functions most commonly used in behavioral science programming, but you will probably want to acquaint yourself with the full list available at your installation.

Alternate names are given below for each of the most used library functions. A particular Fortran compiler will use one or the other set consistently. The first name is the standard Fortran IV convention used by IBM and most other manufacturers, while the name following the title in parentheses is the older Fortran II version, which is used by some CDC Fortran compilers. Note that the newer function names are mode-appropriate, whereas this is not the case for all of the older names.

FREQUENTLY USED LIBRARY FUNCTIONS

SQRT (X) Square Root (SQRTF). The real square root of the real argument X is returned. The argument must not be negative.

ABS (X) Absolute Value (ABSF). The real argument X is returned with a positive sign.

IABS (K) Absolute Value (XABSF). Same as ABS, but integer mode.

AMOD (X,Y) Decimal Remainder (MODF). The decimal-fraction portion of the quotient from dividing the first by the second real argument is returned.

MOD (K, L) Integer Remainder (XMODF). Same as AMOD, but integer mode. The integer remainder is returned.

AMIN1 (A, B, . . . Z) Minimum Value (MIN1F). The minimum (signed) real value of the series of arguments is returned.

MIN0 (I, J, . . . N) Minimum Value (XMIN0F). Same as AMIN1, but integer mode.

AMAX1 (A, B, . . . Z) Maximum Value (MAX1F). Same as AMIN1, but the maximum value is returned.

MAX0 (I, J, . . . N) Maximum Value (XMAX0F). Same as AMAX1, but integer mode. Note the final character in these last four function names is a numeral one or zero.

ALOG(X) Natural Logatithm (LOGF). Returns the natural (base e) logarithm of the real argument X.

EXP (X) Natural Antilogarithm (EXPF). Returns the natural antilogarithm of X, which is e^x.

SIN (X) Sine Function (SINF). Returns the sine of the argument X, which is expressed in radians.

COS (X) Cosine Function (COSF). Returns the cosine of the argument X, which is expressed in radians.

ATAN (X) Arc Tangent Function (ATANF). Computes the arc tangent in radians.

TERMINATING A PROGRAM

The *compilation* of a program normally terminates when an END statement is encountered. Every Fortran program, subroutine, and function subprogram must include this statement as the last one in its card deck:

    END

The *execution* of a program may be terminated by various automatic error-detection checks, but the programmer can terminate execution at any point in the statement sequence by the use of a STOP or a RETURN statement. The RETURN statement is normally used in subroutines or function subprograms to indicate transfer of control back to the calling program, but its use in a program will have the same effect as a STOP statement, which is to terminate execution and transfer control to the computer's monitor system.

    STOP
    RETURN

In some Fortran compilers the END statement serves as a STOP or a RETURN, if neither is included. Other compilers and monitor systems will output an error diagnostic if a specific termination statement is not used.

SUMMARY OF FORTRAN STATEMENTS

In this section we will attempt to summarize all of the Fortran statements described in this chapter, giving an example of each statement. In the next chapter we will systematically approach the construction of Fortran programs, beginning with a very simple problem and gradually working up to a rather complex general-purpose program for intercorrelation. You will probably want to refer to this section repeatedly while studying the next chapter, since it is virtually impossible to retain all of the information presented in this chapter without the benefit of the associations and sense of structure that develops as you apply the statements in solving problems of program construction. If you find later that the information in this summary still leaves you in doubt about the use of a particular statement, make a point of looking it up in the earlier parts of this chapter while the problem is still fresh in your mind.

DIMENSION: Reserves memory areas for array variables. Array names are followed by integer constants in parentheses designating the numbers of rows, columns, and slices for each array.

Summary of Fortran Statements

DIMENSION A(5), KB(2, 3), CC(5, 2, 4)

FORMAT: Describes arrangement of fields in external medium, and determines modes of data transfer by input/output statements.

5 FORMAT (I2, 3X, 5F10.4, 3HΔCΔ, A4)

READ *(Cards):* Inputs data from tab cards according to a referenced FORMAT into variables listed.

READ 10, N, (A(I), I = 1, K), ((B(I, J), I = 1, 2), J = 1, N)

PUNCH: Outputs data to tab cards according to a referenced FORMAT from variables listed.

PUNCH 12, ID, (Z(I), I = 1, 15), T, X, Q

PRINT: Outputs data to a printer according to a referenced FORMAT from variables listed. FORMAT should avoid column 1, except to control printer (1 = page eject; 0 = double space; Δ = single space).

PRINT 9, AVG, SIG, RMAT

REWIND: Rewinds the tape unit specified to its load point.

REWIND 2

WRITE *(external tape:* BCD): Outputs data to tape unit specified according to a referenced FORMAT from variables listed. Records are 120 characters maximum, but may be multiple, depending on FORMAT.

WRITE (3, 20) K, (Z(K, I), I = 1, N)

READ *(external tape:* BCD): Inputs data from tape unit specified according to a referenced FORMAT into variables listed. Records must have been written with an external tape WRITE statement, if prepared by a Fortran program.

READ (2, 15) A, B, ((C(I, J), I = 1, 5), J = 1, 10)

WRITE *(internal tape: binary):* Outputs data to the tape unit specified from the variables listed. One record per statement execution, no FORMAT.

WRITE (3) A, B, (C(I), I = 1, 10), KD, KX, KY

READ *(internal tape: binary):* Inputs data from the tape unit specified to the variables listed. Record must have been written by an internal tape WRITE statement.

READ (2) ((KX(J, I), I = 1, 50), J = 1, 100), A, B, C

=*(replacement)*: Evaluates expression on right side of =, converts mode if necessary and replaces contents of location specified at left of = with the value from the right side.

S(I) = SQRT(S(I) / T − A(I)**2)

84 FORTRAN: VOCABULARY AND GRAMMAR

GO TO *(unconditional):* Transfers control directly to statement specified.

    GO TO 15

GO TO *(conditional):* Transfers control to statement whose position in a series is the value of an integer variable specified.

    GO TO (15, 4, 37), K

IF *(arithmetic):* Transfers control to one of three statements designated, depending on whether the value of a parenthesized expression is negative, zero, or positive, respectively.

    IF (A − 2.0 * B + ABSF(C)) 15, 20, 25

IF *(logical/relational):* Evaluates a parenthesized expression as *true* or *false* and executes a Fortran statement (another l/r IF or DO excluded) which follows the expression, if *true*. If *false*, control goes immediately to the next statement in sequence.

    IF (A .GT. B .AND. C / 2.0 .LE. D) K = K + 1

DO: Initializes a series of statements (loop) ending with the statement specified, designating an index variable, its initial value, terminal value, and increment, if more than one.

    DO 55 I = 1, N, 2

CONTINUE: A marker statement used to complete a DO loop to avoid terminating on an IF, GO TO, or another DO.

    27 CONTINUE

STOP: Causes termination of program execution, and return to the computer's monitor system.

END: Signals the end of program or subprogram compilation. Must be the last card in every program and subprogram deck.

Review Exercises

1. Describe the use of these card fields for Fortran statements: column 1, columns 2–5, column 6, columns 7–72, columns 73–80.
2. Fill in the table with two examples for each cell.

	integer	real	alphameric
constant			
variable			

Review Exercises

3. Punch the following Fortran "program" and submit it for compilation at your installation. Try to predict the errors which the compiler will detect.

        C   PROGRAM ERRORS
             DIMENSION X(5, 2), Y(K)
             A + B = I**5.4
             Z = A * I
             DO 5 I = 10, J + 2
             L = X(K*2, 3 + J)
             IF (I .LT. G) DO 10 J = 1, 10
          5 GO TO K
             END

4. In what ways are the rules for F-mode field specifications more restrictive for output than for input formats?

5. If a data card holds the sequence of symbols shown here, write a READ and a PUNCH statement with their FORMAT statements needed to produce the output shown.
    data card columns 1–12: A062B305C−21
    output card columns 1–17: Δ6.2ΔΔ3.050ΔΔ−21.

6. Fill in the spaces in the matrix, vector, and single cell with the data values which will be placed there.
    DIMENSION X(2, 3), Y(2)
    READ 27, ((X(J, I), I = 1, 2), Y(J), J = 1, 2), Z
    27 FORMAT (7F1.0)
    (data card columns 1–7: 1234567)

7. What value will be computed for C?
    A = 3.5
    B = 7.2
    K = 1.0 + B / A
    C = K**3 / 27 − 1

8. What will be the final value of K?
    K = 5
    DO 25 I = 1, 5
    IF (K .GT. I) K = K − 1
    25 CONTINUE

9. Fill in the final values for cell A and the cells of R by stepping this sequence through, changing the contents of the appropriate cells as you execute each instruction.
    DO 5 I = 1, 3
    A = A + X(I)
    DO 5 J = 1, 3
    5 R(I, J) = R(I, J) + X(I) * X(J)

    X: | 1.0 | 2.0 | 3.0 | A: □   R: (3×3 grid)   I: □   J: □
    (Assume A and R hold zeros initially.)

10. What will be the computed value of K?
    K = SQRT(8.5 + ABS(3.0 * (AMIN1(−13.5, 12.5, −9.4)))) / 3.0

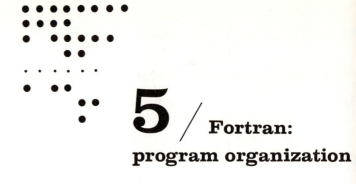

5 / Fortran: program organization

A computer program is a sequence of instructions that the machine can interpret and execute in order to achieve the programmer's purposes. The units of this sequence are statements of the various types described in the previous chapter.

The statements used in this book constitute a limited subset of the Fortran language, and the rules given are more restrictive than necessary for many compilers. These restrictions permit wider applicability across machines and serve to focus attention upon the more important aspects of the language. Programs written in this "basic" Fortran, however, may compile faster and even run faster on some computers, because most of the "frills" in Fortran only enhance programming convenience—often at a cost in efficiency.

The most difficult part of computer programming precedes any use of the Fortran language: stating the problem-solving process completely and unambiguously. Once this has been accomplished, the translation of the steps into a sequence of Fortran statements is relatively easy. Although the discipline involved is severe, those who master the techniques of programming often find that they have acquired a deeper understanding of analytic procedures, as well as vastly increased efficiency in their use.

The purpose of the present chapter is to illustrate the process of constructing programs from statements of the types outlined in Chapter 4, describing in detail the organization of each routine and the functions of the various statements they contain. As in writing any meaningful set of instructions, the *sequence* of the steps is as important as the steps themselves. It is useful to think of computer programming as analogous to giving instructions to a blindingly fast, amazingly accurate, but utterly rigid clerk. This million-dollar clerk has a very limited set of arithmetic and decision-making skills, but can call upon a certain number of prepackaged routines when told to do so (for example, obtaining a square root). The clerk's memory can be compared to a very large blackboard ruled as a grid with some 20,000 cells available for use in problem solving. Each of these cells can hold a number or a set of up to six alphameric characters. The clerk's use of this blackboard is restricted to reading the contents of the cells, or replacing completely the contents of one cell at a time.

The task of the programmer is to write out a sequence of instructions using a particular notation system—Fortran. The clerk has available a special translation routine for converting the Fortran statements to the many specific orders it can understand and execute. Writing out a problem-solving process requires considerable patience and attention to detail, and, if the rules of the language are not followed, the clerk may refuse to attempt the task. If the instructions are valid but in the wrong order, the clerk will go ahead with the job—and produce nonsense with its usual amazing speed. For instance, if you instruct the machine to add the contents of memory locations A and B before you have defined those contents with other instructions, you can hardly expect a meaningful answer. *Something* would be taken from those cells, but normally you would have no idea what, unless your program had specifically defined the contents in some way.

The present chapter is built around a set of twelve programs of gradually increasing complexity. By careful study of the flow charts and Fortran listings, a sense of the logic of program organization should emerge. Although at this stage you will have to consider each step carefully as you trace these routines and as you practice writing programs of your own, eventually you will become fluent in this language. Experienced programmers are often as unconscious of the structure of the language they use as you are of the structure of English when you write a paragraph. The crucial *difference* between ordinary language usage and Fortran programming is the fact that the communication is all in one direction, and the recipient is unable to guess at the meaning of ambiguous statements or to fill out incomplete messages.

FLOW CHARTS

Each of the routines in this book is accompanied by a diagram which describes the sequence of operations involved. These visual aids are called *flow charts* or *block diagrams*. There is no single standard for the symbolic shapes and connectors employed in such charts; the set we have chosen to use is described in Figure 5-1. The purpose of flow charting is to aid understanding of a problem-solving procedure (algorithm), and any set of conventions which achieves this end is as good as any other. Since di-

88 FORTRAN: PROGRAM ORGANIZATION

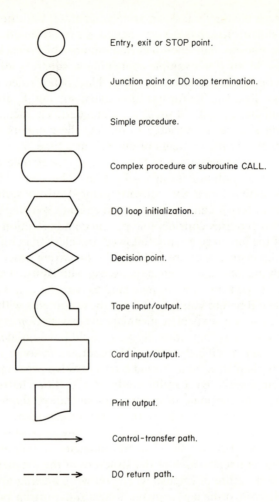

FIGURE 5-1. Flow chart symbols.

agrams such as these are very helpful only to someone other than the programmer who wrote the routine, most programmers do not bother with constructing flow charts except for public documentation. This is not to say that experienced programmers do not often outline the steps they intend to follow before they begin writing a Fortran program. A few short phrases will usually serve this purpose, though, and little is gained through the use of the elaborate special symbols and complete notation of a flow chart.

The flow charts in this book do not include FORMAT or DIMENSION statements, nor do they include definitions of the variable names involved. The diagrams represent only the operational sequences, and must be studied together with the Fortran statement listings to be fully understood. Although tracing through someone else's programs is quite tedious, it can be a very fruitful experience for a student of the language. Try not to leave any one of these routines until you feel that you fully understand the reasons behind every move that is implied. You will probably want to refer frequently to the summary of statements at the end of Chapter 4.

PROGRAM ONE

We will begin with the simplest kind of a problem: add the values 1 and 2 and print the sum. The flow chart and Fortran listing are shown in Figure 5-2.

The first statement simply gives the program a name; in our first example the program name is "ONE." In IBM Fortran systems this is only a comment card, as shown, since programs are named only on system-control cards. In CDC Fortran, however, all programs must begin with a statement such as the first one here (without the "C" in column one.)

The second card contains the first operational statement; it stores the constant 1 in the location named KA. The second statement is also a replacement statement; the constant 2 is stored in location KB. No DIMENSION statement is included in this program because no array variables are involved. KA, KB, and KSUM are all simple variables; their names are labels for single memory cells.

Control next passes to a statement which replaces the previously undefined contents of another simple variable, KSUM, with the sum of the values stored in locations KA and KB. This operation does not affect the contents of either of the locations on the right side of the equals sign.

Finally the value stored in KSUM is printed by the next operational statement in the program, referencing the FORMAT numbered 15. Since the sum is known to be only a single digit (3), the use of an I2 field specification will avoid print position one, which will be occupied by the blank that is inserted in front of the first significant digit in integer-mode output. To be absolutely certain that we will avoid print position one, we might have used the X specification in statement 15:

15 FORMAT (1X, I2)

We put the FORMAT statement after the I/O statement that referenced it in order to aid tracing. It could have been placed anywhere else in the program deck since it is not operational, but only serves as a reference when the PRINT statement is executed.

The last operational statement in the program, STOP, tells the computer

90 FORTRAN: PROGRAM ORGANIZATION

that the execution phase has been completed, and control is returned from the program to the computer's monitoring system. The final statement in the listing, END, is for the benefit of the Fortran compiler, and tells it that the conclusion of an independent routine has been reached.

It is sometimes helpful to use a piece of paper or a blackboard to simulate the various storage locations while tracing a program. In Figure 5-3 are represented the contents of locations 1, 2, KA, KB, and KSUM before and after each step in the program. It is not necessary to draw more than a single set of boxes, the contents of which can be changed as necessary while tracing the program sequence. Boxes for constants are not really necessary either, since the name and content are always the same, and remain unchanged throughout the program. They are included here to emphasize the fact that every constant and variable in a Fortran program is a label for some location(s) in the computer memory.

This problem is, of course, quite artificial; no one needs a computer to add 1 and 2. Even this first program is more complex than necessary, since we could have avoided the use of variables KA and KB and simply defined KSUM with one Fortran statement:

$$KSUM = 1 + 2$$

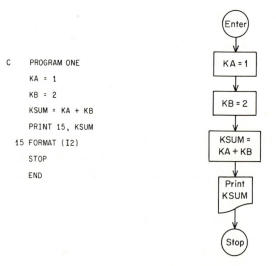

FIGURE 5-2. Program One and flow chart.

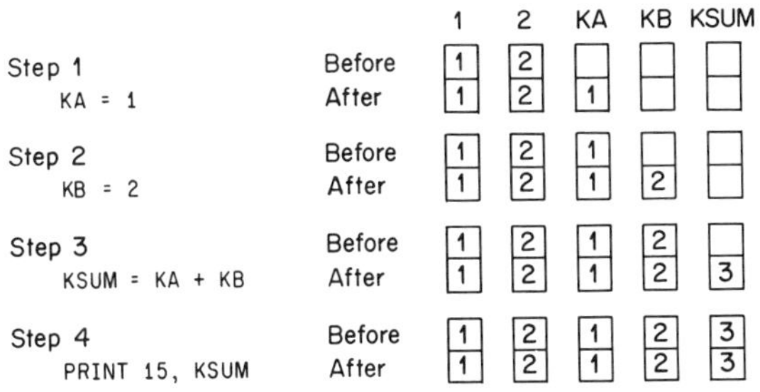

		1	2	KA	KB	KSUM
Step 1 KA = 1	Before After	1 1	2 2	 1		
Step 2 KB = 2	Before After	1 1	2 2	1 1	 2	
Step 3 KSUM = KA + KB	Before After	1 1	2 2	1 1	2 2	 3
Step 4 PRINT 15, KSUM	Before After	1 1	2 2	1 1	2 2	3 3

FIGURE 5-3. Memory-location contents for Program One.

PROGRAM TWO

The only difference between Program TWO, shown in Figure 5-4 and Program ONE, is in the way the contents of KA and KB are defined. Instead of equating the variable names to integer constants, two values are read from a single data card external to the program. This is, of course, a much more useful *type* of program, since we can obtain the sum of any two values without altering the program. For this artificially simple example, however, Program ONE is less bother.

The two definition steps have been replaced by a READ statement and a FORMAT which specifies two single-digit integer fields (columns 1 and 2) in the data card. Because the input values are limited to single-digit numbers, we know that the sum cannot exceed 18. We also know that the values cannot be negative, since separate columns would be needed for minus signs. The possibility of a two-digit output value necessitates a change in the FORMAT statement numbered 15 to be certain that the first printer position is avoided; the field length is simply increased to I3. We had to use separate FORMATS for input and output in this program because of the way we decided to punch the data card. If we were willing to use three columns for each input value, then the following FORMAT could have been used for both input and output, thus shortening the program deck by one card:

15 FORMAT (2I3)

This statement would be referenced both by the READ and PRINT, but the

92   FORTRAN: PROGRAM ORGANIZATION

latter would only output the single value designated by its variable list, ignoring the second field specified in the FORMAT. We would still need to avoid values that would yield a three-character result, in order not to force a symbol into printer position one.

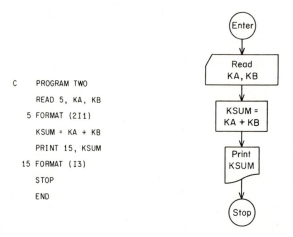

```
C     PROGRAM TWO
      READ 5, KA, KB
5     FORMAT (2I1)
      KSUM = KA + KB
      PRINT 15, KSUM
15    FORMAT (I3)
      STOP
      END
```

FIGURE 5-4. Program Two and flow chart.

PROGRAM THREE

Program THREE (Figure 5-5) is functionally the same as Programs ONE and TWO; two values are added and the sum is printed. We have introduced a DIMENSION statement here to designate a vector of two elements which will hold the input values. The DIMENSION statement reserves two storage locations for the variable name KX. Locations KX(1) and KX(2) will be used here just as KA and KB were used previously. No change in the FORMAT is needed; as before, the values punched in the two data-card fields will be stored in the two designated storage locations in the order of their appearance on the data card and in the READ list. KSUM again is used to hold the sum of the contents of the two locations, and this value is printed as before.

Program ONE is the simplest way to handle the problem. The complexities we are introducing are unnecessary here, but are essential for the more practical problems that are presented later. Programs FOUR and FIVE introduce still other alternative ways of achieving the same goal with which we began this series.

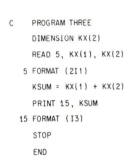
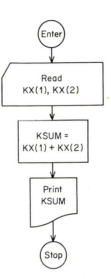

```
      C    PROGRAM THREE
            DIMENSION KX(2)
            READ 5, KX(1), KX(2)
         5  FORMAT (2I1)
            KSUM = KX(1) + KX(2)
            PRINT 15, KSUM
        15  FORMAT (I3)
            STOP
            END
```

FIGURE 5-5. Program Three and flow chart.

PROGRAM FOUR

Program FOUR (Figure 5-6) illustrates the use of a DO loop to obtain the sum of a series of values. An additional variable is needed here for indexing the loop. This variable's name I, appears in the DO statement with its initial and final values, as well as the statement number of the terminal statement in the loop (10). Before the loop is begun, location KSUM must be set to zero, because values are to be accumulated there. The loop will be executed twice before control moves on to the PRINT statement. This is the shortest possible DO loop, consisting only of the DO statement and its terminal statement. Later programs in this series will illustrate longer and more complex DO loops.

The index variable I is used in statement 10 as a subscript for the vector-variable KX. On each pass through the DO loop, location I will contain

94 FORTRAN: PROGRAM ORGANIZATION

a specific integer—either 1 or 2 in this case—and the contents of the appropriate cell in KX will be added to the previous contents of KSUM. *Then* this sum will replace the previous contents of KSUM. KSUM must be set to zero before the loop is started in order to insure the correct result upon completion of the loop, since the initial value in the memory cell is indeterminate.

Three statements in this program replace the single statement in Program THREE which obtains the sum. With only two values the DO loop is less efficient, but with more than five or six values it becomes necessary to specify such repetitive operations by the use of some indexing procedure. The DO loop notation provides an economical way of accomplishing this. In the flow chart we have used a dashed line pointing back toward the DO statement to indicate the return path that is implicitly taken from statement

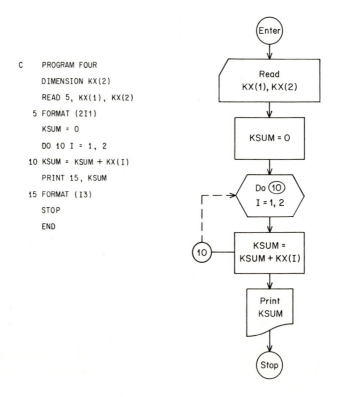

```
      C    PROGRAM FOUR
           DIMENSION KX(2)
           READ 5, KX(1), KX(2)
        5  FORMAT (2I1)
           KSUM = 0
           DO 10 I = 1, 2
       10  KSUM = KSUM + KX(I)
           PRINT 15, KSUM
       15  FORMAT (I3)
           STOP
           END
```

FIGURE 5-6. Program Four and flow chart.

10 after each pass through the loop which does not "satisfy" the indexing instructions. After the final (second) pass through the loop, control automatically proceeds along the solid arrow to the next statement in sequence (PRINT).

PROGRAM FIVE

The only difference between Program FIVE (Figure 5-7) and Program FOUR is in the list of the READ statement. The same input is achieved by this alternative, which illustrates the DO-implying notation of an indexed I/O list. The parentheses enclose the equivalent of a DO loop, with an integer index variable (I) and its limits. Since the use of this variable will be completed before control leaves the READ statement, the same variable name may be used in the summation DO loop later in the program.

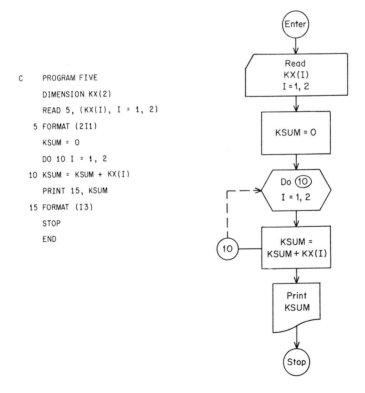

FIGURE 5-7. Program Five and flow chart.

PROGRAM SIX

In Program SIX we begin to work with more useful routines. The task here is to obtain the average of 50 single-digit whole numbers. Since they can all fit on a single data card, we will assume that they have been punched this way, beginning in card-column one. As shown in the flow chart (Figure 5-8) the first step is to read the 50 values into memory. The use of 50 separate variable names would be prohibitively awkward, so we will use a DIMENSION statement to reserve a 50-cell vector for the raw scores. The first operational statement in the program is an indexed READ which transfers the 50 single digit numbers from the data card into the 50 locations collectively named X. The transfer is carried out using real-mode (F) conversion, since we will later want to deal with these values in real mode.

The next step is to set the simple variable named SUM equal to zero, prior to accumulating a total in this cell. Note that this is done in real mode as well, and that all variable names in this program except the index of the DO loop are real-mode names. We could have written this zeroing statement as $SUM = 0$, in effect asking the computer to convert the integer zero to real mode before storing it in SUM, but by using the real-mode version of the constant we save a few machine-language instructions.

After setting SUM to zero we begin a DO loop using the integer variable I as the index. After the loop has been executed 50 times, the total of all 50 values will remain in SUM, and control will pass on automatically to the next statement, which computes the average of the 50 values. The content of SUM is divided by the real constant 50.0, and the result is stored in another cell labeled with the name AVG. The content of SUM is not affected by this operation.

Finally, AVG is printed using real-mode conversion, which is determined by the FORMAT specification F10.4. This field will be ten columns in length with four decimal places. Since the integer portion of the answer in this example cannot exceed one digit, the integer portion of the field (four columns plus the sign column) will be wide enough to avoid anything but a blank in the first printer position. Suppose the contents of AVG turned out to be 2.75 for a particular set of 50 scores. The output line of print would then contain the following characters in columns one through ten:

$\Delta\Delta\Delta\Delta$2.7500

Although the usefulness of this program is restricted by the specific number of items and the data-card FORMAT which are included, it is a practical means of obtaining an answer that would be tedious to compute by hand. With a desk calcu'ator available, most programmers would not bother to write a program such as this. There are other considerations that would also argue against the use of a computer program to solve a problem this small, such as the time spent waiting for the program to be processed by the computation center. Cost would probably be negligible since the program would run only a few seconds. With programs SEVEN, EIGHT, and NINE, the need for a computer will still be debatable, but for the remaining problems in this chapter most programmers would prefer to write programs rather than spend the time necessary to do the computations with a desk calculator.

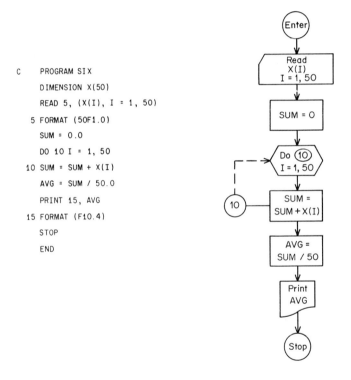

FIGURE 5-8. Program Six and flow chart.

PROGRAM SEVEN

Program SEVEN (Figure 5-9) extends Program SIX to compute the standard deviation (sigma) for the set of 50 scores in addition to their mean. In

98 FORTRAN: PROGRAM ORGANIZATION

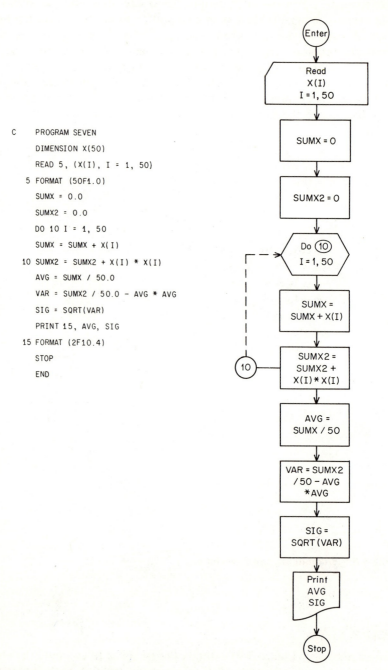

```
C     PROGRAM SEVEN
      DIMENSION X(50)
      READ 5, (X(I), I = 1, 50)
    5 FORMAT (50F1.0)
      SUMX = 0.0
      SUMX2 = 0.0
      DO 10 I = 1, 50
      SUMX = SUMX + X(I)
   10 SUMX2 = SUMX2 + X(I) * X(I)
      AVG = SUMX / 50.0
      VAR = SUMX2 / 50.0 - AVG * AVG
      SIG = SQRT(VAR)
      PRINT 15, AVG, SIG
   15 FORMAT (2F10.4)
      STOP
      END
```

FIGURE 5-9. Program Seven and flow chart.

order to do this, the values of the squared raw scores must be accumulated. The simple variable SUMX2 is used for this purpose; it is zeroed before the accumulation loop is started, and an additional statement is added to the loop to accumulate the squared values. This statement now becomes the terminal statement 10. The middle statement within the loop does not need a statement number. AVG holds the computed mean as in Program SIX, and a new location called VAR is used to hold the variance of the scores, which is computed with the formula

$$\sigma^2 = \frac{\Sigma X^2}{N} - \mu^2$$

Since the mean (AVG) was computed in the previous statement, it may be used in computing the variance. No parentheses are needed in this statement which defines the contents of VAR; SUMX2 will first be divided by the constant 50.0, then AVG will be multiplied by itself (squared) and finally the latter result will be subtracted from the former.

In the next statement the square-root function SQRT is "called" to obtain the value of sigma, which is then stored in a new location named SIG. Although it does not matter in this particular program since we do not output the value, the content of VAR will not be affected by appearing as an argument to the function SQRT.

Finally, the values of AVG and SIG are printed with reference to FORMAT 15, which indicates two F10.4 fields in succession on the same line of print. Since the input values are one-digit numbers, we can be sure that these two output values will be effectively spaced far enough apart to be readable.

PROGRAM EIGHT

Program EIGHT (Figure 5-10) is a simplification of Program SEVEN, and yields the same output values, although some Hollerith labeling has been added.

The first simplification is in the READ statement, where advantage is taken of the rule relaxation that permits use of an array name without subscripting and indexing instructions. Since we want to fill the entire array X with values in the order that they will be transferred from the data card, we can allow the computer to reference the DIMENSION statement to determine the number of values to be input.

Single letters are used for all variable names in this program just to simplify punching and to make the statements more readable. Of course, short names like these restrict the mnemonic value of the variable names.

In statement 10 we have used the exponentiation symbol (**) to indicate squaring a score, instead of multiplying it by itself. Also, we have elimi-

100 FORTRAN: PROGRAM ORGANIZATION

```
C     PROGRAM EIGHT
      DIMENSION X(50)
      READ 5, X
    5 FORMAT (50F1.0)
      A = 0.0
      S = 0.0
      DO 10 I = 1, 50
      A = A + X(I)
   10 S = S + X(I)**2
      A = A / 50.0
      S = SQRT(S / 50.0 - A**2)
      PRINT 15, A, S
   15 FORMAT (4H A =, F10.4, 3X, 3HS =, F10.4)
      STOP
      END
```

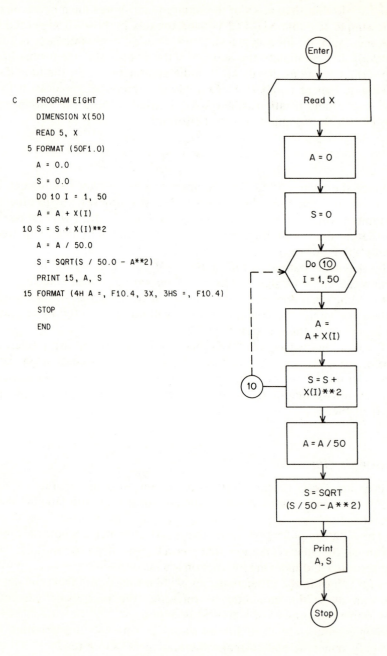

FIGURE 5-10. Program Eight and flow chart.

nated completely the separate computation of the variance, since we do not intend to output this value or use it in any other program statements. The argument to the square-root function which yields sigma thus becomes the arithmetic expression which reduces to the variance. No part of this expression is changed by appearing within these parentheses.

Finally, the values of the mean and sigma are printed. The first field on the single output line is a four-character Hollerith block beginning with blank character which will occupy printer position one. A comma separates this specification from the next, serving to convert the contents of location A to a real-mode output value. Three spaces are then skipped on this same line and another three-character Hollerith block is output, followed by the field specification for the value of variable S. If A and S happened to contain 5.40 and 1.36 for a particular set of 50 input scores, the output line would be as follows:

$$\Delta A\Delta=\Delta\Delta\Delta\Delta 5.4000\Delta\Delta\Delta S\Delta=\Delta\Delta\Delta\Delta 1.3600$$

PROGRAM NINE

The flow chart for Program NINE (Figure 5-12) reflects the expanded task with which we are confronted. The purpose of the program is to compute a Pearson product-moment correlation between two sets of 50 scores — two scores from each of 50 subjects. The method employed is not the one most commonly used with desk calculators, since we want to obtain the means and sigmas of the two variables as by-products of the procedure. Therefore, the formula we will use for the correlation coefficient is:

$$r_{xy} = \frac{\Sigma XY \ / \ N - \mu_x \mu_y}{\sigma_x \sigma_y}$$

The first step in the program is to read the scores for all 50 subjects into the computer memory. Assuming that we have punched one data card containing two scores for each of the 50 subjects, and that we will use separate vectors for the raw scores on each variable, we will need an indexed READ statement that will place the scores alternately in the two vectors as they are input from the data cards. The index variable I will keep track of the subject number during the reading process, and therefore can serve also as the subscript designating the appropriate cells in the X and Y vectors for each subject's scores. To achieve the alternating storage needed, the two storage locations are designated within the loop-implying parentheses, followed by the indexing instructions. The FORMAT only specifies the arrangement of data on one subject's card; it will be repeated automatically 50 times, beginning each repetition at the start of a new data card as they are arranged in the input deck. Figure 5-11 represents this input sequence graphically.

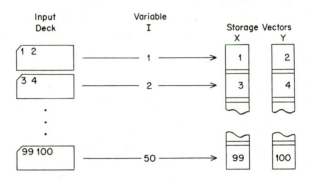

FIGURE 5-11. Input order for Program Nine.

After entering all 100 values into memory, five storage locations are zeroed. In the flow chart this is stated within a single complex-procedure box to save space, but it requires five separate Fortran statements. These locations will hold the five accumulated values needed in later computations. The DO loop ending with statement 10 accomplishes these accumulations over the 50 subject's score pairs. After statement 10 has been executed for the fiftieth time, AX and AY will contain ΣX and ΣY, respectively; SX and SY similarly will contain ΣX^2 and ΣY^2; and R will contain ΣXY.

The next two statements convert the contents of AX and AY to the means of the two variables, which are used in the following pair of statements to compute the corresponding sigmas. Then R is converted to the correlation coefficient using these previously computed statistics. Parentheses are necessary here to force the division by the sigma product to take place last in the evaluation of the expression.

The PRINT statement then outputs all five values with appropriate labeling in five lines of print which might look like this for a particular set of data:

$\Delta AX\Delta = \Delta\Delta\Delta 23.4544\Delta\Delta\Delta AY\Delta = \Delta\Delta\Delta 22.9650$

$\Delta SX\Delta = \Delta\Delta\Delta\Delta 2.2200\Delta\Delta\Delta SY\Delta = \Delta\Delta\Delta\Delta 4.5051$

$\Delta R(XY)\Delta = \Delta\Delta\Delta 0.4250$

A line is skipped after the first and second output lines because a double slash appears in the FORMAT; a single slash would only have ended the current line of print, resulting in single spacing and three lines of output. Note that the parentheses in the Hollerith block of the last line are not operational, but are only symbols which are printed verbatim as part of the block.

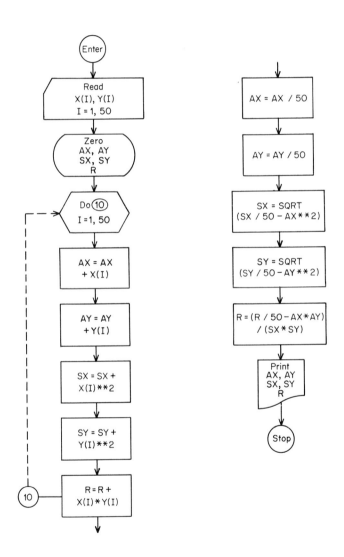

FIGURE 5-12. Flow chart for Program Nine.

```
C          PROGRAM NINE
           DIMENSION X(50), Y(50)
           READ 5, (X(I), Y(I), I = 1,50)
         5 FORMAT (10X, 2F5.0)
           AX = 0.0
           AY = 0.0
           SX = 0.0
           SY = 0.0
           R = 0.0
           DO 10 I = 1,50
           AX = AX + X(I)
           AY = AY + Y(I)
           SX = SX + X(I)**2
           SY = SY + Y(I)**2
        10 R = R + X(I) * Y(I)
           AX = AX / 50.0
           AY = AY / 50.0
           SX = SQRT(SX / 50.0 - AX**2)
           SY = SQRT(SY / 50.0 - AY**2)
           R = (R / 50.0 - AX * AY) / (SX * SY)
           PRINT 15, AX, AY, SX, SY, R
       150 FORMAT (5H AX =, F10.4, 3X, 4HAY =, F10.4 // 5H SX =,
          1 F10.4, 3X, 4HSY =, F10.4 // 8H R(XY) =, F10.4)
           STOP
           END
```

PROGRAM TEN

The problem in Program TEN would require hours of work with a desk calculator, and is therefore unquestionably appropriate for computer solution. Instead of computing only one correlation coefficient, we wish to obtain a matrix of correlations, representing the relationships among all possible pairings of ten variables. The sample size remains 50 cases as before, but each subject now has provided ten scores instead of only two. Ten means and sigmas will have to be computed along with a 10-by-10 matrix of correlation coefficients. What will be the properties of this output matrix? We know already that it will be square. It will also be *symmetric* on either side of the main diagonal, since r_{xy} and r_{yx} are always the same value. The main diagonal will represent r_{xx}, which will always be 1.00. An

Schematic						Example				
r_{11}	r_{12}	r_{13}	r_{14}	r_{15}		1.00	.12	-.56	.00	-.10
r_{21}	r_{22}	r_{23}	r_{24}	r_{25}		.12	1.00	.43	.44	.30
r_{31}	r_{32}	r_{33}	r_{34}	r_{35}		-.56	.43	1.00	.96	.09
r_{41}	r_{42}	r_{43}	r_{44}	r_{45}		.00	.44	.96	1.00	.10
r_{51}	r_{52}	r_{53}	r_{54}	r_{55}		-.10	.30	.09	.10	1.00

FIGURE 5-13. Arrangement of an intercorrelation matrix.

intercorrelation matrix for a five-variable problem is represented schematically and with a set of example values in Figure 5-13.

Programs ELEVEN and TWELVE concern procedures for intercorrelation which do not require storing all of the raw data at once in the computer memory. Program TEN deals with a problem that is small enough to permit input of all raw scores to a data matrix before computations are begun. We will call this matrix X and dimension it with 50 rows (for subjects) and 10 columns (for variables). We will also need to dimension ten-element vectors for the means (vector A) and sigmas (vector S) of the variables, as well as a 10-by-10 matrix for the intercorrelations (matrix R).

The first stage of the program is the zeroing of the A, S, and R arrays. This could have been done after reading the raw data into X, since neither block of operations is dependent on the other. In the flow chart (Figure 5-14) we have indicated this zeroing in a single box, but the process in Fortran requires a pair of coterminous DO loops, which end on statement 5. The index variable I is initialized and used in the next two statements as a subscript for variables A and S. A second index variable J is then initialized, and both integer variables are used to subscript R. The index (J) nearest the terminal statement will proceed through all of its values (1 to 10) before the outer loop is incremented. This results in the zeroing of an element in A, an element in S, and then all elements of the corresponding *row* of R before the I variable is stepped. After statement 5 has been executed 100 times, both DO loops will be satisfied and control will move on to the READ statement.

The single READ statement fills the entire X matrix by using coterminous DO-loop-implying notation. Because of the way we decided to DIMENSION the X matrix, this notation is necessary to achieve the correct storage of scores from 50 data cards, each of which contains 10 values for one subject. If we had dimensioned X(10, 50), then we could have used the following statement to input the 500 raw scores: READ 10, X. The only reason for doing it the hard way was to illustrate a double-indexed READ statement. The FORMAT describes one subject's data card, and will be repeated automatically 50 times—until the READ list is satisfied. In this kind of nested indexing, the inner index variable (J) will proceed through all of its 10 values before the outer index variable (I) is incremented. Storage of scores in the X matrix, therefore, is by rows.

Three coterminous DO loops are next used to accumulate ΣX, ΣX^2, and ΣXY in the cells of A, S, and R. The placement of the accumulation statements in this sequence relative to the DO statements is crucial and should be carefully studied. You may find it helpful to step this process through on a piece of paper or a blackboard, using a smaller (three- or four-variable) example. Note especially the use of variable I to index subjects, while J and K are used to index variables.

The next DO loop, which terminates on statement 20, converts the

106 FORTRAN: PROGRAM ORGANIZATION

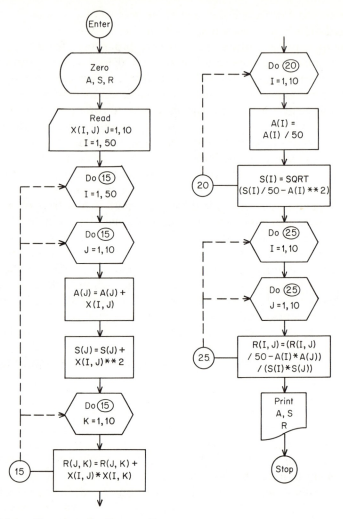

FIGURE 5-14. Flow chart for Program Ten.

contents of the A cells to means and the contents of the S cells to sigmas. After this has been completed, another pair of DO statements terminating on statement 25 is used to compute a correlation coefficient in each cell of the R matrix, utilizing in each case the ΣXY that had been stored there and the appropriate combination of the means and sigmas now stored in cells of A and S vectors.

The program concludes with the printing of the 10 means, 10 sigmas, and the entire 10-by-10 intercorrelation matrix. All 10 means will appear on the first printed line, a line will be skipped, and then all 10 sigmas will be printed. After another line-skip, the Hollerith label R∆MATRIX will be printed. Beginning on the next line of print, because of the slash mark, the first row of the intercorrelation matrix will be printed next. This specification is in parentheses not preceded by a number so that control will not return all the way to the beginning of the FORMAT, but will go back only to skip another line and print another row of R. This will continue until the PRINT statement's output list has been satisfied. Notice that the parenthesized specifications for printing A, S, and R constitute three independent sequences. The single-indexed A loop will be completed before the S loop is begun. Similarly, all S output will be completed before output from R begins. This is the order of the specifications in the FORMAT, fortunately. If the sequences did not correspond in this way, the output, which would proceed according to the order of the PRINT statement, would be erroneously labeled.

This is a complex program, but one which embodies a great many of the most common programming devices used by behavioral scientists in statistical analysis. Full understanding of this routine and the remaining two in this chapter will require considerably more effort than did the earlier programs. It would be advisable to slow down at this point and take the time to study these routines carefully. The techniques explained in the remainder of this chapter will be central to most of the programs presented in later chapters.

```
C       PROGRAM TEN
        DIMENSION X(50,10), A(10), S(10), R(10,10)
        DO 5 I = 1,10
        A(I) = 0.0
        S(I) = 0.0
        DO 5 J = 1,10
      5 R(I,J) = 0.0
        READ 10, ((X(I,J), J = 1,10), I = 1,50)
     10 FORMAT (5X, 10F2.0)
        DO 15 I = 1,50
        DO 15 J = 1,10
        A(J) = A(J) + X(I,J)
        S(J) = S(J) + X(I,J)**2
        DO 15 K = 1,10
     15 R(J,K) = R(J,K) + X(I,J) * X(I,K)
        DO 20 I = 1,10
        A(I) = A(I) / 50.0
     20 S(I) = SQRT(S(I) / 50.0 - A(I)**2)
        DO 25 I = 1,10
        DO 25 J = 1,10
     25 R(I,J) = (R(I,J) / 50.0 - A(I) * A(J)) / (S(I) * S(J))
        OPRINT 30, (A(I), I = 1,10), (S(I), I = 1,10),
       1 ((R(I,J), J = 1,10), I = 1,10)
     300FORMAT (8H MEANS = 10F10.4 // 9H SIGMAS = 10F10.4 //
       1 10H R MATRIX., (/ 10F10.4))
        STOP
        END
```

PROGRAM ELEVEN

It is not at all uncommon in behavioral sciences research to encounter intercorrelation problems which involve so many variables and/or subjects that storage of the entire raw-score matrix in central memory is beyond the capacity of most computers. A different algorithm is needed for these problems, and as often happens, this alternative technique is no less efficient than the more straightforward solution.

Instead of reading all raw scores into a data matrix, the procedure in Program ELEVEN requires storage of only one subject's vector of raw scores at a time. These scores are then used to add the appropriate values to the cells which accumulate sums, sums of squares, and cross-products for all variables and their combinations, and another subject's vector of scores is read in, replacing the previous set. By the time all data have been entered from cards, the accumulator cells will hold all necessary values for computing the required means, sigmas, and intercorrelations, but only the last subject's set of raw scores will remain in memory.

The program (Figure 5-15) begins with the zeroing of the A vector and the R matrix, using a pair of DO loops like those in Program TEN. The S vector is not zeroed because it will be used to hold one subject's raw scores during the accumulation process. Once the accumulation process has been completed, the S vector will be used to hold sigmas, which will be computed from the ΣX^2 values contained in the main diagonal of the R matrix.

This program is written to process a sample of 500 subjects, each of whom has provided 50 one-digit scores (test items, perhaps) which are punched on a data card. The FORMAT (10) which is referenced by the READ statement skips the first 10 columns of the data card, since this field would normally be occupied by the subject's identification code. After a single subject's scores are read into vector S, these values are added to corresponding cells in A, and their cross-products are added to the appropriate cells of R through use of a third DO loop terminating on statement 15.

The next loop, terminating on statement 20, is equivalent to that in Program TEN, except that the sums of squares necessary to compute the sigmas are taken from the main diagonal of matrix R. These values are ΣX^2, since $X_i X_j = X_i^2$ when $i = j$, which is the case for each of the 50 diagonal cells.

The next pair of DO loops, which terminate on statement 25, compute the correlation coefficients. Since the R matrix is symmetrical across the diagonal, we have introduced a refinement that speeds program execution by computing R_{ij} only above and on the diagonal, reflecting the computed values to the corresponding cells across the diagonal by reversed subscripts. This is accomplished by setting the initial parameter for the second "J" loop as I rather than 1. When $i = j$, the reflection statement (25) is redundant, but will still be executed.

Note that the loops terminating on statements 5 and 15 also operate only on cells above and on the main diagonal of the R matrix.

The vectors of means and sigmas are printed next, using repetition factors in front of left parentheses within FORMAT 30 in order to output the two sets of 50 values, 10 per line of print. A slash within each of these

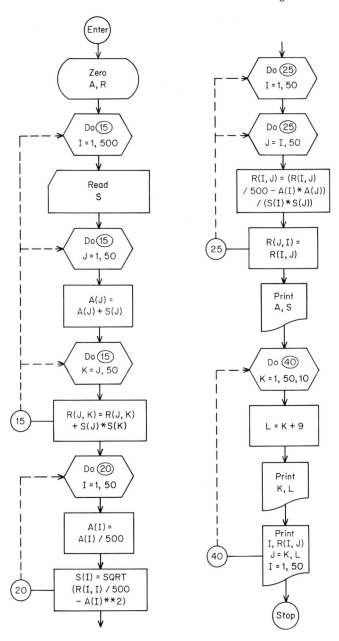

FIGURE 5-15. Flow chart for Program Eleven.

inner parentheses sets is necessary to indicate transfers to new lines of print before repetition of the subformats.

Printing the 50-by-50 intercorrelation matrix R presents more of a

110 FORTRAN: PROGRAM ORGANIZATION

problem. The procedure used here partitions the matrix into five blocks, each of which is 10 columns wide and 50 rows long. Each block begins on a new page because of the 1 in printer-position one in FORMAT 35. The index variable K is given a third parameter in the DO statement so that it can serve to designate the initial column of the current block in PRINT statement 40 while also controlling the number of blocks to be output. The statement L = K + 9 defines the last column in the current block, and is used as the final parameter in the indexing of PRINT statement 40. Before the printing of values from R begins for each block, a labeling line is output which contains the current values of K and L. PRINT statement 40 outputs the index value I, which is the row number, followed by 10 elements from the current block. FORMAT 45 describes a single line of printed output and is repeated 50 times per block under the control of the I index variable in the PRINT statement.

```
C     PROGRAM ELEVEN
      DIMENSION A(50), S(50), R(50,50)
      DO 5 I = 1,50
      A(I) = 0.0
      DO 5 J = 1,50
    5 R(I,J) = 0.0
      DO 15 I = 1,500
      READ 10, S
   10 FORMAT (10X, 50F1.0)
      DO 15 J = 1,50
      A(J) = A(J) + S(J)
      DO 15 K = J,50
   15 R(J,K) = R(J,K) + S(J) * S(K)
      DO 20 I = 1,50
      A(I) = A(I) / 500.0
   20 S(I) = SQRT(R(I,I) / 500.0 - A(I)**2)
      DO 25 I = 1,50
      DO 25 J = I,50
      R(I,J) = (R(I,J) / 500.0 - A(I) * A(J)) / (S(I) * S(J))
   25 R(J,I) = R(I,J)
      PRINT 30, A, S
   30 FORMAT (7H MEANS., 5(/ 10F10.4) // 8H SIGMAS., 5(/ 10F10.4))
      DO 40 K = 1,50,10
      L = K + 9
      PRINT 35, K, L
   35 FORMAT (14H1R MATRIX. COL, I3, 3H TO, I3)
   40 PRINT 45, (I, (R(I,J), J = K,L), I = 1,50)
   45 FORMAT (I5, 10F10.4)
      STOP
      END
```

PROGRAM TWELVE

Program TWELVE (Figure 5-16) is an example of a general-purpose library routine. Without changing any of the program statements, this routine can be employed with any number of variables up to 100, and with any number of subjects. Furthermore, the data-card FORMAT may be varied at will from one problem to another. This generality is achieved through the use of two *control cards*, which precede the data cards in the data deck,

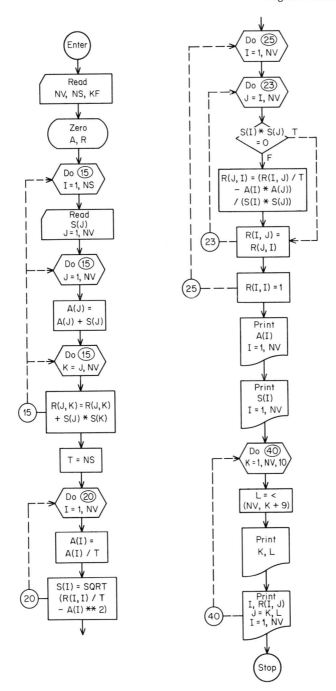

FIGURE 5-16. Flow chart for Program Twelve.

providing the program with the information necessary for correct processing of the data. The output from this program is the same as that produced by Program ELEVEN.

In addition to the vectors A and S and the matrix R, the DIMENSION statement includes a vector named KF, which is used to hold the variable FORMAT read at the start of the program. The later READ statement, used to input data for a single subject, references this vector by name instead of an internal FORMAT such as statement 10 in Program ELEVEN. The first operational statement in the program reads the two control cards. The first of these cards is expected to contain the numbers of variables and subjects as two consecutive five-digit integers. The second control card is expected to contain the data-card FORMAT. If we wished to run the problem solved by Program ELEVEN on this general routine, we would place the following control cards in front of the data deck:

ΔΔΔ50ΔΔ500
(10X, 50F1.0)

After the control information has been stored, vector A and matrix R are zeroed. Note that the entire R matrix is zeroed here (for a reason to be explained later). The limit values in these DO statements are set equal to the previously read number of variables (NV) instead of the dimensioned maximum, since only the first NV locations will be involved in later storage and computations.

The next stage of the routine parallels Program ELEVEN, accumulating sums and cross products for NV variables, reading data for NS subjects in turn into vector S. Since the number of scores per subject is not fixed, an indexed READ statement is necessary here. Again, all DO-loop limits are integer variables rather than predetermined constants.

After statement 15 has been executed for the last time, control passes to the statement that converts the number of subjects to a real-mode value in location T. Then means and sigmas are computed and stored in A and S respectively, as in Program ELEVEN.

The next stage of the program computes the intercorrelations using a slightly different procedure which includes a check for zero variance. This check was not included in Program ELEVEN for the sake of simplicity, and is not needed when the programmer is sure that no variable has zero variation (all subjects having identical scores). In a general-purpose routine such as Program TWELVE, however, it is wise to provide for such possibilities. Since division by zero is a meaningless operation and computers vary in the way they react to such an instruction, the computation of the correlation coefficient is skipped and zero is arbitrarily stored from below the diagonal in the event that either variable of a particular combination has a zero sigma; the product of the two sigmas is used to detect this condition. Note that the computed correlation is stored below the diagonal and reflected above, unlike Program ELEVEN, in order to accommodate this modification smoothly. The first DO statement in this section is terminated on an additional statement (25) which sets the diagonal element to 1.0; this is necessary to preserve the diagonal even when one or more variables has zero variance.

The output stages of Programs ELEVEN and TWELVE are organized similarly except for the use of integer variables instead of predetermined constants as limits for the indexing. The vectors of means and sigmas are printed separately because the FORMAT used in Program ELEVEN is only appropriate for the particular number of variables (50) in that problem. In the present program, the number of such elements to be output is not determined until execution of the program; the use of an inner parenthesis set without a repetition factor in Program TWELVE allows output of as many lines as necessary to accommodate each vector. Note that the computation of L for the matrix-partition output employs the MIN0 Function to insure that this value does not exceed NV, in the event that the final partition is less than 10 columns wide, which will be the case if NV is not exactly divisible by 10.

```
      C      PROGRAM TWELVE
             DIMENSION KF(16), A(100), S(100), R(100,100)
             READ 3, NV, NS, KF
           3 FORMAT (2I5 / 16A5)
             DO 5 I = 1,NV
             A(I) = 0.0
             DO 5 J = 1,NV
           5 R(I,J) = 0.0
             DO 15 I = 1,NS
             READ KF, (S(J), J = 1,NV)
             DO 15 J = 1,NV
             A(J) = A(J) + S(J)
             DO 15 K = J,NV
          15 R(J,K) = R(J,K) + S(J) * S(K)
             T = NS
             DO 20 I = 1,NV
             A(I) = A(I) / T
          20 S(I) = SQRT(R(I,I) / T - A(I)**2)
             DO 25 I = 1,NV
             DO 23 J = I,NV
             IF (S(I) * S(J) .EQ. 0.0) GO TO 23
             R(J,I) = (R(I,J) / T - A(I) * A(J)) / (S(I) * S(J))
          23 R(I,J) = R(J,I)
          25 R(I,I) = 1.0
             PRINT 30, (A(I), I = 1,NV)
          30 FORMAT (7H MEANS., (/ 10F10.4))
             PRINT 31, (S(I), I = 1,NV)
          31 FORMAT (8H SIGMAS., (/ 10F10.4))
             DO 40 K = 1,NV,10
             L = MIN0(NV, K + 9)
             PRINT 35, K, L
          35 FORMAT (14H1R MATRIX. COL, I3, 3H TO, I3)
          40 PRINT 45, (I, (R(I,J), J = K,L), I = 1,NV)
          45 FORMAT (I5, 10F10.4)
             STOP
             END
```

114 FORTRAN: PROGRAM ORGANIZATION

The twelve programs presented in this chapter are obviously a biased and restricted sampling of the programming problems encountered in behavioral sciences research, since their purpose was to introduce progressively greater complexity within a common problem framework. Throughout the rest of this book flow charts will be provided for every program, but the discussions of program construction will be much more limited than those in the present chapter. It will be worth the effort to trace each new program the way we did in this chapter, in order to acquire a comprehensive stock of problem-solving techniques. Sooner or later you will probably need them all, in one form or another.

Review Exercises

1. In Exercise 7 for Chapter 3, you punched a set of 16 data cards. Now write a computer program to read these cards and punch a new deck of cards with the format (A6, 2X, 8I2, I3). Be careful about matching the modes of input/output statements and their formats.
2. Write two programs to compute the mean of the total scores (variable nine) for the 16 subjects in the example deck output in Exercise 1. One version should read all scores before computing; the other needs no DIMENSION statement.
3. Write two programs to compute a mean and sigma for each of the 16 subjects in the example deck, based on his first 8 scores. Print 16 lines, each holding a subject's code number (columns 1–6), his mean, and his sigma. Again, write one version to read all data before computing, and the other to process one subject at a time.
4. Write a program to locate the largest and smallest total score (variable nine) in the example deck of 16 subjects. Print these scores and the code numbers of the subjects who obtained them, with appropriate labeling.
5. Write a program to read the 16 total scores from the example deck into a vector, reorder the elements of the vector so that they are ranked from largest to smallest, and then print the 16 reordered scores. Write another program which employs a substantially different algorithm to accomplish the reordering.

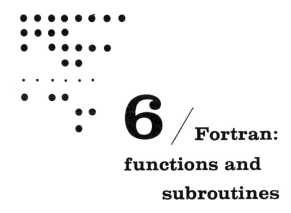

6 / Fortran: functions and subroutines

Functions and subroutines are independently compiled sequences of instructions which may be called into operation by single Fortran statements in programs or other subprograms. The subprogramming concept is a very important part of the Fortran language, since it vastly reduces programming effort and can help in organizing a problem-solving procedure.

We have already employed function subprograms such as SQRT, and have discussed a number of other library functions that are automatically available in Fortran compilers. When a Fortran program is compiled which includes the names of any of these library functions, an already compiled instruction sequence is stored in the computer memory as part of the complete object program. During the execution phase of the processing sequence, control is automatically transferred to the appropriate function's instruction sequence, and is returned to the main program after the function operations are complete. The Fortran programmer is not restricted to the use of functions provided by the compiler, however. He can write his own function subprograms and subroutines to be submitted along with the main program which calls them. This chapter will present the essential rules for building and using such subprograms, and will also include some of the functions and subroutines which the author has developed or adapted for statistical data-processing.

FORMULAS AS FUNCTIONS

The notion of implied standard operational sequences which "return" values computed from arguments which were "sent" to the operational sequence is actually not new to you. Consider the formula for a correlation coefficient:

$$r_{xy} = \frac{\Sigma XY/N - \mu_x \mu_y}{\sigma_x \sigma_y}$$

The symbols μ_x, μ_y, σ_x, σ_y, and r_{xy} all imply such standard computation sequences. The same formula is referenced by the symbols μ_x and μ_y: $\mu_A = \Sigma A/N$. Note that *within* the formula which defines the symbol μ, we normally use some variable name like A even though we understand that the same procedure will yield different values for different variables. Thus, *outside* the formula for μ, we will use the symbol with subscripts appropriate to variables involved in the larger context of another formula such as the one above defining r_{xy}.

The symbol σ also implies a standard operational sequence which employs the definition of μ:

$$\sigma_A = \sqrt{\Sigma A^2/N - \mu_A^2}$$

This nesting of formulas is carried even further when both μ and σ are used to define r, as illustrated in Figure 6-1.

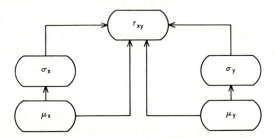

FIGURE 6-1. Nesting formulas to define the correlation coefficient.

Although it might appear that function subprograms for the mean, sigma, and correlation coefficient would be desirable in statistical programming, experience suggests that such functions are not as valuable as they might seem, for various reasons which will be apparent later. Nothing would *prevent* us from writing and using such functions, however, if we wished to do so.

SUBPROGRAM ORGANIZATION

You are already familiar with the procedure for calling a function into operation by employing its name as a pseudovariable in a program statement. We will discuss the calling of subroutines later in this chapter. Let us first consider the construction of the subprogram itself.

Every subprogram begins with a naming statement. Examples follow:

SUBROUTINE ALPHA (A, B, K, L)
SUBROUTINE KOUNT (V, K)
SUBROUTINE P23XY (P, Q, X)
FUNCTION BETA (A, B, C)
FUNCTION K2X2 (KK, LL)
FUNCTION SIGF (X, K)

The key word SUBROUTINE or FUNCTION determines the type of the subprogram. The name of the subprogram is subject to the same restrictions as are variable names: the first character must be alphabetic, and the length is restricted to six characters. The mode of the name is important for functions, but is irrelevant for subroutines. The variable names enclosed in the parentheses following the subprogram name are known as the *arguments* to the function or subroutine. Although these arguments may be otherwise in the calling program, in the name statement of the subprogram itself they may only appear as variable names; constants and subscripts are not permitted. These variable names may designate either simple or array variables. Integer and/or real-mode variable names may be used as arguments, regardless of the mode of the subprogram name.

The most significant characteristic of subprograms is the lack of any necessary correspondence between variable names appearing in the subprogram and those which appear in the routine(s) which call the subprogram. All linkages between variable names in the subprogram and calling routine are determined by comparable *positions* in the argument lists following the name of the subprogram. It is this independence of variable names within subprograms that makes their application so flexible.

Only those locations named in the argument list are linked to the calling routine; all *other* variable names in the subprogram — even if identical to names in the calling routine — will be assigned to different memory locations.

The rest of a subprogram consists of Fortran statements which carry out the operations necessary to achieve its purposes. In the case of functions, this purpose is to define a single value for the function name. Subroutines, however, have a much wider range of applications since they may "return" any number of values. Input/output statements may be used in either kind of subprogram, but are usually employed only in subroutines. To emphasize the fact that the operations within a subroutine are not restricted in any way, we might consider a main program as a special kind of subroutine. In fact, some of the programs to be presented later do little more than control the calling of subroutines and functions, which themselves call other subprograms. Thus a program may be considered as simply a higher-level control subroutine which is, in a sense, "called" by the computer's monitoring system.

When the operational sequence of a subprogram is completed, a RETURN statement is used to transfer control back to the calling program—acting as an unconditional GO TO (the calling program). In some Fortran systems, the END statement will accomplish this transfer in the absence of a RETURN statement. Every subprogram must conclude with an END statement, which signals the compiler that the end of an independent program segment has been reached. Although only one END statement is used, RETURN statements may be inserted at any number of points in a subprogram—wherever transfer of control back to the calling routine is desired.

Typically when a programmer writes a routine which employs functions or subroutines, he writes more than one such subprogram. When the program is submitted for processing, the subprogram card decks are stacked behind the main program deck in any order, and the composite program deck is followed by the data cards. The Fortran compiler translates each independent segment (program, subroutine, or function) into a separate sequence of machine-language instructions, and loads all of these machine language instructions into the computer memory before beginning the execution phase of the processing.

DIMENSIONED ARRAYS

Subprograms which employ array variables must have DIMENSION statements specifying the storage reservations for all array variables used, whether or not they also appear in the argument list. For array variables *not* named in the argument list, the DIMENSION statement reserves memory space in addition to that of the main program. For arrays which *are* named in the argument list, however, no additional space is reserved, since the calling program's DIMENSION statement has already served this purpose. The names in corresponding positions of the argument lists are simply linked to the same memory location(s).

The array-size specifications for such "transmitted" arrays which appear in the subprogram DIMENSION statement only insure comparable subscript referencing within the subprogram, since it is assumed that sufficient memory space has been reserved for the array by the calling program. All that is actually "transmitted" or equated through the argument list is a single memory-location reference for each argument. For array-name arguments, the first cell is implicitly designated. The programmer does not know or care what the actual memory references are; he can simply assume that the variable names which appear in corresponding positions in the argument lists in the calling program and subprogram are equated.

Since storage reservation for arrays named in the argument list is accomplished in the calling program, it really does not matter what size is designated in the DIMENSION statement of the subprogram, *except* to insure comparable subscripting. For vectors, any number of elements may be designated, and in some of the routines presented later you will find vectors designated with only one location, although it is apparent that more space has to be reserved in the calling program. For matrices, however, the number of *rows* designated must match in the calling program and subprogram DIMENSION statements in order to insure comparable subscripting. The number of columns need not correspond, and you will find routines later which specify the number of rows for matrices, but designate only one column. This "minimum condition" way of handling dimensioning in subprograms is not *necessary,* but serves to remind us that the actual storage reservations are accomplished in the calling program. The remarks in this paragraph apply only to arrays which are named in the argument list, since they are the only ones which can share memory with the calling routine. Our only reasons for discussing this topic are to emphasize the fact that subprograms depend on the calling program to have dimensioned sufficient space for their array arguments, and to prevent confusion when you examine the subprograms presented later in this chapter.

MODE AGREEMENT

The Fortran compiler does not compare the modes of variable names appearing in corresponding positions of the argument lists in the calling-program's statement and the subprogram name statement. All that is accomplished by the argument lists is an equating of memory-cell references.

Variables are equated only for the location in memory by appearing in corresponding positions of the argument lists, and are not equated in any other respects; no automatic mode conversion will take place. Thus, if an integer-mode value is stored for a subprogram variable that is equated to a real-mode variable name in the calling program, this location will continue to hold an integer-mode value after control returns to the calling program.

A comparable situation exists with regard to correspondence between a variable name in an input/output statement and the FORMAT specification that is referenced for it. No checking is done by the system, and no automatic conversion takes place. If the modes do not match, the result will be unintelligible.

VARIABLE DIMENSION SPECIFICATIONS

In subprogram DIMENSION statements, most current Fortran compilers permit the use of simple integer variable names in place of the usual integer constants to define the sizes of arrays. Arrays which are dimensioned in this way must be named in the argument list, and the integer variable(s) used to define the array size must also appear in the argument list. As a general rule, these integer variable(s) should not be changed anywhere in the subprogram, but see Subroutine TDRS in Chapter 9 for an exception example. Following our earlier discussion of dimensioning for arrays appearing in the argument list, it is usually necessary to use such variable dimensions only for designating the numbers of rows in matrices. Wherever possible, however, we will use variables in subroutine DIMENSION statements for vectors and for both dimensions of matrices as reminders of the necessary sizes of the corresponding arrays in the calling routines.

SUBROUTINE SUBPROGRAMS

A subroutine subprogram is *called* into operation by means of a separate statement in the calling program. The keyword for this statement is CALL, which precedes the name of the subroutine and its argument list. Examples of CALL statements follow. (They are meant to correspond to the first three examples of subroutine-name statements which appeared earlier in this chapter.)

  CALL ALPHA (A, BETA, 25, LIST(2))
  CALL KOUNT (Z, KAPPA(I))
  CALL P23XY (A, B, 5HMEANS)

As exemplified here, the arguments in a CALL statement are not restricted to variable names alone; they may include constants, subscripted variable names, and even H-mode character strings (maximum of six characters per argument).[1] If these CALL statements were used with the subroutine-name statements previously described, the variables A, BETA, Z, A, and B would have been equated to their positional counterparts A, B, V, P, and Q in the respective subroutines concerned. The location of the integer constant 25 would be equated to the location of variable K in Subroutine ALPHA, and its variable L would be equated with the memory reference for the second element of the main-program vector called LIST. Similarly, K in Subroutine KOUNT would be equated to the Ith cell of vector KAPPA in the calling program. In Subroutine P23XY, the location named X would be equated to the location holding the Hollerith constant MEANS.

You may have already sensed a source of danger in the use of constants as arguments to subprograms. If this is done and the subprogram variable name equated to this constant is used in a statement that changes the value stored in the location concerned, then considerable disruption may occur after control is returned to the main program. Any later use of the same constant in the main program would inadvertently employ the wrong value. We do not advise against use of constants in CALL statements, but only wish to make clear the importance of leaving these values unchanged by subprogram statements.

An example of a program which employs a subroutine is shown in Figure 6-2. This example program illustrates the fact that variables appearing in an

---

[1] Arguments in CALL statements may also be arithmetic expressions or function calls, but we will not employ such arguments in any routines presented in this book.

Function Subprograms   121

```
C     PROGRAM PSUM
C
C     EXAMPLE OF A PROGRAM EMPLOYING A SUBROUTINE SUBPROGRAM.
C
      DIMENSION A(3), B(3)
      READ 5, A, B
    5 FORMAT (3F2.0)
      CALL ADDS (A, ONE)
      CALL ADDS (B, TWO)
      P = ONE * TWO
      PRINT 10, P
   10 FORMAT (F10.4)
      STOP
      END
      SUBROUTINE ADDS (X, S)
      DIMENSION X(3)
      S = X(1) + X(2) + X(3)
      RETURN
      END
```

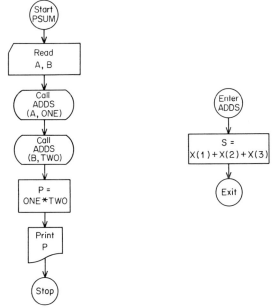

FIGURE 6-2. Example of subroutine usage.

argument list may serve to "transmit" information to a subroutine (arrays A = X and B = X) or may "receive" information computed within the subroutine (ONE = S and TWO = S). Of course, data might simply be replaced by answers in the same locations, if one did not mind losing the input information. To check your understanding of this example, make up some scores and prove to yourself that the program will compute the product of the sums of two sets of three values each.

FUNCTION SUBPROGRAMS

Function subprograms are called implicitly in the same way as library functions by the appearance of the function name in a replacement or IF

122 FORTRAN: FUNCTIONS AND SUBROUTINES

statement. The only difference between these routines and library functions is that the library functions are always available automatically as part of the Fortran system, whereas these routines are written by the programmer as he needs them for particular purposes, and must be included with the program which calls them, as must subroutines, whenever the program is to be executed.

In the calling statement, a list of arguments follows the name of the function, and a value is returned for this name, which appears as a simple variable. In the function subprogram itself, the function name must appear on the left side of the equals sign in at least one replacement statement.[2] In other respects the function subprogram is organized like a subroutine, beginning with a name statement and ending with an END statement, using one or more RETURN statements to transfer control back to the calling

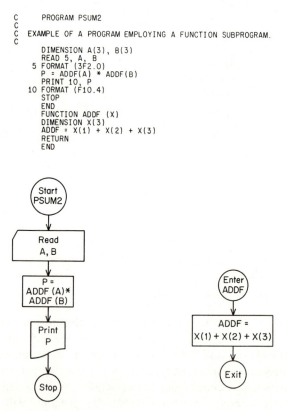

```
C      PROGRAM PSUM2
C
C      EXAMPLE OF A PROGRAM EMPLOYING A FUNCTION SUBPROGRAM.
C
       DIMENSION A(3), B(3)
       READ 5, A, B
     5 FORMAT (3F2.0)
       P = ADDF(A) * ADDF(B)
       PRINT 10, P
    10 FORMAT (F10.4)
       STOP
       END
       FUNCTION ADDF (X)
       DIMENSION X(3)
       ADDF = X(1) + X(2) + X(3)
       RETURN
       END
```

FIGURE 6-3. Example of function usage.

---

[2] This requirement would be satisfied if the function name appeared in an input list or as an argument in a CALL statement, but we will have no occasion to use these methods in any of the routines presented in this book.

program. The following example of a program employing a function subprogram (Figure 6-3) is meant to be a direct parallel with the PSUM Program, and should be compared carefully with that routine.

This program yields exactly the same result as did Program PSUM. As illustrated, the principal difference in usage of functions and subroutines is in the manner of calling them into operation. Subroutines require separate CALL statements, while functions are called by the appearance of the name (with its arguments) as a simple variable in a replacement or IF statement. It should be apparent that the mode of a function name is important since it is directly involved in the computations within the subprogram, as well as being involved in a statement in the calling program where mode consistency is significant. However, the modes of subroutine names are not significant.

STATISTICAL FUNCTIONS AND SUBROUTINES

The remainder of this chapter will concern a series of subprograms which the author has found to be useful in constructing programs for statistical analysis of behavioral-science data. In later chapters this series will be extended to include routines developed for matrix operations and for multivariate analytic techniques.

The routines presented throughout this book have been thoroughly tested on two widely used computer systems (IBM 7040 and CDC 1604), but they should be accepted by the reader only as suggestions for development of his own program library, for at least two reasons. No set of routines can satisfy the needs of all behavioral scientists with respect to trade-off among speed of execution, capacity for variables, arithmetic precision, and storage requirements for object-code. Also, it would be foolish to believe that these routines cannot be improved in efficiency by other programmers. This is inevitably true in one sense, because many conveniences and special capabilities available in certain Fortran systems have purposely been avoided in writing these routines, in order to achieve a wider applicability across Fortran systems.

The reader who wishes to begin by punching all of the routines in this book will have a powerful library of programs and subroutines that he can count on for reliability, at least. It would be unfortunate, however, if he did not then begin to look for ways to make the library more suitable for his own needs, or the needs of his colleagues. He may find that double-precision accuracy—at least in some routines—would be desirable. He might soon realize that certain intermediate results are not being printed, but could be obtained with only minor program changes. The author wishes to encourage such adaptation and extension; the routines presented here are only suggestions, certainly not the only way of programming the procedures concerned, and not even the best way from many points of view.

SUMF (X, KK, NN, ND)

A function subprogram to compute ΣX or ΣX^2 from an array vector.

The arguments to this routine are described in the program listing, and the flow chart (Figure 6-4) outlines the statement sequence. In any one CALL, one of four separate computation loops is used, depending on the signs of certain arguments.

Suppose we wish to obtain the sum of the first 20 elements in a vector called ALPHA in a program we are writing. A single statement calling this function can be used to obtain this sum and store it in a location named ASUM.

$$\text{ASUM} = \text{SUMF(ALPHA, 1, 20, 20)}$$

As a second example, assume a matrix named Z which is dimensioned with 100 rows and 50 columns. We wish to obtain the sum of squares of the 50 values in the fourteenth row of this matrix and store it in SS:

$$\text{SS} = \text{SUMF}(Z, -14, -50, 100)$$

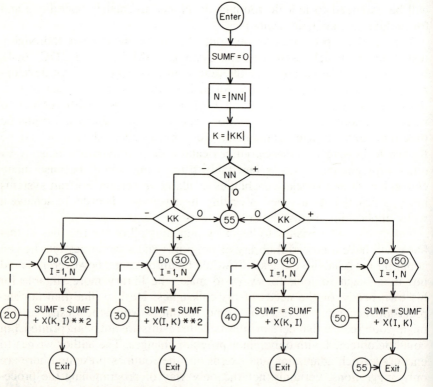

FIGURE 6-4. Function SUMF flow chart.

Statistical Functions and Subroutines

The negative sign on the second argument tells the routine that the vector is a matrix row, while the negative sign on the third argument tells the routine that the sum of squares is to be obtained. Note that this routine can be used only with real-mode arrays. A separate routine would have to be written to accomplish these same operations with integer data. This routine illustrates the use of a variable DIMENSION specification, as well as a "minimum-case" columns specification. It also illustrates one of the infrequent situations in which the use of arithmetic IF statements is more economical than the use of the logical IF form would be.

Some programmers would prefer to use separate arguments to signal the options which are indicated here by the signs of KK and NN. This is a matter of personal preference, since economy in writing these argument lists entails some added risk of error.

```
      FUNCTION SUMF (X, KK, NN, ND)
COMPUTES SUM X OR SUM X**2 FROM A VECTOR.
X = ARRAY CONTAINING THE SCORES TO BE USED.
NN = NUMBER OF VALUES TO BE SUMMED. IF NEGATIVE, SUM X**2 COMPUTED.
KK = ROW OR COLUMN NUMBER IF X IS A MATRIX. SET = 1 IF X IS A VECTOR.
IF KK IS POSITIVE AND NOT 1, IT IS A COLUMN VECTOR.
IF KK IS NEGATIVE AND NOT 1, IT IS A ROW VECTOR.
ND = NUMBER OF ROWS (OR ELEMENTS) DIMENSIONED FOR X IN THE
     CALLING PROGRAM.
      DIMENSION X(ND,1)
      SUMF = 0.0
      N = IABS(NN)
      K = IABS(KK)
      IF (NN) 5,55,10
    5 IF (KK) 15,55,25
   10 IF (KK) 35,55,45
   15 DO 20 I = 1,N
   20 SUMF = SUMF + X(K,I)**2
      RETURN
   25 DO 30 I = 1,N
   30 SUMF = SUMF + X(I,K)**2
      RETURN
   35 DO 40 I = 1,N
   40 SUMF = SUMF + X(K,I)
      RETURN
   45 DO 50 I = 1,N
   50 SUMF = SUMF + X(I,K)
   55 RETURN
      END
```

SUMF2 (X, KK, NN, ND)

A function duplicating the operations of SUMF, but with a less efficient method.

This routine is included here only to illustrate the fact that program efficiency often can be affected seriously by a minor change in procedure. Compare the flow charts in Figures 6-4 and 6-5. The only difference between the two routines is in the use of one versus four separate DO loops, but a substantial savings in execution time is gained by the use of the

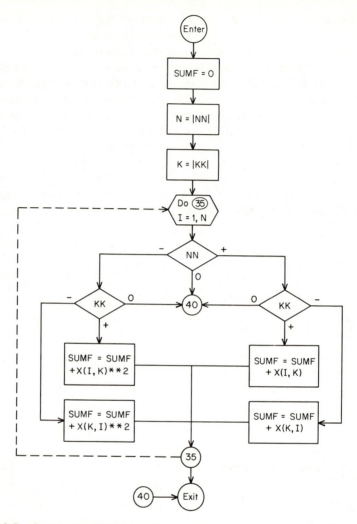

FIGURE 6-5. Function SUMF2 flow chart.

SUMF procedure rather than the one presented here. The reason for the inefficiency of the SUMF2 routine is the fact that the two IF statements are encountered on *each* pass through the DO loop. In SUMF, however, the corresponding IF statements are only encountered once — before one of the DO loops is begun. A general statement as to the comparative speed of these two versions cannot be made due to compiler variations and the fact that the discrepancy increases as a function of the number of elements to be summed.

The question of program efficiency may seem trivial because of the microsecond speeds of modern machines, but for a routine such as this, which may be called thousands of times in the execution of some programs which employ it, the savings in processing time will be substantial in an installation that does a good deal of statistical work. We do not mean to imply that concern for efficiency of operation is always appropriate. While you are learning the Fortran language, and later when you are developing new routines, operational efficiency should be a secondary concern. Once a problem is solved, however, and it becomes apparent that the new routine is going to be used repeatedly, it may be quite worthwhile to rewrite the whole procedure to optimize its operational efficiency. As for the routines contained in this book, it is certainly possible to increase the efficiency of most of them at a cost in flexibility of application.

```
      FUNCTION SUMF2 (X, KK, NN, ND)
C
C  THIS ROUTINE DUPLICATES THE OPERATIONS OF SUMF, BUT LESS EFFICIENTLY,
C     SINCE THE IF STATEMENTS ARE EXECUTED N TIMES.
C
      DIMENSION X(ND,1)
      SUMF2 = 0.0
      N = IABS(NN)
      K = IABS(KK)
      DO 35 I = 1,N
      IF (NN) 5,40,10
    5 IF (KK) 15,40,20
   10 IF (KK) 25,40,30
   15 SUMF2 = SUMF2 + X(K,I)**2
      GO TO 35
   20 SUMF2 = SUMF2 + X(I,K)**2
      GO TO 35
   25 SUMF2 = SUMF2 + X(K,I)
      GO TO 35
   30 SUMF2 = SUMF2 + X(I,K)
   35 CONTINUE
   40 RETURN
      END
```

SCPF (X, Y, KX, KY, N, ND)

A function subprogram to compute the sum of cross-products (scalar product) of two array vectors.

As is apparent in the flow chart for this routine (Figure 6-6), the procedure employed is very similar to that used in SUMF. Two vectors are involved here, however, and the purpose is to obtain the sum of the products of values in their corresponding cells. The significance of this subprogram for matrix operations will be discussed in a later chapter.

Although X and Y are designated as separate arrays in the subprogram, the same matrix (or vector) may be equated to both of them in the calling statement. For example, suppose the calling program included a matrix D dimensioned with 20 rows and 20 columns and we wished to obtain the sum of products of corresponding elements in the third row and the fifth column of this matrix. The following statement would store this scalar product in location SP35:

$$SP35 = SCPF(D, D, -3, 5, 20, 20)$$

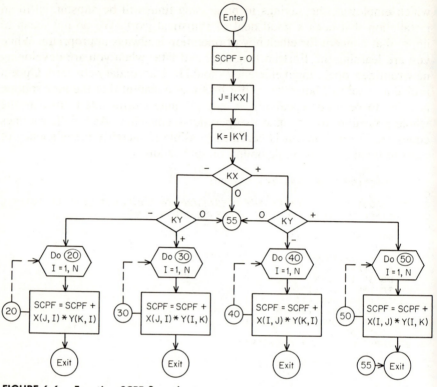

FIGURE 6-6. Function SCPF flow chart.

If we had designated the same vector in the same matrix (D, D, 5, 5, 20, 20), the result obtained would be the sum of squares for the vector concerned and would be identical to what could also be obtained from SUMF(D, 5, −20, 20).

As another example, suppose we had two matrices, R and S, dimensioned with 40 rows and 30 columns each, and we wished to obtain the sum of products of corresponding elements in the second row of R and the third row of S, and store this result in RS23:

$$RS23 = SCPF(R, S, -2, -3, 30, 40)$$

Note that the applications of this routine are restricted to matrices which have equal numbers of rows dimensioned for them, although the numbers of their columns may differ.

```
      FUNCTION SCPF (X, Y, KX, KY, N, ND)
C
C     COMPUTES SUM OF CROSSPRODUCTS (SCALAR PRODUCT) OF TWO VECTORS.
C     X, Y = ARRAYS CONTAINING THE SCORES TO BE USED.
C        THEY MAY BE SENT AS THE SAME ARRAY.
C     KX, KY = ROW OR COLUMN NUMBERS FOR X AND Y, IF MATRICES.
C        SET = 1 IF VECTOR.
```

```
C     IF KX OR KY IS POSITIVE AND NOT 1, IT IS A COLUMN NUMBER.
C     IF KX OR KY IS NEGATIVE AND NOT 1, IT IS A ROW NUMBER.
C     N = THE NUMBER OF PRODUCTS TO BE SUMMED, ELEMENTS OF EACH VECTOR.
C     ND = THE NUMBER OF ROWS (OR ELEMENTS) DIMENSIONED FOR BOTH X AND Y
C        IN CALLING PROGRAM.
C
      DIMENSION X(ND,1), Y(ND,1)
      SCPF = 0.0
      J = IABS(KX)
      K = IABS(KY)
      IF (KX) 5,55,10
    5 IF (KY) 15,55,25
   10 IF (KY) 35,55,45
   15 DO 20 I = 1,N
   20 SCPF = SCPF + X(J,I) * Y(K,I)
      RETURN
   25 DO 30 I = 1,N
   30 SCPF = SCPF + X(J,I) * Y(I,K)
      RETURN
   35 DO 40 I = 1,N
   40 SCPF = SCPF + X(I,J) * Y(K,I)
      RETURN
   45 DO 50 I = 1,N
   50 SCPF = SCPF + X(I,J) * Y(I,K)
   55 RETURN
      END
```

PRBF (DA, DB, FR)

A function subroutine to compute the exact probability of random occurrence of an F ratio.

This routine was adapted from a subroutine written by Jaspen (1965), based on a normalizing transformation of the F distribution (Kelley, 1947; Kendall, 1955).

$$Z = \frac{\left[1 - \dfrac{2}{9B}\right] F^{1/3} - \left[1 - \dfrac{2}{9A}\right]}{\left[\dfrac{2}{9B} F^{2/3} + \dfrac{2}{9A}\right]^{1/2}}$$

where A = degrees of freedom for the numerator of the F ratio
B = degrees of freedom for the denominator of the F ratio
F = the ratio of two independent variances
Z = a normally distributed variable with $\mu = 0$, $\sigma = 1$

With B less than 4, Kelley recommends the following adjustment of the transformed F value:

$$Z' = Z\left[1 + \frac{.08Z^4}{B^3}\right]$$

The probability of random occurrence of an F ratio may be determined from the Z or Z' transformation by means of the following approximation (Hastings, 1955):

$$P = .5/(1 + C_1 Z + C_2 Z^2 + C_3 Z^3 + C_4 Z^4)^4$$

where $C_1 = .196854$

$C_2 = .115194$
$C_3 = .000344$
$C_4 = .019527$

As shown in the flow chart in Figure 6-7, the function PRBF will be returned with a value of 1.0 if any of its arguments are zero. When the F ratio to be evaluated is less than 1.0, the probability of its reciprocal is

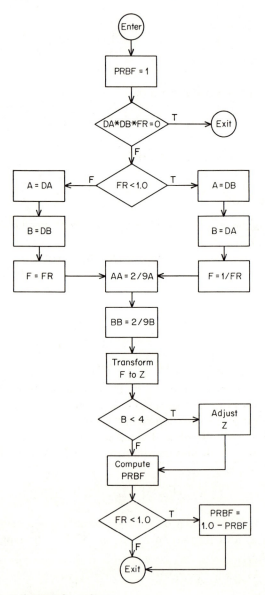

FIGURE 6-7. Function PRBF flow chart.

computed using reversed degrees of freedom and this probability is subtracted from 1.0 before RETURN.

This routine can be used to compute exact probabilities of random occurrence for other statistics by transforming them to F values in the calling statement. Since $F = \chi^2 \;/\; df$ with (df, ∞) degrees of freedom, the probability for a chi-square value may be obtained from:

$$P = PRBF\ (DF,\ 1000.0,\ C\ /\ DF)$$

where C is the chi-square value and DF signifies its degrees of freedom.

Similarly, since $F = t^2$ with (1, df) degrees of freedom, a probability value for a t ratio may be obtained from:

$$P = PRBF\ (1.0,\ DF,\ T**2)$$

where T is the t ratio and DF signifies its degrees of freedom.

Also, since $F = z^2 = t^2$ with ∞ degrees of freedom, the probability for a z value may be obtained from:

$$P = PRBF\ (1.0,\ 1000.0,\ Z**2)$$

where Z is the z value. The constant 1000 is used as an approximation to ∞ in the case of χ^2 and z evaluations.

The probabilities returned by this function are in the form of decimal fractions. Therefore, an F ratio which yielded a probability value of .04 would be considered "statistically significant" since the likelihood of obtaining an F value as large or larger than the one in question would be 4 percent, if in fact the null (random) hypothesis was true.

```
      FUNCTION PRBF (DA, DB, FR)
C
C     COMPUTES EXACT PROBABILITY OF RANDOM OCCURRENCE OF AN F-RATIO.
C     DA = NUMERATOR DEGREES OF FREEDOM.
C     DB = DENOMINATOR DEGREES OF FREEDOM.
C     FR = F-RATIO TO BE EVALUATED.
C     PRBF IS RETURNED AS A DECIMAL-FRACTION PROBABILITY.
C
      PRBF = 1.0
      IF (DA * DB * FR .EQ. 0.0) RETURN
      IF (FR .LT. 1.0) GO TO 5
      A = DA
      B = DB
      F = FR
      GO TO 10
    5 A = DB
      B = DA
      F = 1.0 / FR
   10 AA = 2.0 / (9.0 * A)
      BB = 2.0 / (9.0 * B)
      OZ = ABS(((1.0 - BB) * F**0.333333 - 1.0 + AA) / SQRT(BB * F
     1 **0.666667 + AA))
      IF (B .LT. 4.0) Z = Z * (1.0 + 0.08 * Z**4 / B**3)
      OPRBF = 0.5 / (1.0 + Z * (0.196854 + Z * (0.115194 + Z *
     1 (0.000344 + Z * 0.019527))))**4
      IF (FR .LT. 1.0) PRBF = 1.0 - PRBF
      RETURN
      END
```

132 FORTRAN: FUNCTIONS AND SUBROUTINES

CCDS (KF, KI, KJ, KK, KL, KM)

A subroutine to read and print information from problem control cards.
This subroutine is used by most of the general-purpose statistical programs described in later chapters to input information from three control cards which are required in front of every data deck to be processed.

(1) *Title Control Card.* All 80 columns may be used for alphameric information describing the problem. This card is printed verbatim, beginning on a new page.

(2) *Parameter Control Card.* Five 5-digit fields (columns 1–25) are picked up as five integer numbers and stored in separate simple-variable locations. On return to the calling program these values will be available as number of subjects, number of variables, and so forth, or they may represent up to five single-digit parameters each, which can be broken out as option signals.

(3) *Format Control Card.* The entire card may be used to hold a variable FORMAT for the data cards to follow. This technique permits the same program to be used with widely varying data-card arrangements, since the FORMAT for data input is not specified until the execution phase.

Before returning control to the calling program, this subroutine prints the information contained in all three cards. At the start of the routine the first card is examined to determine whether the contents of columns 1–5 are identical to those of columns 6–10. If this condition is encountered, a STOP statement terminates execution of the program. This check allows control programs to be constructed so that control is sent back to the CALL statement for Subroutine CCDS after processing of a problem is complete. If the user wishes, he may stack problems, each with its own three control cards, behind a single copy of the program. A blank card added after the last problem deck then acts as a dummy Title Control Card which will yield a STOP when read by Subroutine CCDS (Figure 6-8).

INPUT DECK ARRANGEMENT USING SUBROUTINE CCDS

System control cards
Program deck
System control cards
Subroutine and/or function decks, if any
System control cards
Title control card ⎫
Parameter control card ⎬
Format control card ⎬ Problem deck
Other control or key cards, if any ⎬
Data deck ⎭
Blank card, or another problem deck
System control cards

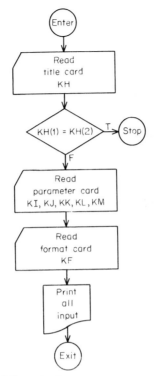

FIGURE 6-8. Subroutine CCDS flow chart.

Note that the Title, Parameter, and Format control cards, as well as any other control cards required by the program concerned, are all treated as part of the "data" deck by the Fortran system, since they are all read under the control of the object program after it has been compiled and receives control from the monitoring system.

```
      SUBROUTINE CCDS (KF, KI, KJ, KK, KL, KM)
C
C     READS AND PRINTS TITLE, PARAMETER, AND FORMAT CONTROL CARDS.
C     KF = VECTOR HOLDING VARIABLE FORMAT ON RETURN.
C     KI, KJ, KK, KL, KM = PARAMETER VALUES.
C     KH = TEMPORARY STORAGE WITHIN THIS ROUTINE.
C     BLANK TITLE CARD YIELDS STOP.
C
      DIMENSION KF(16), KH(16)
      READ 5, KH
    5 FORMAT (16A5)
      IF (KH(1) .EQ. KH(2)) STOP
      READ 10, KI, KJ, KK, KL, KM, KF
   10 FORMAT (5I5 / 16A5)
      PRINT 15, KH, KI, KJ, KK, KL, KM, KF
   15 FORMAT (1H1, 16A5 // 11H PARAMETERS / 13H COL  1- 5 = , I5 /
     1 13H COL  6-10 = , I5 / 13H COL 11-15 = , I5 / 13H COL 16-20 = ,
     2 I5 / 13H COL 21-25 = , I5 // 15H DATA FORMAT = , 16A5)
      RETURN
      END
```

ARRAY OUTPUT SUBROUTINES

PRTS (X, N, M, KH, ND)

A subroutine to print an array.

This subroutine prints the contents of a vector or a matrix in 10-element partitions. As indicated by the flow chart (Figure 6-9), one of two independent paths within the subroutine is taken, depending on the value given for the number of columns. Thus, when $M = 1$, a column vector is specified, but the values will be printed from the vector across the page, 10 elements per line.

The rows and columns of the output are individually index-numbered including an alphameric label which is received as argument KH. In the printing of a matrix, all rows are printed for a 10-column partition before the next set of 10 columns is begun.

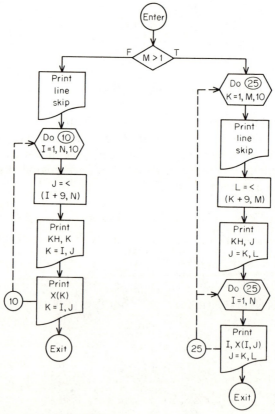

FIGURE 6-9. Subroutine PRTS flow chart.

As examples, the following CALL statements would yield printed output of a vector (D) of 12 elements and a 12-by-15 matrix (Q), respectively.

CALL PRTS (D, 12, 1, 5HDΔVEC, 12)

CALL PRTS (Q, 12, 15, 6HQΔSORT, 15)

Because we assumed that Q was contained in an array dimensioned (15, 15) the last argument in the CALL of PRTS must be 15, even though only the first 12 rows are to be printed.

Note that a line-skip is achieved in this routine by a PRINT statement which has no variable list. When the FORMAT is referenced, a new line is begun, but control then leaves the FORMAT because the "list" is satisfied.

```
      SUBROUTINE PRTS (X, N, M, KH, ND)
C
C     PRINT A MATRIX OR VECTOR IN 10-COLUMN PARTITIONS.
C     X = ARRAY TO BE OUTPUT.
C     N = NUMBER OF ROWS (OR ELEMENTS) OF X TO BE PRINTED.
C     M = NUMBER OF COLUMNS OF X TO BE PRINTED.
C         SET = 1 IF X IS VECTOR.
C     KH = NAME OF ARRAY FOR OUTPUT HEADING, A HOLLERITH
C          CONSTANT IN THE CALL STATEMENT, MAX. = 6 CHARACTERS.
C     ND = NUMBER OF ROWS (OR ELEMENTS) DIMENSIONED FOR X IN THE
C          CALLING PROGRAM.
C
      DIMENSION X(ND, M)
      IF (M .GT. 1) GO TO 20
      PRINT 15
      DO 10 I = 1,N,10
      J = MINO(I + 9, N)
      PRINT 5, KH, (K, K = I,J)
    5 FORMAT (/A7, 10I11)
   10 PRINT 15, (X(K,1), K = I,J)
   15 FORMAT (10X, 10F11.4)
      RETURN
   20 DO 25 K = 1,M,10
      PRINT 15
      L = MINO(K + 9, M)
      PRINT 5, KH, (J, J = K,L)
      DO 25 I = 1,N
   25 PRINT 30, I, (X(I,J), J = K,L)
   30 FORMAT (/I6, 4X, 10F11.4)
      RETURN
      END
```

PCDS (X, N, M, KH, ND)

A subroutine to punch an array.

This routine (Figure 6-10) is organized like Subroutine PRTS, in that separate paths are included for output of vectors and matrices. The partitioning of vectors or matrix rows is by seven-element sets. In matrix output, punching proceeds across rows in blocks of seven; each row is completed before output from the next row is begun. Each row always begins on a new card.

The first ten columns of every card contain the following information:

136 FORTRAN: FUNCTIONS AND SUBROUTINES

Cols. 1–5 : Hollerith label (KH) from the CALL statement
Cols. 6–8 : row number (1 in vector output)
Cols. 9–10: partition-block number within the row or vector

The following examples of CALL statements are for the vector of 12 elements and the 12-by-15 matrix used to illustrate subroutine PRTS:

CALL PCDS (D, 12, 1, 5HDΔVEC, 12)
CALL PCDS (Q, 12, 15, 5HQSORT, 15)

Note that the six-character block in the second CALL statement (6HQ ΔSORT) had to be reduced to five characters to meet the limitations of this routine.

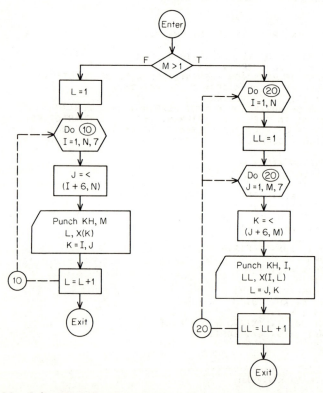

FIGURE 6-10. Subroutine PCDS flow chart.

```
      SUBROUTINE PCDS (X, N, M, KH, ND)
C
C     PUNCHES CARDS FROM AN ARRAY IN 7-ELEMENT BLOCKS. A MATRIX IS
C         PUNCHED BY ROWS, BEGINNING EACH ROW ON A NEW CARD.
C     X = NAME OF ARRAY TO BE OUTPUT.
C     N = NUMBER OF ROWS IF X IS MATRIX, OR ELEMENTS IF A VECTOR.
C     M = NUMBER OF COLUMNS IF X IS MATRIX. SET = 1 FOR A VECTOR.
C     KH = OUTPUT LABEL. HOLLERITH BLOCK (MAX = 5) IN CALL STATEMENT.
C     ND = NUMBER OF ROWS DIMENSIONED FOR X IN CALLING PROGRAM.
C
```

```
      DIMENSION X(ND, M)
      IF (M .GT. 1) GO TO 15
      L = 1
      DO 10 I = 1,N,7
      J = MINO(I + 6, N)
      PUNCH 5, KH, M, L, (X(K,1), K = I,J)
    5 FORMAT (A5, I3, I2, 7F10.4)
   10 L = L + 1
      RETURN
   15 DO 20 I = 1,N
      LL = 1
      DO 20 J = 1,M,7
      K = MINO(J + 6, M)
      PUNCH 5, KH, I, LL, (X(I,L), L = J,K)
   20 LL = LL + 1
      RETURN
      END
```

PTMS (X, N, KH, ND)

A subroutine to punch the upper triangular portion of a symmetric matrix as a vector.

This subroutine accomplishes economical output of matrices that are identical in corresponding cells across the main diagonal. Only the nonredundant values are punched (including the diagonal), and these elements are output as a continuous vector. Output is serial across rows of the square symmetric matrix in memory, beginning in each row at the diagonal element, but not necessarily with a new tab card. In Figure 6-11 the CALL statement would be CALL PTMS (R, 4, 4HDEMO, 15). We are assuming that matrix R is contained within an array dimensioned with 15 rows in the

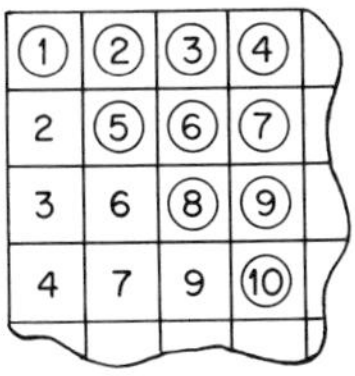

FIGURE 6-11. Elements of a square matrix punched by Subroutine PTMS.

calling program, even though only a four-by-four portion is punched.

The output would consist of two punched cards; the first card would hold the elements whose numbers are circled in the diagram, 1 through 7; and the second card would hold circled elements 8 through 10. Columns 1–4 on each card would contain the Hollerith block DEMO from the CALL statement. Column 10 would contain the card number (1 or 2, in this example). A square symmetric matrix also could be punched using the PCDS subroutine, but the larger the matrix to be output, the more economical this routine becomes (Figure 6-12).

Cards punched by this routine may be read into the appropriate memory locations of a similar matrix by another program, and the original matrix then may be reformed with the following sequence of Fortran statements:

138 FORTRAN: FUNCTIONS AND SUBROUTINES

```
      READ 5, ((R(I, J), J = 1, N), I = 1, N)
   5  FORMAT (10X, 7F10.4)
      DO 10 I = 1, N
      DO 10 J = I, N
  10  R(J, I) = R(I, J)
```

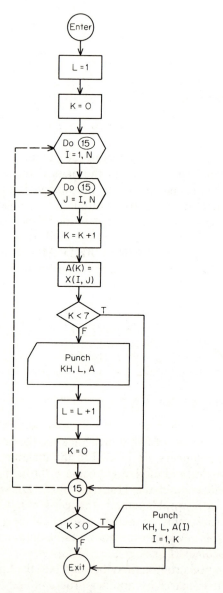

FIGURE 6-12. Subroutine PTMS flow chart.

Array Output Subroutines 139

This sequence, which assumes a predefinition of the variable N representing the size of the matrix R, appears in Program FACTOR in Chapter 9. The flow chart indicates the output technique, which employs a seven-element vector to hold values selected from the matrix for punching on a single card. Whenever this vector is full, a card is punched. A is dimensioned 7 so that it can be referenced without indexing in statement 5. For an example of output produced by this subroutine, see example problem 1 for Program FACTOR in Chapter 9.

```
      SUBROUTINE PTMS (X, N, KH, ND)
C
C     PUNCHES UPPER TRIANGLE (INCLUDING DIAGONAL) OF A SYMMETRIC MATRIX
C        AS A CONTINUOUS VECTOR OF N*(N+1)/2 ELEMENTS, 7 PER CARD.
C     X = NAME OF SYMMETRIC MATRIX.
C     N = ORDER OF MATRIX X.
C     KH = OUTPUT LABEL. HOLLERITH CONSTANT (MAX = 6) IN CALL STATEMENT.
C     A = TEMPORARY STORAGE WITHIN THIS ROUTINE.
C     ND = NUMBER OF ROWS DIMENSIONED FOR X IN CALLING PROGRAM.
C
      DIMENSION X(ND,N), A(7)
      L = 1
      K = 0
      DO 15 I = 1,N
      DO 15 J = I,N
      K = K + 1
      A(K) = X(I,J)
      IF (K .LT. 7) GO TO 15
    5 PUNCH 10, KH, L, A
   10 FORMAT (A6, I4, 7F10.4)
      L = L + 1
      K = 0
   15 CONTINUE
      IF (K .GT. 0) PUNCH 10, KH, L, (A(I), I = 1,K)
      RETURN
      END
```

SUBS (KD, N, KH, ID)

A subroutine to punch a vector of scores for one subject in integer or real mode.

Much of the data processing in behavioral-sciences rescarch involves the conversion or computation of series of scores for individual subjects. This subroutine simplifies programming where punched output of such scores is necessary. Two paths are included for the most frequently used combinations of field-length and mode. Real-mode scores may be punched 7F10.4 per card, or integer scores may be punched 35I2 per card, depending on the sign of N (the number of scores) in the CALL statement (Figure 6-13).

This subroutine capitalizes on the fact that no comparison is made by the compiler between the mode of the vector name (KD) in the PUNCH statement and the mode of output conversion in the FORMAT. Thus, the name of the score vector in the CALL statement may be either integer or real. As long as the sign of N is appropriate, the FORMAT (5 or 20) which matches the mode of the *contents* of KD will be used.

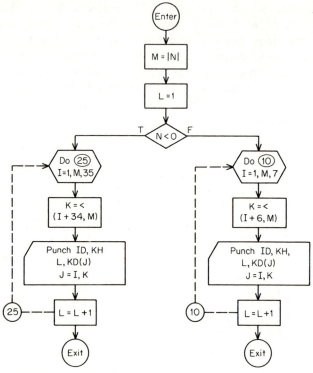

FIGURE 6-13. Subroutine SUBS flow chart.

Each call of this subroutine will output a vector of scores on one or more cards for a single subject. Columns 1–6 on each card will hold the subject code number (ID) as an alphameric block. Columns 7–8 also will hold an alphameric identification block (KH) which permits labeling the type of scores punched. Columns 9–10 will hold the card number when more than one card per subject is necessary for the output vector.

This routine is used in later subroutines and control programs to output standardized scores, factor scores, discriminant scores, and so forth.

```
      SUBROUTINE SUBS (KD, N, KH, ID)
C
C     PUNCHES ONE SUBJECTS SCORE VECTOR IN INTEGER OR REAL MODE.
C     KD = SCORE VECTOR. MAY BE EITHER MODE IN CALL STATEMENT.
C     N = NUMBER OF SCORES TO BE PUNCHED.
C     KH = HOLLERITH OUTPUT LABEL (MAX = 2)
C     ID = HOLLERITH SUBJECT IDENTIFICATION (MAX = 6)
C     IF N IS SENT NEGATIVE, KD IS OUTPUT INTEGER MODE. IF SENT
C        POSITIVE, KD IS OUTPUT REAL MODE.
C
      DIMENSION KD(1)
      M = IABS(N)
      L = 1
      IF (N .LT. 0) GO TO 15
      DO 10 I = 1,M,7
```

```
      K = MINO(I + 6, M)
      PUNCH 5, ID, KH, L, (KD(J), J = I,K)
    5 FORMAT (A6, A2, I2, 7F10.4)
   10 L = L + 1
      RETURN
   15 DO 25 I = 1,M,35
      K = MINO(I + 34, M)
      PUNCH 20, ID, KH, L, (KD(J), J = I,K)
   20 FORMAT (A6, A2, I2, 35I2)
   25 L = L + 1
      RETURN
      END
```

Review Exercises

1. Rewrite Program TEN in Chapter 5 to employ Subprograms SUMF, SCPF, and PRTS.
2. Rewrite Program TWELVE in Chapter 5 to employ Subprograms CCDS and PRTS. Why can Functions SUMF and SCPF not be used here?
3. Rewrite the programs described in Exercise 3 at the end of Chapter 5 to use Subprogram SUMF.
4. Write a function subprogram to return the index number of the highest absolute value in a vector of real numbers. Arguments should be (1) the name of the vector, (2) the number of elements in the vector to be examined.
5. Write a subroutine which will return two means, two sigmas, and a correlation coefficient when sent two vectors of real numbers. Eight arguments will be required: the names for the two score vectors, the number of cases (scores in each vector), the names for the means, the names for the sigmas, and the name of the correlation coefficient location. Use Functions SUMF and SCPF within this routine.

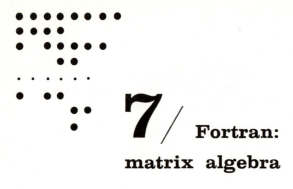

7 / Fortran: matrix algebra

The notation of matrix algebra permits concise expression of complex multivariate statistical procedures. For univariate procedures the familiar *summation notation* is usually preferred because of its flexibility. Matrix notation, however, is commonly used in such journals as *Psychometrika, Educational and Psychological Measurement,* and *Multivariate Behavioral Research.* With the increasing availability of computers, a greater number of researchers can employ the latest advances in statistical methodology — if they can translate matrix formulations into valid computer programs.

The essentials of matrix algebra are presented in this chapter along with equivalent Fortran statement sequences for the basic operations. More detailed discussions of this topic may be found in recent books by Horst (1963) and Fuller (1962).

It will become apparent that the operations implied by matrix algebra notation are not necessarily the most economical in terms of computer programming. In most cases, however, translation from one "language" to another presents few problems. Summation notation is actually much closer to the nature of Fortran statements, but is prohibitively awkward for expressing many common operations with matrices.

DEFINITIONS AND NOTATION

Matrix. A matrix is a series of elements arranged in a rectangular array, with particular numbers of rows and columns. In the notation of matrix algebra a matrix is denoted by a single capital letter. In Fortran coding, of course, a matrix name may contain multiple characters.

Every matrix has a specific *size,* which means the numbers of its rows and columns and not simply the total number of its elements. We will use this term to avoid confusing the term "dimension" with the Fortran DIMENSION statement. Matrices are stored in double-subscripted arrays in Fortran programs, but an array may be dimensioned larger than the size of the matrix stored there.

Most writers do not subscript matrix designators in matrix algebra formulas, but simply predefine the size of each matrix involved. In order to avoid as much confusion as possible in this chapter, we will depart from the usual conventions of matrix algebra notation and add capital-letter or numeric subscripts to each matrix designator. The first subscript will signify the number of rows and the second subscript will indicate the number of columns in the matrix. For example, A_{23} signifies a matrix with two rows and three columns, and B_{IJ} signifies a matrix with I rows and J columns.

Vector. Vectors are special cases of matrices, in which either the number of rows or number of columns is one. A *row vector* has one row and multiple columns. A *column vector* has multiple rows and one column. In Fortran coding, vectors are stored in single-subscripted arrays, and their definition as row or column vectors is only implicit in their use.

The size of a vector is the number of its elements; we will reserve the term "length" for a special usage to be explained later. Even though in Fortran coding row and column vectors are not distinguished, they are differently represented in matrix algebra notation; this will be explained when we discuss matrix transposition.

Although not a common practice, we will add capital letter or numeric subscripts to each vector designator in our matrix algebra notation to indicate the number of elements in the vector. For example, A_5 indicates a vector containing five elements, and B_K indicates a vector of K elements.

Scalar. A scalar may be defined as a matrix with one row and one column, although the rules for operations involving scalars suggest a more unique status for these single values. Because ordinary algebra deals only with operations involving scalars, it is sometimes called *scalar algebra.*

Scalars are stored in unsubscripted (single) memory locations in Fortran coding. In matrix algebra notation they are represented by capital, lower case, or Greek letters. We will use capital letters without subscripts to designate scalars. Since each element of a matrix or vector may be considered a scalar, however, we may occasionally wish to designate a particular element in a vector or matrix. In such cases we will use the lower case form of the vector or matrix designator with subscripts to indicate the particular element of the vector or matrix concerned. For example: P, 2, and .25 each signify scalars, while a_2 indicates the second element in vector A, and b_{ij} indicates the element at the juncture of row i and column j in matrix B.

The various kinds of matrices just discussed are represented conceptually in Figure 7-1.

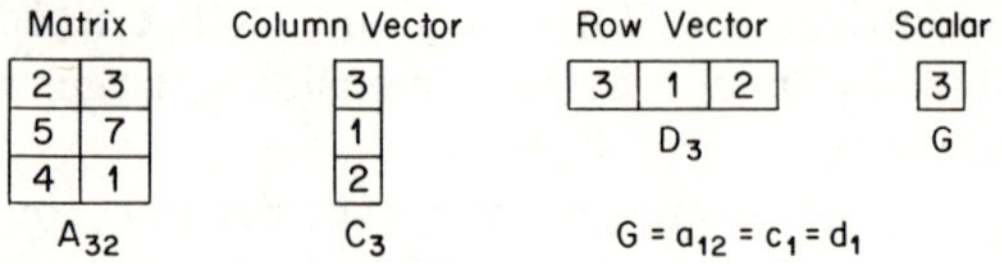

```
    Matrix     Column Vector    Row Vector         Scalar
    ┌─┬─┐         ┌─┐           ┌─┬─┬─┐             ┌─┐
    │2│3│         │3│           │3│1│2│             │3│
    ├─┼─┤         ├─┤           └─┴─┴─┘             └─┘
    │5│7│         │1│             D₃                 G
    ├─┼─┤         ├─┤
    │4│1│         │2│
    └─┴─┘         └─┘
     A₃₂          C₃             G = a₁₂ = c₁ = d₁
```

FIGURE 7-1. Conceptual arrangement of matrices, vectors, and scalars.

EQUALITY OF MATRICES

Two matrices A_{IJ} and B_{IJ} are said to be *equal* only when all of their corresponding elements are equal: $a_{ij} = b_{ij}$ for *all i and j*; therefore, only matrices of the same size can be equal. The column vector C_3 and the row vector D_3 in the previous diagram are *not* equal, even though their elements are equal in value, order, and number.

TRANSPOSE OF A MATRIX

Every matrix A_{IJ} has a transpose A'_{JI} such that $a_{ij} = a'_{ji}$. The transpose of a matrix is a new matrix, designated by the letter of the original matrix with a *prime sign* attached. The transpose of a row vector is a column vector, and vice versa. In the previous diagram D_3 could be designated C'_3, or C_3 could be designated D'_3. It is common practice, however, to refer to a row vector as the transpose of a column vector, reserving the unprimed letters for column vectors only. We will follow this practice henceforth. The transpose of a transposed matrix is the original matrix: $(A'_{JI})'_{IJ} = A_{IJ}$.

Note that we attach subscripts ordered for the transposed version of the matrix. The prime sign thus serves only to remind us that the matrix designated is the transpose of another matrix with the same name and reversed subscripts.

Actual transposition of a matrix in Fortran coding is seldom necessary because of the flexibility afforded by subscript reversal, but a statement sequence to accomplish this purpose is shown with Figure 7-2. The "new"

```
         A₃₂                    A'₂₃ = T₂₃
       ┌─┬─┐                   ┌─┬─┬─┐
       │2│3│                   │2│5│4│
       ├─┼─┤                   ├─┼─┼─┤
       │5│7│                   │3│7│1│
       ├─┼─┤                   └─┴─┴─┘
       │4│1│
       └─┴─┘

           DO 5 I = 1,3
           DO 5 J = 1,2
         5 T(J,I) = A(I,J)
```

FIGURE 7-2. Matrix transposition.

matrix A'_{JI} might be stored anywhere in memory in terms of Fortran array names, and yet be referred to by the same designator letter (A) in matrix algebra notation.

SQUARE AND SYMMETRIC MATRICES

A *square matrix* is one with equal numbers of rows and columns. The size of a square matrix is sometimes called its *order*.

A *symmetric matrix* is a special kind of square matrix which is equal to its transpose, so that $B_{IJ} = B'_{JI}$ when $b_{ij} = b_{ji}$. All *intercorrelation* matrices are symmetric, as are the *cross-products* matrices which are formed during the first stage of the intercorrelation process.

Square

2	4	5
4	3	6
7	2	1

A_{33}

Symmetric

2	4	5
4	3	6
5	6	1

B_{33}

FIGURE 7-3. Square and symmetric matrices.

DIAGONAL, SCALAR, AND IDENTITY MATRICES

A *diagonal matrix* is a symmetric matrix in which all off-diagonal elements (those with unequal subscripts) are zero. Since it is a symmetric matrix, a diagonal matrix is equal to its transpose. There is no standard convention for the representation of diagonal-matrix designators; we will use a delta subscript in place of one of the two identical size subscripts of a square matrix to indicate that it is diagonal. Thus, $P_{\Delta 3}$ will signify a three-by-three diagonal matrix named P.

It is frequently useful to define a diagonal matrix as containing the diagonal elements of another square matrix; we will designate such a diagonal matrix by means of a delta subscript attached to the letter of the original matrix. For instance, $A_{\Delta 3}$ in Figure 7-4 is derived from the diagonal of A_{33} in Figure 7-3. In a similar manner we will subscript the letter for a

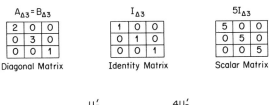

$A_{\Delta 3} = B_{\Delta 3}$

2	0	0
0	3	0
0	0	1

Diagonal Matrix

$I_{\Delta 3}$

1	0	0
0	1	0
0	0	1

Identity Matrix

$5I_{\Delta 3}$

5	0	0
0	5	0
0	0	5

Scalar Matrix

U'_3

| 1 | 1 | 1 |

Unit Vector

$4U'_3$

| 4 | 4 | 4 |

Scalar Vector

FIGURE 7-4. Specialized matrices and vectors.

vector to indicate the construction of a diagonal matrix from the elements of the vector. It is assumed that $V'_I = V_I$ in such cases, since row and column vectors cannot be differentiated after they have been converted to diagonal matrices.

A *scalar matrix* is a diagonal matrix whose diagonal elements are all equal. Since we will later define a scalar matrix as the product of a scalar and an identity matrix, no special notation will be used for it.

An *identity matrix* is a scalar matrix whose diagonal elements are all ones. The usual notation for an identity matrix is the letter I.

A *scalar vector* is a vector whose elements are all equal. Since we will see later that this may be defined as the product of a scalar and a unit vector, no special notation will be used for this type of vector.

A *unit vector* is a vector whose elements are all ones. We will use the letter U to designate a column unit vector, and U' to indicate a row unit vector.

Although these special matrices and vectors are important in matrix algebra notation, computer programming of operations involving them can be greatly simplified by capitalizing on the redundancy involved. In Fortran coding a diagonal matrix is normally stored as a vector of its diagonal elements. Scalar matrices and vectors, as well as identity matrices and vectors, are unnecessary in the coding of matrix operations generally. Scalars are stored as unsubscripted variables, and the uses of identity

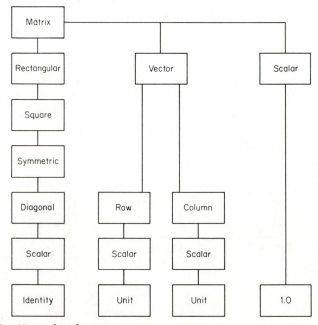

FIGURE 7-5. Hierarchy of matrix types.

Matrix Addition and Subtraction   147

matrices and unit vectors normally resolve to the redundant use of the constant 1.0 in Fortran coding. The various types of matrices and vectors that have just been described are summarized schematically in the hierarchical chart of Figure 7-5.

MATRIX ADDITION AND SUBTRACTION

These operations proceed by scalar addition or subtraction of corresponding elements, and hence are *commutative:* $A + B = B + A$. Only matrices of the same size may be added or subtracted. In Figure 7-6 note that $a_{ij} + b_{ij} = c_{ij}$.

$$A_{23} + B_{23} = C_{23}$$

A_{23}				B_{23}				C_{23}		
1	3	4	+	7	4	2	=	8	7	6
2	3	6		1	6	5		3	9	11

The Fortran coding sequence for this operation is:

```
    DO 5 I = 1,2
    DO 5 J = 1,3
  5 C(I,J) = A(I,J) + B(I,J)
```

FIGURE 7-6. Matrix addition.

Addition and subtraction of vectors follow the same rules (Figure 7-7).

The addition or subtraction of a scalar and a matrix or vector proceeds on an element-by-element basis according to the rules of scalar algebra (Figure 7-8). A scalar in such operations is *not* considered to be a matrix with one row and column, which would prohibit any operations of scalars upon matrices.

$$A_2 + B_2 = C_2$$

A_2		B_2		C_2
6	+	2	=	8
7		3		10

```
    DO 5 I = 1,2
  5 C(I) = A(I) + B(I)
```

FIGURE 7-7. Vector addition.

It should be understood that for any of the previous Fortran sequences, storage of the result matrix could be in one of the original memory arrays, if the contents of that original array need not be retained.

The diagonal elements of a square matrix may be modified through use of a diagonal matrix (Figure 7-9).

$A + B_{23} = C_{23}$

```
     A         B₂₃          C₂₃
   ┌───┐    ┌───┬───┬───┐  ┌───┬───┬───┐
   │ 3 │ +  │ 1 │ 4 │ 5 │  │ 4 │ 7 │ 8 │
   └───┘    ├───┼───┼───┤= ├───┼───┼───┤
            │ 6 │ 2 │ 3 │  │ 9 │ 5 │ 6 │
            └───┴───┴───┘  └───┴───┴───┘
```

```
      DO 5 I = 1,2
      DO 5 J = 1,3
    5 C(I,J) = A + B(I,J)
```

FIGURE 7-8. Addition of scalar and matrix.

$A_{33} - B_{\Delta 3} = C_{33}$

```
     A₃₃           B_Δ₃          C₃₃
  ┌───┬───┬───┐  ┌───┬───┬───┐  ┌───┬───┬───┐
  │ 5 │ 4 │ 7 │  │ 2 │ 0 │ 0 │  │ 3 │ 4 │ 7 │
  ├───┼───┼───┤  ├───┼───┼───┤  ├───┼───┼───┤
  │ 2 │ 1 │ 2 │ -│ 0 │ 1 │ 0 │ =│ 2 │ 0 │ 2 │
  ├───┼───┼───┤  ├───┼───┼───┤  ├───┼───┼───┤
  │ 6 │ 3 │ 8 │  │ 0 │ 0 │ 3 │  │ 6 │ 3 │ 5 │
  └───┴───┴───┘  └───┴───┴───┘  └───┴───┴───┘
```

If the diagonal elements of $B_{\Delta 3}$ were stored in a vector, the Fortran coding would be:

```
      DO 10 I = 1,3
      DO 5 J = 1,3
    5 C(I,J) = A(I,J)
   10 C(I,I) = A(I,I) - B(I)
```

FIGURE 7-9. Modifying diagonal elements of a square matrix.

MATRIX MULTIPLICATION

Matrix multiplication is *not* commutative unless both matrices are symmetric: $A_{KK}B_{KK}$ does not necessarily equal $B_{KK}A_{KK}$. Furthermore, multiplication of some matrix pairs is not possible, since *the number of columns of the first matrix and the number of rows of the second matrix must be equal*. Matrices which meet this requirement are said to be *conformable* for multiplication. *The product matrix will have the number of rows of the first matrix and the number of columns of the second matrix.* Since the order of the matrices is important in multiplication, B_{JK} is said to be *premultiplied* by A_{IJ} in the formula $A_{IJ}B_{JK} = C_{IK}$, or A_{IJ} is said to be *postmultiplied* by B_{JK}.

The product of any matrix and its own transpose is always square:

$$A_{JK}A'_{KJ} = B_{JJ} \text{ and } A'_{KJ}A_{JK} = C_{KK}$$

The product of a symmetric matrix and its transpose will be the same in either order:

$$A'_{KK}A_{KK} = A_{KK}A'_{KK}$$

The transpose of a matrix product is equal to the product of the transposes of the original matrices multiplied in reverse order:

$$(A_{IJ}B_{JK})' = B'_{KJ}A'_{JI}$$

We will continue with this topic after discussing vector products.

Matrix Multiplication   149

Vector Products. The product of a column vector postmultiplied by a row vector is a matrix of all possible products of the scalar elements of the two vectors. This is sometimes called the *outer* or *major product* of the vectors. Note that $a_i b'_j = c_{ij}$ in Figure 7-10. The operation is accomplished in Fortran by means of the two DO loops and a pair of single-subscripted arrays. The SCPF Function cannot be used in this case.

$$A_3 B'_3 = C_{33}$$

```
         A₃           B'₃              C₃₃
        ┌─┐        ┌─┬─┬─┐         ┌──┬─┬──┐
        │3│   ×    │4│2│5│    =    │12│6│15│
        ├─┤        └─┴─┴─┘         ├──┼─┼──┤
        │1│                        │ 4│2│ 5│
        ├─┤                        ├──┼─┼──┤
        │2│                        │ 8│4│10│
        └─┘                        └──┴─┴──┘

         DO 5 I = 1,3
         DO 5 J = 1,3
       5 C(I,J) = A(I) * B(J)
```

FIGURE 7-10. Outer product of two vectors.

The product of a row vector postmultiplied by a column vector is a scalar sum of the products of corresponding scalar elements of the two vectors. This is sometimes called the *inner* or *minor product* of the vectors, and is also known as a *scalar product*. The two vectors in this case must have the same number of elements; this was not necessary, however, for the outer product. The matrix formula $D = A'_3 B_3$ for Figure 7-11 is equivalent to $D = \Sigma AB$ in summation notation. The SCPF Function *can* be used.[1]

$$D = 0.0$$
$$\text{DO } 5 \text{ I} = 1, 3 \qquad \text{or} \qquad D = \text{SCPF}(A, B, 1, 1, 3, ND)$$
$$5 \quad D = D + A(I) * B(I)$$

```
         A'₃              B₃            D
       ┌─┬─┬─┐          ┌─┐           ┌──┐
       │2│3│4│    ×     │3│     =     │32│
       └─┴─┴─┘          ├─┤           └──┘
                        │2│
                        ├─┤
                        │5│
                        └─┘
```

FIGURE 7-11. Inner (scalar) product of two vectors.

The inner product of a vector and its transpose is simply the sum of squares of the vector elements:

Summation notation: $T = \sum\limits^{N} X^2$
Matrix notation: $T = X'_N X_N$

In Fortran either SCPF or SUMF can be used:

$$T = 0.0$$
$$\text{DO } 5 \text{ I} = 1, N \qquad \text{or} \qquad T = \text{SCPF}(X, X, 1, 1, N, ND)$$
$$5 \quad T = T + X(I) * X(I) \qquad \text{or} \qquad T = \text{SUMF}(X, 1, -N, ND)$$

[1]In all examples in this chapter, ND would be determined by the DIMENSION statement.

Matrix Products. The earlier example ($D = A'_3 B_3$) represents the first step in obtaining the product matrix C_{22} in Figure 7-12, in that $D = c_{11}$.

$$A_{23} B_{32} = C_{22}$$

$$\begin{array}{c} A_{23} \\ \begin{array}{|c|c|c|} \hline 2 & 3 & 4 \\ \hline 5 & 2 & 1 \\ \hline \end{array} \end{array} \times \begin{array}{c} B_{32} \\ \begin{array}{|c|c|} \hline 3 & 4 \\ \hline 2 & 3 \\ \hline 5 & 2 \\ \hline \end{array} \end{array} = \begin{array}{c} C_{22} \\ \begin{array}{|c|c|} \hline 32 & 25 \\ \hline 24 & 28 \\ \hline \end{array} \end{array}$$

FIGURE 7-12. Product of two matrices.

Each element of a product matrix is the inner product of a row vector from the first matrix and a column vector from the second matrix being multiplied.

This procedure may be clarified by Figure 7-13 in which we have indicated the various vectors to be multiplied to obtain each element of the product matrix.

$$\begin{array}{c} A_{2K} \\ \begin{array}{|c|} \hline R \\ \hline S \\ \hline \end{array} \end{array} \times \begin{array}{c} B_{K2} \\ \begin{array}{|c|c|} \hline T & U \\ \hline \end{array} \end{array} = \begin{array}{c} C_{22} \\ \begin{array}{|c|c|} \hline RT & RU \\ \hline ST & SU \\ \hline \end{array} \end{array}$$

FIGURE 7-13. Matrix multiplication as a series of scalar products.

In Fortran, matrix multiplication may be coded completely, with the use of Function SCPF, or with Subroutine AXBS as follows:

```
      DO 5 I = 1, 2
      DO 5 J = 1, 2
      C(I, J) = 0.0
      DO 5 K = 1, 3
    5 C(I, J) = C(I, J) + A(I, K) * B(K, J)
```

or

```
      DO 5 I = 1, 2
      DO 5 J = 1, 2
    5 C(I, J) = SCPF(A, B, −I, J, 3, ND)
```

AXBS (A, B, C, KA, KB, N, ND)

A subroutine to compute a matrix product.

This subroutine is described in flow chart form in Figure 7-14. The organization of the routine resembles those of SUMF and SCPF, since options are provided which permit implicit transposition of either of the matrices to be multiplied.

Certain restrictions limit application of this subroutine, and should be clearly understood. The number of rows dimensioned for all three matrices (ND) in the calling program must be the same, to insure correct subscript

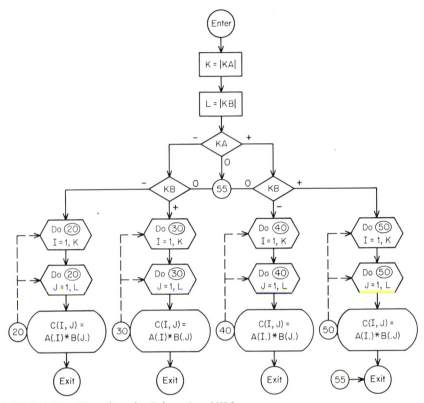

FIGURE 7-14. Flow chart for Subroutine AXBS.

referencing. The output matrix C must occupy a different memory area from either A or B, but A and B *may* be equated to the same matrix in the CALL statement for this routine. For instance, suppose we wished to store the product $X'_{32} X_{23}$ in Q_{33}. The following statement would be used:

CALL AXBS (X, X, Q, −3, 3, 2, ND)

To obtain the matrix product for the earlier example we could have employed the following statement instead of writing out the complete Fortran sequence:

CALL AXBS (A, B, C, 2, 2, 3, ND)

It is very important to recognize the fact that the negative signs on the fourth and/or fifth arguments in the CALL statement do not *actually* transpose the matrices concerned, but only yield a product matrix which is formed *as if* they had been already transposed; the absolute values of these arguments should be the numbers of rows and columns of the product matrix to be obtained.

When it is necessary because of storage limitations to replace one of the

152 FORTRAN: MATRIX ALGEBRA

two original matrices with the product matrix, rather than store the product in a new array, a temporary storage vector is necessary, and AXBS cannot be used. In the following illustration the product matrix is stored in array A.

```
       DO 10 I = 1, 2
       DO 5 J = 1, 3
    5  T(J) = A(I, J)
       DO 10 J = 1, 2
       A(I, J) = 0.0
       DO 10 K = 1, 3
   10  A(I, J) = A(I, J) + T(K) * B(K, J)
```

or

```
       DO 10 I = 1, 2
       DO 5 J = 1, 3
    5  T(J) = A(I, J)
       DO 10 J = 1, 2
   10  A(I, J) = SCPF(T, B, 1, J, 3, ND)
```

This subroutine cannot be used to obtain the product of a matrix and a vector, nor can it be used to obtain the outer product of two vectors. (The inner product may be obtained from Function SCPF.) Computation of the product of a matrix and a vector will be discussed later in this chapter.

A notational convenience is introduced in Figure 7-14 for the designation of a vector within a matrix. The period within a subscript stands for "all elements." Thus, A(.I) designates the entire Ith *column* of matrix A, while B(J.) designates the entire Jth *row* of matrix B. The expression A(.I) * B(J.) denotes the scalar product of the two vectors.

```
      SUBROUTINE AXBS (A, B, C, KA, KB, N, ND)
C
C     COMPUTES MATRIX PRODUCT OF A AND B AND STORES IT IN C.
C     A,B = INPUT MATRICES. C = OUTPUT MATRIX.
C         A AND B MAY BE SENT AS THE SAME MATRIX.
C     KA = NUMBER OF ROWS IN MATRIX PRODUCT C. IF NEGATIVE, ASSUME THE
C         A MATRIX TRANSPOSED.
C     KB = NUMBER OF COLUMNS IN MATRIX PRODUCT C. IF NEGATIVE, ASSUME THE
C         B MATRIX TRANSPOSED.
C     N = NUMBER OF ELEMENTS IN COMMON DIMENSION OF MATRICES AS MULTIPLIE
C     ND = NUMBER OF ROWS DIMENSIONED FOR ALL MATRICES A, B, C,
C         IN CALLING PROGRAM.
C
      DIMENSION A(ND,1), B(ND,1), C(ND,1)
      K = IABS(KA)
      L = IABS(KB)
      IF (KA) 5,55,10
    5 IF (KB) 15,55,25
   10 IF (KB) 35,55,45
   15 DO 20 I = 1,K
      DO 20 J = 1,L
   20 C(I,J) = SCPF(A, B, I, -J, N, ND)
```

```
   RETURN
25 DO 30 I = 1,K
   DO 30 J = 1,L
30 C(I,J) = SCPF(A, B, I, J, N, ND)
   RETURN
35 DO 40 I = 1,K
   DO 40 J = 1,L
40 C(I,J) = SCPF(A, B, -I, -J, N, ND)
   RETURN
45 DO 50 I = 1,K
   DO 50 J = 1,L
50 C(I,J) = SCPF(A, B, -I, J, N, ND)
55 RETURN
   END
```

MATRIX MULTIPLICATION BY A SCALAR

Matrix multiplication by a scalar (shown in Figure 7-15) is equivalent to pre- or postmultiplication by a conformable scalar matrix. However, multiplication by a scalar usually is represented by the conjunction of a scalar symbol and a matrix symbol, and the operation is understood to be the scalar multiplication of each element of the matrix by the scalar quantity. The product matrix is the same size as the original matrix. The operation is considered commutative.

$AB_{23} = C_{23} = B_{23}A$ or $A_{\Delta 2}B_{23} = C_{23} = B_{23}A_{\Delta 3}$

$$\underset{A}{\begin{bmatrix} 3 \end{bmatrix}} \text{ or } \underset{A_{\Delta 2}}{\begin{bmatrix} 3 & 0 \\ 0 & 3 \end{bmatrix}} \times \underset{B_{23}}{\begin{bmatrix} 2 & 4 & 1 \\ 5 & 3 & 2 \end{bmatrix}} = \underset{C_{23}}{\begin{bmatrix} 6 & 12 & 3 \\ 15 & 9 & 6 \end{bmatrix}}$$

```
  DO 5 I = 1,2
  DO 5 J = 1,3
5 C(I,J) = A * B(I,J)
```

FIGURE 7-15. Matrix multiplication by a scalar.

VECTOR MULTIPLICATION BY SCALARS

Vector multiplication by a scalar (shown in Figure 7-16) does not necessitate the concept of a diagonal matrix, since premultiplication of a row vector and postmultiplication of a column vector by a scalar both are operations involving conformable matrices. The operation is typically written as if commutative, however:

$$AB_I = B_IA = C_I \text{ and } AB'_I = B'_IA = C'_I$$

$AB'_3 = C'_3$ $\qquad$ $B_3A = C_3$

$$\underset{A}{\begin{bmatrix} 3 \end{bmatrix}} \times \underset{B'_3}{\begin{bmatrix} 2 & 4 & 1 \end{bmatrix}} = \underset{C'_3}{\begin{bmatrix} 6 & 12 & 3 \end{bmatrix}} \qquad \underset{B_3}{\begin{bmatrix} 2 \\ 4 \\ 1 \end{bmatrix}} \times \underset{A}{\begin{bmatrix} 3 \end{bmatrix}} = \underset{C_3}{\begin{bmatrix} 6 \\ 12 \\ 3 \end{bmatrix}}$$

FIGURE 7-16. Vector multiplication by a scalar.

154 FORTRAN: MATRIX ALGEBRA

Since both row and column vectors are normally stored as single-subscripted arrays in Fortran coding, this operation is even simpler than multiplication of a matrix by a scalar:

```
    DO 5 I = 1, 3
  5 C(I) = A * B(I)
```

The product of a scalar and an identity matrix is a scalar matrix (Figure 7-17), and the product of a scalar and a unit vector is a scalar vector. These operations are normally unnecessary in Fortran coding.

$$AI_{\Delta 2} = A_{\Delta 2} \qquad\qquad AU_2' = A_2'$$

$$A \quad I_{\Delta 2} \quad\;\; A_{\Delta 2} \qquad\qquad A \quad U_2' \quad\; A_2'$$

$$\boxed{3} \times \begin{array}{|c|c|}\hline 1 & 0 \\ \hline 0 & 1 \\ \hline\end{array} = \begin{array}{|c|c|}\hline 3 & 0 \\ \hline 0 & 3 \\ \hline\end{array} \qquad \boxed{3} \times \begin{array}{|c|c|}\hline 1 & 1 \\ \hline\end{array} = \begin{array}{|c|c|}\hline 3 & 3 \\ \hline\end{array}$$

FIGURE 7-17. Product of a scalar and identity matrix.

MATRIX MULTIPLICATION BY VECTORS

The usual requirement of conformability applies here as well as to multiplication of two matrices; therefore, premultiplication of a matrix must be by a row vector and postmultiplication must be by a column vector, yielding row and column vector products, respectively (Figures 7-18 and 7-19).

$$A_2' B_{23} = C_3'$$

$$\begin{array}{c} A_2' \\ \boxed{1\;\;2} \end{array} \times \begin{array}{c} B_{23} \\ \begin{array}{|c|c|c|}\hline 2 & 4 & 1 \\ \hline 3 & 5 & 2 \\ \hline\end{array} \end{array} = \begin{array}{c} C_3' \\ \boxed{8\;\;14\;\;5} \end{array}$$

```
    DO 5 J = 1,3                        DO 5 J = 1,3
    C(J) = 0.0              or        5 C(J) = SCPF(A, B, 1, J, 2, ND)
    DO 5 I = 1,2
  5 C(J) = C(J) + A(I) * B(I,J)
```

FIGURE 7-18. Matrix multiplication by a row vector.

$$B_{23} A_3 = C_2$$

$$\begin{array}{c} B_{23} \\ \begin{array}{|c|c|c|}\hline 2 & 4 & 1 \\ \hline 3 & 5 & 2 \\ \hline\end{array} \end{array} \times \begin{array}{c} A_3 \\ \begin{array}{|c|}\hline 1 \\ \hline 2 \\ \hline 3 \\ \hline\end{array} \end{array} = \begin{array}{c} C_2 \\ \begin{array}{|c|}\hline 13 \\ \hline 19 \\ \hline\end{array} \end{array}$$

```
    DO 5 I = 1,2                        DO 5 I = 1,2
    C(I) = 0.0              or        5 C(I) = SCPF(B, A, -1, 1, 3, ND)
    DO 5 J = 1,3
  5 C(I) = C(I) + B(I,J) * A(J)
```

FIGURE 7-19. Matrix multiplication by a column vector.

Pre- or postmultiplication of a matrix by unit vectors result in vectors of column or row sums, respectively (Figures 7-20 and 7-21).

$U_3'A_{32} = B_2'$

$$\underset{U_3'}{\begin{bmatrix} 1 & 1 & 1 \end{bmatrix}} \times \underset{A_{32}}{\begin{bmatrix} 2 & 4 \\ 1 & 3 \\ 3 & 2 \end{bmatrix}} = \underset{B_2'}{\begin{bmatrix} 6 & 9 \end{bmatrix}}$$

FIGURE 7-20. Matrix multiplication by a row unit vector.

In Fortran coding, a unit vector is not necessary.

```
  DO 5 J = 1, 2
  B(J) = 0.0
  DO 5 I = 1, 3
5 B(J) = B(J) + A(I, J)
```

or

```
  DO 5 J = 1, 2
5 B(J) = SUMF(A, J, 3, ND)
```

$A_{32}U_2 = B_3$

$$\underset{A_{32}}{\begin{bmatrix} 2 & 4 \\ 1 & 3 \\ 3 & 2 \end{bmatrix}} \times \underset{U_2}{\begin{bmatrix} 1 \\ 1 \end{bmatrix}} = \underset{B_3}{\begin{bmatrix} 6 \\ 4 \\ 5 \end{bmatrix}}$$

```
  DO 5 I = 1,3
  B(I) = 0.0
  DO 5 J = 1,2
5 B(I) = B(I) + A(I,J)
```

or

```
  DO 5 I = 1,3
5 B(I) = SUMF(A, -I, 2, ND)
```

FIGURE 7-21. Matrix multiplication by a column unit vector.

MATRIX MULTIPLICATION BY DIAGONAL MATRICES

Premultiplication of a matrix by a diagonal matrix is equivalent to scalar multiplication of each *row* element in the matrix by the corresponding diagonal element (same row) of the diagonal matrix (Figure 7-22).

$A_{\Delta 2}B_{23} = C_{23}$

$$\underset{A_{\Delta 2}}{\begin{bmatrix} 2 & 0 \\ 0 & 3 \end{bmatrix}} \times \underset{B_{23}}{\begin{bmatrix} 3 & 2 & 6 \\ 4 & 5 & 1 \end{bmatrix}} = \underset{C_{23}}{\begin{bmatrix} 6 & 4 & 12 \\ 12 & 15 & 3 \end{bmatrix}}$$

FIGURE 7-22. Matrix premultiplication by a diagonal matrix.

Since diagonal matrices are normally stored as single-subscripted arrays, this operation is equivalent to multiplying the elements of each row of the matrix by the corresponding scalar element of the vector:

```
  DO 5 I = 1, 2
  DO 5 J = 1, 3
5 C(I, J) = A(I) * B(I, J)
```

Postmultiplication of a matrix by a diagonal matrix is equivalent to scalar multiplication of each *column* element in the matrix by the corresponding diagonal element (same column) of the diagonal matrix (Figure 7-23).

$$B_{23} A_{\Delta 3} = C_{23}$$

B_{23}				$A_{\Delta 3}$				C_{23}		
3	2	6	×	2	0	0	=	6	2	18
4	5	1		0	1	0		8	5	3
				0	0	3				

FIGURE 7-23. Matrix postmultiplication by a diagonal matrix.

```
    DO 5 J = 1, 3
    DO 5 I = 1, 2
  5 C(I, J) = B(I, J) * A(J)
```

Multiplication of a matrix by a scalar matrix was discussed previously. Matrix multiplication by an identity matrix yields the original matrix: $A_{JK} I_{\Delta K} = I_{\Delta J} A_{JK} = A_{JK}$, and this also holds for multiplication of vectors by conformable identity matrices.

MATRIX INVERSION

The analog of division in matrix operations is multiplication by a reciprocal. The reciprocal of a matrix is known as its *inverse*, which is the same size as the original matrix. Only square matrices can be inverted, but some square matrices, called *singular* matrices, do not have inverses. The inverse of a matrix is denoted by a -1 superscript attached to the designator, and is defined by the equation $A_{KK}^{-1} A_{KK} = I_{\Delta K}$. There are a number of methods for solving this matrix equation for A_{KK}^{-1}, and one of these, known as the *Gauss-Jordan method,* is available in the form of Subroutine INVS.

INVS (N, X, KP, KR, KC, ND)

A subroutine to compute the inverse of a square matrix.

This routine employs the Gauss-Jordan method; detailed descriptions are presented by Cooley and Lohnes (1962) and by Ralston and Wilf (1960). The inversion of input matrix X is done "in place," destroying the original matrix. If the original matrix is needed later in the calling routine, it must be duplicated into another memory area prior to calling INVS. Although the three temporary storage vectors KP, KR, and KC are assigned integer-mode names in the subroutine, they may be equated to vectors named in either mode in the calling routine, since they are used only for temporary storage. A flow chart of this subroutine is shown in Figure 7-26.

Most of the inverses obtained in behavioral science research are of

Matrix Inversion

$$B_{33} \qquad B_{33}^{-1} \qquad C_{33} = I_{\Delta 3}$$

1	2	1
2	5	5
1	5	11

×

30	-17	5
-17	10	-3
5	-3	1

=

1	0	0
0	1	0
0	0	1

```
      DO 5 I = 1,3
      DO 5 J = 1,3
    5 Q(I,J) = B(I,J)
      CALL INVS (3, Q, X, Y, Z, ND)
      CALL AXBS (B, Q, C, 3, 3, 3, ND)
```

FIGURE 7-24. Product of a matrix and its inverse.

symmetric matrices. Figure 7-24 is typical. Since the inverse is also symmetric, $B_{33} B_{33}^{-1} = B_{33}^{-1} B_{33} = I_{\Delta 3}$.

If both matrices are nonsingular, the following identity holds for matrix inversion as well as matrix transposition: $(AB)^{-1} = B^{-1}A^{-1}$.

The inverse of a diagonal matrix is another diagonal matrix whose elements are scalar reciprocals of the elements of the original matrix. If the diagonal matrix is stored as a vector, the operation may be coded directly without calling INVS (Figure 7-25).

$$A_{\Delta 2} \qquad A_{\Delta 2}^{-1} = B_{\Delta 2}$$

2	0
0	3

1/2	0
0	1/3

```
      DO 5 I = 1,2
    5 B(I) = 1.0 / A(I)
```

FIGURE 7-25. Inverse of a diagonal matrix.

```
      SUBROUTINE INVS (N, X, KP, KR, KC, ND)
C
C     COMPUTES THE INVERSE OF A SQUARE MATRIX.
C     N = ORDER OF THE INPUT MATRIX X.
C     X = SQUARE INPUT MATRIX. RETURNED HOLDING X INVERSE.
C     KP, KR, KC = TEMPORARY STORAGE VECTORS.
C     ND = NUMBER OF ROWS DIMENSIONED FOR X IN CALLING PROGRAM.
C
      DIMENSION X(ND,N), KP(N), KR(N), KC(N)
      DO 5 I = 1,N
    5 KP(I) = 0
      DO 45 I = 1,N
C     SEARCH FOR THE PIVOT ELEMENT.
      T = 0.0
      DO 20 J = 1,N
      IF (KP(J) .EQ. 1) GO TO 20
      DO 15 K = 1,N
      IF (KP(K) - 1) 10,15,60
   10 IF (T .GE. ABS(X(J,K))) GO TO 15
      IR = J
      IC = K
      T = ABS(X(J,K))
   15 CONTINUE
   20 CONTINUE
      KP(IC) = KP(IC) + 1
      IF (IR .EQ. IC) GO TO 30
```

158 FORTRAN: MATRIX ALGEBRA

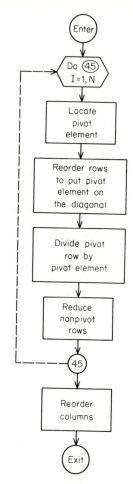

FIGURE 7-26. Flow chart for Subroutine INVS.

```
C   PUT PIVOT ELEMENT ON DIAGONAL BY SWAPPING ROWS.
        DO 25 L = 1,N
        T = X(IR,L)
        X(IR,L) = X(IC,L)
 25     X(IC,L) = T
 30     KR(I) = IR
        KC(I) = IC
C   DIVIDE PIVOT ROW BY PIVOT ELEMENT.
        T = X(IC,IC)
        X(IC,IC) = 1.0
        DO 35 L = 1,N
 35     X(IC,L) = X(IC,L) / T
C   REDUCE NON-PIVOT ROWS.
        DO 45 M = 1,N
        IF (M .EQ. IC) GO TO 45
        T = X(M,IC)
        X(M,IC) = 0.0
        DO 40 L = 1,N
 40     X(M,L) = X(M,L) - X(IC,L) * T
 45     CONTINUE
```

```
C   REORDER COLUMNS.
    DO 55 I = 1,N
    J = N - I + 1
    IF (KR(J) .EQ. KC(J)) GO TO 55
    K = KR(J)
    L = KC(J)
    DO 50 M = 1,N
    T = X(M,K)
    X(M,K) = X(M,L)
 50 X(M,L) = T
 55 CONTINUE
 60 RETURN
    END
```

SQUARE ROOTS AND POWERS OF DIAGONAL MATRICES

The square of a matrix can be written as multiplication by itself $A_{JJ}^2 = A_{JJ} A_{JJ}$. In the case of diagonal matrices, the operation $A_{\Delta J}^2$ is equivalent to scalar squaring of each diagonal element separately to yield a new diagonal matrix (Figure 7-27).

$$A_{\Delta 2} \quad\quad A_{\Delta 2} \quad\quad A_{\Delta 2}^2$$

$$\begin{array}{|c|c|} \hline 2 & 0 \\ \hline 0 & 3 \\ \hline \end{array} \times \begin{array}{|c|c|} \hline 2 & 0 \\ \hline 0 & 3 \\ \hline \end{array} = \begin{array}{|c|c|} \hline 4 & 0 \\ \hline 0 & 9 \\ \hline \end{array}$$

FIGURE 7-27. Square of a diagonal matrix.

When the diagonal matrix is stored as a vector, the Fortran coding would be:

$$\text{DO } 5 \text{ I} = 1, 2$$
$$5 \quad B(I) = A(I) * A(I)$$

The square root of a diagonal matrix (Figure 7-28) may be obtained in the same manner, and is written either under a radical sign, $\sqrt{A_{\Delta K}}$ or more often, with a fractional superscript (exponent), $A_{\Delta K}^{1/2}$. (See Figure 7-29.) Inversion and extraction of the square root of a diagonal matrix may be combined. Note that

$$A_{\Delta K}^{-1/2} = (A_{\Delta K}^{1/2})^{-1} = (A_{\Delta K}^{-1})^{1/2}$$

$$A_{\Delta 2} \quad\quad\quad A_{\Delta 2}^{1/2}$$

$$\begin{array}{|c|c|} \hline 4 & 0 \\ \hline 0 & 9 \\ \hline \end{array} \quad\quad \begin{array}{|c|c|} \hline 2 & 0 \\ \hline 0 & 3 \\ \hline \end{array}$$

```
DO 5 I = 1,2
5 A(I) = SQRT(A(I))
```

FIGURE 7-28. Square root of a diagonal matrix.

$$A_{\Delta 2} \quad\quad\quad A_{\Delta 2}^{-1/2}$$

$$\begin{array}{|c|c|} \hline 4 & 0 \\ \hline 0 & 9 \\ \hline \end{array} \quad\quad \begin{array}{|c|c|} \hline 1/2 & 0 \\ \hline 0 & 1/3 \\ \hline \end{array}$$

```
DO 5 I = 1,2
5 A(I) = 1.0 / SQRT(A(I))
```

FIGURE 7-29. Diagonal matrix with negative fractional exponent.

NORMALIZATION

Vectors, including individual row or column vectors of matrices, are said to be *normalized* if the sum of the squared element-values equals 1.0. This usage of the term "normal" has *no* relationship to the concept of a *normal distribution*. A normalized vector (Figure 7-30) is sometimes said to be of *unit length,* where the term "length" refers to the geometric representation of the vector and not to the number of its elements. In algebraic terms the length of a vector is the square root of the sum of its squared element-values. If P is the length of the vector X, which contains N elements, then

$P = \sqrt{\sum^{N} X^2}$ in summation notation,
$P = (X'_N X_N)^{1/2}$ in matrix notation, and
$P = \text{SQRT(SUMF(X, 1, }-\text{N, ND))}$ in Fortran coding

To normalize a vector of raw scores (X), each of the raw scores would be divided by P. The complete process yielding a normalized vector (Y) is given by the matrix formula:

$$Y_N = (X'_N X_N)^{-1/2} X_N = P^{-1} X_N$$

In Fortran coding the normalization of a vector may be accomplished with the following statement sequence:

```
    P = SQRT(SUMF(X, 1, -N, ND))
    DO 5 I = 1, N
  5 Y(I) = X(I)  /  P
```

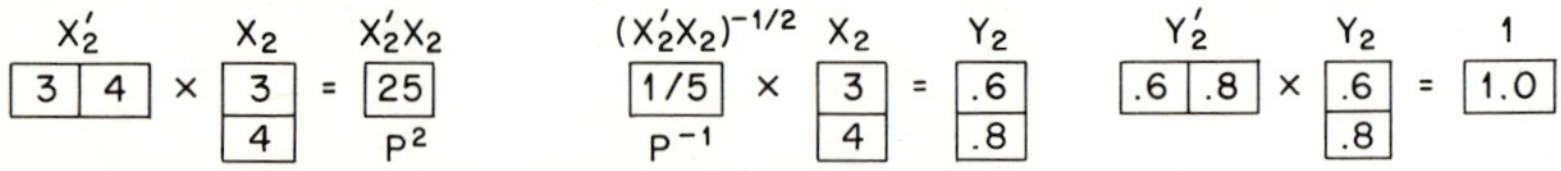

$\begin{array}{c} X'_2 \\ \boxed{3 \mid 4} \end{array} \times \begin{array}{c} X_2 \\ \boxed{\begin{array}{c}3\\4\end{array}} \end{array} = \begin{array}{c} X'_2 X_2 \\ \boxed{25} \\ P^2 \end{array} \quad \begin{array}{c}(X'_2 X_2)^{-1/2}\\ \boxed{1/5} \\ P^{-1}\end{array} \times \begin{array}{c} X_2 \\ \boxed{\begin{array}{c}3\\4\end{array}} \end{array} = \begin{array}{c} Y_2 \\ \boxed{\begin{array}{c}.6\\.8\end{array}} \end{array} \quad \begin{array}{c} Y'_2 \\ \boxed{.6 \mid .8} \end{array} \times \begin{array}{c} Y_2 \\ \boxed{\begin{array}{c}.6\\.8\end{array}} \end{array} = \begin{array}{c} 1 \\ \boxed{1.0} \end{array}$

Note that $Y'_2 Y_2 = 1.0$ in the last part of the diagram.

FIGURE 7-30. Normalization of a vector.

Now let us generalize the normalization sequence to deal with all rows or all columns of a matrix simultaneously. The key to the following formulas is the fact that the diagonal of the product of the raw-score matrix premultiplied by its transpose will contain column sums of squares, while the diagonal of the product of the raw-score matrix postmultiplied by its transpose will contain row sums of squares.

To normalize *columns* of a matrix:

$$Y_{NK} = X_{NK}(X'_{KN} X_{NK})_{\Delta K}^{-1/2}$$

To normalize *rows* of a matrix:

$$Y_{NK} = (X_{NK}X'_{KN})_{\Delta N}^{-1/2} X_{NK}$$

In Fortran, these procedures are coded as follows:

```
          BY COLUMNS
       DO 5 J = 1, K
       P = SQRT(SUMF(X, J, -N, ND))
       DO 5 I = 1, N
5      Y(I, J) = X(I, J)  /  P

          BY ROWS
       DO 5 I = 1, N
       P = SQRT(SUMF(X, -I, -K, ND))
       DO 5 J = 1, K
5      Y(I, J) = X(I, J)  /  P
```

STANDARDIZATION

Standardization is familiar to most students of statistics as conversion to z scores by means of the formula $z = (x - \mu)/\sigma$, where μ is the mean of the scores, and σ is their standard deviation. Conversion of a vector of raw scores to z-score form changes the length of the vector to the square root of the number of its elements ($N^{1/2}$), and *also* changes the sum of the elements to zero. This is accomplished through the use of μ and σ, which are defined as follows:

In summation notation:

$$\mu = \overset{N}{\Sigma} X/N \quad \text{and} \quad \sigma = \sqrt{\overset{N}{\Sigma} X^2/N - \mu^2}$$

In matrix notation:

$$M = U'_N X_N N^{-1} \quad \text{and} \quad S = (X'_N X_N N^{-1} - M^2)^{1/2}$$
$$Z_N = (X_N - M) S^{-1}$$

Figure 7-31 illustrates computation of M and S, conversion to z scores and proof that $Z'_N Z_N = N$.

To standardize columns or rows of a matrix to z-score form, vectors of means and sigmas are usually computed as part of the process, although it is not necessary to retain them, as in the following sequences.

```
              BY COLUMNS
       T = N
       DO 5 J = 1, K
       CM(J) = SUMF(X, J, N, ND)  /  T
       CS(J) = SQRT(SUMF(X, J, -N, ND)  /  T - CM(J)**2)
       DO 5 I = 1, N
5      ZC(I, J) = (X(I, J) - CM(J))  /  CS(J)
```

BY ROWS

```
      T = N
      DO 5 I = 1, N
      RM(I) = SUMF(X, -I, K, ND)  /  T
      RS(I) = SQRT(SUMF(X, -I, -K, ND)  /  T - RM(I)**2)
      DO 5 J = 1, K
    5 ZR(I, J) = (X(I, J) - RM(I))  /  RS(I)
```

$$\underset{U'_N}{\boxed{1\ 1}} \times \underset{X_N}{\boxed{\begin{array}{c}3\\4\end{array}}} \times \underset{N^{-1}}{\boxed{1/2}} = \underset{M}{\boxed{3.5}} \qquad \underset{X'_N}{\boxed{3\ 4}} \times \underset{X_N}{\boxed{\begin{array}{c}3\\4\end{array}}} \times \underset{N^{-1}}{\boxed{1/2}} - \underset{M^2}{\boxed{12.25}} = \underset{S^2}{\boxed{.25}} \quad \underset{S}{\boxed{.5}}$$

$$\underset{X_N}{\boxed{\begin{array}{c}3\\4\end{array}}} - \underset{M}{\boxed{3.5}} = \underset{X_N-M}{\boxed{\begin{array}{c}-.5\\.5\end{array}}} \times \underset{S^{-1}}{\boxed{2}} = \underset{Z_N}{\boxed{\begin{array}{c}-1.0\\1.0\end{array}}} \quad \underset{Z'_N}{\boxed{-1.0\ 1.0}} \times \underset{Z_N}{\boxed{\begin{array}{c}-1.0\\1.0\end{array}}} = \underset{N}{\boxed{2}}$$

The Fortran sequence for standardizing a vector is:

```
      T = N
      XM = SUMF(X, 1, N, ND) / T
      XS = SQRT(SUMF(X, 1, -N, ND) / T - XM**2)
      DO 5 I = 1, N
    5 Z(I) = (X(I) - XM) / XS
```

FIGURE 7-31. Standardization of a vector.

This chapter has presented only the most essential topics and terminology of matrix algebra. Some authors employ a much greater variety of specialized matrices which simplify the specification of certain complex matrix manipulations. With the foundation presented in this chapter you should be able to extend your understanding with little difficulty by further reading in the references cited earlier. As we have seen, matrix notation is concise and consistent from a mathematical point of view, but would be clumsy and wasteful if coded literally in the Fortran language. The more familiar you are with matrix *operations,* the more you will be able to capitalize on the systematic redundancy in matrix notation to increase the efficiency of your Fortran programs.

Almost all computer installations have available a library of matrix manipulating subroutines such as AXBS and INVS. For their System/360 machines, IBM supplies an extensive subroutine package that includes a wide variety of routines for matrix operations, as well as a group of programs for multivariate statistical analysis. The subroutines presented in this book may duplicate very closely some of those already available at your installation. In other cases, however, they may differ to some extent. These differences may be in flexibility of application, in speed of execution, in storage requirements, or in accuracy of results. Only you can decide the importance of these differences—after careful comparison of the routines concerned.

In later chapters we will present a number of other subroutines which involve operations upon matrices. Some of these are of limited usefulness in that they only serve to partition a complex procedure, and facilitate rebuilding of programs. Others, such as the routines which extract eigenroots and vectors, are much more general in application. Rather than attempt to bring all of the important matrix-manipulation routines together in this chapter, we have scattered them throughout the coming chapters to be discussed within the contexts of their most common applications.

Review Exercises

1. Reconstruct from memory the chart in Figure 7-5, which lists the various kinds of matrices and vectors. Give an example of each type.
2. Define the following terms by means of examples:
   a. matrix transposition
   b. matrix equality and conformability
   c. matrix multiplication
   d. outer, inner, and scalar vector products
   e. pre- and postmultiplication
   f. matrix inversion and singularity

```
       A           B         C        D        E
   ┌───┬───┐   ┌───┬───┐   ┌───┐   ┌───┬───┐   ┌───┐
   │ 1 │ 2 │   │ 2 │ 3 │   │ 2 │   │ 1 │ 1 │   │ 2 │
   ├───┼───┤   ├───┼───┤   ├───┤   └───┴───┘   └───┘
   │ 3 │ 4 │   │ 3 │ 2 │   │ 3 │
   └───┴───┘   └───┴───┘   └───┘
```

3. Write a computer program to compute the product ABCDE, using Subroutines AXBS and PRTS. Calculate the correct answer by hand to check the output.
4. Rewrite the raw-score formula for the correlation coefficient as a single *matrix* formula employing only unit vectors, two raw-score vectors X_N and Y_N, and the scalar N.

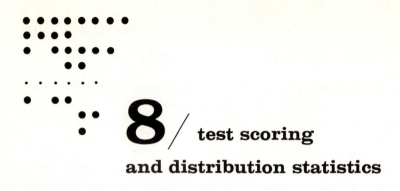

8 / test scoring and distribution statistics

Most of the data collected by behavioral scientists for research purposes are elicited by paper-and-pencil instruments which contain a series of items. Each of these items requires a selection from two or more supplied alternatives. Most Americans have been asked to complete such forms, which are widely used in academic and industrial settings as well as for opinion surveys. The terminology in this area is quite varied, but from the psychometric standpoint three major types of items may be identified.

MULTIPLE-CHOICE TESTS

Multiple-choice tests seek to measure the respondent's ability or knowledge by requiring the selection of predetermined "right" choices from the alternatives supplied. The following item is a typical example:

> The capital city of New York State is
> a. New York City
> b. Albany
> c. Wyoming
> d. Chicago
> e. Buffalo

For each such item the subject's score may be considered as 1 (right choice) or 0 (wrong choice). These converted item scores are added over items to yield a number which reflects the subject's ability to select correct choices. These total scores have the properties of at least ordinal measurement, and are typically assumed to meet the requirements of interval scaling.

Programs for scoring such tests usually assume that the item choices are recorded as choice-position integers. For instance, a respondent's choice of "Wyoming" would be recorded on his data card as the number 3 (choice c). The scoring program would use a vector containing the choice numbers of the right answers to compare against each respondent's vector of choice numbers, and would compute the total number of choices which agreed with the correct-choice key. It would be possible, of course, for the choices to be recorded as alphabetic characters rather than numbers; the matching process would be the same.

QUESTIONNAIRES

The term "questionnaire" is commonly used for an instrument which seeks information about the respondent's personal history or opinions. Although the item format resembles that of the multiple-choice test, the accompanying instructions make clear the fact that there are no "right answers" to the items. Typical biographical and opinion items are shown here:

> *Marital Status*
> a. single d. widowed
> b engaged e. separated
> c. married f. divorced

> The best automobile design this year is:
> a. Chevrolet
> b. Ford
> c. Plymouth

Data from instruments of this type are usually examined on an item-by-item basis, and no attempt is made to compute a summary score for each respondent, since the data have only the characteristics of a nominal scale of measurement. This does not mean that machine processing is unnecessary. With large samples of respondents, the computation of frequency distributions for items singly and in comparison is vastly simplified by the use of tab cards and computer programs.

RATING SCALES

The item format for rating scales may resemble the previous types or may emphasize the fact that the respondent is being asked to evaluate something by placing it on a scale—a dimension defined by an ordered series of alternatives. For example:

> When I was in high school I enjoyed
> a. math more than English
> b. both about equally
> c. English more than math

166 TEST SCORING AND DISTRIBUTION STATISTICS

	High		*Medium*		*Low*	
My self-confidence is	7	6	5	4	3	2	1

She is the best teacher I ever had.   TRUE true false FALSE

T F   Smoking cigarettes is sinful.

The United Nations
good:___:___:___:___:___:___:___: bad
slow:___:___:___:___:___:___:___: fast
strong:___:___:___:___:___:___:___: weak

These items have in common the characteristics of ordinal data. The choices are transferred to tab cards as integer numbers which reflect more than simply the alternative chosen; the numbers may be added to yield a score with ordinal and perhaps interval-scale qualities. In the first example, a score of 1 (alternative *a*) would mean a less positive attitude toward English than would a 2 (alternative *b*), which in turn would be lower than a score of 3 (alternative *c*). By combining scores from similar items reflecting attitudes toward quantitative versus verbal activities, one might obtain a single score on a general quantitative-verbal dimension.

In the second example, the item response directly reflects the respondent's self-rating on a "self-confidence" scale.

The circled choice in the third example could be numbered 4, 3, 2, or 1 to reflect degree of liking for the teacher in question.

The fourth example (true-false) is typical of many personality inventories. Each such item is scored 1 = true or 0 = false and scores are accumulated to reflect a composite attitude.

The last example illustrates Osgood's (1957) *Semantic Differential* technique. Each object word *(The United Nations)* is followed by a series of rating scales (usually 12 or more) bordered by polar adjectives. The respondent's check mark on each scale is recorded as a number (1–7). Such data may be analyzed in terms of respondents, object words, or individual adjective-pair scales.

To summarize: *multiple-choice tests* provide unordered alternatives and require selection of the "best" or "correct" answer. *Questionnaires* present unordered alternatives, but do not seek particular choices to the items. Finally, *rating scales* present ordered alternatives, and the ordinal position of the choice is treated directly as a score.

DATA RECORDING

Item scores (choice numbers) may be punched directly from questionnaire forms as integers in successive card columns in most cases, since few instruments provide more than nine alternatives for any item. If we reserve the first five columns for the subject's code number, 75 item scores may be recorded on one card. It is usually advisable to punch integers for the choices, reserving the zero (blank column) for missing answers.

Until recently, electrographic test-scoring machines were widely used for recording subject's responses to multiple-choice tests and for some questionnaires. These answer sheets required the use of special lead pencils to blacken spaces outlined with pairs of dashed lines.

a. ====
b. ====
c. ====
d. ====
e. ====

Item scores still had to be key-punched from these answer sheets, but special scoring machines could be used to obtain counts of predetermined right answers, if that was the investigator's only interest in the data.

In 1963 IBM introduced the 1230 Optical Mark Scoring Reader, which also requires the use of special answer sheets. A standard five-choice 150-item form is shown on a following page.

The new system provides at least three major advantages over the older electrographic technique. No special pencils are needed, the scoring machine is entirely automatic, and the reader can be attached directly to a special key-punch machine (354) which will automatically record 150 item responses on a single data card for each subject. The format for this item-data card may be adjusted, but we will assume that columns 1–5 are reserved for a subject-code number.

Since a tab card holds only 80 characters, five of which we are reserving for subject identification, the 1230 reader obviously must use a special code (shown in the table) for recording two item scores per card column. The choices for each *pair* of items are converted to a single alphameric character, which occupies one of the output-card columns. Thus, each row of the answer sheet yields four item scores which are recorded in two columns of the output card. A subroutine which decodes IBM 1230 output cards is described here. It can be incorporated into any scoring and/or analysis program that is intended to process such data cards.

1230 (KEY, INPUT, ITEM, N, KODE)

A subroutine to decode IBM 1230 "Special" Marking Code data cards.

A special key card with characters in certain columns from 1 to 55 must be read by the calling program and stored prior to the first CALL of this subroutine. This 55-element vector is transmitted to the routine as vector KEY, to be used as a reference in the decoding process. The subroutine is called once for each data card to be processed. In the calling program, the characters representing the subject's choices on the N items are read (A mode) into a vector equated to INPUT. The subject's code number is also

168   TEST SCORING AND DISTRIBUTION STATISTICS

transmitted (KODE) to permit his identification by an error-print in case the data are mispunched or misread. The subroutine returns a list of the choice-position integers for the N items in vector ITEM (Figure 8-1).

SPECIAL 1230 MARKING CODE

Item Responses		Punched in		Item Responses		Punched in	
First	Second	Card Column		First	Second	Card Column	
1	1	0–5	(V)	4	4	11–8–3	($)
1	2	0–6	(W)	4	5	11–8–4	(*)
1	3	0–7	(X)	5	1	1	(1)
1	4	0–3	(T)	5	2	2	(2)
1	5	0–4	(U)	5	3	9	(9)
2	1	11–5	(N)	5	4	0–8–3	(,)
2	2	11–6	(O)	5	5	0–8–4	(()
2	3	11–7	(P)	1		0	(0)
2	4	11–3	(L)	2		11	(–)
2	5	11–4	(M)	3		8	(8)
3	1	11–1	(J)	4		11–8	(Q)
3	2	11–2	(K)	5		0–8	(Y)
3	3	11–9	(R)		1	5	(5)
3	4	8–3	(=)		2	6	(6)
3	5	8–4	(@)		3	7	(7)
4	1	0–1	(/)		4	3	(3)
4	2	0–2	(S)		5	4	(4)
4	3	0–9	(Z)			blank	

The decoding technique used here is not immediately obvious. Each *possible* input character is located in a particular cell of the KEY vector. The two-digit number corresponding to the *index* of that cell, when split into two separate digits, defines the pair of item-choices represented by the character. Thus, whenever a character from INPUT is the letter S, it will match cell 42 of vector KEY, and the two item scores will be known to have been 4 and 2.

```
      SUBROUTINE I230 (KEY, INPUT, ITEM, N, KODE)
C
C     TRANSLATE DATA FROM IBM1230 SPECIAL MARKING CODE.
C     KEY = DECODING SYMBOL VECTOR.
C     INPUT = DATA TO BE DECODED (2 ITEMS PER CELL).
C     ITEM = OUTPUT VECTOR OF ITEM-CHOICE INTEGERS.
C     N = NUMBER OF ITEMS REPRESENTED IN INPUT.
C     KODE = SUBJECT-CODE BLOCK.
C
      DIMENSION KEY(55), INPUT(75), ITEM(150)
      K = 1
      DO 20 I = 1,N,2
      DO 5 J = 1,55
      IF (KEY(J) .EQ. INPUT(K)) GO TO 15
    5 CONTINUE
      PRINT 10, KODE
   10 FORMAT (18H0ERROR FOR SUBJECT, A7)
      STOP
   15 IF (J .EQ. 6) J = 0
      ITEM (I+1) = MOD(J, 10)
      ITEM(I) = J / 10
   20 K = K + 1
      RETURN
      END
```

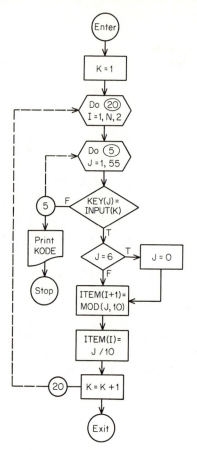

FIGURE 8-1. Flow chart for Subroutine 1230.

PROGRAM TESTAT

Program TESTAT has a wide range of applications, but in one sense it illustrates the impossibility of constructing a program which will meet all needs for test scoring or item analysis. Many of the programming techniques employed, however, are generally useful and will reappear in later programs.

Probably the most important programming concept involved here is that of the *key card*. A sequence of values or symbols is read and stored in the computer memory prior to the reading of the data cards to be processed. These values then serve as a reference vector during the processing of one subject's data. Key cards and their corresponding storage vectors are used in Program TESTAT to provide the decoding key for 1230-card input, to indicate the items for which scaling is to be reversed, to indicate the correct-choice numbers, and to assign items to subscales. In the processing of any particular problem, only the necessary key cards — as indicated by Parameter Control Card signals — are read into memory (Figure 8-2).

The program begins by calling Subroutine CCDS to input a Title, Parameter, and Format Control Card. If the data cards to follow were punched by the IBM 1230-534 machine, column 11 on the Parameter card should be set = 1, and the format should specify $(N + 1) / 2$ single-character (A1) fields. If the item scores were key punched directly as integer digits, however, column 11 should be zero or blank and the format should specify N integer-mode score fields (I1) where N represents the number of items (columns 1-5 on the Parameter card).

This program illustrates the breakdown of five-digit integer numbers returned by Subroutine CCDS into single-digit parameter values through the use of integer division and the MOD Function. Note also the manner in which the index number of the total score (KT) is set to follow the last subscale (if any). The 1230-key card is read immediately after the format card if column 11 = 1. Next the key card for directionality reversal is read if column 13 is nonzero; the value in column 13 should be the number of choices per item in this case. The next key card read will be a list of the correct-choice numbers if column 14 = 1. If column 11 = 1 also, this key card should be a 1230 card in the same format as the data cards. This key card can be produced easily by including a key answer sheet along with the subjects' answer sheets when they are processed by the IBM 1230 machine. Finally, if column 15 is nonzero on the Parameter card, a key card containing a subscale number for each item will be read. Following these control and key cards in the problem deck will be the data cards for the respondents to be scored.

ARRANGEMENT OF THE INPUT DECK FOR PROGRAM TESTAT

System Control Card(s)
Program and Subprogram Decks
System Control Card(s) _____
Title Control Card
Parameter Control Card
Format Control Card
IBM 1230 Key Card (optional)   Problem deck
Directionality-Reversal Key Card (optional)
Correct-Choice Key Card (optional)
Subscale-Assignment Key Card (optional)
Data Cards for Respondents _____
Next Problem Deck or a Blank Card
System Control Cards

172 TEST SCORING AND DISTRIBUTION STATISTICS

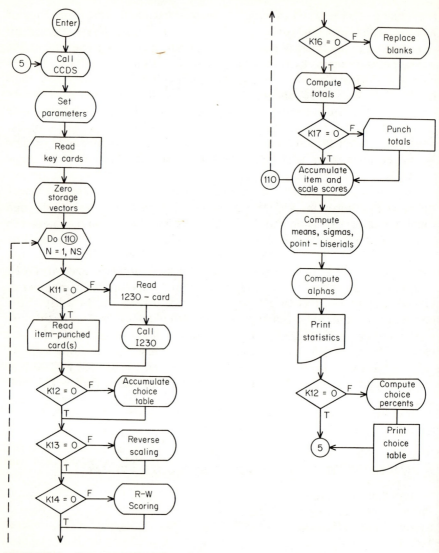

FIGURE 8-2. Program TESTAT flow chart.

As noted among the comments in the program listing, any or all of the four key cards may be omitted, depending on the nature of the processing problem. A standard format is assumed for the last three key cards: (5X, 75I1). Vectors to hold alpha coefficients (A), numbers of items per subscale (F), scale means (AT) and sigmas (ST) are zeroed next. If a subscale key card was input, the numbers of items per subscale are computed next and stored in vector F. The KTth location in F holds the total number of items. The next loop zeros vectors for item means (AI) and sigmas (SI), item-total correlations (RT), and item-scale correlations (RS), as well as the choice-distribution matrix (KP). If no subscale or right-answer key cards are input, the respective vectors are zeroed to avoid confusion in the printed output.

The subject-data input begins next. Subroutine I230 is used if 1230-card input is indicated by parameter column 11. The item choices are registered in table KP if parameter column 12 = 1. The directionality of selected item scales is reversed next if parameter column 13 is nonzero. This is accomplished by subtracting the choice number from K13 + 1, when the value of K13 is the number of choices (scale points) per item. Thus, with a 7-point rating scale, an item value of 6 would be changed to 2, 3 would be changed to 5, and so forth, for those items whose key-card signal = 1.

The next step is right-wrong scoring if parameter column 14 = 1; the choice numbers are converted to 1 if they match the key card and 0 if they do not. The next step is to replace blank (item score = 0) responses with the contents of parameter column 16, if this parameter is not zero. This option permits insertion of a middle-of-the-scale score for blank items in rating scale data (see example problem two).

Subscale and total scores are accumulated in vector XT. Item scores are converted to real-mode and stored in vector XI before accumulation to avoid repetitive mode conversions. The subject's scale and total scores are punched next if parameter column 17 = 1. Then item, scale, and total scores are added to the appropriate accumulation vectors. At this point in the program all data input is complete, and output cards have been punched, if required.

Item, scale, and total means and sigmas are computed next, as well as point-biserial correlations between items and the scale scores to which they have been assigned. Vector RT thus holds a correlation of every item with the total of all items, while vector RS holds a correlation of every item with some particular subtotal. This loop also accumulates the sum of item sigmas for each scale and the total; alpha coefficients are computed next, before the output printing starts.

The alpha coefficient of internal consistency (Cronbach, 1951) reflects the degree of reliability among the items of a scale, in terms of overlapping variance. The formula is a generalization of the Kuder-Richardson Formula 20 for dichotomous items:

$$\alpha = \frac{K}{K-1}\left[\frac{\sigma_T^2 - \sum_{I}^{K}\sigma_I^2}{\sigma_T^2}\right]$$

where K = the number of items in the scale
I = item
T = total (or subscale total)

The final stage in the program is the printing of scale and total item

174   TEST SCORING AND DISTRIBUTION STATISTICS

counts, means, and sigmas, and alpha coefficients. A table of item means, sigmas, scale assignments (if any), and correlations with scale sums and total score is next printed. If parameter column $12 = 1$, the percentages of the sample using each possible item choice are printed, along with the corresponding values from the reversal and correct-choice key vectors.

```
C         PROGRAM TESTAT
C
C   ITEM ANALYSIS AND SCORING OF CHOICE-RESPONSE INSTRUMENTS.
C   PARAMETER CONTROL-CARD FIELDS.
C         COL 1 - 5. NUMBER OF ITEMS (MAX = 150)
C         COL 6 - 10. NUMBER OF SUBJECTS
C         COL 11. DATA INPUT OPTION. 0 = ITEM-PUNCHED, 1 = 1230-CARDS.
C         COL 12. 1 = PRINT CHOICE DISTRIBUTIONS, AS PUNCHED.
C         COL 13. ENTER NUMBER OF CHOICES PER ITEM IF DIRECTIONALITY IS TO
C                 BE REVERSED FOR KEYED ITEMS. IF BLANK, NO DIRECTIONALITY
C                 KEY CARD WILL BE EXPECTED. (MAX CHOICES = 5 FOR 1230-CARD
C                 INPUT, 9 OTHERWISE)
C         COL 14. 1 = CONVERT CHOICES TO 1 = RIGHT, 0 = WRONG, USING
C                 CORRECT-CHOICE KEY.
C         COL 15. NUMBER OF SUBSCALES (MAX = 9) 0 = TOTAL ONLY.
C         COL 16. CONSTANT TO REPLACE BLANK ITEMS.
C         COL 17. 1 = PUNCH CARDS FOR SUBJECTS (SUBTOTALS AND TOTAL SCORE).
C   FORMAT CONTROL CARD MUST SPECIFY A SUBJECT ID BLOCK (MAX = A6)
C         BEFORE ITEM-SCORE FIELDS. USE A-MODE FOR 1230-CARD INPUT,
C         BUT SPECIFY INTEGER FIELDS FOR ITEM-PUNCHED INPUT.
C   KEY CARDS REQUIRED BY SELECTED OPTIONS FOLLOW THE FORMAT CONTROL CARD.
C         1. 1230 CONVERSION KEY (SEE TEXT). WHEN COL 11 = 1.
C         2. DIRECTIONALITY KEY (1 = REVERSE). WHEN COL 13 = NON-ZERO.
C         3. RIGHT-WRONG SCORING KEY (CORRECT-CHOICE NUMBERS). WHEN COL 14 = 1
C            IF COL 11 = 1, KEY CARD SHOULD BE A 1230 CARD.
C         4. SUBSCALING KEY (SCALE NUMBERS). WHEN COL 15 = NON-ZERO.
C         ANY OR ALL OF THESE CARDS MAY BE OMITTED. NO. 2, 3, 4 BEGIN WITH
C            COL 6 = ITEM 1, AND MAY CONTINUE TO A SECOND CARD IF NECESSARY.
C   SUBPROGRAMS REQUIRED ARE CCDS, PRTS, AND I230.
C
          DIMENSION KC(55), KD(150), KE(150), KF(16), KG(150), KX(75),
         1 KI(150), KP(150,10), A(10), F(10), AT(10), ST(10), AI(150),
         2 SI(150), RT(150), RS(150), XT(10), XI(150)
        5 CALL CCDS (KF, NI, NS, KA, KB, I)
C   SET PARAMETERS.
          K11 = KA / 10000
          K12 = MOD(KA / 1000, 10)
          K13 = MOD(KA / 100, 10)
          K14 = MOD(KA / 10, 10)
          K15 = MOD(KA, 10)
          K16 = KB / 10000
          K17 = MOD(KB / 1000, 10)
          NC = (NI + 1) / 2
          KT = K15 + 1
C   READ KEY CARDS.
          IF (K11 .EQ. 1) READ 10, KC
       10 FORMAT (55A1)
          IF (K13 .GT. 0) READ 15, (KD(I), I = 1,NI)
       15 FORMAT (5X, 75I1)
          IF (K14 .EQ. 0) GO TO 18
          IF (K11 .EQ. 0) GO TO 17
          READ KF, ID, (KX(I), I = 1,NC)
          CALL I230 (KC, KX, KE, NI, ID)
          GO TO 18
       17 READ 15, (KE(I), I = 1,NI)
       18 IF (K15 .GT. 0) READ 15, (KG(I), I = 1,NI)
```

```
C     ZERO STORAGE VECTORS.
      DO 20 I = 1,KT
      A(I) = 0.0
      F(I) = 0.0
      AT(I) = 0.0
   20 ST(I) = 0.0
      IF (K15 .EQ. 0) GO TO 30
      DO 25 I = 1,NI
      K = KG(I)
   25 F(K) = F(K) + 1.0
   30 F(KT) = NI
      DO 35 I = 1,NI
      IF (K13 .EQ. 0) KD(I) = 0
      IF (K14 .EQ. 0) KE(I) = 0
      IF (K15 .EQ. 0) KG(I) = 0
      AI(I) = 0.0
      SI(I) = 0.0
      RT(I) = 0.0
      RS(I) = 0.0
      DO 35 J = 1,10
   35 KP(I,J) = 0
      DO 110 N = 1,NS
C     DATA INPUT OPTION.
      IF (K11 .EQ. 0) GO TO 40
      READ KF, ID, (KX(I), I = 1,NC)
      CALL I230 (KC, KX, KI, NI, ID)
      GO TO 45
   40 READ KF, ID, (KI(I), I = 1,NI)
C     CHOICE DISTRIBUTION ACCUMULATION.
   45 IF (K12 .EQ. 0) GO TO 55
      DO 50 I = 1,NI
      J = KI(I) + 1
   50 KP(I,J) = KP(I,J) + 1
C     DIRECTIONALITY REVERSAL.
   55 IF (K13 .EQ. 0) GO TO 65
      DO 60 I = 1,NI
      IF (KI(I) .GT. 0 .AND. KD(I) .EQ. 1) KI(I) = K13 + 1 - KI(I)
   60 CONTINUE
C     RIGHT-WRONG SCORING.
   65 IF (K14 .EQ. 0) GO TO 75
      DO 70 I = 1,NI
      KK = 1
      IF (KE(I) .NE. KI(I)) KK = 0
   70 KI(I) = KK
C     BLANK-ITEM REPLACEMENT.
   75 IF (K16 .EQ. 0) GO TO 85
      DO 80 I = 1,NI
      IF (KI(I) .EQ. 0) KI(I) = K16
   80 CONTINUE
C     SUBSCALE AND TOTAL COMPUTATION, AND PUNCHED OUTPUT.
   85 DO 90 I = 1,KT
   90 XT(I) = 0.0
      DO 95 I = 1,NI
      XI(I) = KI(I)
      IF (K15 .EQ. 0) GO TO 95
      J = KG(I)
      XT(J) = XT(J) + XI(I)
   95 XT(KT) = XT(KT) + XI(I)
      IF (K17 .EQ. 1) PUNCH 100, ID, (XT(I), I = 1,KT)
  100 FORMAT (A6, 4H QS , 10F7.0)
C     ACCUMULATE ITEM AND SCALE SUMS.
      DO 105 I = 1,KT
      AT(I) = AT(I) + XT(I)
  105 ST(I) = ST(I) + XT(I)**2
      DO 110 I = 1,NI
```

```
      AI(I) = AI(I) + XI(I)
      SI(I) = SI(I) + XI(I)**2
      IF (K15 .EQ. 0) GO TO 110
      J = KG(I)
      RS(I) = RS(I) + XT(J) * XI(I)
  110 RT(I) = RT(I) + XT(KT) * XI(I)
C   COMPUTE MEANS, SIGMAS, BISERIALS.
      SN = NS
      DO 115 I = 1,KT
      AT(I) = AT(I) / SN
  115 ST(I) = SQRT(ST(I) / SN - AT(I)**2)
      DO 120 I = 1,NI
      AI(I) = AI(I) / SN
      Q = SI(I) / SN - AI(I)**2
      SI(I) = SQRT(Q)
      RT(I) = (RT(I) / SN - AT(KT) * AI(I)) / (ST(KT) * SI(I))
      IF (K15 .EQ. 0) GO TO 120
      J = KG(I)
      RS(I) = (RS(I) / SN - AT(J) * AI(I)) / (ST(J) * SI(I))
      A(J) = A(J) + Q
  120 A(KT) = A(KT) + Q
C   COMPUTE ALPHA COEFFICIENTS, AND PRINT RESULTS.
      DO 125 I = 1,KT
      Q = ST(I)**2
  125 A(I) = (F(I) / (F(I) - 1.0)) * ((Q - A(I)) / Q)
      CALL PRTS (F, KT, 1, 6HITEM N, 10)
      CALL PRTS (AT, KT, 1, 5HMEANS, 10)
      CALL PRTS (ST, KT, 1, 6HSIGMAS, 10)
      CALL PRTS (A, KT, 1, 6HALPHAS, 10)
      PRINT 130
  130 FORMAT ( /45H1ITEM  SCALE   MEAN   SIGMA  R(TOTAL) R(SCALE))
      PRINT 135, (I, KG(I), AI(I), SI(I), RT(I), RS(I), I = 1,NI)
  135 FORMAT (I4, I6, F8.2, F7.3, F9.4, F10.4)
      IF (K12 .EQ. 0) GO TO 5
C   COMPUTE CHOICE PERCENTAGES AND PRINT.
      DO 140 I = 1,NI
      DO 140 J = 1,10
      P = KP(I,J)
  140 KP(I,J) = P / SN * 100.0 + 0.4999
      PRINT 145, (I, I = 1,9)
  145 FORMAT (36H1CHOICE DISTRIBUTIONS (PERCENTAGES). //
     1 21H ITEM  REV  KEY ZERO, 9I5 / 1X)
      PRINT 150, (I, KD(I), KE(I), (KP(I,J), J = 1,10), I = 1,NI)
  150 FORMAT (I4, 2I5, 2I6, 8I5)
      GO TO 5
      END
```

EXAMPLE PROBLEM 1

Example Problem 1 illustrates the use of data cards punched by the IBM 1230-534 machine. Although 20 items are indicated on the Parameter card, the format specifies only 10 A-mode fields, since each character represents two items. The 1230-decoding-key card and a right-answer-key card come next in the input deck, followed by data cards for 16 subjects. As indicated by the Title card, these scores might represent answers to a classroom examination.

EXAMPLE PROBLEM 2

Example Problem 2 exemplifies the use of item-punched data cards with a 48-item rating-type *Self Report Inventory* (Bown, 1961) which is scored for

Output Listings   177

eight subscales and a total. Of the 48 items, 25 require scale reversal as part of the scoring system. Since item-score values will be accumulated to form Likert-scale (Likert, 1932) scores and a general total, no right-wrong scoring key card is used. The cards output by this program will be used to illustrate the operation of most of the programs to be presented in subsequent chapters.

OUTPUT LISTINGS

Because some of the output from the programs in this book was obtained from an IBM 7040 system, while other listings were obtained from a CDC 1604 computer, a certain amount of inconsistency may be noted from time to time in minor details of the output format. The IBM system inserts leading integer zeros before all decimal fractions, while the CDC system omits them.

Paging may be determined by the presence of the numeral 1 in print position one. This column of the printed output is normally omitted from printed output, but is included here for purposes of illustration.

```
    *** INPUT DATA DECK ***
TESTAT EXAMPLE PROBLEM 1. POP QUIZ
00020000161101001
(A5,10A1)
56734     OVWXTU     -NOPLM     8JKR=-     Q/SZ$*     Y129,(          1230 KEY CARD
KEY   NW9V=V-OKW
S01PQV21W=1RORK
S02PQN212=VUWKW
S03PQO671=V*-KW
S04PQNW9W=V-OS6
S05PQN$9W=VR-TW
S06PQJT(V=V-LKW
S07PQNKRV=NRNKW
S08PQO2MVRXRL2W
S09PQN29V=N-NT=
S10PQOU9V=VMLKW
S11PQ-T9J$5--KW
S12PQJW(2=K7O6K
S13PQ50Y5=V4P6W
S14PQNV9J=V-LKW
S15PQNW9V=V-LKW
S16PQK/91=OXPYW
TESTAT EXAMPLE PROBLEM 2. SRI SCORING
00048000160050831
(A6, 4X, 48I1)
REVER1011010101010000101011010101010101001110101101
SCALE257843165278431678314625317852461435628571843726
S01SRI       242242414231535415234235142534133313331254133 31
S02SRI       1522 141514231531514111152515151515 151114151151
S03SRI       212152525221541145235412423244153255512221522 51
S04SRI       141151544151525245151411514152515251541115151151
S05SRI       112211424151515345 1 512415142 1 45454211 151121
S06SRI       111241514152515155152511153311233555 51115151121
S07SRI       12125151 4525153543432135151434151451422141 51151
S08SRI       141241414232415335231412525251524252452115251151
S09SRI       141131525121515325142511521151314151352134141552
```

```
S10SRI     2311514151515153551525125153511425 551115151151
S11SRI     15215142513151512514151253514252425254213425125 2
S12SRI     1412514351515452552323125152514242513511115251142
S13SRI     1412525241424254452532225152522525244221525215 3
S14SRI     1412515 515152525315121251514151425 251115141141
S15SRI     2411415441525252551423125151325152425211151411 52
S16SRI     2411315142513151551531125253412151523311151411 51
```

*** PUNCHED OUTPUT ***

```
S01PQ  QS  12.
S02PQ  QS  14.
S03PQ  QS  14.
S04PQ  QS  17.
S05PQ  QS  13.
S06PQ  QS  16.
S07PQ  QS  15.
S08PQ  QS  11.
S09PQ  QS  13.
S10PQ  QS  16.
S11PQ  QS  14.
S12PQ  QS  10.
S13PQ  QS  13.
S14PQ  QS  17.
S15PQ  QS  19.
S16PQ  QS   8.
S01SRI QS  25.  21.  22.  20.  26.  26.  19.  23.  1
S02SRI QS  26.  30.  30.  26.  28.  20.  24.  28.  2
S03SRI QS  20.  25.  20.  23.  18.  24.  21.  29.  1
S04SRI QS  30.  28.  29.  29.  28.  23.  28.  30.  2
S05SRI QS  23.  25.  29.  19.  20.  27.  28.  28.  1
S06SRI QS  28.  27.  30.  22.  19.  25.  30.  26.  2
S07SRI QS  28.  24.  27.  27.  17.  21.  30.  26.  2
S08SRI QS  25.  29.  29.  27.  26.  25.  26.  25.  2
S09SRI QS  26.  30.  30.  24.  29.  24.  14.  29.  2
S10SRI QS  28.  29.  30.  26.  25.  28.  30.  28.  2
S11SRI QS  24.  28.  30.  29.  27.  23.  21.  28.  2
S12SRI QS  26.  29.  26.  27.  28.  19.  30.  27.  2
S13SRI QS  30.  27.  26.  24.  25.  21.  28.  25.  2
S14SRI QS  29.  29.  29.  28.  25.  19.  30.  27.  2
S15SRI QS  29.  25.  28.  26.  24.  21.  30.  29.  2
S16SRI QS  29.  26.  30.  20.  25.  20.  30.  28.  2
```

*** PRINTED OUTPUT ***

1TESTAT EXAMPLE PROBLEM 1. POP QUIZ

```
PARAMETERS
COL  1- 5 =      20
COL  6-10 =      16
COL 11-15 =   11010
COL 16-20 =    1000
COL 21-25 =       0

DATA FORMAT = (A5,10A1)

    ITEM N            1
                20.0000
```

MEANS   1
              13.8750

SIGMAS   1
               2.7358

ALPHAS   1
                .5362

1ITEM	SCALE	MEAN	SIGMA	R(TOTAL)	R(SCALE)
1	0	.69	.464	.5114	.0000
2	0	.69	.464	.3142	.0000
3	0	.50	.500	.5026	.0000
4	0	.56	.496	.0058	.0000
5	0	.81	.390	.0951	.0000
6	0	.63	.484	.3421	.0000
7	0	.56	.496	.3281	.0000
8	0	.69	.464	.1663	.0000
9	0	.94	.242	-.0118	.0000
10	0	.94	.242	.2713	.0000
11	0	.63	.484	.5309	.0000
12	0	.81	.390	.7390	.0000
13	0	.63	.484	.3893	.0000
14	0	.63	.484	.6725	.0000
15	0	.94	.242	-.0118	.0000
16	0	.25	.433	-.1319	.0000
17	0	.56	.496	.5584	.0000
18	0	.75	.433	.5012	.0000
19	0	.75	.433	.1847	.0000
20	0	.94	.242	.0826	.0000

1CHOICE DISTRIBUTIONS (PERCENTAGES).

ITEM	REV	KEY	ZERO	1	2	3	4	5	6	7	8	9
1	0	2	6	6	69	19	0	0	0	0	0	0
2	0	1	6	69	25	0	0	0	0	0	0	0
3	0	1	6	50	0	6	12	25	0	0	0	0
4	0	2	6	12	56	0	19	6	0	0	0	0
5	0	5	6	0	6	6	0	81	0	0	0	0
6	0	3	6	12	0	62	0	19	0	0	0	0
7	0	1	6	56	0	12	0	25	0	0	0	0
8	0	1	0	69	31	0	0	0	0	0	0	0
9	0	3	0	0	0	94	6	0	0	0	0	0
10	0	4	0	0	0	6	94	0	0	0	0	0
11	0	1	6	62	19	6	0	6	0	0	0	0
12	0	1	0	81	12	6	0	0	0	0	0	0
13	0	3	12	12	6	62	6	0	0	0	0	0
14	0	5	0	0	0	37	0	62	0	0	0	0
15	0	2	0	6	94	0	0	0	0	0	0	0
16	0	2	19	12	25	12	31	0	0	0	0	0
17	0	3	12	12	0	56	6	12	0	0	0	0
18	0	2	6	0	75	6	12	0	0	0	0	0
19	0	1	6	75	0	19	0	0	0	0	0	0
20	0	2	0	0	94	0	6	0	0	0	0	0

1TESTAT EXAMPLE PROBLEM 2. SRI SCORING

```
PARAMETERS
COL  1- 5 =      48
COL  6-10 =      16
COL 11-15 =     508
COL 16-20 =   31000
COL 21-25 =       0
```

DATA FORMAT = (A6, 4X, 48I1)

ITEM N	1	2	3	4	5	6	7	8	9
	5.0000	6.0000	6.0000	6.0000	6.0000	6.0000	6.0000	6.0000	48.0000
MEANS	1	2	3	4	5	6	7	8	9
	26.6250	27.0000	27.8125	24.8125	24.3750	22.8750	26.1875	27.2500	206.9375
SIGMAS	1	2	3	4	5	6	7	8	9
	2.6897	2.4238	2.9202	3.1269	3.6891	2.7585	4.8117	1.7854	11.9188
ALPHAS	1	2	3	4	5	6	7	8	9
	.6117	.4484	.8125	.4689	.7433	.1626	.8763	.3176	.7604

ITEM	SCALE	MEAN	SIGMA	R(TOTAL)	R(SCALE)
1	2	4.69	.464	.3245	.5007
2	5	3.38	1.317	.4355	.8844
3	7	4.69	.464	.5848	.5027
4	8	4.44	.496	.1738	.7233
5	4	4.13	1.111	.1705	.6544
6	3	4.81	.390	.7095	.8465
7	1	4.56	.496	-.0258	.4391
8	6	4.06	1.029	-.3259	.3551
9	5	4.38	.599	.1607	.4734
10	2	4.56	.788	.4429	.5235
11	7	4.13	1.111	.5339	.9075
12	8	4.63	.484	-.0799	.3254
13	4	4.63	.696	-.1234	.1687
14	3	4.25	1.031	.4286	.8254
15	1	4.75	.968	.5835	.6360
16	6	2.38	.992	-.0932	.2227
17	7	3.75	1.436	.2948	.8117
18	8	4.81	.527	-.1114	.1163
19	3	4.56	.609	.4869	.6214
20	1	4.06	.827	.5966	.7975
21	4	3.81	1.073	.7856	.6412
22	6	3.44	1.413	-.0726	.8159
23	2	4.88	.331	.4103	.4678
24	5	4.13	.599	.4734	.3462
25	3	4.88	.331	.5530	.4287
26	1	4.56	.609	.0909	.4720
27	7	4.50	1.061	.3189	.7899
28	8	4.31	.768	.0431	.3077
29	5	4.31	.768	.3094	.7087
30	2	4.25	.901	.7403	.7438
31	4	3.81	1.184	.1586	.6825
32	6	4.69	.464	-.1393	.0672
33	1	4.25	.750	.1905	.2943
34	4	3.94	.827	.4182	.4548
35	3	4.56	.864	.8048	.8843
36	5	3.38	1.409	.3104	.8990
37	6	3.69	1.402	.0587	.5718
38	2	4.25	.901	.1585	.6579
39	8	4.50	.612	.5009	.6288
40	5	4.81	.390	.4677	.5697
41	7	4.63	.696	.3588	.8795
42	1	4.44	.864	.5855	.7970
43	8	4.56	.788	.4163	.7440
44	4	4.50	1.000	.4483	.4098
45	3	4.75	.559	.7293	.8136
46	7	4.50	1.061	.3832	.9001
47	2	4.38	1.053	.2956	.3427
48	6	4.63	.599	-.0908	.3118

PROGRAM DISTAT

Program DISTAT is intended to provide descriptive statistical information about each of a series of variables, based on a particular sample of subjects. It will also punch a new deck of data cards containing ordinal (percentile) or interval-scale standard scores derived from the input data. The following formulas are used to compute the statistical indexes:

N = number of subjects in the sample
MEAN = M = μ = $\Sigma X/N$

SIGMA = σ = standard deviation (population parameter)
$= \sqrt{\Sigma X^2/N - \mu^2}$

STD.DEV. = S = standard deviation (sample statistic)
$= \sqrt{(\Sigma X^2 - NM^2) / (N-1)}$

SIGMA(M) = σ_M = standard error of the mean (population parameter)
$= \sigma / \sqrt{N}$

S.D.(M) = S_M = standard error of the mean (sample statistic)
$= S / \sqrt{N}$

SUMX = ΣX = sum of all scores

SUMX2 = ΣX^2 = sum of all squared scores

SKEWNESS = $\dfrac{U3}{U2 \sqrt{U2} \text{ (SES)}}$ = critical ratio for skewness

KURTOSIS = $\left[\dfrac{U4}{(U2)^2} - 3\right]\left[\dfrac{1}{2SES}\right]$ = critical ratio for kurtosis

The formulas for skewness and kurtosis employ the first four moments of the distribution and the standard error for skewness (SES) which are defined as follows (McNemar, 1962):

U1 = μ U2 = σ^2
U3 = $\Sigma X^3/N - 3(\Sigma X^2/N)\mu + 2\mu^2$
U4 = $\Sigma X^4/N - 4(\Sigma X^3/N)\mu + 6(\Sigma X^2/N)\mu^2 - 3\mu^4$
SES = $\sqrt{6/N}$

The critical ratios may be interpreted as z scores, and probabilities are automatically computed with Function PRBF and printed for them. The sign of the critical ratio indicates the direction of skewness. For example, if the skewness value for a particular distribution was −2.58, the scores would tend to pile up at the high end of the scale. The probability would be .01 that the sample had been drawn randomly from a population of scores which were symmetrically distributed around the mean. Similarly, the sign of the critical ratio for kurtosis indicates whether the distribution is abnormally flat (platykurtic) or peaked (leptokurtic). For instance, a critical ratio for kurtosis of −1.96 indicates an unusually flattened distribution; the probability printed would be .05 in this case. A normally distributed, large sample of z scores will have a mean = 0.0, sigma = 1.0, skewness = 0.0, and kurtosis = 0.0.

The population parameters σ and σ_M are appropriate measures if the data are considered as the entire population, while S and S_M should be used as estimates of the population parameters when the data are considered a sample drawn at random from some infinite population.

Also printed for each variable will be a distribution of raw scores, their frequencies and percentages of N, and their percentile and standard score ($\mu = 50$, $\sigma = 10$) equivalents. If the scores in a particular distribution are integer values between zero and 99 (inclusive), the raw-score values printed will be exact; in all other cases the distribution will be grouped to yield a maximum of 100 intervals, and the raw-scores printed will be approximations of the midpoints of these intervals.

It should be apparent from the formula for z that conversion of the input scores to this standard-score form changes only the scaling of the scores, and does not affect the *shape* of the distribution, with regard to its third and fourth (or higher) moments: $z = (x - \mu) / \sigma$

The same thing may be said of conversion to standard scores with $\mu = 50$ and $\sigma = 10$, since this is a linear transformation of z scores which have $\mu = 0$ and $\sigma = 1$: $T = z(10) + 50$.

In percentile conversion, however, the new distribution will tend toward rectangularity, regardless of the shape of the distribution of raw scores.

The program's operational sequence is described by the flow chart in Figure 8-3. The routine begins by calling Subroutine CCDS, which returns the data-card format and three parameters. I and J in this CALL statement are dummy variables. After rewinding the temporary data-storage tape (unit 2), the KI vector (data-range signals), part of the A matrix (statistics), and the N matrix (frequencies) are zeroed.

As the data are read, they are output on magnetic tape and the first four powers of each score are computed and added to cells of A. The scores are then checked to see that they are integer and within the 0–99 range. If either of these conditions is not met, the cell of KI corresponding to the variable number of the score is set $= 1$ to serve as a signal later in the program. Distribution statistics are computed next and the results are held in A.

In the next section the data tape is rewound and read. As each subject's data are input, they are converted to z scores (vector D) and to T scores (vector KD) temporarily. The frequency-distribution table is built up by using an integer index (K) derived from the raw score (1 is added to avoid a zero index) or from the T value in KD if the signal in KI $= 1$. Standard scores (z or T) are output in this loop if selected by the option KC.

Percentiles are computed and stored in matrix M in the next section, using the following formula:

$$P_x = (2(CF) + X)(50/N)$$

where X = the frequency of the raw-score value
CF = cumulative frequency below score X
N = total number of subjects

Probabilities for skewness and kurtosis are computed next, and the descriptive statistics in A are printed. The tables of frequencies, percent-

184 TEST SCORING AND DISTRIBUTION STATISTICS

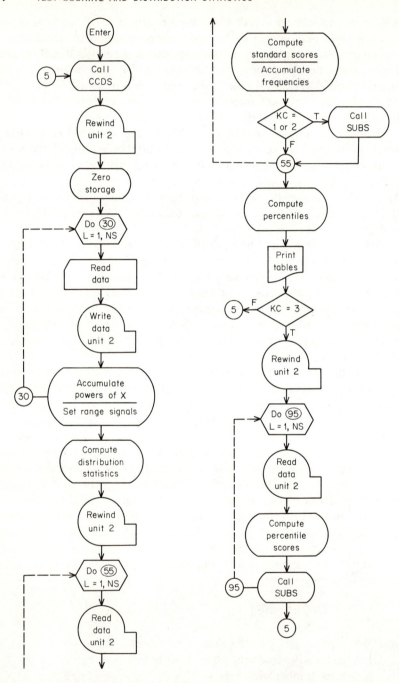

FIGURE 8-3. Program DISTAT flow chart.

ages, percentile and T-score equivalents are then printed. In this sequence raw-score values or approximations with zero frequencies are skipped; the computations are carried out in accordance with the signal in vector KI. If the option KC = 3 the next section of the program computes and punches percentile scores for each subject.

Although this program could be used with data cards that hold many item scores, such as those input to Program TESTAT, it would yield a considerable amount of relatively useless printed output, compared to TESTAT. This program is intended for use with variables that have a reasonably wide range of values—for which the statistical indexes computed will have some meaning and usefulness.

COMPUTER SYSTEMS WITHOUT TAPE UNITS

Almost all computer systems with large enough core storage units to accommodate the programs in this book also have magnetic tape units for temporary data storage. Many of these programs require the use of temporary tape storage. Some computers employ other types of devices such as magnetic discs. It should be relatively easy to adapt the programs to use these other storage devices if tapes are not available. Smaller computers may have no auxiliary storage devices. To accomplish the purposes of the programs in this book, extensive rewriting of some programs would be necessary. Probably, one would find it best to break the processes of a large package program into subunits which would operate as independent programs producing intermediate output on tab cards.

EXAMPLE PROBLEM

In order to conserve space, we have used only the first scale score and the total score on the output cards from Program TESTAT (problem two) to illustrate the output from Program DISTAT. Thus, two variables are indicated on the parameter card, and the format only specifies two score fields. The printed tables illustrate the use of data which do (scale 1) and do not (total) satisfy the integer/range criteria in the program. The punched output illustrates the use of the Z-score option.

```
C      PROGRAM DISTAT
C
C    CONTROL PROGRAM FOR DISTRIBUTION STATISTICS AND STANDARD SCORES.
C    PARAMETER CONTROL-CARD FIELDS.
C       COL 1-5. NUMBER OF VARIABLES (MAX = 70).
C       COL 6-10. NUMBER OF SUBJECTS.
C       COL 15. OUTPUT OPTION FOR STANDARD SCORES. 1 = Z-SCORES,
C          2 = STANDARD SCORES (M=50,S=10), 3 = PERCENTILES.
C    TAPE UNIT 2 IS USED FOR TEMPORARY STORAGE (SCRATCH).
C    SEE DESCRIPTION OF SUBROUTINE SUBS FOR MORE DETAIL REGARDING OUTPUT.
C    FORMAT MUST SPECIFY ID FIELD BEFORE SCORE FIELDS.
C    SUBROUTINES REQUIRED ARE CCDS, PRBF, AND SUBS.
C
```

186 TEST SCORING AND DISTRIBUTION STATISTICS

```
      ODIMENSION KF(16), KI(70), D(70), KD(70), A(70,9), N(100,70),
     1M(100,70)
    5 CALL CCDS (KF, NV, NS, KC, I, J)
      REWIND 2
      DO 15 I = 1,NV
      KI(I) = 0
      DO 10 J = 6,9
   10 A(I,J) = 0.0
      DO 15 J = 1,100
   15 N(J,I) = 0
C  INPUT DATA, ACCUMULATE POWERS OF X, SET RANGE SIGNALS.
      DO 30 L = 1,NS
      READ KF, ID, (D(I), I = 1,NV)
      WRITE (2) ID, (D(I), I = 1,NV)
      DO 30 I = 1,NV
      DO 20 J = 1,4
   20 A(I,J+5) = A(I,J+5) + D(I)**J
      IF (D(I) .GT. 99.0 .OR. D(I) .LT. 1.0) GO TO 25
      IF (AMOD(D(I), 1.0) .EQ. 0.0) GO TO 30
   25 KI(I) = 1
   30 CONTINUE
C  COMPUTE DISTRIBUTION STATISTICS.
      T = NS
      SE = SQRT(6.0 / T)
      DO 35 I = 1,NV
      A(I,1) = A(I,6) / T
      U2 = A(I,7) / T - A(I,1)**2
      A(I,2) = SQRT(U2)
      A(I,3) = SQRT((A(I,7) - T * A(I,1)**2) / (T - 1.0))
      A(I,4) = A(I,2) / SQRT(T)
      A(I,5) = A(I,3) / SQRT(T)
      U3 = A(I,8) / T - 3.0 * A(I,1) * A(I,7) / T + 2.0 * A(I,1)**3
      OU4 = A(I,9) / T - 4.0 * A(I,1) * A(I,8) / T + 6.0 * A(I,1)**2
     1 * A(I,7) / T - 3.0 * A(I,1)**4
      A(I,8) = (U3 / (U2 * A(I,2))) / SE
   35 A(I,9) = (U4 / U2**2 - 3.0) / (SE + SE)
C  ACCUMULATE FREQUENCIES, PUNCH STANDARD SCORES.
      REWIND 2
      DO 55 L = 1,NS
      READ (2) ID, (D(I), I = 1,NV)
      DO 40 I = 1,NV
      K = D(I) + 1.0
      D(I) = (D(I) - A(I,1)) / A(I,2)
      KD(I) = AMAX1(1.0, AMIN1(99.0, D(I) * 10.0 + 50.5))
      IF (KI(I) .EQ. 1) K = KD(I)
   40 N(K,I) = N(K,I) + 1
      IF (KC .EQ. 0) GO TO 55
      GO TO (45, 50, 55), KC
   45 CALL SUBS (D, NV, 1HZ, ID)
      GO TO 55
   50 CALL SUBS (KD, -NV, 1HT, ID)
   55 CONTINUE
C  COMPUTE PERCENTILES AND PRINT OUTPUT.
      C = 50.0 / T
      DO 85 J = 1,NV
      CF = 0.0
      DO 60 I = 1,100
      X = N(I,J)
      M(I,J) = AMAX1(1.0, AMIN1(99.0, (2.0 * CF + X) * C + 0.5))
   60 CF = CF + X
      PS = PRBF(1.0, 1000.0, A(J,8)**2)
      PK = PRBF(1.0, 1000.0, A(J,9)**2)
      PRINT 65, J, (A(J,I), I = 1,8), PS, A(J,9), PK
  650FORMAT (9H1VARIABLE, I3, 24X, 6HMEAN =, F19.4 /
```

Example Problem

```
    1 8HOSIGMA =, F18.4, 10X, 10HSTD.DEV. =, F15.4/
    2 11HOSIGMA(M) =, F15.4, 10X, 9HS.D.(M) =, F16.4 /
    3 8HOSUM X =, F18.4, 10X, 8HSUM X2 =, F17.4 /
    4 11HOSKEWNESS =, F15.4, 5H (P =, F7.4, 1H) /
    5 11HOKURTOSIS =, F15.4, 5H (P =, F7.4, 1H) //
    657H   RAW SCORE  FREQUENCY  PERCENTAGE  PERCENTILE   STANDARD / 1X)
      DO 85 I = 1,100
      IF (N(I,J) .EQ. 0) GO TO 85
      X = N(I,J)
      KP = X / T * 100.0 + 0.5
      IF (KI(J) .EQ. 1) GO TO 70
      X = I - 1
      KS = AMAX1(1.0, AMIN1(99.0, (X - A(J,1)) / A(J,2) * 10.0 + 50.5))
      GO TO 75
   70 KS = I
      X = I
      X = A(J,2) * (X - 50.0) / 10.0 + A(J,1)
   75 PRINT 80, X, N(I,J), KP, M(I,J), KS
   80 FORMAT (F12.4, I7, 2I12, I11)
   85 CONTINUE
      IF (KC .NE. 3) GO TO 5
C COMPUTE AND PUNCH PERCENTILE SCORES.
      REWIND 2
      DO 95 L = 1,NS
      READ (2) ID, (D(I), I = 1,NV)
      DO 90 I = 1,NV
      K = D(I) + 1.0
      IF (KI(I) .EQ. 0) GO TO 90
      K = AMAX1(1.0, AMIN1(99.0, (D(I) - A(I,1)) / A(I,2) *
     1 10.0 + 50.5))
   90 KD(I) = M(K,I)
   95 CALL SUBS (KD, -NV, 1HP, ID)
      GO TO 5
      END
```

*** INPUT DATA DECK ***

```
DISTAT TEST PROBLEM
000020001600001
(A6, 4X, F7.0, 49X, F7.0)
S01SRI QS    25.    21.    22.    20.    26.    26.    19.    23.    182.
S02SRI QS    26.    30.    30.    26.    28.    20.    24.    28.    212.
S03SRI QS    20.    25.    20.    23.    18.    24.    21.    29.    180.
S04SRI QS    30.    28.    29.    29.    28.    23.    28.    30.    225.
S05SRI QS    23.    25.    29.    19.    20.    27.    28.    28.    199.
S06SRI QS    28.    27.    30.    22.    19.    25.    30.    26.    207.
S07SRI QS    28.    24.    27.    27.    17.    21.    30.    26.    200.
S08SRI QS    25.    29.    29.    27.    26.    25.    26.    25.    212.
S09SRI QS    26.    30.    30.    24.    29.    24.    14.    29.    206.
S10SRI QS    28.    29.    30.    26.    25.    28.    30.    28.    224.
S11SRI QS    24.    28.    30.    29.    27.    23.    21.    28.    210.
S12SRI QS    26.    29.    26.    27.    28.    19.    30.    27.    212.
S13SRI QS    30.    27.    26.    24.    25.    21.    28.    25.    206.
S14SRI QS    29.    29.    29.    28.    25.    19.    30.    27.    216.
S15SRI QS    29.    25.    28.    26.    24.    21.    30.    29.    212.
S16SRI QS    29.    26.    30.    20.    25.    20.    30.    28.    208.
```

*** PUNCHED OUTPUT ***

```
S01SRIZ   1    -0.6042    -2.0923
S02SRIZ   1    -0.2324     0.4247
S03SRIZ   1    -2.4631    -2.2601
S04SRIZ   1     1.2548     1.5155
S05SRIZ   1    -1.3477    -0.6660
```

```
S06SRIZ    1     0.5112      0.0052
S07SRIZ    1     0.5112     -0.5821
S08SRIZ    1    -0.6042      0.4247
S09SRIZ    1    -0.2324     -0.0787
S10SRIZ    1     0.5112      1.4316
S11SRIZ    1    -0.9760      0.2569
S12SRIZ    1    -0.2324      0.4247
S13SRIZ    1     1.2548     -0.0787
S14SRIZ    1     0.8830      0.7604
S15SRIZ    1     0.8830      0.4247
S16SRIZ    1     0.8830      0.0891
```

*** PRINTED OUTPUT ***

1DISTAT TEST PROBLEM

PARAMETERS
COL 1- 5 =   2
COL 6-10 =   16
COL 11-15 =   1
COL 16-20 =   0
COL 21-25 =   0

DATA FORMAT = (A6, 4X, F7.0, 49X, F7.0)

1VARIABLE   1   MEAN =   26.6250

0SIGMA =   2.6897   STD.DEV. =   2.7779

0SIGMA(M) =   .6724   S.D.(M) =   .6945

0SUM X =   426.0000   SUM X2 =   11458.0000

0SKEWNESS =   -1.2638 (P =   .2038)

0KURTOSIS =   .0141 (P =   .9857)

RAW SCORE	FREQUENCY	PERCENTAGE	PERCENTILE	STANDARD
20.0000	1	6	3	25
23.0000	1	6	9	37
24.0000	1	6	16	40
25.0000	2	13	25	44
26.0000	3	19	41	48
28.0000	3	19	59	55
29.0000	3	19	78	59
30.0000	2	13	94	63

1VARIABLE   2   MEAN =   206.9375

0SIGMA =   11.9188   STD.DEV. =   12.3097

0SIGMA(M) =   2.9797   S.D.(M) =   3.0774

0SUM X =   3311.0000   SUM X2 =   687443.0000

0SKEWNESS =   -1.4308 (P =   .1489)

0KURTOSIS =   .3832 (P =   .7037)

RAW SCORE	FREQUENCY	PERCENTAGE	PERCENTILE	STANDARD
179.5242	1	6	3	27
181.9079	1	6	9	29
198.5943	1	6	16	43
199.7862	1	6	22	44
205.7456	2	13	31	49
206.9375	1	6	41	50
208.1294	1	6	47	51
210.5132	1	6	53	53
211.7050	4	25	69	54
216.4726	1	6	84	58
223.6239	1	6	91	64
224.8158	1	6	97	65

Review Exercises

1. Distinguish by definitions and examples among (1) multiple-choice tests, (2) questionnaires, and (3) rating scales.
2. In the first example problem for Program TESTAT, which item is the most difficult? What does the item-total correlation for this item suggest? Which item has the highest correlation? This item is also quite easy; do all easy items have high correlations?
3. Describe the control cards for using Program TESTAT to score 100 subjects who answered the following Semantic Differential form: There are 15 items, five measuring each of Osgood's factors. The order of item assignment to factors is E, A, P, E, A, P, and so forth. In addition, all odd-numbered items are reversed on the page (high end = low factor value). Data are punched as one-digit numbers from 1 through 7, one digit per item. Blanks should be replaced by scale-point 4 in the program. Obtain three factor scores and a total score for each subject. Data-card format begins with a five-character ID, followed by five blank columns, then 15 digits.
4. What modifications of Program DISTAT would be required to include an option to omit the printed output?
5. A common problem in data processing is the conversion of a sample of scores using a nonlinear transformation. Write a program to compute squared-score transforms of the test problem data for Program DISTAT, punched as a new data deck. Run these new scores on Program DISTAT. What effect had the transformation on the measures of skewness?

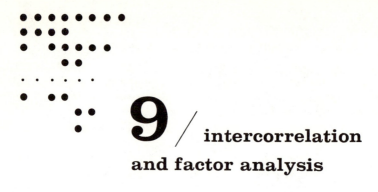

9 / intercorrelation and factor analysis

The procedures to be described in this chapter are all based on the fundamental concept of covariation—the tendency for measures on two dimensions to vary together. The correlation coefficient is a standardized index of this tendency, varying between limits of ±1.00, with an expected value of 0.00 when the dimensions are unrelated. We have already described the construction of a correlation matrix, which systematically represents the relationship pattern among more than two variables. Later in this chapter we will discuss techniques known by the generic name *factor analysis* which analyze the intercorrelation matrix to yield a new set of independent dimensions defined solely in terms of the original variables. We will also present a technique which permits comparison of factor structures obtained from different samples of subjects.

The programs in this chapter vividly demonstrate the ability of the computer to facilitate analysis of quantitative data. Anyone who has ever calculated a Pearson correlation with 100 subjects will appreciate the fact that a computer can compute 10,000 of them in a few minutes. With more complex techniques the significance of the computer's speed is even more striking. A factor analysis that once required months of error-filled drudgery with a desk calculator is now achieved in less than half an hour, and without error. The sudden practicality of complex analytic methods and ease of computing the simpler statistical indexes also introduces certain dangers to the orderly development of the behavioral sciences.

We do not mean to imply, for example, either that the value of an analysis can be measured in terms of its complexity or that analysis of data is the most significant aspect of research. *When* complex analytic techniques are appropriate, however, they can now be used as easily as the simpler methods. Because of their current easy availability, the complex methods are probably misapplied more often today than ever before; but we hope that the meaningful applications compensate for the mistakes sufficiently to raise the general level of our research.

Another kind of danger arises with the ease of computing the simpler statistics. Instead of computing only a few correlation coefficients between the more promising pairs of variables in an exploratory investigation, it is actually easier to compute an intercorrelation matrix of all the variables. The chances for serendipitous discovery in such matrices are greatly enhanced, as well as the risk of false generalization from an unreplicated observation. The computer's power, then, does not release the research worker from any of his responsibilities for caution and common sense in gathering data, selecting analytic procedures, and drawing conclusions from his results. If anything, it complicates his task by expanding the possibilities open to him. The machine's role should be that of an extremely accurate and efficient research assistant; to expect anything more from it would be unwise.

The first section of this chapter will concern a set of three subroutines for intercorrelation. A program for auto- and cross-lag intercorrelation of repeated-measurement data will be described next. The third section will concern a package program for intercorrelation and factor analysis of the intercorrelation matrix. The final section describes a program which compares factor structures obtained from two different samples of subjects. Few research workers will be entirely satisfied with the options and output, and you will probably want to rewrite them yourself as you become familiar with the special capabilities of the Fortran system at your own installation. The flow charts, comment statements and modular construction of the programs are all intended to aid such modifications.

INTERCORRELATION SUBROUTINES

The three routines in this section could be converted easily to serve as independent programs within a statistical library. They are presented here as subroutines because intercorrelation is the initial process for a number of multivariate statistical procedures. All three of them are available at option within the framework of Program FACTOR, which will be discussed in a later section of this chapter.

The first of these subroutines, CORS, is organized very much like Program TWELVE in Chapter 5. Instead of reading control cards, however, it receives parameter information and a variable data-format vector through its argument list from the calling program. It also provides the option of writing a binary tape record of each subject's raw data as they are read from the input deck.

The second subroutine, MDRS, reads an option-control card prior to reading the subjects' data cards. For those variables indicated on the option card, zero or blank raw-score fields are interpreted as missing data, and the computations of means, sigmas, and intercorrelations are appropriately adjusted to ignore such cases.

The third subroutine in this set, TDRS, computes means, sigmas, and intercorrelations for subjects rather than variables, which is to say that the data matrix is effectively transposed prior to the usual intercorrelation procedure. Like Subroutine CORS, the MDRS and TDRS Subroutines receive parameter values and a data format as arguments from the program that calls them.

All three of these routines employ the same formula—the same computational procedure—for the correlation coefficient, as described in earlier chapters. Neither does the form of the data used affect the computational method. If the scores for both variables are dichotomous (one and zero, for instance), the resulting coefficient will be identical to that computed with the familiar short-cut equation for the *phi coefficient*. Similarly, if the data consist of independent sets of rank numbers, the resulting value will be the *rank-order correlation* called *rho*. Finally, if one variable is dichotomous and the other is continuous, the result will be a *point-biserial correlation*. The procedure for computing these correlations is always the same; only the nature of the data determines the appropriate name for the result. Methods of evaluating the statistical significance of these various correlations are *not* the same, however, and are described in most comprehensive introductory statistics texts, such as Young and Veldman (1965).

CORS (NS, NV, R, A, S, KF, KT, ND)

A subroutine to compute means, sigmas, and intercorrelations from raw data on cards, with optional data-tape output.

This subroutine should be compared to Program TWELVE in Chapter 5, since both routines have the same general purposes. In this routine arguments defining the numbers of subjects and variables are transmitted from the main program along with the data-card format in vector KF. In the main program, these arguments might have been defined by calling Subroutine CCDS. The binary data-tape option is intended to save the subjects' raw scores for later use by the main program in computing composite scores developed from analysis of the intercorrelation matrix, as exemplified in Program FACTOR later in this chapter. The data deck read by this routine would include one or more cards for each of NS subjects, and the scores for the series of NV variables would be punched in the same order and field-format across each subjects card(s). The format contained in vector KF would describe the arrangement of the data card(s) and would specify NV fields, preceded by an A-mode subject-identification field

Intercorrelation Subroutines 193

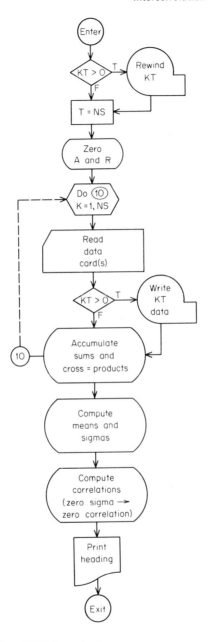

FIGURE 9-1. Subroutine CORS flow chart.

(maximum of six characters). If the value of argument KT is not received as zero, it will be interpreted as the number of a tape unit which will be rewound initially and then written with one binary record for each subject

194   INTERCORRELATION AND FACTOR ANALYSIS

in the sample as the data cards are read. A typical CALL statement for this subroutine is:

CALL CORS (N, K, R, A, S, KF, 2, 100)

Assuming that N and K have the values 140 and 23 respectively, and the vector KF holds the data-card format, the subroutine will input an ID block and 23 scores for each of 140 subjects, putting 140 binary records of raw data on unit 2. A 23-by-23 intercorrelation matrix will be formed in matrix R, which is dimensioned with 100 rows in the calling program. Vectors A and S will be returned holding means and sigmas for the 23 variables.

Because of the READ statement in this subroutine, the data-card format must specify an alphameric field for subject identification as the first field to be read, even if no data tape is to be made. For example, the variable format specifications received in vector KF for the previous example might have been: (A6, 4X, 10F1.0, 13F2.1).

Note that vector KF is dimensioned with 16 locations to permit the variable name to be used without subscripting, as required in the READ statement reference to it. Also, because vector S is dimensioned with NV locations, no indexing is needed in the variable lists of the READ and WRITE statements (Figure 9-1).

```
      SUBROUTINE CORS (NS, NV, R, A, S, KF, KT, ND)
C
C     COMPUTE MEANS, SIGMAS, AND INTERCORRELATION MATRIX FROM RAW DATA ON
C        CARDS. OPTIONAL OUTPUT OF BINARY DATA TAPE.
C     NS = NUMBER OF SUBJECTS.
C     NV = NUMBER OF VARIABLES, THE ORDER OF R.
C     R  = OUTPUT INTERCORRELATION MATRIX.
C     A  = OUTPUT VECTOR OF MEANS.
C     S  = OUTPUT VECTOR OF SIGMAS.
C     KF = VARIABLE FORMAT FOR DATA CARDS. IDENTIFICATION
C           FIELD MUST BE INCLUDED.
C     KT = TAPE UNIT FOR BINARY OUTPUT DATA TAPE. NO OUTPUT IF SENT ZERO.
C     ND = ROWS DIMENSIONED FOR R IN CALLING PROGRAM.
C
      DIMENSION R(ND,NV), A(NV), S(NV), KF(16)
      IF (KT .GT. 0) REWIND KT
      T = NS
      DO 5 I = 1,NV
      A(I) = 0.0
      DO 5 J = 1,NV
    5 R(I,J) = 0.0
      DO 10 K = 1,NS
      READ KF, ID, S
      IF (KT .GT. 0) WRITE (KT) ID, S
      DO 10 I = 1,NV
      A(I) = A(I) + S(I)
      DO 10 J = I,NV
   10 R(I,J) = R(I,J) + S(I) * S(J)
      DO 15 I = 1,NV
      A(I) = A(I) / T
   15 S(I) = SQRT(R(I,I) / T - A(I)**2)
      DO 25 I = 1,NV
      DO 20 J = I,NV
      IF (S(I) * S(J) .EQ. 0.0) GO TO 20
      R(J,I) = (R(I,J) / T - A(I) * A(J)) / (S(I) * S(J))
```

```
   20 R(I,J) = R(J,I)
   25 R(I,I) = 1.0
      PRINT 30
   30 FORMAT (// 27H INTERCORRELATION ANALYSIS.)
      RETURN
      END
```

MDRS (NS, NV, R, A, S, X, M, KF, ND)

A subroutine to compute means, sigmas, and intercorrelations, treating zero scores for selected variables as missing data.

The complexity of the flow chart for this subroutine reflects that of the problem itself. Since each combination of variables might require computation of statistics and a correlation coefficient from a different subset of the NS subjects, the values of $\Sigma X, \Sigma X^2, \Sigma Y, \Sigma Y^2, N$, and ΣXY for each possible combination must be separately stored. Therefore, a square matrix (A) is needed for the means, and another (S) is required for sigmas. The matrix R will contain the correlation coefficients above its diagonal and the N's upon which they are based below the diagonal in corresponding cells (reversed subscripts).

In all three matrices the values in the diagonal cells are based on the variables considered independently. For instance, in a particular problem 20 out of 23 subjects may have valid scores on variable two. Cell R(2, 2) will contain the value 20.0, even though all cells involving variable two below the diagonal might hold numbers less than 20.0 because fewer than 20 subjects have valid scores *both* for variable two and each of the other variables concerned. The storage of values in the three matrices for three variables is diagrammed in Figure 9-2.

Matrix A			Matrix S			Matrix R		
μ_1	$\mu_{1(2)}$	$\mu_{1(3)}$	σ_1	$\sigma_{1(2)}$	$\sigma_{1(3)}$	N_1	r_{12}	r_{13}
$\mu_{2(1)}$	μ_2	$\mu_{2(3)}$	$\sigma_{2(1)}$	σ_2	$\sigma_{2(3)}$	N_{12}	N_2	r_{23}
$\mu_{3(1)}$	$\mu_{3(2)}$	μ_3	$\sigma_{3(1)}$	$\sigma_{3(2)}$	σ_3	N_{13}	N_{23}	N_3

FIGURE 9-2. Arrangement of values in matrices A, S, and R.

For example, the correlation coefficient between variables two and three is computed with the following formula, referencing the matrices shown in Figure 9-2. The accumulated sum of cross-products $\Sigma X_2 X_3$ is held in cell R(2, 3) until it is replaced finally by the correlation coefficient.

$$r_{23} = \frac{\Sigma X_2 X_3 / N_{23} - \mu_{2(3)} \mu_{3(2)}}{\sigma_{2(3)} \sigma_{3(2)}}$$

Because of the use of the option card which is read at the start of the subroutine, only selected variables need to be handled so as to exclude zero scores. Of course, if zero was to be a valid score for all variables, this subroutine would be unnecessarily complex, and CORS should be used

196 INTERCORRELATION AND FACTOR ANALYSIS

instead. The option-card format (5) specifies all 80 columns as single-digit integer values. If NV exceeds 80, this format will be repeated automatically and more than one option card will be needed to hold all of the signals. Note that the variable name (M) for this option-signal vector is integer-mode. Since this vector is not used to return results to the calling program, it can be equated through the argument list to a vector named for either mode in the calling program (Figure 9-3).

```
      SUBROUTINE MDRS (NS, NV, R, A, S, X, M, KF, ND)
C
C     COMPUTES MEANS, SIGMAS, AND INTERCORRELATIONS, TREATING ZERO SCORES
C        FOR SELECTED VARIABLES AS MISSING DATA.
C     NS = NUMBER OF SUBJECTS.
C     NV = NUMBER OF VARIABLES.
C     R = PRINTED WITH CORRELATIONS ABOVE AND CONTINGENT N BELOW
C        DIAGONAL IN CORRESPONDING POSITIONS. SINGLE-VARIABLE N IN DIAGONAL
C     A, S = STORAGE MATRICES FOR CONTINGENT MEANS AND SIGMAS.
C     X = TEMPORARY STORAGE VECTOR FOR RAW DATA.
C     M = VECTOR OF OPTION SIGNALS READ FROM A CONTROL CARD IMMEDIATELY
C        PRECEDING THE DATA DECK.  COL 1-NV = 1 COL PER VARIABLE (1 = ZERO
C        MEANS MISSING DATA, 0 = ZERO IS LEGITIMATE SCORE.)
C     KF = VARIABLE-FORMAT VECTOR. SPECIFY ONLY SCORE-FIELDS.
C     ND = NUMBER OF ROWS DIMENSIONED FOR R, A, S IN CALLING PROGRAM.
C
      DIMENSION R(ND,NV), A(ND,NV), S(ND,NV), X(NV), M(NV), KF(16)
      READ 5, M
    5 FORMAT (80I1)
      DO 10 I = 1,NV
      DO 10 J = 1,NV
      R(I,J) = 0.0
      A(I,J) = 0.0
   10 S(I,J) = 0.0
      DO 30 N = 1,NS
      READ KF, X
      DO 30 I = 1,NV
      IF (M(I) .EQ. 0) GO TO 15
      IF (X(I) .EQ. 0.0) GO TO 30
   15 R(I,I) = R(I,I) + 1.0
      A(I,I) = A(I,I) + X(I)
      S(I,I) = S(I,I) + X(I)**2
      DO 25 J = I,NV
      IF (I .EQ. J) GO TO 25
      IF (M(J) .EQ. 0) GO TO 20
      IF (X(J) .EQ. 0.0) GO TO 25
   20 R(I,J) = R(I,J) + X(I) * X(J)
      R(J,I) = R(J,I) + 1.0
      A(I,J) = A(I,J) + X(I)
      A(J,I) = A(J,I) + X(J)
      S(I,J) = S(I,J) + X(I)**2
      S(J,I) = S(J,I) + X(J)**2
   25 CONTINUE
   30 CONTINUE
      DO 35 I = 1,NV
      DO 35 J = I,NV
      A(I,J) = A(I,J) / R(J,I)
      S(I,J) = SQRT (S(I,J) / R(J,I) - A(I,J)**2)
      IF (I .EQ. J) GO TO 35
      A(J,I) = A(J,I) / R(J,I)
      S(J,I) = SQRT (S(J,I) / R(J,I) - A(J,I)**2)
   35 CONTINUE
      DO 45 I = 1,NV
      DO 45 J = I,NV
      IF (I .EQ. J) GO TO 45
```

Intercorrelation Subroutines

```
      IF (S(I,J) * S(J,I) .GT. 0.0) GO TO 40
      R(I,J) = 0.0
      GO TO 45
   40 R(I,J) = (R(I,J) / R(J,I) - A(I,J) * A(J,I)) / (S(I,J) * S(J,I))
   45 CONTINUE
      PRINT 50, M
  500FORMAT (//45H INTERCORRELATION ANALYSIS (INCOMPLETE DATA).,
     1 // 11H OPTIONS.  , (80I1))
      RETURN
      END
```

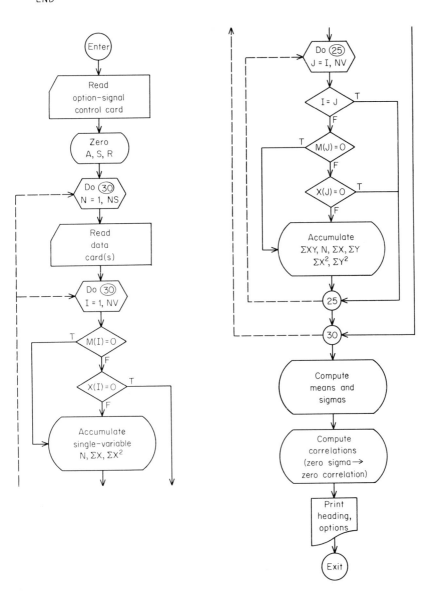

FIGURE 9-3. Subroutine MDRS flow chart.

TDRS (NS, NV, R, D, A, S, VA, VS, KF, ND)

A subroutine to compute means, sigmas, and intercorrelations among subject's score profiles after normative standardization.

This subroutine is designed to handle a common problem in behavioral research with a minimum of data processing. Assuming that data on a series of variables have been punched across one or more cards per subject in the usual manner, the problem requires computation of an intercorrelation matrix which reverses the usual roles of subjects and variables. If a data matrix is conceptualized with NS rows and NV columns, we want to intercorrelate the rows rather than the columns.

In order to avoid distortion of the intercorrelations of rows by differences in the scaling of the variables concerned, we will also want to standardize the scores in each column of the data matrix before starting the intercorrelation process. If this routine was not available, we could achieve its purpose by running the original data deck with Program DISTAT to get standard scores. The resulting data deck of standard scores would then have to be repunched so that NS scores were placed across cards for each of the NV variables. This new deck could then be submitted to a program employing Subroutine CORS to compute the intercorrelations. Subroutine TDRS accomplishes all of this from input of the original data deck.

A matrix named D is used to hold all of the raw data, which is read into memory before any computations are begun. The columns of this matrix represent the variables and rows represent subjects. Means and sigmas are computed for the NV columns, and these statistics are then used to convert the scores in matrix D to z-score scaling. The intercorrelation of the NS rows of the rescaled D matrix is then begun, yielding another set of means and sigmas (for rows) as well as the intercorrelation matrix (Figure 9-4).

Because the values of NS and NV are swapped just before return of control to the calling program, these arguments will not be the same as those originally sent, and constants must not be used in the CALL statement for these arguments. A typical CALL statement would be:

CALL TDRS (NA, NB, R, X, A, S, AA, SS, KF, 90)

If the values in NA and NB were 70 (subjects) and 25 (variables) prior to calling the subroutine, they would be NA = 25 and NB = 70 after control was returned. Matrix R would hold a 70-by-70 matrix of intercorrelations, vectors A and S would hold 70 means and 70 sigmas, and vectors AA and SS would hold 25 raw-score means and sigmas. Matrix D would continue to hold the standardized raw-score matrix.

This technique enables the research worker to measure the degrees of similarity among all pairs of subjects' score profiles within the sample. The standardization of columns of the data matrix prior to intercorrelation of subjects removes the potentially distorting effect of differences in variabil-

Intercorrelation Subroutines 199

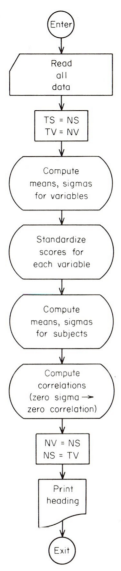

FIGURE 9-4. Subroutine TDRS flow chart.

ity among the score variables that make up the profiles. It should be understood that a correlation of subject profiles reflects only similarity of *shape* and is not a measure of *distance* between score profiles, since the average levels of the scores in each pair of profiles are equated during the computation of the correlation coefficients. Program HGROUP, described in a later chapter, provides an alternative approach to measuring profile similarity.

200 INTERCORRELATION AND FACTOR ANALYSIS

```
      SUBROUTINE TDRS (NS, NV, R, D, A, S, VA, VS, KF, ND)
C
C     COMPUTES MEANS, SIGMAS, CORRELATIONS OF SUBJECTS SCORE PROFILES AFTE
C     STANDARDIZING SCORES ON EACH VARIABLE.
C     NS = NUMBER OF SUBJECTS. RETURNED AS NV.
C     NV = NUMBER OF VARIABLES. RETURNED AS NS.
C     R = MATRIX OF SUBJECT INTERCORRELATIONS.
          ORDER = ORIGINAL NS = RETURNED NV.
C     D = STORAGE MATRIX FOR RAW DATA. RETURNED AS Z-SCORES.
C     A,S = RETURNED AS VECTORS OF SUBJECT MEANS AND SIGMAS.
C     VA,VS = RETURNED AS VECTORS OF VARIABLE MEANS AND SIGMAS.
C     KF = VARIABLE FORMAT VECTOR. SPECIFY ONLY SCORE FIELDS FOR VARIABLES
C     ND = NUMBER OF ROWS DIMENSIONED FOR R AND D IN THE CALLING PROGRAM.
C
      DIMENSION R(ND,NS), D(ND,NV), A(NS), S(NS), VA(NV), VS(NV), KF(16
      DO 5 I = 1,NS
    5 READ KF, (D(I,J), J = 1,NV)
      TS = NS
      TV = NV
      DO 10 J = 1,NV
      VA(J) = SUMF(D, J, NS, ND) / TS
      VS(J) = SQRT(SUMF(D, J, -NS, ND) / TS - VA(J)**2)
      DO 10 I = 1,NS
   10 D(I,J) = (D(I,J) - VA(J)) / VS(J)
      DO 15 I = 1,NS
      A(I) = SUMF(D, -I, NV, ND) / TV
   15 S(I) = SQRT(SUMF(D, -I, -NV, ND) / TV - A(I)**2)
      DO 25 I = 1,NS
      DO 20 J = I,NS
      R(I,J) = 0.0
      IF (S(I) * S(J) .EQ. 0.0) GO TO 20
      R(I,J) = (SCPF(D, D, -I, -J, NV, ND) / TV - A(I) * A(J))
     1 / (S(I) * S(J))
   20 R(J,I) = R(I,J)
   25 R(I,I) = 1.0
      NV = NS
      NS = TV
      PRINT 30
   30 FORMAT (// 45H INTERCORRELATION ANALYSIS (TRANSPOSED DATA).)
      RETURN
      END
```

PROGRAM LAGCOR: AUTO- AND CROSS-LAG INTERCORRELATION

Program LAGCOR computes intercorrelation matrices with the same basic formula for the correlation coefficient that was employed in Subroutines CORS, MDRS, and TDRS. Instead of correlating a set of variables using pairs of scores contributed by a series of subjects, the present program assumes that the scores were obtained by repeated measurements of the same subject. The problem is to determine whether cyclic fluctuations are present in the series of measurements by correlating each series of scores against itself and against those on each of the other variables after the whole series has been "slipped" one or more measurement periods.

For example, suppose that test X and test Y are given to one subject each day for five days in a row. The notion of lagging one variable against another (or against itself, when X = Y) is illustrated by the diagram in Figure 9-5.

Program Lagcor: Auto- and Cross-Lag Intercorrelation

```
   No Lag          Lag = 1        Lag = 1
                                (reversed)

   X    Y          X    Y         X    Y
  ┌──┬──┐          (25)           (20)
  │25│20│         ┌──┬──┐        ┌──┬──┐
  ├──┼──┤         │24│20│        │25│19│
  │24│19│         ├──┼──┤        ├──┼──┤
  ├──┼──┤         │22│19│        │24│25│
  │22│25│         ├──┼──┤        ├──┼──┤
  ├──┼──┤         │26│25│        │22│20│
  │26│20│         ├──┼──┤        ├──┼──┤
  ├──┼──┤         │23│20│        │26│18│
  │23│18│         └──┴──┘        └──┴──┘
  └──┴──┘          (18)           (23)

   N = 5           N = 4          N = 4
```

FIGURE 9-5. Example of lagged relationship of repeated measures.

Note that for any degree of lag, two different correlations can be computed, depending on which variable is lagged. The N for the two correlations at a given degree of lag will be less than the total number of repeated measurements by a value equal to the degree of lag. When no lag is imposed, this procedure yields a correlation matrix identical to that produced by Subroutine CORS, if measurement times are considered as "subjects."

The LAGCOR Program outputs a matrix of intercorrelations for each degree of lag from zero to a limit specified by a Parameter Control Card option. In the diagonal elements of these matrices will be found the autocorrelations resulting from lagging each variable against itself. On either side of the diagonal will be located the two correlations obtained by lagging each of the variables in all possible pairings (Figure 9-6).

Two options are provided for data input to permit more flexibility in punching the data into tab cards: The repeated measurements on a single variable may be punched across one or more cards, beginning the series of scores for each variable on a new data card. Or alternatively, the scores punched across each card may represent scores on each of a group of variables, with the scores for each measurement period beginning on a new card. The program is listed with limits of 35 variables and 400 repeated measurements, but these may be changed easily by revising only the DIMENSION statement and the two statements which follow it.

The data are read into a matrix called D as the first step in this program. The columns of D represent variables to be intercorrelated while the rows represent repeated measurements of these variables. Thus, all of the data are obtained from a single source. We implied earlier that this might be a single subject, but it could also be a group of subjects, if group means were entered as the scores to be analyzed. The source of the scores could be measured every day for a series of days. The time between measures could just as well be seconds, minutes, or months, as long as it was regular throughout the series of measurements. More extended discussions of autocorrelation and its applications may be found in Holtzman (1963) and in Ralston and Wilf (1960).

202 INTERCORRELATION AND FACTOR ANALYSIS

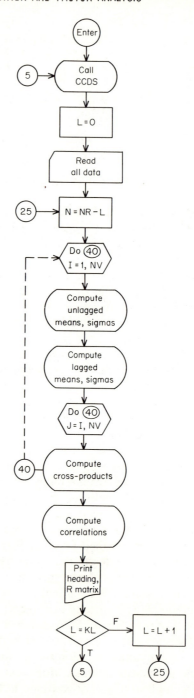

FIGURE 9-6. Program LAGCOR flow chart.

The computational sequence in this program is quite complex because of the need to re-store elements of D for the lagged variable. This is necessary in order to use the SUMF and SCPF Functions which begin indexing from the first locations of the vectors sent to them.

EXAMPLE PROBLEM

The example problem for this program uses the deck of 16 cards punched by Program TESTAT (problem 2). For the sake of demonstration, let us suppose that the 16 cards do not represent 16 different people, but are instead 16 repeated measurements of the same person with the SRI instrument. If this assumption is made, then the input option must be set to obtain auto- and cross-lag intercorrelations of the nine scores punched across each card (column 20 = 1). The output should be compared with that yielded by the CORS Subroutine on page 228, since the first matrix (lag = 0) is identical to that produced by ordinary intercorrelation of the same variables.

```
      PROGRAM LAGCOR
CONTROL PROGRAM FOR AUTO AND CROSS-LAG INTERCORRELATION.
PARAMETER CONTROL-CARD FIELDS.
   COL 1-5.  NUMBER OF VARIABLES TO BE INTERCORRELATED (MAX = 35).
   COL 6-10. NUMBER OF REPEATED MEASURES OF EACH VARIABLE (MAX = 400).
   COL 11-15. MAXIMUM DEGREE OF LAG (MAX = REPEATED MEASURES - 2).
   COL 20.  0 = REPEATED MEASURES PUNCHED ACROSS EACH CARD, EACH VARIABLE
               BEGINS ON A NEW CARD.
            1 = VARIABLES PUNCHED ACROSS EACH CARD, EACH MEASUREMENT TIME
               BEGINS ON A NEW CARD.
FORMAT SPECIFIES SCORE FIELDS AS DATA ARE PUNCHED ACROSS CARDS.
SUBPROGRAMS REQUIRED ARE CCDS, SUMF, SCPF, PRTS.

    ODIMENSION KF(16), D(400,35), X(400), Y(400), R(35,35),
   1 A(35), S(35), AL(35), SL(35)
      NDA = 400
      NDB = 35
    5 CALL CCDS (KF, NV, NR, KL, KT, L)
      IF (KT .EQ. 1) GO TO 15
      DO 10 J = 1,NV
   10 READ KF, (D(I,J), I = 1,NR)
      GO TO 25
   15 DO 20 I = 1,NR
   20 READ KF, (D(I,J), J = 1,NV)
   25 N = NR - L
      T = N
      DO 40 I = 1,NV
      A(I) = SUMF(D, I, N, NDA) / T
      S(I) = SQRT(SUMF(D, I, -N, NDA) / T - A(I)**2)
      DO 30 K = 1,N
      M = K + L
   30 X(K) = D(M,I)
      AL(I) = SUMF(X, 1, N, NDA) / T
      SL(I) = SQRT(SUMF(X, 1, -N, NDA) / T - AL(I)**2)
```

```
            DO 40 J = I,NV
            DO 35 K = 1,N
            M = K + L
         35 Y(K) = D(M,J)
            R(I,J) = SCPF(D, Y, I, 1, N, NDA)
         40 R(J,I) = SCPF(D, X, J, 1, N, NDA)
            DO 60 I = 1,NV
            DO 60 J = I,NV
            IF (S(I) * SL(J) .GT. 0.0) GO TO 45
            R(I,J) = 0.0
            GO TO 50
         45 R(I,J) = (R(I,J) / T - A(I) * AL(J)) / (S(I) * SL(J))
         50 IF (I .EQ. J) GO TO 60
            IF (S(J) * SL(I) .GT. 0.0) GO TO 55
            R(J,I) = 0.0
            GO TO 60
         55 R(J,I) = (R(J,I) / T - A(J) * AL(I)) / (S(J) * SL(I))
         60 CONTINUE
            PRINT 65, L, N
         65 FORMAT (6H1LAG =, I3, 15H FOR ROWS.  N =, I4)
            CALL PRTS (R, NV, NV, 6HLAGCOR, NDB)
            IF (L .EQ. KL) GO TO 5
            L = L + 1
            GO TO 25
            END


      *** INPUT DATA DECK ***

LAGCOR EXAMPLE PROBLEM
00009000160000100001
(10X, 9F7.0)
S01SRI QS        25.     21.     22.     20.     26.     26.     19.     23.     182
S02SRI QS        26.     30.     30.     26.     28.     20.     24.     28.     212
S03SRI QS        20.     25.     20.     23.     18.     24.     21.     29.     180
S04SRI QS        30.     28.     29.     29.     28.     23.     28.     30.     225
S05SRI QS        23.     25.     29.     19.     20.     27.     28.     28.     199
S06SRI QS        28.     27.     30.     22.     19.     25.     30.     26.     207
S07SRI QS        28.     24.     27.     27.     17.     21.     30.     26.     200
S08SRI QS        25.     29.     29.     27.     26.     25.     26.     25.     212
S09SRI QS        26.     30.     30.     24.     29.     24.     14.     29.     206
S10SRI QS        28.     29.     30.     26.     25.     28.     30.     28.     224
S11SRI QS        24.     28.     30.     29.     27.     23.     21.     28.     210
S12SRI QS        26.     29.     26.     27.     28.     19.     30.     27.     212
S13SRI QS        30.     27.     26.     24.     25.     21.     28.     25.     206
S14SRI QS        29.     29.     29.     28.     25.     19.     30.     27.     216
S15SRI QS        29.     25.     28.     26.     24.     21.     30.     29.     212
S16SRI QS        29.     26.     30.     20.     25.     20.     30.     28.     208


       *** PRINTED OUTPUT ***


1LAGCOR EXAMPLE PROBLEM

  PARAMETERS
  COL  1- 5 =        9
  COL  6-10 =       16
  COL 11-15 =        1
  COL 16-20 =        1
  COL 21-25 =        0

  DATA FORMAT = (10X, 9F7.0)
```

Example Problem

LAGCOR

	1	2	3	4	5	6	7	8	9
1	1.0000	.1821	.4685	.2666	.2409	-.3938	.5560	-.0325	.6504
2	.1821	1.0000	.6181	.5525	.5452	-.2150	.0161	.3900	.7247
3	.4685	.6181	1.0000	.2631	.3198	-.0495	.2694	.3087	.7880
4	.2666	.5525	.2631	1.0000	.3529	-.3723	.1394	.2547	.6168
5	.2409	.5452	.3198	.3529	1.0000	-.2104	-.3032	.1091	.4909
6	-.3938	-.2150	-.0495	-.3723	-.2104	1.0000	-.2808	-.1079	-.2055
7	.5560	.0161	.2694	.1394	-.3032	-.2808	1.0000	-.0127	.4743
8	-.0325	.3900	.3087	.2547	.1091	-.1079	-.0127	1.0000	.3679
9	.6504	.7247	.7880	.6168	.4909	-.2055	.4743	.3679	1.0000

ILAG = 1 FOR ROWS. N = 15

LAGCOR

	1	2	3	4	5	6	7	8	9
1	-.1719	-.3559	.0438	-.2323	-.2661	-.0784	.1254	-.2158	-.2598
2	-.2024	-.2838	-.4162	-.0464	-.1929	.2589	-.1616	.1743	-.2730
3	-.3887	-.3628	-.2351	-.2914	-.4444	.2591	-.0524	-.1756	-.4546
4	-.2826	-.1262	-.2643	-.1614	.2048	.0220	-.1439	.0918	-.1807
5	-.2851	.0546	-.2572	-.3172	.0864	.0300	-.1846	.2448	-.2282
6	-.1128	.3104	.4959	.1957	.0881	.2259	-.2685	.0913	.1933
7	.0436	-.4812	.0042	-.2075	-.3032	-.2281	.0080	-.3907	-.3604
8	-.0822	-.4383	-.1068	-.3608	-.2671	.4539	.3332	.2100	-.0344
9	-.3485	-.4226	-.1813	-.3596	-.2683	.1399	-.1166	-.0593	-.4402

FACTOR ANALYSIS

The procedures included under factor analysis have been applied to a wide variety of problems in the behavioral sciences since the advent of modern computing machinery. Although the motivation for the use of these techniques occasionally seems to be more a matter of curiosity than one of planned hypothesis seeking or testing, the usefulness of the method has been repeatedly demonstrated. The general goal of factor analysis is the reduction of a set of variables used to gather data from subjects to a smaller set of new, uncorrelated variables which are defined solely in terms of the original dimensions, and which retain the most "important" information contained in the original data. Factors, then, are variables or dimensions of the same general nature as those variables from which they were derived. They may be used to describe subjects also, but at a higher level of abstraction. In some situations factor analysis may be considered a procedure for exposing the essential determining constructs behind a set of observable behaviors.

As an idealized example, we will use a problem suggested by Cooley and Lohnes (1962). Suppose that we measured a very large number of rectangles of randomly different sizes by obtaining scores on each of five variables for each rectangle. The five variables we will use are:

(1) the length
(2) twice the length plus the width
(3) the length plus the width
(4) twice the width plus the length
(5) the width

"Subjects" in our example would be individual rectangles, each of which would contribute five scores to the data matrix. The first step in the processing would be to obtain an intercorrelation matrix for the five variables; this matrix (R) will be the starting point for the factor analysis. Since the computation of the correlation coefficient implicitly equates the variables for centrality and variability, all information present in the raw-data matrix which was tied to the scaling of the five variables is no longer available for analysis. The matrix R represents only the pattern of relationships among the five original variables. Figure 9-7 contains the in-

Intercorrelations

	1	2	3	4	5
L:1	1.00	.92	.71	.38	.00
2L+W:2	.92	1.00	.92	.71	.38
L+W:3	.71	.92	1.00	.92	.71
2W+L:4	.38	.71	.92	1.00	.92
W:5	.00	.38	.71	.92	1.00

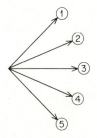

FIGURE 9-7. Intercorrelation of five rectangle scores.

tercorrelation matrix which would be expected, as well as the geometric representation of the five variables. A correlation coefficient can be interpreted as the cosine of the angle between two vectors that stand for the variables concerned (Harmon, 1960, p. 62). Since it is possible to accurately represent *all* of the relationships among the five variables in our problem by means of a *two*-dimensional model, we already have a hint of the outcome of the factor analysis to be performed. Another hint is available to us from the definitions of the five variables, since only two unknowns are represented throughout the set of definitions.

ROOTS AND VECTORS OF A MATRIX

The second major step in the factor-analytic procedure is known to mathematicians as *extraction of eigenroots and vectors*. In our example, which is the most commonly used type of factor analysis, these roots and vectors are extracted from the intercorrelation matrix (R). Other forms of factor analysis operate upon other initial matrices; we will consider one of the variants, the image-covariance matrix (G), later on in this chapter.

Many different techniques have been developed for extracting the roots and vectors of a matrix. Probably the most widely used method is called the Jacobi solution (Cooley and Lohnes, 1962; Ralston and Wilf, 1960). Although both accurate and relatively fast, the Fortran programs for this method are long and complex, and the method requires the extraction of all possible roots and vectors from the basic matrix being analyzed. "All" in this case means a number of factors equal to the number of original variables. In most applications of factor analysis in behavioral sciences research, many fewer than all possible factors are usually needed. The Subroutine SEVS permits extraction of only the necessary number of factors, according to a predetermined criterion, and is therefore more efficient; it also has the advantage of a concise, relatively simple Fortran program.

SEVS (NV, NF, C, R, V, E, P, ND)

A subroutine to extract eigenroots and denormal vectors from a symmetric matrix.

This routine is based on a procedure outlined by Horst (1962, 1965), who attributes it originally to Hotelling (1933). Two methods of limiting the number of factors to be extracted by this routine are available. The argument NF may be sent as a value less than NV (the order of the input matrix R), thus setting an absolute limit on the number of factors to be extracted. Alternatively, the argument C may be given some arbitrary value such as 1.0 for the size of the minimum eigenvalue (eigenroot) to be extracted. Since the roots are extracted automatically in the order of their size, factor extraction will cease if a root is obtained which is less than this criterion value.

208 INTERCORRELATION AND FACTOR ANALYSIS

As indicated by the flow chart, the R matrix is "deflated" after extraction of each root and vector by subtracting the outer product formed from the vector. Consequently, the matrix R is destroyed by this routine as the eigenroots are collected in vector E and the vectors are collected as columns of matrix V (Figure 9-8).

The *trace* of the input matrix is computed at the start of the program; this is defined as the sum of the diagonal elements of the input matrix. If all possible roots and vectors are extracted from the input matrix (R), the sum of the roots will be equal to the trace.[1] As part of the subroutine's operation, the percentages of trace accounted for by each root are stored in P and the total percentage of trace extracted by the NF extracted factors is also computed. Since the value of NF will be changed if the criterion C halts extraction, this argument must not appear as a constant in the CALL statement for this subroutine.

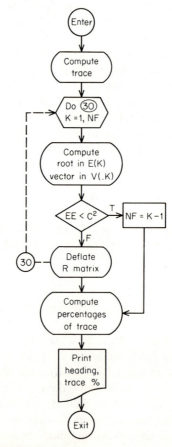

FIGURE 9-8. Subroutine SEVS flow chart.

[1] An exception to this rule will be explained later.

Roots and Vectors of a Matrix   209

The number of iterations for the factor-estimation process is arbitrarily set at 25; this will yield more than enough accuracy for most behavioral research applications. This value can be reset easily, however, to speed the operation of the routine, or to obtain greater accuracy. Changes in this value will affect the accuracy of the vectors to a much greater extent than that of the roots.

The vectors returned by this routine are not normalized, and are sometimes known as *factor loadings*. Since the sum of squared loadings for a given column of the output matrix will equal the eigenroot for that factor, these factor-loading vectors can be easily normalized after return to the calling program. The term *eigenvector* is usually reserved for the normalized version of a factor-loading vector.

```
      SUBROUTINE SEVS (NV, NF, C, R, V, E, P, ND)

      EXTRACT ROOTS AND DENORMAL VECTORS FROM A SYMMETRIC MATRIX.
      NV = THE ORDER OF R.
      NF = INPUT AS MAX. NUMBER OF FACTORS TO BE EXTRACTED, OUTPUT AS NUMBER
           EXTRACTED WITH ROOTS .GT. C.
      C = MINIMUM EIGENVALUE TO BE EXTRACTED.
      R = SYMMETRIC INPUT MATRIX. DESTROYED IN PROCESSING.
      V = OUTPUT MATRIX OF COLUMN VECTORS OF LOADINGS.
      E = OUTPUT VECTOR OF ROOTS.
      P = OUTPUT VECTOR OF PERCENTAGES OF TRACE FOR FACTORS.
      ND = NUMBER OF ROWS DIMENSIONED FOR R AND V IN CALLING PROGRAM.
           DIMENSION R(ND,NV), V(ND,NF), E(NF), P(NV)
      COMPUTE TRACE.
           T = 0.0
           DO 5 I = 1,NV
      5    T = T + R(I,I)
           DO 30 K = 1,NF
      COMPUTE ROOT IN E(K) AND VECTOR IN V(.K).
           DO 10 I = 1,NV
      10   P(I) = 1.0
           E(K) = 1.0
           DO 25 M = 1,25
           DO 15 I = 1,NV
      15   V(I,K) = P(I) / E(K)
           DO 20 I = 1,NV
      20   P(I) = SCPF(R, V, -I, K, NV, ND)
           EE = SCPF(P, V, 1, K, NV, ND)
      25   E(K) = SQRT(ABS(EE))
           IF (EE .LT. C * C) GO TO 35
      DEFLATE R MATRIX.
           DO 30 I = 1,NV
           DO 30 J = 1,NV
      30   R(I,J) = R(I,J) - V(I,K) * V(J,K)
           GO TO 40
      35   NF = K - 1
      COMPUTE PERCENTS OF TRACE.
      40   DO 45 I = 1,NF
      45   P(I) = E(I) / T * 100.0
           EV = SUMF(P, 1, NF, ND)
           PRINT 50, T, EV, NF
      50   FORMAT (// 25H PRINCIPAL AXIS ANALYSIS. // 8H TRACE =, F10.4 //
         1 F7.2, 31H PCT. OF TRACE WAS EXTRACTED BY, I3, 7H ROOTS.)
           RETURN
           END
```

210 INTERCORRELATION AND FACTOR ANALYSIS

This subroutine is intended only for analysis of a symmetric matrix. A slightly more complex version of this same procedure will be presented in Chapter 10 when we encounter the need to analyze a square but nonsymmetric matrix into its roots and vectors.

The extraction of roots and vectors from a matrix may be viewed as the *construction* of a new space which is maximally representative of the space defined by the original variables, but utilizes a minimum number of independent dimensions. From another point of view, extraction of roots and vectors could be said to achieve a stepwise *reduction* of the M-dimensional space defined by the original variables to one which contains only the number of independent dimensions necessary to represent the information contained in the original matrix. Operationally, we may consider the SEVS routine as defining successive dimensions which account for a maximum amount of the variation remaining in the R matrix at each stage of its reduction.

The eigenroots and vectors yielded by the factor-extraction process have certain important properties which are most easily described in matrix algebra notation. We will use M to denote the number of variables to be factored (the order of the correlation matrix: R_{MM}). The letter K will designate the number of factors (roots and vectors) extracted; K has a maximum value of M. The *trace* of the original matrix (T) is the sum of the diagonal elements of R:

$$T = U'_M R_{\Delta M} U_M$$

If the original matrix consists of intercorrelations, the maximum value of T = M, since the diagonal elements of R are all equal to 1.0. The trace of R will also equal the sum of the eigenvalues (E) when all factors are extracted:

$$T = U'_M R_{\Delta M} U_M = U'_K E_K \text{ when } K = M$$

Before going any further we should qualify our assertion that the trace of a square matrix will equal the sum of all of its roots. This is true only if we assume — as we will throughout this chapter — that the *rank* of the matrix is equal to its *order*. When a matrix contains some columns (or rows) which are exactly predictable from a linear combination of the other columns (or rows) we say that these particular vectors are linearly *dependent*. The rank of a matrix is the number of its linearly *independent* rows or columns, whichever is smaller. Thus, for the SRI example data, an R matrix of the nine variables has a rank of eight, since the total score is linearly dependent on the eight subscale scores. Also, a correlation matrix of the 16 subjects using the first eight variables would have a rank of eight, although the order of this R matrix would be 16.

The sum of the roots available from a matrix is equal to its rank, although its order may be larger. If the rank of a matrix of order 10 is only six, the last four roots (and vectors) will be zeros. To state the rule more

Roots and Vectors of a Matrix 211

generally, then, we may say that the trace of a correlation matrix will equal its order; but the sum of its roots will be equal to its rank, which in turn, is equal to or less than its order. In the following discussion we will assume that the rank and order of R are equal (M).

When K is less than M, the sum of the eigenvalues can be used to determine the percentage of the variance (trace) in R extracted by the K factors:

$$P = U'_K E_K T^{-1} 100$$

The most important property of the matrix of factor loadings (V_{MK}) is the fact that the columns of this matrix are independent, which implies that the inner product of this matrix with itself will be a diagonal matrix. We mentioned earlier that each eigenvalue is equal to the sum of squares of the elements in its corresponding vector of factor loadings. Therefore, the diagonal elements of the inner product of V with itself should be eigenvalues:

$$E_{\Delta K} = V'_{KM} V_{MK}$$

The column vectors of factor loadings in matrix V may be normalized by use of the eigenvalues to yield a new matrix of eigenvectors:

$$F_{MK} = V_{MK} E_{\Delta K}^{-1/2}$$

Since the *lengths* of these column vectors are 1.0, the inner product of matrix F with its transpose will be the identity matrix:

$$F'_{KM} F_{MK} = I_{\Delta K}$$

When all M possible factors are extracted from R, then the following basic equations will be valid:

$$R_{MM} V_{MK} = V_{MK} E_{\Delta K} \text{ when } K = M$$
$$R_{MM} F_{MK} = F_{MK} E_{\Delta K} \text{ when } K = M$$

From these equations may be derived definitions of the *outer* products of the loading and eigenvector matrices:

$$V_{MK} V'_{KM} = F_{MK} E_{\Delta K} F'_{KM} = R_{MM} \text{ when } K = M$$
$$F_{MK} F'_{KM} = I_{\Delta M} \text{ when } K = M$$

However, when K is less than M, the matrix reproduced from the outer products of V and F may only approximate the R and I matrices, respectively.

$$\hat{R}_{MM} = V_{MK} V'_{KM} = F_{MK} E_{\Delta K} F'_{KM}$$

The fewer the number of factors necessary to achieve a close correspondence between $\hat{R}$ and R, the stronger the "structure" of R may be said to be. Some data matrices will yield an exact reproduction of R with less than M factors, in which case the rank of R is less than its order, and we

212 INTERCORRELATION AND FACTOR ANALYSIS

know that some of the information provided by the set of M variables is redundant, in that fewer than M variables represent all of the information that is present in the set. One such situation arises when one obtains correlations from a data matrix with fewer subjects than variables. The maximum rank of the correlation matrix will be equal to the minimum dimension of the data matrix from which the correlations are computed.

Even when all M factors are necessary to reproduce R, we usually wish to retain only those factors which represent "important" independent aspects of the information represented in R. Kaiser (1960) recommends the use of only those factors with eigenvalues exceeding 1.0 when a correlation matrix is factored. Intuitive justification for this cutting value may be found in the limiting case where $R = I$, and no structure is represented. In this special case, M factors will be available, each with an eigenvalue of 1.0.

This procedure for extracting the roots and vectors of a matrix is usually called *principal-axis analysis* or *principal-components analysis*. A number of other factor-extraction methods have been developed, but this procedure is usually preferred because of its mathematical elegance.

RECTANGLES EXAMPLE: STAGE II

Returning to the example we began earlier, we may expect the results shown in Figure 9-9 if we submit the intercorrelation matrix shown in Figure 9-7 to Subroutine SEVS. At this stage we can represent the factor structure with a two-dimensional diagram with orthogonal reference axes corresponding to the two extracted principal-axis factors. The original variables are now located in this space at points determined by using the factor-loading values on each axis as coordinates.

The factor loadings indicate the degrees of relationship between the five original scores and each of the new factor variables.

These coefficients may be meaningfully interpreted as correlations of the factor variables with the observed variables. We have identified two prin-

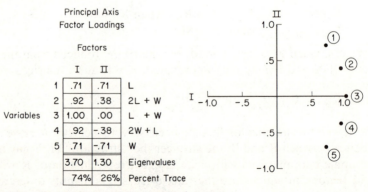

FIGURE 9-9. Principal axes of five rectangle scores.

cipal-axis factors which account for 100 percent of the original variation in R, but we have yet to determine the nature of these factors. The first axis loads most heavily on the sum of *length* and *width* and least on the simple *length* and *width* scores. We might wish to call this factor "Area." The second factor seems to oppose length and width at opposite extremes of another dimension, and might be called "Length versus Width." Although the number of factors meets our earlier expectations, we might have expected a "length" and a "width" factor to emerge instead of the obtained results. This is not an uncommon happening, and we will return to this problem after discussing the topic of factor scores.

PRINCIPAL AXIS FACTOR SCORES

The factors extracted in the procedure just described may be considered dimensional variables of the same general kind as those originally used to describe the sample of rectangles. It should be possible to obtain a pair of scores for each rectangle on these two new factor variables. Standard score weights for the principal-axis factors may be obtained by postmultiplying the factor loading matrix by the inverse of the diagonal matrix of eigenvalues. If the original scores for the rectangles are rescaled as z scores, then the following formula expresses the method of computing principal-axis factor scores (Hotelling, 1933):

$$X_{NK} = Z_{NM} V_{MK} E_{\Delta K}^{-1}$$

The factor scores obtained by this method will have a mean of zero and sigma of 1 for each factor variable, and the correlation of the two factor variables will be zero. Furthermore, if we now correlate these factor variables with each of the five original variables, we will obtain the factor-loading matrix, in line with our earlier remark that factor loadings may be interpreted as correlation coefficients.

Since all of the original variance was accounted for by these two factors, we could use only two scores per subject instead of five in any prediction problem requiring the original information about the rectangles. Even though the names of these factor variables are somewhat less than satisfactory, their scores contain all of the original information.

ROTATION OF FACTOR AXES

The factor-loading matrix obtained from a principal-axis factor analysis reflects the characteristics of the extraction procedure, which maximizes the variance in each successive column of the matrix. The first of these principal axes is easily interpreted; it represents the central focus of the set of original variables, and is often quite important from a psychological standpoint. The remaining principal-axis factors, however, are usually much less interpretable.

The orientation of the factor axes within the space they define is entirely arbitrary, and the principal-axis solution or orientation is only one of an infinite variety of mathematically equivalent ways of expressing the relationships between factors and original variables. An alternate criterion for orienting the factor axes is called "simple structure" and is defined as a solution in which the variances of all the factor vectors are maximized simultaneously, rather than successively. In other words, each column is "simplified" as much as possible in keeping with the restrictions of orthogonality of columns. An ideal simple-structure matrix would have only one non zero loading in each row.

VORS (NV, NF, V, A, B, C, ND)

A subroutine for orthogonal Varimax rotation of factor axes.

This routine was adapted from Kaiser's (1959) explanation of the Varimax method. The input matrix V contains NF columns of factor-loadings (normally from a principal-axis analysis of NV variables), and is returned holding the output matrix of loadings for the rotated solution. Each possible pair of factor vectors is rotated to maximize the column-variance criterion in turn until a complete pass through all combinations does not result in any rotations of more than one degree. The percentages of trace are recomputed for each factor vector and returned in vector A, and comparable percentages are computed for each row of the rotated matrix and are returned in vector B. These latter coefficients, when computed as proportions (row sums of squares from the loading matrix), are known as *communalities,* and are not affected by the rotation process. This coefficient will be a maximum of 1.0 (100 percent) only when all of the variance of the particular variable is completely accounted for by the extracted factors (Figure 9-10).

```
      SUBROUTINE VORS (NV, NF, V, A, B, C, ND)
C
C     VARIMAX (ORTHOGONAL) ROTATION OF A FACTOR-LOADING MATRIX.
C     NV = NUMBER OF VARIABLES (ROWS) OF THE MATRIX.
C     NF = NUMBER OF FACTORS (COLUMNS) OF THE MATRIX.
C     V = MATRIX OF LOADINGS TO BE ROTATED.
C     A = PERCENTAGES OF VARIATION FOR ROTATED FACTORS.
C     B = COMMUNALITIES FOR VARIABLES, AS PERCENTAGES.
C     C = TEMPORARY STORAGE VECTOR.
C     ND = NUMBER OF ROWS DIMENSIONED FOR V IN CALLING PROGRAM.
      DIMENSION V(ND,NF), A(NV), B(NV), C(NV)
      T = NV
C     NORMALIZE ROWS OF V.
      DO 5 I = 1,NV
      B(I) = SQRT(SUMF(V, -I, -NF, ND))
      DO 5 J = 1,NF
    5 V(I,J) = V(I,J) / B(I)
   10 KR = 0
      DO 40 M = 1,NF
      DO 40 N = M,NF
      IF (M .EQ. N) GO TO 40
C     COMPUTE ANGLE OF ROTATION.
      DO 15 I = 1,NV
      A(I) = V(I,M)**2 - V(I,N)**2
```

```
   15 C(I) = 2.0 * V(I,M) * V(I,N)
      AA = SUMF(A, 1, NV, ND)
      BB = SUMF(C, 1, NV, ND)
      CC = SUMF(A, 1, -NV, ND) - SUMF(C, 1, -NV, ND)
      DD = SCPF(A, C, 1, 1, NV, ND) * 2.0
      XN = DD - 2.0 * AA * BB / T
      XD = CC - (AA**2 - BB**2) / T
      Y = ATAN(XN / XD)
      IF (XD .GE. 0.0) GO TO 20
      IF (XN .GE. 0.0) Y = Y + 6.2832
      Y = Y - 3.1416
   20 Y = Y / 4.0
      IF (ABS(Y) .LT. 0.0175) GO TO 40
C  ROTATE PAIR OF AXES.
      CY = COS(Y)
      SY = SIN(Y)
      KR = 1
      DO 35 I = 1,NV
      Q = V(I,M) * CY + V(I,N) * SY
      V(I,N) = V(I,N) * CY - V(I,M) * SY
   35 V(I,M) = Q
   40 CONTINUE
      IF (KR .GT. 0) GO TO 10
C  DENORMALIZE ROWS OF V. COMPUTE PCT. T AND C.
      DO 50 J = 1,NF
      DO 45 I = 1,NV
   45 V(I,J) = V(I,J) * B(I)
   50 A(J) = SUMF(V, J, -NV, ND) / T * 100.0
      DO 55 I = 1,NV
   55 B(I) = B(I)**2 * 100.0
      PRINT 60
   60 FORMAT (// 27H VARIMAX ROTATION ANALYSIS.)
      RETURN
      END
```

RECTANGLES EXAMPLE: STAGE III

The application of the Varimax rotation procedure to the principal-axis factor-loading matrix shown in Figure 9-9 should equalize the emphasis on the two major sources of information (length and width) which we know are equally represented in the five original variables. This result is exactly what appears in the rotated factor-loading matrix shown in Figure 9-11. These "new" factor variables are obviously representative of *length* and *width*.

VARIMAX ROTATED FACTOR SCORES

The computational procedure used in Program FACTOR was derived from a formula suggested by Kaiser (1962):

$$Y_{NK} = Z_{NM} V_{MK} E_{\Delta K}^{-2} V'_{KM} W_{MK}$$

where V is a matrix of unrotated loadings
E is a diagonal matrix of roots
W is the Varimax-rotated matrix of loadings

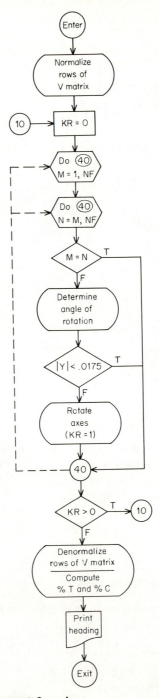

FIGURE 9-10. Subroutine VORS flow chart.

Varimax Rotated Factor Scores 217

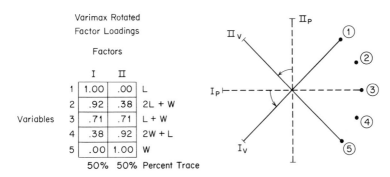

FIGURE 9-11. Varimax-rotated axes of five rectangle scores.

This formula should be compared with the one given earlier for principal-axis factor scores:

$$X_{NK} = Z_{NM} V_{MK} E_{\Delta K}^{-1}$$

Both formulas employ the matrix of raw scores standardized by columns (variables). If we consider the matrix $V_{MK} E_{\Delta K}^{-1}$ as principal-axis factor-score *weights*, then it is easily seen that Kaiser's formula uses the outer-product matrix of this weight matrix to adjust the Varimax loadings to get weights for the rotated factors.

It may be helpful to approach the concept of Varimax rotation and factor scoring from another direction. The rotation of the principal axes may be formulated as postmultiplication of the principal-axis loadings by an *orthogonal transformation matrix* Q_{KK}. This transformation matrix is never actually computed in Program FACTOR, but it is useful in explaining the notion of rotation. The most significant property of an orthogonal matrix is that its inner product is the identity matrix:

$$Q'_{KK} Q_{KK} = I_{\Delta K}$$

Rotation of the principal-axis matrix with this matrix thus retains the orthogonal relationship of the reference axes, although the relationships between these axes and the test vectors may be altered considerably:

$$W_{MK} = V_{MK} Q_{KK}$$

The Varimax procedure may be considered a method of finding the particular Q matrix which achieves a rotation of V closest to simple structure.

It is now possible to derive a parallel definition of rotated factor scores from Kaiser's formula and the definition of W given above:

$$Y_{NK} = Z_{NM} V_{MK} E_{\Delta K}^{-1} E_{\Delta K}^{-1} V'_{KM} V_{MK} Q_{KK}$$

Since $V'_{KM} V_{MK} = E_{\Delta K}$:

$$Y_{NK} = Z_{NM} V_{MK} E_{\Delta K}^{-1} Q_{KK}$$

Since $X_{NK} = Z_{NM} V_{MK} E_{\Delta K}^{-1}$:

$$Y_{NK} = X_{NK} Q_{KK}$$

Varimax factor scores can be defined simply as principal-axis factor scores postmultiplied by the same transformation matrix used to rotate the principal-axis factor loadings. Although conceptually simple, computation of the transformation matrix Q is less practical than the procedure used in Program FACTOR.

IMAGE ANALYSIS

The principal-axis method outlined previously was based on the assumption that all of the variation contained in the correlation matrix was worthy of consideration in deriving factor dimensions from the original variables. Many writers have understood that this assumption is quite unrealistic in most practical research situations, where much of the variation represented in the raw data is known to be unique to individual variables, and hence only confusing in the search for *common* aspects of the behaviors measured by the individual variables. Various attempts have been made to adjust the correlation matrix so as to evade the unique portions of the variance of the original variables. Usually these attempts have amounted to insertion of some kind of communality estimates in place of the 1.0 diagonal elements of the R matrix.

Guttman's (1953) image theory provides an elegant solution to this "communality" problem. As implemented by the contributions of Harris (1962) and Kaiser (1963), image theory defines a matrix called G solely in terms of the R matrix. This G matrix contains image covariances which represent relationships between only the common portions of the original variation, where "common" means "shared by two or more variables." The total amount of common variation for an original variable is the square of the multiple correlation attained by predicting it from all other variables in the set. This proportion is found in the diagonal element of G for that variable. All off-diagonal elements in G are also adjusted to reflect only common covariation. Unlike other attempts to adjust the R matrix, the G matrix retains the mathematical properties that allow it to be completely factored into M roots and vectors by the same principal-axis procedure that was described previously for use with the R matrix. The matrix formula for G is:

$$G_{MM} = R_{MM} + S_{\Delta M} R_{MM}^{-1} S_{\Delta M} - 2 S_{\Delta M}$$

where $S_{\Delta M} = (R_{\Delta M}^{-1})_{\Delta M}^{-1}$

Extraction of roots and vectors of G may be accomplished with Subroutine SEVS, and the resulting matrix of principal-axis loadings may be rotated with Subroutine VORS. Computation of principal-axis and Varimax factor scores requires the use of a weight-modification matrix (Kaiser, 1958), which is defined by:

$$P_{MM} = I_{\Delta M} - R_{MM}^{-1} S_{\Delta M}$$

This matrix is used in computing factor scores as follows:

$$X_{NK} = Z_{NM} P_{MM} V_{MK} E_{\Delta K}^{-1} \text{ (Principal axis scores)}$$
$$Y_{NK} = Z_{NM} P_{MM} V_{MK} E_{\Delta K}^{-2} V'_{KM} W_{MK} \text{ (Varimax rotated scores)}$$

The trace of the G matrix will usually be less than that of the corresponding R matrix, since some of the variation will be unique. This would *not* be the case for the rectangles example, however, since each variable in the set of five is exactly predictable from a combination of others in the set. Therefore, an image analysis would be impossible, since the R matrix would be singular, and G could not be computed. When some of the variation is unique to single variables, the number of factors extracted under the usual criterion of an eigenvalue of 1.0 will yield fewer factors than will analysis of the R matrix. Kaiser (1963) has suggested extracting and rotating a number of factors equal to one half the number of original variables.

Image analysis is particularly suited to item-analysis problems, where the investigator is quite certain that each of the important factors is represented by more than one item. Many factor-analytic problems, however, involve analysis of data where an important factor is represented by only one of the original variables. An image analysis of such data could not register such a factor, since most of its variation would not be shared by other variables in the set.

The factor-analytic models presented in this chapter might be called "parametric" as opposed to other "statistical" models of factor analysis that have been proposed (Horst, 1965; Kaiser and Caffrey, 1965). This means that the technique treats the data as if they represented completely the population of interest to the investigator, in terms of both subjects and variables. In other words, the methods outlined here serve to *describe* a particular set of data, reorganizing and reducing it to essentials by means of criteria internal to the analytic system. The generalizability of the results to other samples of subjects and/or variables remains an open question—untestable except by replication of the analysis.

PROGRAM FACTOR

Program FACTOR includes a variety of relatively independent processes within a single sequential framework of options. For installations that do not permit the construction of a program library tape, a routine as large as this may be rather impractical as a general-purpose program. Although some behavioral research problems require the use of the entire option sequence—from raw data through factor scoring—the use of only the first (intercorrelation) stage may be more practically handled with a separate program which serves only this function. The entire program deck for FACTOR, with all of its subprogram decks, is quite large—even after the Fortran program has been compiled into the form of a binary object deck. The program has been constructed in modular form to simplify the reconstruction of smaller package programs, if this is considered desirable.

The flow chart (Figure 9-12) is very general, in that most of the output

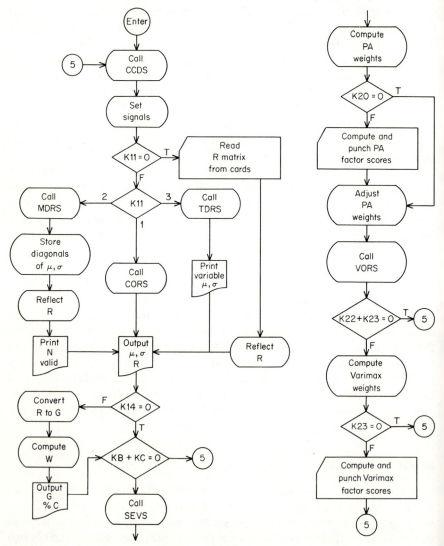

FIGURE 9-12. Program FACTOR flow chart.

options are not shown, and many of the computational processes are only named in the diagram. Although it requires considerable concentration, tracing the Fortran statement sequence in terms of the matrix formulations presented earlier can be a profitable experience yielding greater comprehension of the statistical procedures as well as added sophistication in Fortran programming.

The program begins with the usual CALL of Subroutine CCDS, followed by the expansion of the last three parameter fields (KA, KB, KC) into a series of separate option signals. The first stage of the program develops a correlation matrix in R and vectors of means and sigmas in X and Y (unless R is read from cards). Subroutine CORS, MDRS, or TDRS may be used for this purpose. If optioned, the contents of the R matrix (intercorrelations) are converted to image covariances and the results are output.

At this point a check is made to see whether a factor analysis is required; if parameters K16 through K23 are zero, control returns to CCDS. If a factor analysis is to be performed, Subroutine SEVS is called to extract the roots and vectors (loadings) from the R matrix. After output of these results, principal-axis factor-score weights are computed. These are adjusted by the contents of the W matrix if R had been converted earlier to G. After optional output of these weights, scratch tape 2 is rewound if principal-axis factor-scores are to be computed; the raw data are assumed to have been previously written on this tape by Subroutine CORS. As each subject's raw data are input from tape 2, they are converted to z scores and factor scores are then computed in z-scaled and T-scaled form. At option, one of these sets may be punched completely, or only the first factor score may be punched. The principal-axis weights are adjusted next in preparation for use in computing Varimax weights. This adjustment matrix ($V_{MK}E_{\Delta K}^{-2}V'_{KM}$ or $W_{MM}V_{MK}E_{\Delta K}^{-2}V'_{KM}$) is held in memory area W during the rotation process.

The next step in the processing sequence is Varimax rotation of the principal axes extracted by Subroutine SEVS. Subroutine VORS carries out these rotations. After optional output of the results, a check on the last two signals is made to determine whether processing is complete. If factor-score weights are required, the Varimax-loading matrix is premultiplied by the adjustment matrix and the resulting weight matrix is optionally output. If optioned, Varimax-rotated factor scores are computed next, after rewinding the data tape on unit 2. The procedure is the same as that for principal-axis factor scores, except that the option for the first factor only has been omitted.

EXAMPLE PROBLEMS FOR PROGRAM FACTOR

The first problem uses as data the SRI scores punched by Program TESTAT (problem two). Only the first eight subscales are used as variables.

The total score could have been included also, but we wished to obtain factors that could be compared directly with those obtained in the image analysis of the second problem.

The output illustrates the punching of an intercorrelation matrix by Subroutine PTMS. An eigenvalue cutoff of 1.0 was used, which yielded three factors. Principal-axis loadings were punched, as well as the first principal-axis factor score for each subject. Varimax loadings and factor scores were also punched.

The second example problem uses the same data as did the first problem, but an image analysis is performed. The total score could not be included in this case because it is a linear combination of the eight subscales, and the 9-by-9 R matrix would be singular—preventing computation of the G matrix, since R^{-1} is required in the conversion process. Note that if we had not specified the extraction of three factors in this case, the 1.0 criterion would have led to the extraction of only one factor from the G matrix.

Only Varimax loadings and factor scores were punched for this problem.

The third example problem illustrates intercorrelation with the MDRS Subroutine, which permits the exclusion of zero scores for selected variables. In order to demonstrate the operation of this subroutine, a few scores have been arbitrarily removed for even-numbered variables in the previously used data deck. The results should be compared with those obtained in problem one.

The fourth example problem illustrates the use of Subroutine TDRS. The complete data deck is used, and intercorrelations of the 16 subjects rather than 8 variables are output.

```
C      PROGRAM FACTOR
C
C      INTERCORRELATION AND FACTOR ANALYSIS CONTROL PROGRAM.
C      PARAMETER CONTROL-CARD FIELDS.
C         COL 1-5. NUMBER OF VARIABLES (MAX = 70).
C         COL 6-10. NUMBER OF SUBJECTS (MAX = 70 FOR TDRS OPTION ONLY).
C         COL 11. CORRELATION OPTION. 0 = READ R MATRIX AS PUNCHED BY PTMS,
C              1 = NORMAL INTERCORRELATION (CORS),
C              2 = MISSING-DATA INTERCORRELATION (MDRS),
C              3 = TRANSPOSED-DATA INTERCORRELATION (TDRS).
C         COL 12. OUTPUT OF MEANS AND SIGMAS (SEE BELOW).
C         COL 13. OUTPUT OF INTERCORRELATION MATRIX (SEE BELOW).
C         COL 14. 1 = CONVERT R MATRIX TO G (IMAGE COVARIANCES).
C         COL 15. OUTPUT OF G MATRIX (SEE BELOW).
C         COL 16-17. EIGENVALUE CUTOFF OPTION. 0 = ALL NV FACTORS,
C              1 = FACTORS WHOSE ROOTS EXCEED 1.0, 2+ = EXTRACT THAT MANY FACTOR
C         COL 18. OUTPUT OF PRINCIPAL-AXIS FACTOR LOADINGS (SEE BELOW).
C         COL 19. OUTPUT OF PRINCIPAL-AXIS FACTOR-SCORE WEIGHTS (SEE BELOW).
C         COL 20. PRINCIPAL-AXIS FACTOR-SCORE OPTION. 0 = NONE,
C              1 = REAL-MODE (7 PER CARD), 2 = INTEGER-MODE (35 PER CARD),
C              3 = FIRST FACTOR ONLY (REAL MODE).
C         COL 21. OUTPUT OF VARIMAX-LOADING MATRIX (SEE BELOW).
C         COL 22. OUTPUT OF VARIMAX FACTOR-SCORE WEIGHTS (SEE BELOW).
C         COL 23. VARIMAX-ROTATED FACTOR-SCORE OPTION. 0 = NONE,
C              1 = REAL MODE, 2 = INTEGER MODE.
C      OUTPUT OPTIONS. 0 = NONE, 1 = PRINT ONLY,
C         2 = PUNCH ONLY, 3 = BOTH PRINT AND PUNCH.
```

Example Problems for Program Factor 223

```
C     FORMAT CONTROL CARD SPECIFIES ONLY FIELDS FOR NV SCORES,
C        EXCEPT WHEN COL 11 = 1. CORS OPTION (COL 11 = 1) REQUIRES
C        A-MODE ID FIELD BEFORE FIRST SCORE.
C     WHEN COL 11 = 2 (MDRS) AN OPTION-SIGNAL CARD IMMEDIATELY FOLLOWS FORMAT
C        CONTROL CARD, PRECEDING THE DATA CARDS.
C     TAPE UNIT 2 IS USED FOR TEMPORARY STORAGE (SCRATCH).
C     FACTOR SCORES CAN BE COMPUTED ONLY WHEN COL 11 = 1 (CORS).
C     SUBPROGRAMS REQUIRED ARE SUMF, SCPF, CCDS, PRTS, PCDS, PTMS, SUBS,
C        AXBS, INVS, CORS, MDRS, TDRS, SEVS, VORS.
C
      ODIMENSION KF(16), R(70,70), V(70,70), W(70,70), X(70), Y(70),
     1 Z(70), KS(70), A(70), S(70)
      ND = 70
    5 CALL CCDS (KF, NV, NS, KA, KB, KC)
      K11 = KA / 10000
      K12 = MOD (KA / 1000, 10)
      K13 = MOD (KA / 100, 10)
      K14 = MOD (KA / 10, 10)
      K15 = MOD (KA, 10)
      KEV = KB / 1000
      K18 = MOD (KB / 100, 10)
      K19 = MOD (KB / 10, 10)
      K20 = MOD (KB, 10)
      K21 = KC / 10000
      K22 = MOD (KC / 1000, 10)
      K23 = MOD (KC / 100, 10)
      VN = NV
      IF (K11 .GT. 0) GO TO (15, 20, 30), K11
C     INPUT R MATRIX FROM CARDS.
      READ KF, ((R(I,J), J = I,NV), I = 1,NV)
      DO 10 I = 1,NV
      DO 10 J = I,NV
   10 R(J,I) = R(I,J)
      GO TO 45
C     COMPUTE R MATRIX FROM RAW DATA.
   15 KTD = 0
      IF (K20 + K23 .GT. 0) KTD = 2
      CALL CORS (NS, NV, R, A, S, KF, KTD, ND)
      GO TO 35
   20 CALL MDRS (NS, NV, R, V, W, X, Y, KF, ND)
      DO 25 I = 1,NV
      A(I) = V(I,I)
      S(I) = W(I,I)
      Z(I) = R(I,I)
      R(I,I) = 1.0
      DO 25 J = I,NV
   25 R(J,I) = R(I,J)
      CALL PRTS (Z, NV, 1, 5HVALID, ND)
      GO TO 35
   30 CALL TDRS (NS, NV, R, V, A, S, X, Y, KF, ND)
      CALL PRTS (X, NS, 1, 6HVMEANS, ND)
      CALL PRTS (Y, NS, 1, 6HVSIGMA, ND)
C     OUTPUT MEANS, SIGMAS, AND INTERCORRELATIONS.
   35 IF (K12 .EQ. 0 .OR. K12 .EQ. 2) GO TO 40
      CALL PRTS (A, NV, 1, 5HMEANS, ND)
      CALL PRTS (S, NV, 1, 6HSIGMAS, ND)
   40 IF (K12 .LE. 1) GO TO 45
      CALL PCDS (A, NV, 1, 5HMEANS, ND)
      CALL PCDS (S, NV, 1, 5HSIGMA, ND)
   45 IF (K13 .GT. 1) CALL PTMS (R, NV, 5HR MAT, ND)
      IF (K13 .EQ. 1 .OR. K13 .EQ. 3) CALL PRTS (R, NV, NV, 5HR MAT, ND)
      IF (K14 .EQ. 0) GO TO 85
C     CONVERT R TO G. W = WEIGHT-MODIFICATION MATRIX.
      DO 50 I = 1,NV
      DO 50 J = 1,NV
```

224 INTERCORRELATION AND FACTOR ANALYSIS

```
   50 W(I,J) = R(I,J)
      CALL INVS (NV, W, X, Y, Z, ND)
      DO 55 I = 1,NV
   55 Y(I) = 1.0 / W(I,I)
      DO 65 I = 1,NV
      DO 60 J = 1,NV
   60 R(I,J) = R(I,J) + Y(I) * W(I,J) * Y(J)
   65 R(I,I) = R(I,I) - 2.0 * Y(I)
      DO 75 I = 1,NV
      DO 70 J = 1,NV
   70 W(I,J) = -W(I,J) * Y(J)
      W(I,I) = W(I,I) + 1.0
   75 X(I) = R(I,I) * 100.0
      CV = SUMF(X, 1, NV, ND) / VN
      PRINT 80, CV
   80 FORMAT (// 58H CONVERSION OF R (CORRELATIONS) TO G (IMAGE COVARI
     1CES). // F7.2, 35H PCT. OF TOTAL VARIATION IS COMMON.)
      CALL PRTS (X, NV, 1, 6HPCT. C, ND)
      IF (K15 .GT. 1) CALL PTMS (R, NV, 5HG MAT, ND)
      IF (K15 .EQ. 1 .OR. K15 .EQ. 3) CALL PRTS (R, NV, NV, 5HG MAT, N
   85 IF (KB + KC .EQ. 0) GO TO 5
C  PRINCIPAL-AXIS ANALYSIS.
      NF = NV
      C = KEV
      IF (KEV .LE. 1) GO TO 90
      NF = KEV
      C = 0.0
   90 CALL SEVS (NV, NF, C, R, V, X, Y, ND)
      CALL PRTS (X, NF, 1, 6HEROOTS, ND)
      CALL PRTS (Y, NF, 1, 6HPCT. T, ND)
      IF (K18 .GT. 1) CALL PCDS (V, NV, NF, 5HPLOAD, ND)
      IF (K18 .EQ. 1 .OR. K18 .EQ. 3) CALL PRTS(V, NV, NF, 6HP LOAD, N
C  COMPUTE PRINCIPAL-AXIS FACTOR-SCORE WEIGHTS.
      IF (K14 .EQ. 1) GO TO 100
      DO 95 J = 1,NF
      DO 95 I = 1,NV
   95 R(I,J) = V(I,J) / X(J)
      GO TO 110
  100 CALL AXBS (W, V, R, NV, NF, NV, ND)
      DO 105 J = 1,NF
      DO 105 I = 1,NV
  105 R(I,J) = R(I,J) / X(J)
  110 IF (K19 .GT. 1) CALL PCDS (R, NV, NF, 5HP WTS, ND)
      IF (K19 .EQ. 1 .OR. K19 .EQ. 3) CALL PRTS (R, NV, NF, 5HP WTS, N
      IF (K20 .EQ. 0) GO TO 130
C  COMPUTE PRINCIPAL-AXIS FACTOR-SCORES FOR ALL SUBJECTS.
      REWIND 2
      DO 125 I = 1,NS
      READ (2) ID, (Z(J), J = 1,NV)
      DO 115 J = 1,NV
  115 Z(J) = (Z(J) - A(J)) / S(J)
      DO 120 K = 1,NF
      Y(K) = SCPF(Z, R, 1, K, NV, ND)
  120 KS(K) = AMAX1(1.0, AMIN1(99.0, Y(K) * 10.0 + 50.5))
      IF (K20 .EQ. 1) CALL SUBS (Y, NF, 2HPA, ID)
      IF (K20 .EQ. 2) CALL SUBS (KS, -NF, 2HPA, ID)
      IF (K20 .EQ. 3) CALL SUBS (Y, 1, 2HPA, ID)
  125 CONTINUE
C  ADJUST PA WEIGHTS FOR MODIFYING VARIMAX LOADINGS.
  130 DO 135 J = 1,NF
      DO 135 I = 1,NV
  135 R(I,J) = R(I,J) / X(J)
      CALL AXBS (R, V, W, NV, -NV, NF, ND)
C  VARIMAX ROTATION OF PRINCIPAL AXES.
      CALL VORS (NV, NF, V, X, Y, Z, ND)
```

Example Problems for Program Factor

```
      CALL PRTS (X, NF, 1, 6HPCT. V, ND)
      CALL PRTS (Y, NV, 1, 6HPCT. C, ND)
      IF (K21 .GT. 1) CALL PCDS (V, NV, NF, 5HVLOAD, ND)
      IF (K21 .EQ. 1 .OR. K21 .EQ. 3) CALL PRTS(V, NV, NF, 6HV LOAD, ND)
      IF (K22 + K23 .EQ. 0) GO TO 5
C     COMPUTE VARIMAX FACTOR-SCORE WEIGHTS AND FACTOR SCORES.
      CALL AXBS (W, V, R, NV, NF, NV, ND)
      IF (K22 .GT. 1) CALL PCDS (R, NV, NF, 5HV WTS, ND)
      IF (K22 .EQ. 1 .OR. K22 .EQ. 3) CALL PRTS (R, NV, NF, 5HV WTS, ND)
      IF (K23 .EQ. 0) GO TO 5
      REWIND 2
      DO 150 I = 1,NS
      READ (2) ID, (Z(J), J = 1,NV)
      DO 140 J = 1,NV
  140 Z(J) = (Z(J) - A(J)) / S(J)
      DO 145 K = 1,NF
      Y(K) = SCPF(Z, R, 1, K, NV, ND)
  145 KS(K) = AMAX1(1.0, AMIN1(99.0, Y(K) * 10.0 + 50.5))
      IF (K23 .EQ. 1) CALL SUBS (Y, NF, 2HVR, ID)
      IF (K23 .EQ. 2) CALL SUBS (KS, -NF, 2HVR, ID)
  150 CONTINUE
      GO TO 5
      END


*** INPUT DATA DECK ***

FACTOR EXAMPLE PROBLEM 1. PRINCIPAL COMPONENTS ANALYSIS.
00008000161130001313311
(A6, 4X, 8F7.0)
S01SRI QS     25.      21.      22.      20.      26.      26.      19.      23.      182.
S02SRI QS     26.      30.      30.      26.      28.      20.      24.      28.      212.
S03SRI QS     20.      25.      20.      23.      18.      24.      21.      29.      180.
S04SRI QS     30.      28.      29.      29.      28.      23.      28.      30.      225.
S05SRI QS     23.      25.      29.      19.      20.      27.      28.      28.      199.
S06SRI QS     28.      27.      30.      22.      19.      25.      30.      26.      207.
S07SRI QS     28.      24.      27.      27.      17.      21.      30.      26.      200.
S08SRI QS     25.      29.      29.      27.      26.      25.      26.      25.      212.
S09SRI QS     26.      30.      30.      24.      29.      24.      14.      29.      206.
S10SRI QS     28.      29.      30.      26.      25.      28.      30.      28.      224.
S11SRI QS     24.      28.      30.      29.      27.      23.      21.      28.      210.
S12SRI QS     26.      29.      26.      27.      28.      19.      30.      27.      212.
S13SRI QS     30.      27.      26.      24.      25.      21.      28.      25.      206.
S14SRI QS     29.      29.      29.      28.      25.      19.      30.      27.      216.
S15SRI QS     29.      25.      28.      26.      24.      21.      30.      29.      212.
S16SRI QS     29.      26.      30.      20.      25.      20.      30.      28.      208.
FACTOR EXAMPLE PROBLEM 2. IMAGE ANALYSIS.
00008000161001103100301
(A6, 4X, 8F7.0)
S01SRI QS     25.      21.      22.      20.      26.      26.      19.      23.      182.
S02SRI QS     26.      30.      30.      26.      28.      20.      24.      28.      212.
S03SRI QS     20.      25.      20.      23.      18.      24.      21.      29.      180.
S04SRI QS     30.      28.      29.      29.      28.      23.      28.      30.      225.
S05SRI QS     23.      25.      29.      19.      20.      27.      28.      28.      199.
S06SRI QS     28.      27.      30.      22.      19.      25.      30.      26.      207.
S07SRI QS     28.      24.      27.      27.      17.      21.      30.      26.      200.
S08SRI QS     25.      29.      29.      27.      26.      25.      26.      25.      212.
S09SRI QS     26.      30.      30.      24.      29.      24.      14.      29.      206.
S10SRI QS     28.      29.      30.      26.      25.      28.      30.      28.      224.
S11SRI QS     24.      28.      30.      29.      27.      23.      21.      28.      210.
S12SRI QS     26.      29.      26.      27.      28.      19.      30.      27.      212.
S13SRI QS     30.      27.      26.      24.      25.      21.      28.      25.      206.
S14SRI QS     29.      29.      29.      28.      25.      19.      30.      27.      216.
S15SRI QS     29.      25.      28.      26.      24.      21.      30.      29.      212.
S16SRI QS     29.      26.      30.      20.      25.      20.      30.      28.      208.
```

226 INTERCORRELATION AND FACTOR ANALYSIS

```
FACTOR EXAMPLE PROBLEM 3. MISSING-DATA INTERCORRELATION.
0000800016211
(10X, 8F7.0)
01010101
S01SRI QS    25.            22.            26.            19.            18
S02SRI QS    26.    30.     30.    26.     28.    20.     24.    28.     21
S03SRI QS    20.            20.    23.     18.            21.    29.     18
S04SRI QS    30.    28.     29.    29.     28.    23.     28.    30.     22
S05SRI QS    23.    25.     29.            20.    27.     28.            19
S06SRI QS    28.    27.     30.    22.     19.    25.     30.    26.     20
S07SRI QS    28.    24.     27.    27.     17.    21.     30.    26.     20
S08SRI QS    25.    29.     29.    27.     26.    25.     26.    25.     21
S09SRI QS    26.            30.    24.     29.    24.     14.    29.     20
S10SRI QS    28.    29.     30.    26.     25.    28.     30.    28.     2.
S11SRI QS    24.    28.     30.            27.    23.     21.    28.     21
S12SRI QS    26.    29.     26.    27.     28.    19.     30.    27.     21
S13SRI QS    30.    27.     26.    24.     25.            28.    25.     20
S14SRI QS    29.    29.     29.    28.     25.    19.     30.    27.     21
S15SRI QS    29.    25.     28.    26.     24.    21.     30.            21
S16SRI QS    29.    26.     30.    20.     25.    20.     30.    28.     20
FACTOR EXAMPLE PROBLEM 4. TRANSPOSED-DATA INTERCORRELATION.
0000800016311
(10X, 8F7.0)
S01SRI QS    25.    21.     22.    20.     26.    26.     19.    23.     18
S02SRI QS    26.    30.     30.    26.     28.    20.     24.    28.     21
S03SRI QS    20.    25.     20.    23.     18.    24.     21.    29.     18
S04SRI QS    30.    28.     29.    29.     28.    23.     28.    30.     22
S05SRI QS    23.    25.     29.    19.     20.    27.     28.    28.     19
S06SRI QS    28.    27.     30.    22.     19.    25.     30.    26.     20
S07SRI QS    28.    24.     27.    27.     17.    21.     30.    26.     20
S08SRI QS    25.    29.     29.    27.     26.    25.     26.    25.     21
S09SRI QS    26.    30.     30.    24.     29.    24.     14.    29.     20
S10SRI QS    28.    29.     30.    26.     25.    28.     30.    28.     2.
S11SRI QS    24.    28.     30.    29.     27.    23.     21.    28.     21
S12SRI QS    26.    29.     26.    27.     28.    19.     30.    27.     21
S13SRI QS    30.    27.     26.    24.     25.    21.     28.    25.     20
S14SRI QS    29.    29.     29.    28.     25.    19.     30.    27.     21
S15SRI QS    29.    25.     28.    26.     24.    21.     30.    29.     21
S16SRI QS    29.    26.     30.    20.     25.    20.     30.    28.     20


         *** PUNCHED OUTPUT ***

R  MAT     1    1.0000    .1821    .4685    .2666    .2409   -.3938
R  MAT     2    -.0325   1.0000    .6181    .5525    .5452   -.2150
R  MAT     3    .3900    1.0000    .2631    .3198   -.0495    .2694
R  MAT     4    1.0000    .3529   -.3723    .1394    .2547   1.0000
R  MAT     5    -.3032    .1091   1.0000   -.2808   -.1079   1.0000
R  MAT     6    1.0000
PLOAD  1   1    .6125    -.5973   -.0671
PLOAD  2   1    .8053     .3803    .1170
PLOAD  3   1    .7276    -.0057    .4985
PLOAD  4   1    .7010     .0999   -.2562
PLOAD  5   1    .5851     .4818   -.3833
PLOAD  6   1   -.5046     .3246    .5609
PLOAD  7   1    .3157    -.8384    .2452
PLOAD  8   1    .4227     .3319    .4579
S01SRIPA   1   -2.2887
S02SRIPA   1    .9592
```

```
S03SRIPA   1    -1.9416
S04SRIPA   1     1.2527
S05SRIPA   1    -1.2498
S06SRIPA   1     -.3628
S07SRIPA   1     -.4344
S08SRIPA   1      .1386
S09SRIPA   1      .4657
S10SRIPA   1      .4721
S11SRIPA   1      .4962
S12SRIPA   1      .6972
S13SRIPA   1      .0559
S14SRIPA   1     1.1010
S15SRIPA   1      .3895
S16SRIPA   1      .2492
VLOAD    1 1    0.3061    -0.7943     0.1087
VLOAD    2 1    0.5657    -0.0117     0.6976
VLOAD    3 1    0.1505    -0.3568     0.7924
VLOAD    4 1    0.6778    -0.1892     0.2679
VLOAD    5 1    0.7860     0.2145     0.2400
VLOAD    6 1   -0.6428     0.4626     0.2175
VLOAD    7 1   -0.1727    -0.9097     0.0734
VLOAD    8 1    0.0594     0.0809     0.6989
S01SRIVR   1   -0.3187     1.2922    -2.5469
S02SRIVR   1    1.1415     0.3271     0.5430
S03SRIVR   1   -1.0338     1.7241    -0.8415
S04SRIVR   1    0.7112    -0.4360     0.9777
S05SRIVR   1   -2.2945     0.3851     0.7925
S06SRIVR   1   -1.4459    -0.9011     0.3913
S07SRIVR   1   -0.5785    -1.3046    -1.0051
S08SRIVR   1    0.3277     0.3967     0.1438
S09SRIVR   1    0.7936     1.8264     1.1870
S10SRIVR   1   -0.7461    -0.2224     1.4808
S11SRIVR   1    0.8065     1.0308     0.6530
S12SRIVR   1    1.3574    -0.2812    -0.5779
S13SRIVR   1    0.5913    -0.8190    -1.1665
S14SRIVR   1    1.0392    -1.0638    -0.1000
S15SRIVR   1   -0.0087    -0.9377    -0.0095
S16SRIVR   1   -0.3421    -1.0165     0.0781
VLOAD    1 1    0.3298    -0.6608    -0.0047
VLOAD    2 1    0.7591    -0.0842    -0.2812
VLOAD    3 1    0.3650    -0.3315    -0.4698
VLOAD    4 1    0.2829    -0.1715    -0.4918
VLOAD    5 1   -0.3234     0.1163    -0.5949
VLOAD    6 1   -0.0142     0.3293     0.3484
VLOAD    7 1   -0.1425    -0.6675    -0.0970
VLOAD    8 1    0.3541     0.0123    -0.1422
S01SRIVR   1   -1.4230     1.2810     1.2574
S02SRIVR   1    1.2530     0.3690    -0.5114
S03SRIVR   1   -1.8844     1.9049    -0.0710
S04SRIVR   1    0.3160    -0.6640    -0.9851
S05SRIVR   1    0.4235     0.3126     2.2006
S06SRIVR   1   -0.7139    -0.8058     0.0475
S07SRIVR   1   -0.9905    -1.1918     0.7959
S08SRIVR   1    0.9460     0.3996     0.2396
S09SRIVR   1    0.4543     1.8045    -1.8406
S10SRIVR   1    0.2061    -0.3975    -0.5542
S11SRIVR   1    1.8932     0.9072     0.8245
S12SRIVR   1    0.5304    -0.2037    -0.3414
S13SRIVR   1   -1.4096    -0.6678    -1.3597
S14SRIVR   1    0.2203    -0.9722    -0.8225
S15SRIVR   1   -0.0192    -1.0603     0.5317
S16SRIVR   1    0.1978    -1.0158     0.5887
```

```
*** PRINTED OUTPUT ***

1FACTOR EXAMPLE PROBLEM 1. PRINCIPAL COMPONENTS ANALYSIS.

PARAMETERS
COL  1- 5  =        8
COL  6-10  =       16
COL 11-15  =    11300
COL 16-20  =     1313
COL 21-25  =    31100

DATA FORMAT = (A6, 4X, 8F7.0)

INTERCORRELATION ANALYSIS.
```

	1	2	3	4	5	6	7	8
MEANS	26.6250	27.0000	27.8125	24.8125	24.3750	22.8750	26.1875	27.2500
SIGMAS	2.6897	2.4238	2.9202	3.1269	3.6891	2.7585	4.8117	1.7854
R MAT	1	2	3	4	5	6	7	8
1	1.0000	.1821	.4685	.2666	.2409	-.3938	.5560	-.0325
2	.1821	1.0000	.6181	.5525	.5452	-.2150	.0161	.3900
3	.4685	.6181	1.0000	.2631	.3198	-.0495	.2694	.3087
4	.2666	.5525	.2631	1.0000	.3529	-.3723	.1394	.2547
5	.2409	.5452	.3198	.3529	1.0000	-.2104	-.3032	.1091
6	-.3938	-.2150	-.0495	-.3723	-.2104	1.0000	-.2808	-.1079
7	.5560	.0161	.2694	.1394	-.3032	-.2808	1.0000	-.0127
8	-.0325	.3900	.3087	.2547	.1091	-.1079	-.0127	1.0000

PRINCIPAL AXIS ANALYSIS.

TRACE =   8.0000

70.57 PCT. OF TRACE WAS EXTRACTED BY   3 ROOTS.

EROOTS	1	2	3
	2.9197	1.6620	1.0636

PCT. T	1	2	3
	36.4964	20.7751	13.2948

P LOAD	1	2	3
1	.6125	-.5973	-.0671
2	.8053	.3803	.1170
3	.7276	-.0057	.4985
4	.7010	.0999	-.2562
5	.5851	.4818	-.3833
6	-.5046	.3246	.5609
7	.3157	-.8384	.2452
8	.4227	.3319	.4579

P WTS	1	2	3
1	.2098	-.3594	-.0631
2	.2758	.2288	.1100
3	.2492	-.0034	.4687
4	.2401	.0601	-.2408
5	.2004	.2899	-.3604
6	-.1728	.1953	.5274
7	.1081	-.5044	.2306
8	.1448	.1997	.4305

INTERCORRELATION AND FACTOR ANALYSIS

VARIMAX ROTATION ANALYSIS.

	1	2	3	4	5	6	7	8
PCT. V	24.5008	23.6034	22.4619					
PCT. C	73.6493	80.6836	77.7905	56.6943	72.1384	67.4511	86.2730	49.8490

V LOAD	1	2	3
1	.3061	-.7943	.1087
2	.5657	-.0117	.6976
3	.1505	-.3568	.7924
4	.6778	-.1892	.2679
5	.7860	.2145	.2400
6	-.6428	.4626	.2175
7	-.1727	-.9097	.0734
8	.0594	.0809	.6939

V WTS	1	2	3
1	.0920	-.4082	-.0457
2	.1715	.0791	.3238
3	-.1533	-.1477	.4862
4	.3440	-.0290	-.0099
5	.4590	.2045	-.0399
6	-.4283	.2070	.3461
7	-.2165	-.5191	.0554

```
1FACTOR EXAMPLE PROBLEM 2.  IMAGE ANALYSIS.

PARAMETERS
COL  1- 5 =        8
COL  6-10 =       16
COL 11-15 =    10011
COL 16-20 =     3100
COL 21-25 =    30100

DATA FORMAT = (A6, 4X, 8F7.0)
```

INTERCORRELATION ANALYSIS.

CONVERSION OF R (CORRELATIONS) TO G (IMAGE COVARIANCES).

49.70 PCT. OF TOTAL VARIATION IS COMMON.

PCT. C	1 61.1463	2 67.5998	3 60.9144	4 40.6880	5 56.0397	6 32.8896	7 56.2511	8 22.0993
G MAT	1	2	3	4	5	6	7	8
1	.6115	.2977	.2981	.2078	.0756	-.2537	.3440	.0537
2	.2977	.6760	.4183	.3694	.3958	-.1564	.0191	.3133
3	.2981	.4183	.6091	.3565	.3192	-.2133	.2219	.1917
4	.2078	.3694	.3565	.4069	.3192	-.2694	.1001	.1845
5	.0756	.3958	.3192	.3221	.5604	-.1448	.0480	.1780
6	-.2537	-.1564	-.2133	-.2694	-.1448	.3289	.1877	-.0138
7	.3440	.0191	.2219	.1001	-.0480	-.1877	.5625	.0210
8	.0537	.3133	.1917	.1845	.1780	-.0138	.0210	.2210

232 INTERCORRELATION AND FACTOR ANALYSIS

```
PRINCIPAL AXIS ANALYSIS.

TRACE =    3.9763

84.15 PCT. OF TRACE WAS EXTRACTED BY 3 ROOTS.

EROOTS         1          2          3
            2.1091      .9052      .3317

PCT. T         1          2          3
           53.0423    22.7652    8.3416
```

P LOAD	1	2	3
1	.5149	-.4551	.2704
2	.6984	.2924	.2987
3	.6752	-.0349	-.0814
4	.5635	.0802	-.1655
5	.5221	.3765	-.2401
6	-.3745	.2004	.2227
7	.2727	-.6236	-.1099
8	.3092	.1848	.1267

```
VARIMAX ROTATION ANALYSIS.

PCT. V         1          2          3          4          5          6          7          8
           14.3584    14.3834    13.0833    35.1324    47.2000    23.0014    47.5320    14.5774

PCT. C         1          2          3
           54.5392    66.2382    46.3801
```

V LOAD	1	2	3
1	.3298	-.6608	-.0047
2	.7591	-.0842	-.2812
3	.3650	-.3315	-.4698
4	.2829	-.1715	-.4918
5	.3234	.1163	-.5949
6	-.0142	.3293	.3484
7	-.1425	-.6675	-.0970

(Note that the "P LOAD" matrix was printed just before the Varimax output in the original listing, and not as shown here.)

```
1FACTOR EXAMPLE PROBLEM 3. MISSING-DATA INTERCORRELATION.

PARAMETERS
COL  1- 5 =        8
COL  6-10 =       16
COL 11-15 =    21100
COL 16-20 =        0
COL 21-25 =        0

DATA FORMAT = (10X, 8F7.0)

INTERCORRELATION ANALYSIS (INCOMPLETE DATA).

OPTIONS. 01010101
```

	1	2	3	4	5	6	7	8
VALID	16.0000	13.0000	16.0000	13.0000	16.0000	13.0000	16.0000	13.0000
MEANS	26.6250	27.3846	27.8125	25.3077	24.3750	22.6923	26.1875	27.3846
SIGMAS	2.6897	1.8203	2.9202	2.4615	3.6891	2.8658	4.8117	1.4956
R MAT	1	2	3	4	5	6	7	8
1	1.0000	-.1065	.4685	.1688	.2409	-.3492	.5560	-.2152
2	-.1065	1.0000	.2514	.3179	.7521	-.0584	-.3619	.2372
3	.4585	.2514	1.0000	.0805	.3198	.4328	.2694	-.0143
4	.1588	.3179	.0805	1.0000	.2988	-.0886	.1751	.0211
5	.2409	.7521	.3198	.2988	1.0000	-.2226	-.3032	.2911
6	-.3492	-.0584	.4328	-.0886	-.2226	1.0000	-.1504	-.0065
7	.5560	-.3619	.2694	.1751	-.3032	-.1504	1.0000	-.4335
8	-.2152	.2372	-.0143	.0211	.2911	-.0065	-.4335	1.0000

```
1FACTOR EXAMPLE PROBLEM 4. TRANSPOSED-DATA INTERCORRELATION.

PARAMETERS
COL  1- 5 =      8
COL  6-10 =     16
COL 11-15 =  31100
COL 16-20 =      0
COL 21-25 =      0

DATA FORMAT = (10X, 8F7.0)

INTERCORRELATION ANALYSIS (TRANSPOSED DATA).
```

	1	2	3	4	5	6	7	8
VMEANS	26.6250	27.0000	27.8125	24.8125	24.3750	22.8750	26.1875	27.2500

	1	2	3	4	5	6	7	8
VSIGMA	2.6897	2.4238	2.9202	3.1269	3.6891	2.7585	4.8117	1.7854

	1	2	3	4	5	6	7	8	9	10
MEANS	-1.1138	.2550	-.9952	.7948	-.3149	-.0292	-.3615	.1549	.2004	.7131

	11	12	13	14	15	16
MEANS	.2030	.1127	-.1274	.3189	.1866	.0025

	1	2	3	4	5	6	7	8	9	10
SIGMAS	1.2387	.7251	1.2038	.5163	1.0774	.8261	.9281	.6970	1.1730	.4827

	11	12	13	14	15	16
SIGMAS	.7902	.7980	.7175	.7501	.6511	.8514

R MAT	1	2	3	4	5	6	7	8	9	10
1	1.0000	-.5282	-.0118	-.2568	.1603	.0047	-.2344	.2810	.0203	.4020
2	-.5282	1.0000	-.2670	.2688	-.5098	-.5694	-.5138	.1322	.5893	-.6431
3	-.0118	-.2670	1.0000	.0918	.3998	-.2115	-.1275	-.1629	-.0872	.3303
4	-.2568	.2688	.0918	1.0000	-.5983	-.6593	.1246	-.6212	-.1460	-.7739
5	.1603	-.5098	.3998	-.5983	1.0000	.5756	-.0791	-.0876	-.0826	.7397
6	.0047	-.5694	-.2115	-.6593	.5756	1.0000	.4641	.0447	-.4493	.6789
7	-.2344	-.5138	-.1275	.1246	-.0791	.4641	1.0000	-.2046	-.7966	.0256
8	.2810	.1322	-.1629	-.6212	-.0876	.0447	-.2046	1.0000	.1171	.3732
9	.0203	.5893	-.0872	-.1460	-.0826	-.4493	-.7966	.1171	1.0000	-.0891
10	.4020	-.6431	.3303	-.7739	.7397	.6789	.0256	.3732	-.0891	1.0000
11	-.1533	.5916	.1658	.2131	-.2503	-.6215	-.3913	.4043	.6309	-.2359
12	-.3475	.5739	-.1585	.3038	-.6780	-.5641	-.0735	.0932	-.1652	-.6993
13	.2087	-.1012	-.6521	.0408	-.5476	.1668	.2943	.0225	-.4068	-.2383
14	-.6027	.4755	-.5334	.3670	-.7516	-.1391	.4120	-.0553	-.3069	-.6931
15	-.2902	-.1999	-.0630	.6669	-.1612	-.0540	.5930	-.8232	-.4954	-.5339
16	-.2254	.0657	-.4984	.0654	.1414	.2988	.0613	-.6188	-.1961	-.3133

236 INTERCORRELATION AND FACTOR ANALYSIS

R MAT	11	12	13	14	15	16
1	-.1533	-.3475	.2087	-.6027	-.2902	-.2256
2	.5916	.5739	-.1012	.4755	-.1999	.065
3	.1658	-.1585	-.6521	-.5334	-.0630	-.4984
4	.2131	.3038	.0408	.3670	.6669	.0654
5	-.2503	-.6780	-.5476	-.7516	-.1612	.1414
6	-.6215	-.5641	.1668	-.1391	-.0540	.2988
7	-.3913	-.0735	.2943	.4120	.5930	.0611
8	.4043	.0932	.0225	-.0553	-.8232	-.6188
9	.6309	-.1652	-.4068	-.3069	-.4954	-.1961
10	-.2359	-.6993	-.2383	-.6931	-.5339	-.3131
11	1.0000	.1147	-.5901	-.0476	-.3630	-.5835
12	.1147	1.0000	.3544	.7176	.1244	.0202
13	-.5901	.3544	1.0000	.5515	.1787	.3175
14	-.0476	.7176	.5515	1.0000	.3748	.2408
15	-.3630	.1244	.1787	.3748	1.0000	.5211
16	-.5835	.0202	.3175	.2408	.5211	1.0000

COMPARISON OF FACTORS

The factor structure obtained from a given set of variables (tests) is obviously a function of the particular sample of subjects that contributed the data used to form the intercorrelation matrix. Once a factor structure has been determined, the question of its stability over random samples — "factorial invariance" — quite naturally arises. One may question the stability of the structure over changes in the variables factored or over changes in the sample of subjects. The latter question is more common in behavioral research. Changes in subject samples may be random, or may involve specific subpopulations such as males and females. The two samples of data might also be obtained from the same subjects tested on two occasions with the same variables. Comparison of factor structures derived from different sets of variables (tests) is reasonable only if a one-to-one correspondence of some sort can be established between variables in the two sets. Even then, two tests with the same name (anxiety, for example) may be quite dissimilar in their functional relationships to other variables.

When the same group of subjects has been tested twice with the same set of variables, the most direct way of determining the stability of the factor structure over time would be to carry out a separate factor analysis of each set of data, obtaining two sets of factor scores for each subject. Intercorrelation of these two sets of factor variables would indicate the stability of the factor structure over time.

When the two factor structures to be compared are based on *different* samples of subjects, correlation of factor scores is no longer possible, and another approach to the question of factorial invariance must be used. The program described in this section is based on a method developed by Kaiser (1960).[2] It accepts as input two factor-loading matrices derived from the same set of variables (or from comparable variables, if one is willing to make the necessary assumptions). Typically the two factor structures represent random or specific (male and female) subpopulations.

Although Kaiser has extended the use of the technique to oblique factor structure, the program (RELATE) to be presented here is intended only for orthogonal sets of reference vectors such as those produced by Program FACTOR. The procedure is to arbitrarily equate the origins and factor-vector orientations of the two structures, and then to determine analytically the degree of *rotation* of the factor axes of one of the structures which will result in a maximum degree of overlap between corresponding *test vectors* in the two structures. The degree of rotation necessary to achieve this criterion is expressed as a matrix of cosines of the angles between all pairs of factor axes in the two structures. These cosines may be interpreted as correlations between the factor variables derived from the two analyses.

Since the matrix of cosines is actually a transformation matrix which will carry one structure of test vectors into maximum contiguity with the other, it may be applied directly to one of the original factor structures to achieve this rotation. The resulting matrix of factor loadings could then be used to derive weights for factor-score computation.

Although the rotation accomplished by this method minimizes the angles between corresponding test vectors in the two structures, one may question the success of this reorientation. The final step in the procedure yields a matrix of cosines between all pairs of *test vectors* after the reorientation of one of the matrices is accomplished with the initial factor-cosine matrix. The diagonal elements of this matrix are indices of the constancy of individual tests across the two analyses.

AN EXAMPLE

Before we undertake an explanation of the operation of Program RELATE, we will discuss an example of the application of this technique, using a geometric representation of the two factor structures to illustrate the rotation process. In this example each structure has only two reference axes. The two original factor-loading matrices and the rotated loadings for the

---

[2] The author wishes to thank Dr. Steven Hunka of the University of Alberta for bringing this technique to his attention. Professor Kaiser provided the matrix formulas as well as very helpful criticisms of this section, for which the author wishes to express his appreciation — without evading responsibility for the explanation presented here.

second matrix are shown here, along with the matrix of cosines among the factor vectors and the series of cosines between test vectors after reorientation of the second matrix.

Variables	A Loadings I	A Loadings II	B Loadings I	B Loadings II	Rotated B Loadings I	Rotated B Loadings II
1	.72	−.55	−.15	.93	.83	−.45
2	.51	.17	−.52	.44	.67	.14
3	.60	.32	−.70	.15	.55	.46
4	.34	.34	−.71	.18	.58	.45
5	.45	.31	−.58	.29	.59	.28
6	.28	.29	−.64	.04	.43	.48

Factor Relationships

	I_B	II_B
I_A	−.62	.79
II_A	−.79	−.62

Correlations between Test Vectors of the Original A and Rotated B Structures

1	2	3	4	5	6
.99	.99	.98	.99	.99	1.00

Figure 9-13 illustrates the two factor structures in a common factor space—one with the same origin and colinear factor vectors. Figure 9-14 indicates the effect of rotating the B structure to achieve maximum test vector overlap.

PROGRAM RELATE

Program RELATE is intended for comparing factor structures which have orthogonal reference axes. Normally, the same number of factors will be available for both matrices, although the program will handle unequal numbers of factors if the matrix containing the larger number of factors is entered first. In any case the number of variables (tests) must be the same, and the variables must be arranged in each structure in the same order. Normally the same variables will be represented in the two structures, but this is not mandatory. The subjects who provide the raw data for the two analyses will represent two random or specific subpopulations ordinarily, but the same subjects may be used in both analyses in some situations.

The first step in the program is the reading of the A and B factor-loading matrices from cards. The same format is required for both matrices. If punched output from Program FACTOR is entered, the contents of the Format Control Card will be (10X, 7F10.4). The two factor-loading matrices are immediately normalized by rows upon entry. This extends the test vectors to the same (1.0) length, in order to equalize the contribution of each test to the determination of the amount of rotation necessary. The lengths of the test vectors of the B structure are saved in vector G for use later in the program.

The next step is the computation of the matrix of cosines among the

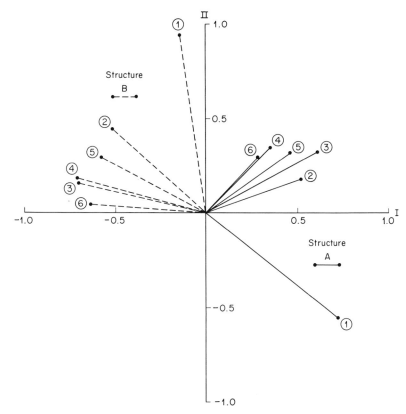

FIGURE 9-13. Test vectors of structures A and B in a common factor space.

factor vectors of the two structures. These cosines represent the relationships between the factors after the two sets of test vectors have been aligned for maximum contiguity. This matrix is also the transformation matrix for reorienting the B structure. It is defined by the formula:

$$C_{JI} = (A'_{IK}B_{KJ})'_{JI} V_{IJ} E_{\Delta J}^{-1.5} V'_{JI}$$

where $E_{\Delta J}$ and V_{IJ} are the roots and loadings for all J possible factors of the following matrix:

$$A'_{IK}B_{KJ}(A'_{IK}B_{KJ})'_{JI}$$

where I = the number of factors in the A matrix
J = the number of factors in the B matrix
K = the number of variables factored in each analysis

The reason that only J factors are possible is that in the situation where I and J are unequal, the factor space common to the two structures will shrink to the rank of the second matrix (B).

The roots (E) and loadings (V) of A'B(A'B)' are obtained by calling Subroutine SEVS. The cosine matrix is computed and stored in transposed

240 INTERCORRELATION AND FACTOR ANALYSIS

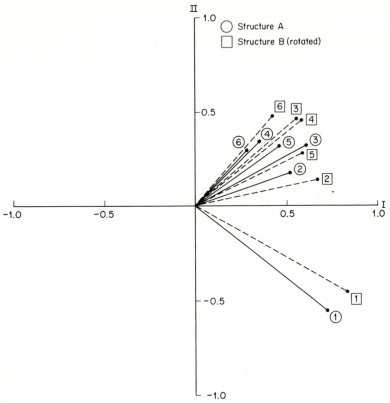

FIGURE 9-14. Test vectors of original structure A and structure B after rotation to maximize test-vector contiguity.

form (C'_{IJ}) to simplify its output. After printing, the cosine matrix is premultiplied by the original B matrix, which effectively rotates its factor axes to the position that produces maximum contiguity between the two sets of corresponding test vectors.

$$Q_{KI} = B_{KJ}C_{JI}$$

Note that this "new" B matrix of loadings (Q) will have as many factor columns as the A matrix. The newly rotated B matrix is stored in denormalized form for printing and punching (Figure 9-15).

The final step in the program is the computation of a series of cosines which reflect the proximity of corresponding test vectors in the original A matrix and the rotated B matrix. These cosines are the diagonal elements of the matrix product $A_{KI}C'_{IJ}B'_{JK}$, in which the latter part of the product is the transpose of the new B matrix of loadings. Therefore, the test-vector correlations are the diagonal elements of $A_{KI}Q'_{IK}$. The normalized version of matrix Q is used in these computations.

Two kinds of answers may thus be given to the question of factorial

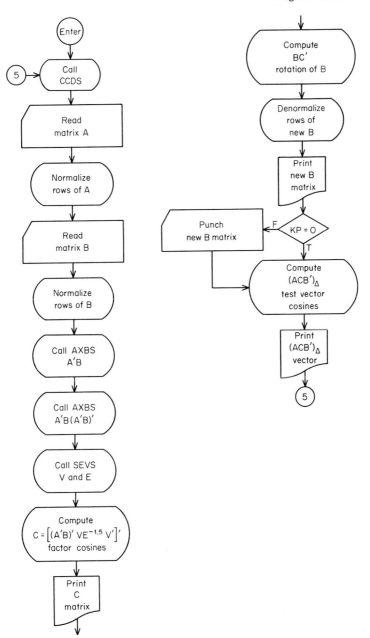

FIGURE 9-15. Program RELATE flow chart.

invariance: (1) the matrix of cosines among factor axes tells us how similar were the factors of the original structures, and (2) the series of cosines among test vectors tells us how closely together the two sets of test vectors can be brought by rotation of one of the original sets of factor axes.

EXAMPLE PROBLEM

The Varimax-rotated matrices of loadings from the first two problems for Program FACTOR will be employed to illustrate the operation of this program. Each of the structures includes three factors, obtained by principal components analysis of the intercorrelations and the image covariances of the same set of eight test variables. Although the factor axes in these two structures do not correspond in the same order, their similarity is very strong in that the "rotation" necessary to align them amounted to little more than the reflection of one factor axis and the relabeling of axes I and III.

The list of test-vector correlations, however, illustrates the fact that two factor structures may be aligned closely even though certain tests do not correspond very well (tests 1 and 3). In the present example, the suggestion is that the content or "meaning" of the factors derived in the two analyses differs primarily in terms of their determination by these two tests.

```
C      PROGRAM RELATE
C
C      CONTROL PROGRAM FOR FACTOR COMPARISON.
C      PARAMETER CONTROL CARD FIELDS.
C         COL 1-5. NUMBER OF VARIABLES (TESTS) IN EACH LOADING MATRIX.
C         COL 6-10. NUMBER OF FACTORS IN FIRST (A) MATRIX ENTERED.
C         COL 11-15. NUMBER OF FACTORS IN SECOND (B) MATRIX.
C         COL 20. 1 = PUNCH RE-ROTATED SECOND MATRIX.
C      MAX VARIABLES = 70. MAX FACTORS = 25 PER MATRIX.
C      IF NUMBERS OF FACTORS IN A AND B DIFFER, ENTER LARGER MATRIX AS A.
C      FORMAT WOULD BE (10X, 7F10.4) FOR LOADINGS FROM PROGRAM FACTOR.
C      REQUIRES SUBPROGRAMS SUMF, SCPF, CCDS, PRTS, PCDS, AXBS, SEVS.
C
      ODIMENSION KF(16), A(70,25), B(70,25), C(70,25), D(70,25), E(25),
     1 F(25), G(25), V(70,25)
       ND = 70
     5 CALL CCDS (KF, NV, NA, NB, KP, I)
C      READ AND NORMALIZE MATRIX A BY ROWS.
       DO 10 I = 1,NV
       READ KF, (A(I,J), J = 1,NA)
       P = 1.0 / SQRT(SUMF(A, -I, -NA, ND))
       DO 10 J = 1,NA
    10 A(I,J) = A(I,J) * P
C      READ AND NORMALIZE MATRIX B BY ROWS. SAVE LENGTHS IN G.
       DO 15 I = 1,NV
       READ KF, (B(I,J), J = 1,NB)
       G(I) = SQRT(SUMF(B, -I, -NB, ND))
       DO 15 J = 1,NB
    15 B(I,J) = B(I,J) / G(I)
C      COMPUTE COSINES BETWEEN FACTOR AXES AND PRINT.
       CALL AXBS (A, B, C, -NA, NB, NV, ND)
       CALL AXBS (C, C, D, NA, -NA, NB, ND)
       CALL SEVS (NA, NB, 0.0, D, V, E, F, ND)
       CALL AXBS (C, V, D, -NB, NB, NA, ND)
       DO 20 J = 1,NB
       EE = E(J)**(-1.5)
       DO 20 I = 1,NB
    20 D(I,J) = D(I,J) * EE
       CALL AXBS (V, D, C, NA, -NA, NB, ND)
       PRINT 25
    25 FORMAT (// 26H COSINES AMONG FACTOR AXES)
       CALL PRTS (C, NA, NB, 6HA BY B, ND)
C      COMPUTE ROTATED B MATRIX AND OUTPUT IN DENORMAL FORM.
```

Example Problem

```
      CALL AXBS (B, C, D, NV, -NA, NB, ND)
      DO 30 I = 1,NV
      DO 30 J = 1,NA
   30 V(I,J) = D(I,J) * G(I)
      CALL PRTS (V, NV, NA, 5HNEW B, ND)
      IF (KP .NE. 0) CALL PCDS (V, NV, NA, 5HNEW B, ND)
C  COMPUTE COSINES BETWEEN CORRESPONDING TEST VECTORS AND PRINT.
      DO 35 I = 1,NV
   35 G(I) = SCPF(A, D, -I, -I, NA, ND)
      CALL PRTS (G, NV, 1, 6HTEST R, ND)
      GO TO 5
      END
```

*** INPUT DATA DECK ***

```
RELATE EXAMPLE PROBLEM.
000080000300003000001
(10X, 7F10.4)
VLOAD  1 1    0.3061   -0.7943    0.1087
VLOAD  2 1    0.5657   -0.0117    0.6976
VLOAD  3 1    0.1505   -0.3568    0.7924
VLOAD  4 1    0.6778   -0.1892    0.2679
VLOAD  5 1    0.7860    0.2145    0.2400
VLOAD  6 1   -0.6428    0.4626    0.2175
VLOAD  7 1   -0.1727   -0.9097    0.0734
VLOAD  8 1    0.0594    0.0809    0.6989
VLOAD  1 1    0.3298   -0.6608   -0.0047
VLOAD  2 1    0.7591   -0.0842   -0.2812
VLOAD  3 1    0.3650   -0.3315   -0.4698
VLOAD  4 1    0.2829   -0.1715   -0.4918
VLOAD  5 1    0.3234    0.1163   -0.5949
VLOAD  6 1   -0.0142    0.3293    0.3484
VLOAD  7 1   -0.1425   -0.6675   -0.0970
VLOAD  8 1    0.3541    0.0123   -0.1422
```

*** PUNCHED OUTPUT ***

```
NEW B  1 1    0.0281   -0.6446    0.3593
NEW B  2 1    0.3219   -0.0469    0.7460
NEW B  3 1    0.4915   -0.3111    0.3543
NEW B  4 1    0.5077   -0.1550    0.2638
NEW B  5 1    0.6102    0.1351    0.2854
NEW B  6 1   -0.3516    0.3260   -0.0107
NEW B  7 1    0.0952   -0.6728   -0.1165
NEW B  8 1    0.1607    0.0297    0.3450
```

*** PRINTED OUTPUT ***

1RELATE EXAMPLE PROBLEM

```
PARAMETERS
COL  1- 5 =     8
COL  6-10 =     3
COL 11-15 =     3
COL 16-20 =     1
COL 21-25 =     0

DATA FORMAT = (10X, 7F10.4)
```

PRINCIPAL AXIS ANALYSIS.

TRACE =   26.1548

100.00 PCT. OF TRACE WAS EXTRACTED BY   3 ROOTS.

COSINES AMONG FACTOR AXES

A BY B	1	2	3
1	.0532	-.0089	-.9985
2	.0467	.9989	-.0064
3	.9975	-.0463	.0535

NEW B	1	2	3
1	.0281	-.6446	.3593
2	.3219	-.0469	.7460
3	.4915	-.3111	.3543
4	.5077	-.1550	.2638
5	.6102	.1351	.2854
6	-.3516	.3260	-.0107
7	.0952	-.6728	-.1165
8	.1607	.0297	.3450

TEST R	1	2	3	4	5	6	7	8
	.8831	.9618	.7753	.9950	.9889	.9507	.9168	.9389

Review Exercises

1. Convert Subroutine CORS to a general-purpose program. Include an option for punched output, but do not include the binary data-tape option.
2. Write a special-purpose program to prove that $VV' = R$ when all factors have been extracted.
3. Intercorrelate the eight raw-score variables with the three rotated factor score variables, using the input deck and punched output from Program FACTOR example problem one. Predict the nature of (1) the intercorrelations of the factor variables, and (2) the correlations between raw-score and factor-score variables.
4. Run the principal-axis and rotated loadings from Program FACTOR example problem one as input to the RELATE Program. The factor cosine matrix in this case is the "transformation" matrix for the orthogonal rotation. Predict the values of the cosines between test vectors.

10 / analysis of variance

The fundamental concept of the previous chapter was the notion of covariation—the tendency for measures on two dimensions to vary together. The present chapter is concerned with a group of analytic methods based on a different concept: *the ability of variables, singly or as a set, to differentiate among two or more groups of individuals and/or repeated trials of individuals.* Analysis of variance is typically considered as a method for determining the "significance" of observed differences among the means of particular groups of scores. In this sense, the scores are measures on a "dependent variable," while a basis for defining subject groups is termed an "independent variable." In order to extend the concept of traditional analysis of variance directly to the method called *discriminant analysis,* we prefer to use the conceptual model stated earlier, instead of the more common notion of testing differences among means. Another reason for adopting this approach will become apparent in the next chapter when we discuss the relationship between linear regression models and analysis of variance procedures.

The first two programs in this chapter implement the most commonly employed traditional analysis of variance designs. The third program extends the elementary single-classification design to the use of multiple "dependent" variables as differentiators of subject groups. Extensive discussion of the computational formulas for these procedures has been avoided, since most advanced statistical texts discuss them thoroughly (Cooley and Lohnes, 1962; Edwards, 1960; McNemar, 1962; Winer, 1962). Readers familiar with complex analysis of variance models may be disappointed by the "elementary" nature of the designs programmed in this chapter. There are a number of reasons for restricting presentation of programs of this type. First of all, space limitations prohibit comprehensive coverage of the field. Most users in the behavioral sciences will find the programs included here adequate for most of their research problems. Also, it is our personal belief that the multiple-regression approach to complex research problems is more powerful than traditional analysis of variance techniques, and will ultimately prove to be more practical as well (Bottenberg and Ward, 1963).

PROGRAM ANOVAR

The design implemented by Program ANOVAR is basically groups-by-trials analysis of variance, but when only one trial is involved it resolves to ordinary single-classification analysis of variance, and when only one group is defined (with multiple trials) the design becomes subjects-by-trials. Because with two groups of subjects single-classification analysis of variance is equivalent to the t test for independent groups, this program will accomplish such purposes. Similarly, with two trials, a subjects-by-trials analysis of variance is equivalent to a t test for correlated observations. The program allows unequal numbers of subjects in multiple groups, and also includes an option which permits designation of particular dependent variables for which zero scores are to be treated as missing data.

The basic design for this program is illustrated by the example in Figure 10-1, in which each of nine subjects has been measured twice on a dependent variable. Also shown are the results of reducing the design by considering only trial one, and by considering all subjects as members of a single group. The asterisks indicate terms for which F ratios would be appropriately computed to test the significance of the effects concerned. Each X stands for a single score on the dependent variable being analyzed.

INPUT DECK ORGANIZATION

The input deck order for this program is listed here. A group-control

		T_1	T_2	Source	Degrees of Freedom	
	S_1	X	X	Total	17	
	S_2	X	X	Between Subjects	8	
G_1	S_3	X	X	Groups	1	*
	S_4	X	X	Error (G)	7	
	S_5	X	X	Within Subjects	9	
	S_6	X	X	Trials	1	*
G_2	S_7	X	X	GT Interaction	1	*
	S_8	X	X	Error (T)	7	
	S_9	X	X			

FIGURE 10-1A. Groups-by-trials design.

248 ANALYSIS OF VARIANCE

		T_1	Source	Degrees of Freedom
G_1	S_1	X	Total	8
	S_2	X	Groups	1 *
	S_3	X	Error (G)	7
	S_4	X		
	S_5	X	(With two groups, $F = t^2$ for an	
	S_6	X	independent-groups t-test.)	
G_2	S_7	X		
	S_8	X		
	S_9	X		

FIGURE 10-1B. Single-classification design.

		T_1	T_2	Source	Degrees of Freedom
	S_1	X	X	Total	17
	S_2	X	X	Between Subjects	8
	S_3	X	X	Trials	1 *
	S_4	X	X	Error (T)	8
G_1	S_5	X	X		
	S_6	X	X	(With two trials, $F = t^2$ for a	
	S_7	X	X	correlated-observations t-test.)	
	S_8	X	X		
	S_9	X	X		

FIGURE 10-1C. Subjects-by-trials design.

card is required before the first data-card of each group, even when only one group of subjects is required by the design. The optional control card for missing data is arranged like that for Subroutine MDRS, described in the previous chapter. Beginning with column one, each dependent variable is assigned a single-column signal: 0 if zero scores (and blank fields) are to be considered valid scores, or 1 if zero scores are to signify missing data. When multiple trials are a part of the design and the missing-data option = 1, valid scores must be available for all trials to include a subject in the analysis.

System Control Card(s)
Program Deck (with subroutines)
System Control Card(s)
Title Control Card
Parameter Control Card
Format Control Card
Missing-Data Option-Signal Card (if required)
Group Control Card (Group One)
Data-Card Deck (Group One)
Group Control Card (Group Two)
Data-Card Deck (Group Two)
Blank (or Title Control Card for next problem)
System Control Card(s)

Arrangement of the data on the subjects' cards is no problem when only one trial is involved; the scores for the series of dependent variables are punched across each subject's card(s) in the same order. Care must be exercised, however, when multiple trials and multiple dependent variables are involved. The program reads (NV * NT) scores for each subject. These scores must be arranged so that the scores on all dependent variables for trial one precede all of the scores for subsequent trials; the same rule applies to subsequent trials. The easiest way to handle this is to punch each trial series of scores for the various dependent variables on separate cards, using one card per trial, and arrange the trial cards sequentially for each subject. This is illustrated here for three subjects, three dependent variables and two trials, along with the alternative arrangement of each subject's set of six scores on a single card.

$(S_1) (T_1): V_1 V_2 V_3$
$(S_1) (T_2): V_1 V_2 V_3$
$(S_2) (T_1): V_1 V_2 V_3$
$(S_2) (T_2): V_1 V_2 V_3$
$(S_3) (T_1): V_1 V_2 V_3$
$(S_3) (T_2): V_1 V_2 V_3$

or

$(S_1) (T_1): V_1 V_2 V_3 (T_2): V_1 V_2 V_3$
$(S_2) (T_1): V_1 V_2 V_3 (T_2): V_1 V_2 V_3$
$(S_3) (T_1): V_1 V_2 V_3 (T_2): V_1 V_2 V_3$

Because the data-input loop is indexed by subjects, it is not possible to put more than one subject's scores on a single card. The format need not specify all cards for a single subject when multiple cards per subject are employed; automatic format repetition may be relied upon if all cards have the same field arrangement.

PROGRAM ORGANIZATION

As indicated by Figure 10-2, all data are input to the computer memory and certain sums are accumulated for each variable before the series of analyses of the dependent variables is begun. Vectors TQ and SQ, and matrices C and G are used to hold total sums of squares, subject sums of squares, cell sums and cell N for all variables as the data are read from cards. Note that a cell N is reduced if optioned whenever a zero score is encountered, and a later check is made for each variable to insure that at least one subject per group remains before each analysis is begun.

Following data input, a loop indexing the dependent variables is initialized and sums of squares are accumulated for the G and GT effects. Various cell sums are computed, along with the correction factor, and then all eight possible sums of squares and degrees-of-freedom terms are completed. Sums of squares are converted to mean squares by division by their degrees of freedom. The three possible F ratios are computed along with their probabilities of chance occurrence. After computing all cell means, output of the source table and means is begun. This output is selective,

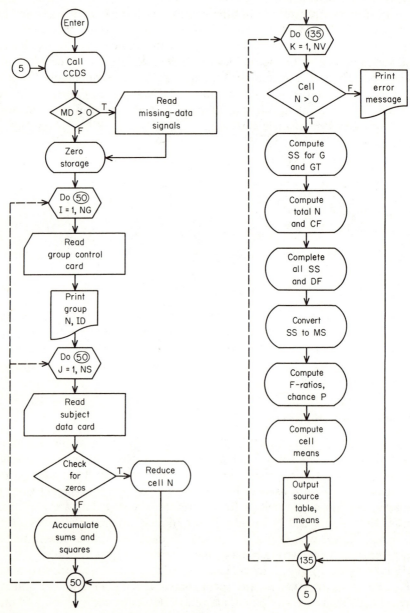

FIGURE 10-2. Program ANOVAR flow chart.

depending on the nature of the design being utilized. Control returns to begin analysis of another dependent variable when statement 135 is encountered.

EXAMPLE PROBLEMS

The first example problem illustrates single-classification analysis of variance of the first two variables, using the data deck employed previously to illustrate Program FACTOR with missing-data correlation (problem three). Note that scores have been removed for variable two, but not for variable one. The missing-data option card indicates that both variables are to be analyzed under the restriction that zero score fields indicate missing data. Since all scores for variable one are in fact nonzero, the first signal could just as well have been a zero. Note that the N and therefore the degrees of freedom for the second analysis have been adjusted because of the three subjects who had zero scores on the second variable.

The second example problem illustrates a subjects-by-trials design. In this case, the even-numbered subjects are considered as trial-two data cards for the odd-numbered subjects. Again, data is available for all *eight* subjects on the first variable, but scores for "trial one" are missing for three subjects on variable two. Note that only the Total, Trials, and Error (T) terms are printed for this design. If necessary, the between-subjects effect could be computed by subtraction of sums of squares. (A sum of squares may be computed for any effect by multiplying the mean square by its degrees of freedom.)

The third example problem illustrates the full design with multiple groups and multiple trials. Only one dependent variable has been analyzed here; the scores on variable two have been interpreted as representing the second trial for each subject. Because scores on the second trial (variable two) are absent for three of the 16 subjects, and the option-card field for variable one contains a 1, the N has been appropriately reduced and degrees of freedom adjusted.

```
C     PROGRAM ANOVAR
C
C     ANALYSIS OF VARIANCE WITH MULTIPLE GROUPS AND/OR MULTIPLE TRIALS.
C     PARAMETER CONTROL CARD FIELDS.
C         COL 1-5 = NUMBER OF DEPENDENT VARIABLES TO BE ANALYZED (MAX = 70).
C         COL 6-10 = NUMBER OF INDEPENDENT GROUPS OF SUBJECTS (MAX = 10).
C         COL 11-15 = NUMBER OF TRIALS PER SUBJECT
C             (REPEATED MEASURES) (MAX = 10).
C         COL 20 = 1 IF MISSING-DATA SIGNAL CARD PRECEDES DATA.
C     GROUP CONTROL CARD MUST PRECEDE EACH SEGMENT OF DATA DECK,
C         EVEN WITH ONE GROUP.  (COL 1-5 = NUMBER OF SUBJECTS,
C         COL 6-80 = ALPHAMERIC GROUP TITLE)
C     FIRST 3 PARAMETER FIELDS MUST ALWAYS EXCEED ZERO.
C     MISSING DATA SIGNAL CARD BEGINS WITH COL 1 = VARIABLE 1,
C         ONE COLUMN PER VARIABLE. (0 = ZERO IS MEANINGFUL SCORE,
```

252   ANALYSIS OF VARIANCE

```
C     1 = ZERO SIGNIFIES MISSING DATA).
C     FORMAT SHOULD SPECIFY (VARIABLES * TRIALS) SCORE-FIELDS, UNLESS EACH
C        TRIAL BEGINS A NEW CARD WITH THE SAME LAYOUT.
C     WITH MULTIPLE TREATMENTS, ALL DEPENDENT VARIABLES FOR A GIVEN TRIAL MUS
C        PRECEDE SCORES FOR ALL SUBSEQUENT TRIALS WITHIN
         EACH SUBJECTS DATA LIST.
C     SUBPROGRAMS REQUIRED ARE SUMF, PRBF, CCDS, PRTS.
C
      ODIMENSION KF(16), KH(15), M(70), X(700), G(10,70), C(10,10,70),
     1 TQ(70), SQ(70), GM(10), TM(10), CM(10,10), S(8), D(8), F(8), P(8)
      ND = 10
    5 CALL CCDS (KF, NV, NG, NT, MD, I)
      IF (MD .GT. 0) READ 10, M
   10 FORMAT (80I1)
      DO 15 K = 1,NV
      TQ(K) = 0.0
      SQ(K) = 0.0
      DO 15 I = 1,NG
      DO 15 J = 1,NT
   15 C(I,J,K) = 0.0
      NX = NV * NT
C     INPUT DATA, ACCUMULATE SUMX, SUMX2, N FOR ALL VARIABLES.
      DO 50 I = 1,NG
      READ 20, NS, KH
   20 FORMAT (I5, 15A5)
      PRINT 25, I, NS, KH
   25 FORMAT (/ 6H GROUP, I2, I6, 11H SUBJECTS.  , 15A5)
      DO 30 J = 1,NV
   30 G(I,J) = NS
      DO 50 J = 1,NS
      READ KF, (X(K), K = 1,NX)
      DO 50 K = 1,NV
      IF (MD * M(K) .EQ. 0) GO TO 40
      DO 35 L = K,NX,NV
      IF (X(L) .GT. 0.0) GO TO 35
      G(I,K) = G(I,K) - 1.0
      GO TO 50
   35 CONTINUE
   40 N = 1
      XX = 0.0
      DO 45 L = K,NX,NV
      XX = XX + X(L)
      TQ(K) = TQ(K) + X(L)**2
      C(I,N,K) = C(I,N,K) + X(L)
   45 N = N + 1
      SQ(K) = SQ(K) + XX**2
   50 CONTINUE
      GN = NG
      TN = NT
      DO 135 K = 1,NV
C     BEGIN ANALYSIS OF ONE DEPENDENT VARIABLE.
      S(3) = 0.0
      S(7) = 0.0
C     COMPUTE CERTAIN SUMS OF SQUARES AND CELL SUMS.
      DO 70 I = 1,NG
      IF (G(I,K) .GT. 1.0) GO TO 60
      PRINT 55, K
   55 FORMAT (9H1VARIABLE, I3, 20H. INSUFFICIENT DATA.)
      GO TO 135
   60 DO 65 J = 1,NT
      CM(I,J) = C(I,J,K)
   65 S(7) = S(7) + CM(I,J)**2 / G(I,K)
      GM(I) = SUMF(CM, -I, NT, ND)
   70 S(3) = S(3) + GM(I)**2 / (G(I,K) * TN)
      SN = SUMF(G, K, NG, ND)
```

```
      CF = SUMF(GM, 1, NG, ND)**2 / (SN * TN)
      DO 75 J = 1,NT
   75 TM(J) = SUMF(CM, J, NG, ND)
C  COMPLETE ALL SUMS OF SQUARES AND DEGREES OF FREEDOM.
      S(1) = TQ(K) - CF
      D(1) = SN * TN - 1.0
      S(2) = SQ(K) / TN - CF
      D(2) = SN - 1.0
      S(3) = S(3) - CF
      D(3) = GN - 1.0
      S(4) = S(2) - S(3)
      D(4) = SN - GN
      S(5) = S(1) - S(2)
      D(5) = D(1) - D(2)
      S(6) = SUMF(TM, 1, -NT, ND) / SN - CF
      D(6) = TN - 1.0
      S(7) = S(7) - CF - S(3) - S(6)
      D(7) = D(3) * D(6)
      S(8) = S(5) - S(6) - S(7)
      D(8) = D(4) * D(6)
C  CONVERT SUMS OF SQUARES TO MEAN SQUARES.
      DO 80 J = 1,8
      IF (D(J) .GT. 0.0) S(J) = S(J) / D(J)
   80 CONTINUE
C  COMPUTE F-RATIOS AND PROBABILITIES.
      F(3) = S(3) / S(4)
      P(3) = PRBF(D(3), D(4), F(3))
      F(6) = S(6) / S(8)
      P(6) = PRBF(D(6), D(8), F(6))
      F(7) = S(7) / S(8)
      P(7) = PRBF(D(7), D(8), F(7))
C  COMPUTE CELL MEANS.
      DO 85 I = 1,NG
      GM(I) = GM(I) / (G(I,K) * TN)
      DO 85 J = 1,NT
   85 CM(I,J) = CM(I,J) / G(I,K)
      DO 90 J = 1,NT
   90 TM(J) = TM(J) / SN
C  BEGIN OUTPUT OF SOURCE TABLE AND MEANS.
      PRINT 95, K, S(1), D(1)
   95 0FORMAT (/// 9H VARIABLE, I3, 10H ANALYSIS. //
     1 7H SOURCE, 5X, 11HMEAN SQUARE, 5X, 4HD.F., 5X,
     2 7HF-RATIO, 8X, 1HP // 6H TOTAL, F17.4, F9.0)
      IF (D(7) .GT. 0.0) PRINT 100, S(2), D(2)
  100 FORMAT (/ 8H BETWEEN, F15.4, F9.0)
      IF (NG .GT. 1) PRINT 105, S(3), D(3), F(3), P(3), S(4), D(4)
  105 FORMAT (/ 8H  GROUPS, F15.4, F9.0, F12.3, F11.4 //
     1 11H  ERROR (G), F12.4, F9.0)
      IF (D(7) .GT. 0.0) PRINT 110, S(5), D(5)
  110 FORMAT (/ 7H WITHIN, F16.4, F9.0)
      IF (NT .GT. 1) PRINT 115, S(6), D(6), F(6), P(6)
  115 FORMAT (/ 8H  TRIALS, F15.4, F9.0, F12.3, F11.4)
      IF (D(7) .GT. 0.0) PRINT 120, S(7), D(7), F(7), P(7)
  120 FORMAT (/ 8H  G BY T, F15.4, F9.0, F12.3, F11.4)
      IF (NT .GT. 1) PRINT 125, S(8), D(8)
  125 FORMAT (/ 11H  ERROR (T), F12.4, F9.0)
      IF (NG .GT. 1) CALL PRTS (GM, NG, 1, 6HG MEAN, ND)
      IF (MD .EQ. 1) PRINT 130, (G(I,K), I = 1,NG)
  130 FORMAT (/ 8H N VALID, F9.0, 9F11.0)
      IF (NT .GT. 1) CALL PRTS (TM, NT, 1, 6HT MEAN, ND)
      IF (D(7) .GT. 0.0) CALL PRTS (CM, NG, NT, 6HG BY T, ND)
  135 CONTINUE
      GO TO 5
      END
```

254 ANALYSIS OF VARIANCE

*** INPUT DATA DECK ***

```
ANOVAR EXAMPLE PROBLEM 1.  TWO GROUPS, ONE TRIAL.
00002000020000100001
(10X, 2F7.0)
11
00008 SUBJECTS 1-8.
S01SRI QS     25.              22.              26.              19.              182
S02SRI QS     26.     30.      30.     26.      28.     20.      24.     28.      212
S03SRI QS     20.              20.     23.      18.              21.     29.      180
S04SRI QS     30.     28.      29.     29.      28.     23.      28.     30.      225
S05SRI QS     23.     25.      29.              20.     27.      28.              199
S06SRI QS     28.     27.      30.     22.      19.     25.      30.     26.      207
S07SRI QS     28.     24.      27.     27.      17.     21.      30.     26.      200
S08SRI QS     25.     29.      29.     27.      26.     25.      26.     25.      212
00008 SUBJECTS 9-16.
S09SRI QS     26.              30.     24.      29.     24.      14.     29.      206
S10SRI QS     28.     29.      30.     26.      25.     28.      30.     28.      224
S11SRI QS     24.     28.      30.              27.     23.      21.     28.      210
S12SRI QS     26.     29.      26.     27.      28.     19.      30.     27.      212
S13SRI QS     30.     27.      26.     24.      25.              28.     25.      206
S14SRI QS     29.     29.      29.     28.      25.     19.      30.     27.      216
S15SRI QS     29.     25.      28.     26.      24.     21.      30.              212
S16SRI QS     29.     26.      30.     20.      25.     20.      30.     28.      208
ANOVAR EXAMPLE PROBLEM 2.  ONE GROUP, TWO TRIALS.
00002000010000200001
(10X, 2F7.0)
11
00008 EVEN-NUMBERED SUBJECTS CONSIDERED TRIAL TWO.
S01SRI QS     25.              22.              26.              19.              182
S02SRI QS     26.     30.      30.     26.      28.     20.      24.     28.      212
S03SRI QS     20.              20.     23.      18.              21.     29.      180
S04SRI QS     30.     28.      29.     29.      28.     23.      28.     30.      225
S05SRI QS     23.     25.      29.              20.     27.      28.              199
S06SRI QS     28.     27.      30.     22.      19.     25.      30.     26.      207
S07SRI QS     28.     24.      27.     27.      17.     21.      30.     26.      200
S08SRI QS     25.     29.      29.     27.      26.     25.      26.     25.      212
S09SRI QS     26.              30.     24.      29.     24.      14.     29.      206
S10SRI QS     28.     29.      30.     26.      25.     28.      30.     28.      224
S11SRI QS     24.     28.      30.              27.     23.      21.     28.      210
S12SRI QS     26.     29.      26.     27.      28.     19.      30.     27.      212
S13SRI QS     30.     27.      26.     24.      25.              28.     25.      206
S14SRI QS     29.     29.      29.     28.      25.     19.      30.     27.      216
S15SRI QS     29.     25.      28.     26.      24.     21.      30.              212
S16SRI QS     29.     26.      30.     20.      25.     20.      30.     28.      208
ANOVAR EXAMPLE PROBLEM 3.  TWO GROUPS, TWO TRIALS.
00001000020000200001
(10X, 2F7.0)
1
00008 SUBJECTS 1-8. VARIABLE TWO CONSIDERED TRIAL TWO.
S01SRI QS     25.              22.              26.              19.              182
S02SRI QS     26.     30.      30.     26.      28.     20.      24.     28.      212
S03SRI QS     20.              20.     23.      18.              21.     29.      180
S04SRI QS     30.     28.      29.     29.      28.     23.      28.     30.      225
S05SRI QS     23.     25.      29.              20.     27.      28.              199
S06SRI QS     28.     27.      30.     22.      19.     25.      30.     26.      207
S07SRI QS     28.     24.      27.     27.      17.     21.      30.     26.      200
S08SRI QS     25.     29.      29.     27.      26.     25.      26.     25.      212
00008 SUBJECTS 9-16. V2 = T2, AS IN G1.
S09SRI QS     26.              30.     24.      29.     24.      14.     29.      206
S10SRI QS     28.     29.      30.     26.      25.     28.      30.     28.      224
S11SRI QS     24.     28.      30.              27.     23.      21.     28.      210
S12SRI QS     26.     29.      26.     27.      28.     19.      30.     27.      212
S13SRI QS     30.     27.      26.     24.      25.              28.     25.      206
```

Example Problems   255

```
14SRI QS    29.   29.   29.   28.   25.   19.   30.   27.   216.
15SRI QS    29.   25.   28.   26.   24.   21.   30.         212.
16SRI QS    29.   26.   30.   20.   25.   20.   30.   28.   208.
```

*** PRINTED OUTPUT ***

1ANOVAR EXAMPLE PROBLEM 1. TWO GROUPS, ONE TRIAL.

PARAMETERS
COL 1- 5 =   2
COL 6-10 =   2
COL 11-15 =   1
COL 16-20 =   1
COL 21-25 =   0

DATA FORMAT = (10X, 2F7.0)

GROUP 1   8 SUBJECTS.   SUBJECTS 1-8.

GROUP 2   8 SUBJECTS.   SUBJECTS 9-16.

VARIABLE   1 ANALYSIS.

SOURCE	MEAN SQUARE	D.F.	F-RATIO	P
TOTAL	7.7167	15.		
GROUPS	16.0000	1.	2.246	.1534
ERROR (G)	7.1250	14.		

G MEAN   1   2
             25.6250   27.6250

N VALID   8.   8.

VARIABLE   2 ANALYSIS.

SOURCE	MEAN SQUARE	D.F.	F-RATIO	P
TOTAL	3.5897	12.		
GROUPS	.5293	1.	.137	.7182
ERROR (G)	3.8680	11.		

G MEAN   1   2
             27.1667   27.5714

N VALID   6.   7.

1ANOVAR EXAMPLE PROBLEM 2. ONE GROUP, TWO TRIALS.

PARAMETERS
COL 1- 5 =   2
COL 6-10 =   1
COL 11-15 =   2

ANALYSIS OF VARIANCE

```
COL 16-20 =     1
COL 21-25 =     0
```

DATA FORMAT = (10X, 2F7.0)

GROUP 1   8 SUBJECTS. EVEN-NUMBERED SUBJECTS CONSIDERED TRIAL TWO.

VARIABLE 1 ANALYSIS.

SOURCE	MEAN SQUARE	D.F.	F-RATIO	P
TOTAL	7.7167	15.		
TRIALS	16.0000	1.	2.000	.1987
ERROR (T)	8.0000	7.		
N VALID	8.			

T MEAN	1	2
	25.6250	27.6250

VARIABLE 2 ANALYSIS.

SOURCE	MEAN SQUARE	D.F.	F-RATIO	P
TOTAL	3.4333	9.		
TRIALS	12.1000	1.	8.963	.0405
ERROR (T)	1.3500	4.		
N VALID	5.			

T MEAN	1	2
	25.8000	28.0000

1ANOVAR EXAMPLE PROBLEM 3. TWO GROUPS, TWO TRIALS.

```
PARAMETERS
COL  1- 5 =     1
COL  6-10 =     2
COL 11-15 =     2
COL 16-20 =     1
COL 21-25 =     0
```

DATA FORMAT = (10X, 2F7.0)

GROUP 1   8 SUBJECTS. SUBJECTS 1-8. VARIABLE TWO CONSIDERED TRIAL TW

GROUP 2   8 SUBJECTS. SUBJECTS 9-16. V2 = T2, AS IN G1.

VARIABLE 1 ANALYSIS.

SOURCE	MEAN SQUARE	D.F.	F-RATIO	P
TOTAL	4.2354	25.		

Program AVAR23   257

BETWEEN	3.9487	12.			
GROUPS	4.1108	1.	1.045	.3301	
ERROR (G)	3.9340	11.			
WITHIN	4.5000	13.			
TRIALS	.0385	1.	.007	.9308	
G BY T	.9973	1.	.191	.6731	
ERROR (T)	5.2240	11.			

G MEAN	1	2
	26.9167	27.7143
N VALID	6.	7.

T MEAN	1	2
	27.3077	27.3846

G BY T	1	2
1	26.6667	27.1667
2	27.8571	27.5714

PROGRAM AVAR23

The designs implemented by Program AVAR23 extend single-classification analysis of variance to permit classification of subjects into "levels" on two or three independent variables simultaneously. Tests of significance are computed for the general effects of each of the two or three "factors," as well as for their interactive effects upon the dependent variable.

The computational procedure used in this program differs from those for factorial analysis of variance presented in most statistics texts. The method used in this program is described by Winer (1962, p. 222), and has the definite advantage of permitting unequal numbers of subjects to be used in each cell of the design. When all cells have equal N, however, the procedure yields results equivalent to the ordinary computational formulas. The adjustments that are made for unequal N are analogous to filling empty score-spaces with the means of the other cell scores; this method is appropriate only when the user can assume that the unequalness of cell Ns is random — not representative of systematic differences in the composition of the populations to which inferences are to be made.[1]

Figure 10-3 illustrates a double and a triple-classification design with two levels for each factor and two subjects per cell, along with the partitioning

[1] This assumption could be tested by chi-square analysis of the cell frequencies, which is discussed in Chapter 12.

258 ANALYSIS OF VARIANCE

					Cell	Source	Degrees of Freedom	
A_1	B_1	–	S_1	–	S_2	1	Total	12
	B_2	S_3	S_4	S_5	S_6	2	Between cells	3
							A factor	1 *
A_2	B_1	–	S_7	S_8	S_9	3	B factor	1 *
	B_2	S_{10}	S_{11}	S_{12}	S_{13}	4	AB interaction	1 *
							Within cells	9

FIGURE 10-3A. Double-classification design.

						Cell	Source	Degrees of Freedom	
A_1	B_1	C_1	S_1	S_2		1	Total	15	
		C_2	S_3	S_4		2	Between cells	7	
	B_2	C_1	S_5	S_6		3	A factor	1 *	
		C_2	S_7	S_8		4	B factor	1 *	
							C factor	1 *	
A_2	B_1	C_1	S_9	S_{10}		5	AB interaction	1 *	
		C_2	S_{11}	S_{12}		6	AC interaction	1 *	
	B_2	C_1	S_{13}	S_{14}		7	BC interaction	1 *	
		C_2	S_{15}	S_{16}		8	ABC interaction	1 *	
							Within cells	8	

FIGURE 10-3B. Triple-classification design.

of sums of squares in each design. The double-classification design illustrates unequal cell Ns. The "factors" A, B, or C in these designs might represent such variables as sex, social class, ethnic origin, level of anxiety, experimental treatment, drug dosage, and so forth. Although any continuous dimension could be subdivided to define groups of subjects, the user should remember that *any* differences among levels on a given factor will be registered by the F test—including nonlinear relationships with the dependent variable. The scores which are entered into the cells of these designs (S_i) are measures of the single dependent variable to be analyzed into independent components functionally attributable to each of the independent variables and their interactions. The dependent variable is usually a well-differentiated continuum, such as questionnaire score. Raw test scores may be used, such as those of the example problems in this chapter, or composite scores such as the factor variables derived from Program FACTOR may be employed as dependent variables.

INPUT DECK ARRANGEMENT

Each subject's set of dependent-variable scores begins on a new card. The sequence of subject cards is illustrated here for a 2-by-2-by-2 design, with two dependent variables. This deck arrangement is the same as that used for the second example problem later in this section.

Unequal cell Ns can be handled in two different ways with this program.

If desired, a group-control card can be placed in front of the data cards for *every* ABC cell in the design, and varying numbers of *data cards* may then be used for the various cells (see example problem one). The alternative method avoids the use of group-control cards. Equal numbers of data cards are required for each cell, but scorefields may be left blank to indicate missing data. A missing-data option card is required after the format card in this case. If zero is to be a meaningful score, the group-control card method would have to be used for unequal cell frequencies. When all cells are complete for all variables, no missing-data option or group-control cards are needed.

$(A_1 B_1 C_1 S_1) \, V_1 V_2$
$(A_1 B_1 C_1 S_2) \, V_1 V_2$
$(A_1 B_1 C_2 S_1) \, V_1 V_2$
$(A_1 B_1 C_2 S_2) \, V_1 V_2$
$(A_1 B_2 C_1 S_1) \, V_1 V_2$
$(A_1 B_2 C_1 S_2) \, V_1 V_2$
$(A_1 B_2 C_2 S_1) \, V_1 V_2$
$(A_1 B_2 C_2 S_2) \, V_1 V_2$
$(A_2 B_1 C_1 S_1) \, V_1 V_2$
$(A_2 B_1 C_1 S_2) \, V_1 V_2$
$(A_2 B_1 C_2 S_1) \, V_1 V_2$
$(A_2 B_1 C_2 S_2) \, V_1 V_2$
$(A_2 B_2 C_1 S_1) \, V_1 V_2$
$(A_2 B_2 C_1 S_2) \, V_1 V_2$
$(A_2 B_2 C_2 S_1) \, V_1 V_2$
$(A_2 B_2 C_2 S_2) \, V_1 V_2$

PROGRAM ORGANIZATION

After calling CCDS to input parameters, certain accumulators are zeroed and the missing-data option signals are read, if required. Data input is controlled by group-control cards or by a general cell-N parameter. As the data are input, they are checked for zero scores (at option) and cell means and Ns are taped for all variables simultaneously. The cell-N reciprocals and cell variances are accumulated also during this stage.

After converting certain parameters to real mode and setting the known degrees-of-freedom cells, the series of analyses of the dependent variables is begun. The initial step for each variable is to determine whether any cell N has dropped to zero; the analysis of such a variable is skipped. The next section amounts to a straightforward computation of a triple-classification analysis of variance with one score (cell mean) per cell. Means for all main effects and interaction cells are also computed during this part of the process (Figure 10-4).

260 ANALYSIS OF VARIANCE

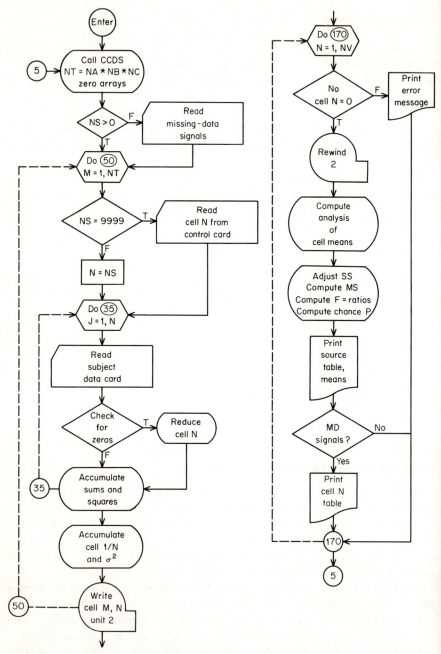

FIGURE 10-4. Program AVAR23 flow chart.

Sums of squares are adjusted with the correction factor and by the harmonic mean of all cell frequencies, and are then converted to mean

Example Problems   261

squares. Note that the total sum of squares is computed by addition of its components, unlike the usual computational procedure. F ratios and corresponding probabilities are computed next for all seven possible effects and output printing of the source table is begun. Only the components shown in Figure 10-3 are printed, depending on the design. After printing all appropriate mean values, a matrix of cell frequencies is printed if they were unequal.

EXAMPLE PROBLEMS

The first example uses 13 data cards to fill a 2-by-2 design with varying numbers of subjects per cell; the use of group control cards to handle unequal cell Ns is illustrated, and only variable two is analyzed.

The second example problem demonstrates a 2-by-2-by-2 analysis with two subjects per cell. No group control cards are used, and the missing-data option is used to handle unequal cell Ns. Both variables one and two are analyzed in this example.

```
C     PROGRAM AVAR23
C
C     DOUBLE OR TRIPLE-CLASSIFICATION ANALYSIS OF VARIANCE.
C     PARAMETER CONTROL-CARD FIELDS.
C         COL 1-5 = NUMBER OF DEPENDENT VARIABLES TO BE ANALYZED (MAX = 70).
C         COL 6-10 = NUMBER OF LEVELS FOR THE A FACTOR (MAX = 10).
C         COL 11-15 = NUMBER OF LEVELS FOR THE B FACTOR (MAX = 10).
C         COL 16-20 = NUMBER OF LEVELS FOR THE C FACTOR (MAX = 10).
C             SET = 1 FOR DOUBLE-CLASSIFICATION DESIGN.
C         COL 21-25 = NUMBER OF SUBJECTS PER ABC CELL, IF CELL N ARE ALL EQUAL.
C             FOR UNEQUAL CELL N SET = 9999 AND ADD A GROUP-CONTROL
C             CARD IN FRONT OF EACH CELL-SET OF DATA CARDS (COL 1-5 = CELL N).
C             IF ZERO SCORES ARE TO BE TREATED AS MISSING DATA FOR ANY VARIABLE,
C             ADD MINUS SIGN TO THIS FIELD AND ADD OPTION-SIGNAL CARD AFTER
C             FORMAT CONTROL CARD (1 = ZERO MEANS MISSING, 0 = ZERO VALID.
C         COL 1 = VARIABLE 1, ETC).
C     FORMAT MUST SPECIFY NV SCORE FIELDS (FOR ONE SUBJECT).
C     ORDER OF CELLS IN DATA DECK = A1B1C1, A1B1C2, A1B2C1, ETC.
C     TAPE UNIT 2 IS USED FOR TEMPORARY STORAGE (SCRATCH).
C     SUBPROGRAMS REQUIRED ARE PRBF, CCDS, PRTS.
C
      ODIMENSION KF(16), KH(15), ZM(70), S(10), D(10), F(10), P(10),
     1 A(10), B(10), C(10), AB(10,10), AC(10,10), BC(10,10),
     2 ABC(10,10,10), W(70), R(70), T(70), X(70), SX(70), SQ(70), G(70),
     3 GN(10,10,10)
      ND = 10
    5 CALL CCDS (KF, NV, NA, NB, NC, NS)
      NT = NA * NB * NC
C     ZERO ACCUMULATORS AND READ MISSING-DATA OPTIONS.
      DO 10 I = 1,NV
      ZM(I) = 0.0
      T(I) = 0.0
      R(I) = 0.0
   10 W(I) = 0.0
      IF (NS .GT. 0) GO TO 20
      NS = IABS(NS)
      READ 15, (ZM(I), I = 1,NV)
   15 FORMAT (80F1.0)
   20 REWIND 2
```

ANALYSIS OF VARIANCE

```
C     INPUT DATA, CHECK, ACCUMULATE SUMS.
      DO 50 M = 1,NT
      N = NS
      IF (N .EQ. 9999) READ 25, N
   25 FORMAT (I5)
      DO 30 I = 1,NV
      SX(I) = 0.0
      SQ(I) = 0.0
   30 G(I) = N
      DO 35 I = 1,N
      READ KF, (X(J), J = 1,NV)
      DO 35 J = 1,NV
      IF (ZM(J) .EQ. 1.0 .AND. X(J) .EQ. 0.0) G(J) = G(J) - 1.0
      SX(J) = SX(J) + X(J)
   35 SQ(J) = SQ(J) + X(J)**2
      DO 45 I = 1,NV
      IF (G(I) .GT. 0.0) GO TO 40
      ZM(I) = 2.0
      GO TO 45
C     ACCUMULATE (1/CELL N) AND CELL VARIANCE.
   40 W(I) = W(I) + (SQ(I) - SX(I)**2 / G(I))
      R(I) = R(I) + 1.0 / G(I)
C     COMPUTE AND TAPE CELL MEAN AND N FOR ALL VARIABLES.
      SX(I) = SX(I) / G(I)
   45 T(I) = T(I) + G(I)
   50 WRITE (2) SX, G
C     SET PARAMETERS AND DEGREES OF FREEDOM.
      TN = NT
      AN = NA
      BN = NB
      CN = NC
      D(2) = TN - 1.0
      D(3) = AN - 1.0
      D(4) = BN - 1.0
      D(5) = CN - 1.0
      D(6) = D(3) * D(4)
      D(7) = D(3) * D(5)
      D(8) = D(4) * D(5)
      D(9) = D(3) * D(8)
C     BEGIN ANALYSES OF DEPENDENT VARIABLES.
      DO 170 N = 1,NV
      IF (ZM(N) .LT. 2.0) GO TO 60
      PRINT 55, N
   55 FORMAT ( 31H1INSUFFICIENT DATA FOR VARIABLE, I3)
      GO TO 170
   60 REWIND 2
      DO 65 I = 1,10
      S(I) = 0.0
      A(I) = 0.0
      B(I) = 0.0
      C(I) = 0.0
      DO 65 J = 1,10
      AB(I,J) = 0.0
      AC(I,J) = 0.0
   65 BC(I,J) = 0.0
      D(1) = T(N) - 1.0
      D(10) = T(N) - TN
C     COMPUTE 1-SCORE-PER-CELL ANALYSIS AND CELL MEANS.
      DO 70 I = 1,NA
      DO 70 J = 1,NB
      DO 70 K = 1,NC
      READ (2) SX, G
      GN(I,J,K) = G(N)
      S(2) = S(2) + SX(N)**2
      A(I) = A(I) + SX(N)
```

```
         B(J) = B(J) + SX(N)
         C(K) = C(K) + SX(N)
         AB(I,J) = AB(I,J) + SX(N)
         AC(I,K) = AC(I,K) + SX(N)
         BC(J,K) = BC(J,K) + SX(N)
      70 ABC(I,J,K) = SX(N)
         DO 80 I = 1,NA
         S(3) = S(3) + A(I)**2 / (BN * CN)
         A(I) = A(I) / (BN * CN)
         DO 75 J = 1,NB
         S(6) = S(6) + AB(I,J)**2 / CN
      75 AB(I,J) = AB(I,J) / CN
         DO 80 K = 1,NC
         S(7) = S(7) + AC(I,K)**2 / BN
      80 AC(I,K) = AC(I,K) / BN
         DO 85 J = 1,NB
         S(4) = S(4) + B(J)**2 / (AN * CN)
         B(J) = B(J) / (AN * CN)
         DO 85 K = 1,NC
         S(8) = S(8) + BC(J,K)**2 / AN
      85 BC(J,K) = BC(J,K) / AN
         CF = 0.0
         DO 90 K = 1,NC
         CF = CF + C(K)
         S(5) = S(5) + C(K)**2 / (AN * BN)
      90 C(K) = C(K) / (AN * BN)
         CF = CF * CF / TN
C     ADJUST SUMS OF SQUARES AND COMPLETE COMPUTATION.
         DO 95 I = 2,9
      95 S(I) = (S(I) - CF) * TN / R(N)
         S(6) = S(6) - S(3) - S(4)
         S(7) = S(7) - S(3) - S(5)
         S(8) = S(8) - S(4) - S(5)
         S(9) = S(2) - S(3) - S(4) - S(5) - S(6) - S(7) - S(8)
         S(10) = W(N)
         S(1) = S(2) + S(10)
C     CONVERT SUMS OF SQUARES TO MEAN SQUARES.
         DO 100 I = 1,10
         IF (D(I) .GT. 0.0) S(I) = S(I) / D(I)
     100 CONTINUE
C     COMPUTE F-RATIOS AND PROBABILITIES.
         DO 105 I = 3,9
         F(I) = S(I) / S(10)
     105 P(I) = PRBF(D(I), D(10), F(I))
C     PRINT SOURCE TABLE AND RELEVANT CELL MEANS.
         OPRINT 110, N, (S(I), D(I), I = 1,3), F(3), P(3), S(4), D(4), F(4),
        1 P(4)
     1100FORMAT (///21H ANALYSIS OF VARIABLE, I3 // 7H SOURCE, 16X, 4HM.S.,
        1 7X, 4HD.F., 4X, 7HF-RATIO, 8X, 1HP // 6H TOTAL, F21.3, F10.0 //
        2 8H BETWEEN, F19.3, F10.0 / 3X, 1HA, F23.3, F10.0, 2F12.4 /
        3 3X, 1HB, F23.3, F10.0, 2F12.4)
         IF (NC .GT. 1) PRINT 115, S(5), D(5), F(5), P(5)
     115 FORMAT (3X, 1HC, F23.3, F10.0, 2F12.4)
         PRINT 120, S(6), D(6), F(6), P(6)
     120 FORMAT (3X, 2HAB, F22.3, F10.0, 2F12.4)
         IF (NC .GT. 1) PRINT 125, (S(I), D(I), F(I), P(I), I = 7,9)
     1250FORMAT (3X, 2HAC, F22.3, F10.0, 2F12.4 / 3X, 2HBC, F22.3,
        1 F10.0, 2F12.4 / 3X, 3HABC, F21.3, F10.0, 2F12.4)
         PRINT 130, S(10), D(10)
     130 FORMAT (/ 7H WITHIN, F20.3, F10.0 /// 23H MEANS FOR ALL EFFECTS.)
         CALL PRTS (A, NA, 1, 6HA MAIN, ND)
         CALL PRTS (B, NB, 1, 6HB MAIN, ND)
         IF (NC .GT. 1) CALL PRTS (C, NC, 1, 6HC MAIN, ND)
         CALL PRTS (AB, NA, NB, 6HA BY B, ND)
         IF (NC .EQ. 1) GO TO 150
```

264 ANALYSIS OF VARIANCE

```
      CALL PRTS (AC, NA, NC, 6HA BY C, ND)
      CALL PRTS (BC, NB, NC, 6HB BY C, ND)
      PRINT 135
  135 FORMAT (// 31H CELL MEANS. BLOCKS = C LEVELS.)
      DO 145 K = 1,NC
      DO 140 I = 1,NA
      DO 140 J = 1,NB
  140 AB(I,J) = ABC(I,J,K)
  145 CALL PRTS (AB, NA, NB, 2HAB, ND)
  150 IF (ZM(N) .EQ. 0.0) GO TO 170
C     PRINT CELL N MATRIX.
      PRINT 155
  155 FORMAT (// 38H SUBJECTS PER CELL. BLOCKS = C LEVELS.)
      DO 165 K = 1,NC
      DO 160 I = 1,NA
      DO 160 J = 1,NB
  160 AB(I,J) = GN(I,J,K)
  165 CALL PRTS (AB, NA, NB, 2HAB, ND)
  170 CONTINUE
      GO TO 5
      END


*** INPUT DATA DECK ***

AVAR23 EXAMPLE PROBLEM ONE. DOUBLE CLASSIFICATION.
00001000020000200001099999
(17X, F7.0)
00002 GROUP   A1B1
S02SRI QS     26.    30.    30.    26.    28.    20.    24.    28.    212.
S04SRI QS     30.    28.    29.    29.    28.    23.    28.    30.    225.
00004 GROUP   A1B2
S05SRI QS     23.    25.    29.           20.    27.    28.           199.
S06SRI QS     28.    27.    30.    22.    19.    25.    30.    26.    207.
S07SRI QS     28.    24.    27.    27.    17.    21.    30.    26.    200.
S08SRI QS     25.    29.    29.    27.    26.    25.    26.    25.    212.
00003 GROUP   A2B1
S10SRI QS     28.    29.    30.    26.    25.    28.    30.    28.    224.
S11SRI QS     24.    28.    30.           27.    23.    21.    28.    210.
S12SRI QS     26.    29.    26.    27.    28.    19.    30.    27.    212.
00004 GROUP   A2B2
S13SRI QS     30.    27.    26.    24.    25.           28.    25.    206.
S14SRI QS     29.    29.    29.    28.    25.    19.    30.    27.    216.
S15SRI QS     29.    25.    28.    26.    24.    21.    30.           212.
S16SRI QS     29.    26.    30.    20.    25.    20.    30.    28.    208.
AVAR23 EXAMPLE PROBLEM TWO. TRIPLE CLASSIFICATION.
00002000020000200002    -2
(10X, 2F7.0)
11
S01SRI QS     25.           22.           26.           19.           182.
S02SRI QS     26.    30.    30.    26.    28.    20.    24.    28.    212.
S03SRI QS     20.           20.    23.    18.           21.    29.    180.
S04SRI QS     30.    28.    29.    29.    28.    23.    28.    30.    225.
S05SRI QS     23.    25.    29.           20.    27.    28.           199.
S06SRI QS     28.    27.    30.    22.    19.    25.    30.    26.    207.
S07SRI QS     28.    24.    27.    27.    17.    21.    30.    26.    200.
S08SRI QS     25.    29.    29.    27.    26.    25.    26.    25.    212.
S09SRI QS     26.           30.    24.    29.    24.    14.    29.    206.
S10SRI QS     28.    29.    30.    26.    25.    28.    30.    28.    224.
S11SRI QS     24.    28.    30.           27.    23.    21.    28.    210.
S12SRI QS     26.    29.    26.    27.    28.    19.    30.    27.    212.
S13SRI QS     30.    27.    26.    24.    25.           28.    25.    206.
S14SRI QS     29.    29.    29.    28.    25.    19.    30.    27.    216.
S15SRI QS     29.    25.    28.    26.    24.    21.    30.           212.
S16SRI QS     29.    26.    30.    20.    25.    20.    30.    28.    208.
```

*** PRINTED OUTPUT ***

1AVAR23 EXAMPLE PROBLEM ONE. DOUBLE CLASSIFICATION.

PARAMETERS
COL 1- 5 =   1
COL 6-10 =   2
COL 11-15 =   2
COL 16-20 =   1
COL 21-25 =   9999

DATA FORMAT = (17X, F7.0)

ANALYSIS OF VARIABLE   1

SOURCE	M.S.	D.F.	F-RATIO	P
TOTAL	3.587	12.		
BETWEEN	5.625	3.		
A	.021	1.	.0072	.9321
B	16.333	1.	5.6178	.0403
AB	.521	1.	.1791	.6836
WITHIN	2.907	9.		

MEANS FOR ALL EFFECTS.

A MAIN   1   2
            27.6250   27.7083

B MAIN   1   2
            28.8333   26.5000

A BY B   1   2

   1   29.0000   26.2500

   2   28.6667   26.7500

1AVAR23 EXAMPLE PROBLEM TWO. TRIPLE CLASSIFICATION.

PARAMETERS
COL 1- 5 =   2
COL 6-10 =   2
COL 11-15 =   2
COL 16-20 =   2
COL 21-25 =   -2

DATA FORMAT = (10X, 2F7.0)

ANALYSIS OF VARIABLE   1

SOURCE	M.S.	D.F.	F-RATIO	P
TOTAL	7.717	15.		

266 ANALYSIS OF VARIANCE

```
BETWEEN         6.250       7.
   A           16.000       1.    1.7778    .2177
   B           16.000       1.    1.7778    .2177
   C            1.000       1.     .1111    .7450
   AB           6.250       1.     .6944    .5667
   AC           2.250       1.     .2500    .6342
   BC           2.250       1.     .2500    .6342
   ABC           .000       1.     .0000   1.0000

WITHIN          9.000       8.
```

MEANS FOR ALL EFFECTS.

```
A MAIN         1          2
            25.6250    27.6250


B MAIN         1          2
            25.6250    27.6250


C MAIN         1          2
            26.8750    26.3750

A BY B         1          2

   1        25.2500    26.0000

   2        26.0000    29.2500


A BY C         1          2

   1        25.5000    25.7500

   2        28.2500    27.0000


B BY C         1          2

   1        26.2500    25.0000

   2        27.5000    27.7500
```

CELL MEANS. BLOCKS = C LEVELS.

```
AB             1          2

   1        25.5000    25.5000

   2        27.0000    29.5000


AB             1          2

   1        25.0000    26.5000

   2        25.0000    29.0000
```

SUBJECTS PER CELL. BLOCKS = C LEVELS.

AB	1	2
1	2.0000	2.0000
2	2.0000	2.0000

AB	1	2
1	2.0000	2.0000
2	2.0000	2.0000

ANALYSIS OF VARIABLE 2

SOURCE	M.S.	D.F.	F-RATIO	P
TOTAL	3.515	12.		
BETWEEN	3.526	7.		
A	.045	1.	.0130	.9098
B	16.409	1.	4.6883	.0815
C	3.682	1.	1.0519	.3538
AB	.409	1.	.1169	.7431
AC	.409	1.	.1169	.7431
BC	.045	1.	.0130	.9098
ABC	3.682	1.	1.0519	.3538
WITHIN	3.500	5.		

MEANS FOR ALL EFFECTS.

A MAIN	1	2
	27.6250	27.7500

B MAIN	1	2
	28.8750	26.5000

C MAIN	1	2
	28.2500	27.1250

A BY B	1	2
1	29.0000	26.2500
2	28.7500	26.7500

A BY C	1	2
1	28.0000	27.2500
2	28.5000	27.0000

B BY C	1	2
1	29.5000	28.2500

ANALYSIS OF VARIANCE

           2   27.0000   26.0000

CELL MEANS. BLOCKS = C LEVELS.

AB	1	2
1	30.0000	26.0000
2	29.0000	28.0000

AB	1	2
1	28.0000	26.5000
2	28.5000	25.5000

SUBJECTS PER CELL. BLOCKS = C LEVELS.

AB	1	2
1	1.0000	2.0000
2	1.0000	2.0000

AB	1	2
1	1.0000	2.0000
2	2.0000	2.0000

MULTIPLE DISCRIMINANT ANALYSIS

This statistical technique may be conceptualized as an extension of single-classification analysis of variance to include simultaneously a group of dependent variables. The problem is to determine the extent and manner in which two or more previously defined groups of subjects may be differentiated by a set of dependent variables operating together. With two groups of subjects this separation can be represented only along a single dimension, but with more than two groups the differentiation may be described in terms of multiple independent dimensions. The *maximum* number of these "factors" or reference axes necessary to represent group differences will be the number of groups minus one, or the number of variables, whichever is smaller.

The procedure used in Program DSCRIM is based on the work of Cooley and Lohnes (1962), although certain major modifications have been made. The direct factoring of $W^{-1}A$ and the internal computation of correlations between original variables and discriminant functions are the responsibility of the author.

The notation of matrix algebra is the most convenient vehicle for describing the computational sequence. For each group of subjects, the matrices P, T, and W are formed in turn from the raw scores (X) by the following methods:

$P_{MM} = X'_{MN} X_{NM}$ raw cross-products
$T_M = X'_{MN} U_N$ raw sums
$W_{MM} = P_{MM} - T_M T'_M N^{-1}$ deviation cross-products

where N = the number of subjects in the group
M = the number of variables

These matrices and the total N are accumulated over all groups and the following matrices are developed from them. P, T, W, and N henceforth refer to the accumulated matrices.

$C_{MM} = N^{-1}(P_{MM} - T_M T'_M N^{-1})$ covariance matrix
$A_{MM} = N C_{MM} - W_{MM}$ among-groups matrix

Although W^{-1} and A are symmetric matrices, their product is not. The discriminant functions are the eigenvectors of this product matrix $W^{-1}A$, and cannot be extracted with Subroutine SEVS. A subroutine for extracting the roots and vectors of a square by asymmetric matrix follows.

AEVS (NV, NF, C, Λ, V, E, X, Y, Z, ND)

A subroutine to extract roots and vectors from a square asymmetric matrix.

This subroutine is organized very much like Subroutine SEVS, except that both "right" and "left" eigenvectors are extracted and their outer product is used to deflate the A matrix after extraction of each root. The right (column) vectors are returned by the routine in denormalized form as columns of matrix V. The vector E is returned holding the corresponding roots which are the sums of squares of these column vectors. The deflation technique used here is described by Whyte (1958). It is worth noting that if the input matrix A is symmetric, the right and left vectors are identical and the computational formulas may be reduced to those of Subroutine SEVS. An arbitrary limit of 25 iterations has been imposed on the estimation of each root, which yields more than enough accuracy for most problems in the behavioral sciences (Figure 10-5).

```
      SUBROUTINE AEVS (NV, NF, C, A, V, E, X, Y, Z, ND)
C
C     EXTRACT ROOTS AND DENORMAL VECTORS FROM A NON-SYMMETRIC SQUARE MATRIX.
C     NV = THE ORDER OF A.
C     NF = INPUT AS MAX. NUMBER OF FACTORS TO BE EXTRACTED. OUTPUT AS
C          NUMBER EXTRACTED WHICH EXCEEDED MINIMUM C.
C     C = MINIMUM EIGENVALUE TO BE EXTRACTED.
C     A = SQUARE INPUT MATRIX. DESTROYED IN PROCESSING.
C     V = OUTPUT MATRIX OF COLUMN VECTORS OF LOADINGS.
C     E = OUTPUT VECTOR OF ROOTS.
C     X = OUTPUT VECTOR OF PERCENTAGES OF TRACE FOR FACTORS.
C     Y,Z = TEMPORARY STORAGE VECTORS.
```

270 ANALYSIS OF VARIANCE

```
C   ND = NUMBER OF ROWS DIMENSIONED FOR A AND V IN CALLING PROGRAM.
C
    DIMENSION A(ND,NV), V(ND,NF), E(NF), X(NV), Y(NV), Z(NV)
C   COMPUTE TRACE.
    T = 0.0
    DO 5 I = 1,NV
  5 T = T + A(I,I)
    DO 30 K = 1,NF
C   ROOTS IN E(K) AND EK, VECTORS IN V(.,K) AND Z.
    DO 10 I = 1,NV
    X(I) = 1.0
 10 Y(I) = 1.0
    E(K) = 1.0
    EK = 1.0
    DO 25 M = 1,25
    DO 15 I = 1,NV
    V(I,K) = X(I) / E(K)
 15 Z(I) = Y(I) / EK
    DO 20 I = 1,NV
    X(I) = SCPF(A, V, -I, K, NV, ND)
 20 Y(I) = SCPF(A, Z, I, 1, NV, ND)
    E2 = SCPF(X, V, 1, K, NV, ND)
    E(K) = SQRT(ABS(E2))
 25 EK = SQRT(ABS(SCPF(Y, Z, 1, 1, NV, ND)))
    IF (E2 .LT. C * C) GO TO 35
C   DEFLATE R MATRIX.
    D = E(K) / SCPF(V, Z, K, 1, NV, ND)
    DO 30 I = 1,NV
    DO 30 J = 1,NV
 30 A(I,J) = A(I,J) - V(I,K) * Z(J) * D
    GO TO 40
 35 NF = K - 1
C   COMPUTE PERCENTS OF TRACE.
 40 DO 45 I = 1,NF
 45 X(I) = E(I) / T * 100.0
    EV = SUMF(X, 1, NF, ND)
    PRINT 50, T, EV, NF
500 FORMAT (// 45H PRINCIPAL AXIS ANALYSIS (ASYMMETRIC MATRIX). //
   1 18H TRACE =, F10.4 // F7.2, 31H PCT. OF TRACE WAS EXTRACTED BY, I3
   2 7H ROOTS.)
    RETURN
    END
```

An intuitive approach to understanding the discriminant analysis procedure is suggested by interpreting the $W^{-1}A$ matrix as analogous to an F ratio in single-classification analysis of variance; F is the ratio of terms representing within-group and among-group variation also. If the F ratio can be considered an index of the ability of a dependent variable to discriminate (separate) the predetermined groups of subjects, then the factoring of the $W^{-1}A$ matrix may be construed as the partitioning of the discriminating power of the set of dependent variables into independent components, which may perhaps lead to or support hypotheses about underlying sources of the variation among the groups.

The vectors obtained from $W^{-1}A$ by Subroutine AEVS are also analogous to factor dimensions in that they are independent axes defining a K-fold space. The nature of this space, however, is such that when points representing the groups are located within it, these points are separated from each other to a maximum degree. Points representing each individual

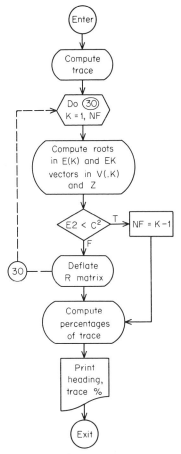

FIGURE 10-5. Subroutine AEVS flow chart.

subject in the sample may also be located within this space. In order to obtain the coordinates for these points, the vectors returned by Subroutine AEVS are normalized and the resulting eigenvectors of $W^{-1}A$ are then multiplied directly by each subject's vector of raw scores on the original variables to obtain a set of discriminant scores. We will use the letter K to indicate the number of discriminant axes and also the number of discriminant scores per subject. The vectors returned by Subroutine AEVS are normalized by:

$$B_{MK} = V_{MK} E_{\Delta K}^{-1/2}$$

Discriminant scores for all subjects are represented by:

$$D_{NK} = X_{NM} B_{MK}$$

Just as individual subjects may be located by sets of discriminant scores, so also may groups be located at their *centroids* in the discriminant space. The coordinates of these centroids or multivariate means are computed from a matrix H containing the means of each of the L groups on each of the M original variables, using the same eigenvectors:

$$G_{LK} = H_{LM}B_{MK}$$

The coefficients contained in the eigenvectors of $W^{-1}A$ do not necessarily reflect the relationships between the original variables and the discriminant-function variables. To compute correlations between these two sets of dimensions in order to determine the "nature" of the discriminant functions, we could obtain discriminant scores for all subjects and directly compute the correlations we seek. It is more economical from a programming standpoint, however, to use the covariance matrix C as a basis for accomplishing this by the following method:

$$S_{\Delta M} = C_{\Delta M}^{1/2} \quad \text{(sigmas of the original variables)}$$
$$Q_{\Delta K} = (B'_{KM}C_{MM}B_{MK})_{\Delta K}^{1/2} \quad \text{(sigmas of the discriminant variables)}$$
$$R_{MK} = S_{\Delta M}^{-1}C_{MM}B_{MK}Q_{\Delta K}^{-1}$$

These correlation coefficients may be interpreted in much the same way as factor loadings, to describe the discriminant dimensions in terms of the names of the original variables.

Although the maximum number of discriminant axes (K) are obtained from Subroutine AEVS and are used in all of the previously described computations, they will be successively less important in that they will account for successively less of the differences among the predefined groups of subjects on the original dimensions. A statistical test is available to determine the extent to which the discrimination of the groups obtained would be likely by chance alone, as well as tests for the significance of group separation along each of the discriminant axes. Wilk's Lambda is defined by

$$\prod_{}^{K} [1/(E+1)]$$

where the symbol Π means the product of all K terms, and is tested with an F ratio (Cooley and Lohnes, 1962, p. 125) which indicates the significance of overall group differentiation. Chi-square tests of the significance of each discriminant function are computed from formulas derived from Rao (1952, p. 373).

When only one discriminant dimension is significant, subject scores and group centroids can be adequately represented at points on a single linear dimension scaled in terms of the discriminant scores. When two functions are significant, a two-dimensional plot (graph) is required, as illustrated in Figure 10-6, where we have plotted the subject points and group centroids for the example problem. The discrimination effected here is artificially

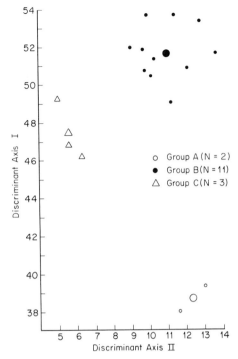

FIGURE 10-6. Group centroids and subject points for example problem.

strong, because the grouping of subjects was determined by output from Program HGROUP (presented in a later chapter) which clusters subjects so as to maximize group differences.

PROGRAM ORGANIZATION

After obtaining parameters and the data-card format from the CCDS Subroutine, the C and W matrices are zeroed, since they will hold raw and deviation cross-products accumulated over groups. As each group of subjects is input from data cards punched in the usual manner with scores for variables across each subject's card(s), the sum of scores on each variable is stored in matrix S and a within-group matrix is computed and added to W. Raw cross-products are added to matrix C. Raw sums of squares are saved in Q for the later univariate analyses, and the covariance, among and within-group matrices are computed. $W^{-1}A$ is computed next and submitted to Subroutine AEVS. Discriminant score weights are computed and output, followed by computation of correlations between original variables and discriminant functions.

Wilks' Lambda is computed and tested for significance, followed by the chi-square tests of each discriminant function. Group centroids are computed next, and then univariate analyses of variance are computed for each

274 ANALYSIS OF VARIANCE

of the original variables for comparison purposes. Finally, discriminant scores are computed for each subject, if optioned (Figure 10-7).

EXAMPLE PROBLEM

This example problem is artificial in that the subjects have been clustered by an analytic routine (Program HGROUP) which maximizes group differ-

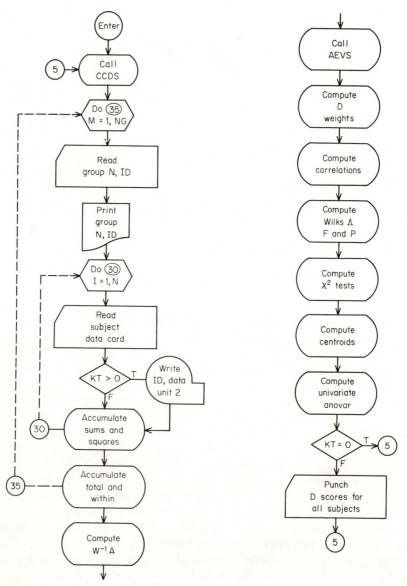

FIGURE 10-7. Program DSCRIM flow chart.

Example Problem 275

ences. Most of the subjects compose group B, while two other groups of relatively deviant score-profile types are composed of only two and three subjects respectively. Both of the discriminant functions yield significant chi-square values. Most of the variables load the first discriminant axis, while the second discriminant function appears to be determined largely by variable five. Inspection of the results of the univariate analyses indicates that variables six, seven, and eight do not by themselves separate the groups. Their contributions to the composite discriminant functions, on the other hand, are indicated by their weights in the vectors used to compute the discriminant scores (punched output listing), as well as by their correlations with the discriminant-function variables (printed output).

```
C       PROGRAM DSCRIM
C
C   MULTIPLE DISCRIMINANT ANALYSIS CONTROL PROGRAM.
C   PARAMETERS ARE DEFINED BELOW.
C       COL 1-5.  NUMBER OF PREDICTOR VARIABLES.  MAX = 70.
C       COL 6-10. NUMBER OF GROUPS OF SUBJECTS.   MAX = 10.
C       COL 15.  1 = PUNCH DISCRIMINANT FUNCTION WEIGHTS.
C       COL 20.  1 = PUNCH DISCRIMINANT SCORES FOR SUBJECTS.
C   TAPE UNIT 2 IS USED FOR TEMPORARY STORAGE (SCRATCH).
C   FORMAT MUST SPECIFY ID FIELD BEFORE SCORE FIELDS.
C   A GROUP CONTROL CARD IS REQUIRED BEFORE EACH SET OF DATA CARDS.
C       (COL 1-5 = GROUP N, COL 6-80 = ALPHAMERIC GROUP IDENTIFICATION)
C   SUBROUTINES AND FUNCTIONS REQUIRED ARE
C       SUMF, SCPF, PRBF, CCDS, PRTS, PCDS, SUBS, AXBS, INVS, AEVS.
C
       ODIMENSION A(70,70), W(70,70), C(70,70), S(70,10), T(70),
      1 V(70), X(70), Y(70), Z(70), Q(70), G(10), KF(16), KH(15)
       N1 = 70
       N2 = 10
     5 CALL CCDS (KF, NV, NG, KW, KT, I)
       DO 10 I = 1,NV
       DO 10 J = I,NV
       C(I,J) = 0.0
    10 W(I,J) = 0.0
       IF (KT .GT. 0) REWIND 2
C   INPUT DATA, ACCUMULATE SUMS AND CROSS-PRODUCTS.
       DO 35 M = 1,NG
       READ 15, N, KH
    15 FORMAT (I5, 15A5)
       PRINT 20, M, N, KH
    20 FORMAT (/ 6H GROUP, I2, I8, 10H SUBJECTS., 2X, 15A5)
       G(M) = N
       DO 25 I = 1,NV
       S(I,M) = 0.0
       DO 25 J = I,NV
    25 A(I,J) = 0.0
       DO 30 I = 1,N
       READ KF, ID, (X(J), J = 1,NV)
       IF (KT .GT. 0) WRITE (2) ID, (X(J), J = 1,NV)
       DO 30 J = 1,NV
       S(J,M) = S(J,M) + X(J)
       DO 30 K = J,NV
    30 A(J,K) = A(J,K) + X(J) * X(K)
       DO 35 I = 1,N
       DO 35 J = I,NV
       C(I,J) = C(I,J) + A(I,J)
    35 W(I,J) = W(I,J) + (A(I,J) - S(I,M) * S(J,M) / G(M))
       TN = SUMF(G, 1, NG, N2)
```

ANALYSIS OF VARIANCE

```
         DO 40 I = 1,NV
         T(I) = SUMF(S, -I, NG, N1) / TN
      40 Q(I) = C(I,I)
C COMPUTE COVARIANCE, AMONG, AND WITHIN MATRICES.
         DO 45 I = 1,NV
         DO 45 J = 1,NV
         C(I,J) = C(I,J) / TN - T(I) * T(J)
         C(J,I) = C(I,J)
         A(I,J) = C(I,J) * TN - W(I,J)
         A(J,I) = A(I,J)
      45 W(J,I) = W(I,J)
C COMPUTE AND FACTOR W INVERSE A.
         CALL INVS (NV, W, X, Y, Z, N1)
         DO 55 I = 1,NV
         DO 50 J = 1,NV
      50 X(J) = W(I,J)
         DO 55 J = 1,NV
      55 W(I,J) = SCPF(X, A, 1, J, NV, N1)
         NF = MIN0(NG - 1, NV)
         CALL AEVS (NV, NF, 0.0, W, A, V, X, Y, Z, N1)
C COMPUTE AND OUTPUT DISCRIMINANT-SCORE WEIGHTS.
         DO 60 J = 1,NF
         E = 1.0 / SQRT(V(J))
         DO 60 I = 1,NV
      60 A(I,J) = A(I,J) * E
         IF (KW .EQ. 1) CALL PCDS (A, NV, NF, 5HD WTS, N1)
C COMPUTE CORRELATIONS OF DISCRIMINANT AND ORIGINAL VARIABLES.
         DO 65 I = 1,NV
      65 X(I) = SQRT(C(I,I))
         CALL AXBS (C, A, W, NV, NF, NV, N1)
         DO 70 I = 1,NF
      70 Y(I) = SQRT(SCPF(A, W, I, I, NV, N1))
         DO 75 I = 1,NV
         DO 75 J = 1,NF
      75 C(I,J) = W(I,J) / (X(I) * Y(J))
C COMPUTE WILKS LAMBDA, F-RATIO, AND PROBABILITY.
         TR = SUMF(V, 1, NF, N1)
         XL = 1.0
         DO 80 I = 1,NF
         X(I) = V(I) / TR * 100.0
      80 XL = XL * (1.0 / (1.0 + V(I)))
         VN = NV
         GN = NG
         GM = GN - 1.0
         SS = SQRT((VN**2 * GM**2 - 4.0) / (VN**2 + GM**2 - 5.0))
         YY = XL**(1.0 / SS)
         FA = VN * GM
         FB = ((TN - 1.0) - (VN + GN) / 2.0) * SS - (VN * GM - 2.0) / 2.0
         F = (FB * (1.0 - YY)) / (YY * FA)
         P = PRBF(FA, FB, F)
         PRINT 85, XL, FA, FB, F, P
      85 FORMAT (// 15H WILKS LAMBDA =, F10.3 // 7H D.F. =, F5.0,
        1 14H AND, F7.0 // 10H F-RATIO =, F8.3, 5X, 3HP =, F7.4)
C COMPUTE CHI-SQUARE TESTS AND PROBABILITIES.
         DF = VN + GN
         CC = TN - DF / 2.0
         DO 90 I = 1,NF
         CS = CC * ALOG(1.0 + V(I))
         DF = DF - 2.0
         P = PRBF(DF, 1000.0, CS / DF)
      90 PRINT 95, I, X(I), CS, DF, P
      95 FORMAT (/ 5H0ROOT, I2, F10.2, 14H PCT. VARIANCE //
        1 13H CHI-SQUARE =, F10.3, 5X, 6HD.F. =, F5.0, 5X, 3HP =, F7.4)
C COMPUTE CENTROIDS.
         DO 100 I = 1,NV
```

```
      T(I) = T(I) * TN
      DO 100 J = 1,NG
  100 S(I,J) = S(I,J) / G(J)
      CALL AXBS (S, A, W, -NG, NF, NV, N1)
      CALL PRTS (W, NG, NF, 5HCENT., N1)
      CALL PRTS (C, NV, NF, 6HCOREL., N1)
C COMPUTE UNIVARIATE ANALYSES OF VARIANCE.
      DFW = TN - GN
      PRINT 105, GM, DFW
  1050FORMAT (// 26H UNIVARIATE F-TESTS. DFB =, F3.0,
     16H DFW =, F6.0 /// 18H VARIABLE   F-RATIO, 6X, 1HP)
      DO 115 I = 1,NV
      B = 0.0
      DO 110 J = 1,NG
  110 B = B + S(I,J)**2 * G(J)
      CC = T(I)**2 / TN
      F = ((B - CC) * DFW) / ((Q(I) - B) * GM)
      P = PRBF(GM, DFW, F)
  115 PRINT 120, I, F, P
  120 FORMAT (/ I6, F12.4, F10.4)
      CALL PRTS (S, NV, NG, 6HG MEAN, N1)
      IF (KT .EQ. 0) GO TO 5
C COMPUTE AND PUNCH DISCRIMINANT SCORES FOR SUBJECTS.
      REWIND 2
      NT = TN
      DO 130 I = 1,NT
      READ (2) ID, (X(J), J = 1,NV)
      DO 125 J = 1,NF
  125 Y(J) = SCPF(X, A, 1, J, NV, N1)
  130 CALL SUBS (Y, NF, 2HDS, ID)
      GO TO 5
      END
```

*** INPUT DATA DECK ***

```
SCRIM EXAMPLE PROBLEM
0008000030000100001
(6, 4X, 8F7.0)
0002 GROUP A (SUBJECTS 1,3)
01SRI QS      25.     21.     22.     20.     26.     26.     19.     23.    182.
03SRI QS      20.     25.     20.     23.     18.     24.     21.     29.    180.
0011 GROUP B
02SRI QS      26.     30.     30.     26.     28.     20.     24.     28.    212.
04SRI QS      30.     28.     29.     29.     28.     23.     28.     30.    225.
08SRI QS      25.     29.     29.     27.     26.     25.     26.     25.    212.
09SRI QS      26.     30.     30.     24.     29.     24.     14.     29.    206.
0SRI QS       28.     29.     30.     26.     25.     28.     30.     28.    224.
1SRI QS       24.     28.     30.     29.     27.     23.     21.     28.    210.
2SRI QS       26.     29.     26.     27.     28.     19.     30.     27.    212.
3SRI QS       30.     27.     26.     24.     25.     21.     28.     25.    206.
4SRI QS       29.     29.     29.     28.     25.     19.     30.     27.    216.
5SRI QS       29.     25.     28.     26.     24.     21.     30.     29.    212.
6SRI QS       29.     26.     30.     20.     25.     20.     30.     28.    208.
0003 GROUP C (SUBJECTS 5,6,7)
5SRI QS       23.     25.     29.     19.     20.     27.     28.     28.    199.
6SRI QS       28.     27.     30.     22.     19.     25.     30.     26.    207.
7SRI QS       28.     24.     27.     27.     17.     21.     30.     26.    200.
```

*** PUNCHED OUTPUT ***

```
WTS  1 1    0.1493    0.0793
WTS  2 1    0.4072    0.1362
```

ANALYSIS OF VARIANCE

```
D WTS   3  1     0.7722    -0.7207
D WTS   4  1     0.1295     0.0220
D WTS   5  1     0.3040     0.6024
D WTS   6  1    -0.2430     0.0371
D WTS   7  1     0.1965     0.0022
D WTS   8  1     0.0940     0.3017
S01SRIDS   1    39.3387    13.0350
S03SRIDS   1    38.0763    11.6115
S02SRIDS   1    53.6254    11.2088
S04SRIDS   1    53.2692    12.7634
S08SRIDS   1    50.7143     9.8157
S09SRIDS   1    50.8275    12.1953
S10SRIDS   1    51.8393     9.7334
S11SRIDS   1    51.2787    10.3458
S12SRIDS   1    51.5870    13.6516
S13SRIDS   1    49.0022    11.2895
S14SRIDS   1    53.5689     9.9422
S15SRIDS   1    50.3068    10.1490
S16SRIDS   1    51.9342     8.9757
S05SRIDS   1    46.1157     6.3051
S06SRIDS   1    49.2242     5.0439
S07SRIDS   1    46.6980     5.5540
```

*** PRINTED OUTPUT ***

1DSCRIM EXAMPLE PROBLEM

```
PARAMETERS
COL   1- 5 =      8
COL   6-10 =      3
COL  11-15 =      1
COL  16-20 =      1
COL  21-25 =      0
```

DATA FORMAT = (A6, 4X, 8F7.0)

GROUP 1   2 SUBJECTS.   GROUP A (SUBJECTS 1,3)

GROUP 2   11 SUBJECTS.   GROUP B

GROUP 3   3 SUBJECTS.   GROUP C (SUBJECTS 5,6,7)

PRINCIPAL AXIS ANALYSIS (ASYMMETRIC MATRIX).

TRACE =   14.2884

100.00 PCT. OF TRACE WAS EXTRACTED BY 2 ROOTS.

WILKS LAMBDA =   .019

D.F. = 16. AND   12.

F-RATIO =   4.665   P = .0055

0ROOT 1   76.37 PCT. VARIANCE

   CHI-SQUARE =   26.014   D.F. =   9.   P = .0026

0ROOT 2   23.63 PCT. VARIANCE

   CHI-SQUARE =   15.501   D.F. =   7.   P = .0306

NT.	1	2
1	38.7080	12.3233
2	51.6326	10.9155
3	47.3464	5.6344

REL.	1	2
1	.6235	-.0843
2	.7825	.2026
3	.8591	-.3633
4	.5501	.2559
5	.5551	.7363
6	-.4058	-.2013
7	.3773	-.4533
8	.3388	.1039

IVARIATE F-TESTS. DFB = 2. DFW = 13.

RIABLE	F-RATIO	P
1	3.6818	.0531
2	9.4517	.0032
3	22.7658	.0002
4	3.1689	.0746
5	15.2042	.0006
6	1.4475	.2703
7	2.6416	.1078
8	.8321	.5397

MEAN	1	2	3
1	22.5000	27.4545	26.3333
2	23.0000	28.1818	25.3333
3	21.0000	28.8182	28.6667
4	21.5000	26.0000	22.6667
5	22.0000	26.3636	18.6667
6	25.0000	22.0909	24.3333
7	20.0000	26.4545	29.3333
8	26.0000	27.6364	26.6667

Review Exercises

1. Make out the necessary control cards for Program ANOVAR to carry out the three analyses shown in Figure 10-1. Assume that each score is punched in separate tab card (columns 9–10). This would result in data decks of 18 cards each for problems *a* and *c*, and nine cards for problem *b*.
2. Were any of the F ratios computed for the ANOVAR and AVAR23 example problems significant at the traditional 5 percent level?
3. Consider the three rotated factor variables produced in Chapter 9 by the first example problem for Program FACTOR. If these factor scores were used as three repeated measures of one group of subjects, what F ratio would be expected from Program ANOVAR?
4. Will the use of standardized scores as data affect the results of the discriminant analysis? Answer the question empirically also by obtaining standard scores for the example data (all subjects) with Program DISTAT, and then using the output cards instead of the original scores as input to Program DSCRIM.

11 / regression analysis

The essential concept underlying the techniques to be discussed in this chapter is covariation. Unlike the descriptive methods given in Chapter 9, the goals of these procedures are primarily predictive.

Most behavioral scientists are familiar with the multiple-regression model in which a single criterion variable is predicted from a *set* of predictor variables, yielding a multiple-correlation coefficient: $r_{y \cdot x_1 x_2 \cdots x_n}$. Just as the square of an ordinary correlation coefficient indicates the amount of variation shared by the two correlated variables, the square of a multiple-correlation coefficient may be interpreted as the proportion of the variance of the criterion variable that is "explained" by the predictors, in the sense that it is predictable. The solution of a multiple-correlation problem involves the determination of a set of weights—one for each predictor variable—which can be applied to each subject's set of predictor scores to yield a series of composite predicted criterion scores. The multiple-correlation coefficient is actually the correlation which would be obtained if the actual and predicted criterion scores were used to compute an ordinary correlation coefficient.

The equation used to compute a subject's criterion score may be expressed as:

$$\hat{Y} = W_1 X_1 + W_2 X_2 + \cdots + W_K X_K$$

where $\hat{Y}$ is the predicted criterion score
  W_i is a weight for a predictor
  X_i is a predictor score
  K is the number of predictor variables

We can define a subject's *actual* criterion score as:

$$Y = \hat{Y} + E = W_1X_1 + W_2X_2 + \cdots + W_KX_K + E$$

where E is the error of prediction: $Y - \hat{Y}$. The multiple-correlation technique seeks a set of weights (W_i) which, when applied to the raw scores of each subject in turn, will yield a set of E values with a minimum sum of squares (minimum prediction error).

Although the notation and mathematics of multiple correlation are known to most behavioral scientists, the uses of this model to carry out analysis of variance and covariance designs are seldom seen in the literature. Actually, the linear-regression approach to analysis of variance offers the investigator the possibility of making much more precise tests of his hypotheses without many of the usual assumptions of traditional analysis of variance procedures. We will not attempt to illustrate more than a few of the wide variety of possible applications of this method, but interested readers should obtain a copy of a lucid monograph on the topic by Bottenberg and Ward (1963).[1]

Multiple correlation is a special case of a more general statistical model called *canonical correlation,* in which two sets of variables are related to each other in as many independent ways as are possible. We will discuss this more general model for multivariate correlational analysis and program for its implementation before taking up the topic of multiple linear regression analysis.

CANONICAL CORRELATION ANALYSIS

The discussion that follows is based in part upon the work of Cooley and Lohnes (1962) and Koons (1962), although we have modified certain equations in an attempt to reconcile inconsistencies and to simplify other published formulations of this procedure.

The goal of canonical analysis is to define the primary independent dimensions which relate one set of variables to another set of variables. The technique is primarily descriptive, although the method used involves finding sets of weights which will yield two composite variables (one for each set of original variables) which will correlate maximally. The two sets of variables might consist of subscales from two personality inventories, ratings of home and schoolroom behavior of children, biochemical and psychological test performances. The output of a canonical analysis should suggest answers to questions concerning the *number* of ways in which the two sets of measures are related, the *strengths* of the relationships, and the *nature* of the relationships so defined.

The maximum number of *independent* multivariate relationships which

[1] See also: Ward (1962).

can be defined between two sets of original variables is equal in number to the smaller of the two sets. Thus, two canonical correlations can be determined between a set of three variables on one side and a set of two variables on the other side. The term "independent" as used here implies that the composite scores for successive canonical variables will be uncorrelated on each side, and when cross-correlated will yield a diagonal matrix of canonical correlation coefficients. Again, we must partition information from raw scores into independent components. In this case the information concerns the relationships existing between two sets of variables. Each canonical "root" will be associated with two vectors of weights, which may be applied to the original scores on their respective sides to yield the composite canonical scores. For example, consider a problem involving two variables on one side and three on the other. Equations defining the two canonical scores for a single subject for one root may be expressed as follows:

$$P = A_1 X_1 + A_2 X_2 + A_3 X_3$$
$$Q = B_1 Y_1 + B_2 Y_2$$

where P and Q are composite canonical scores
X_i and Y_i are original-variable scores
A_i and B_i are weights which yield a maximum correlation of variables P and Q

As an aside, consider what happens to these equations and the canonical analysis model when there is only a single variable in the B set, and therefore only one root:

$$P = A_1 X_1 + A_2 X_2 + A_3 X_3$$
$$Q = B_1 Y_1 = Y$$

The optimum weight for the Y variable is 1.0, and the problem reduces to the well-known multiple correlation task of determining the set of weights (A_i) which will yield the maximum possible correlation between a criterion variable (Y) and a weighted composite (P) of a set of predictor variables (X_i). Note also that when *both* sides are composed of single variables, the weights are both 1.0 and we simply compute an ordinary correlation coefficient to determine the degree of relationship between the two variables.

Computational Procedure. Figure 11-1 represents a supermatrix of

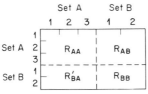

FIGURE 11-1. Supermatrix of intercorrelations.

correlations between all possible pairs of the variables within and between the two sets. This supermatrix may be partitioned to define three sub matrices (R_{AA}, R_{AB}, and R_{BB}) which serve as the starting elements for the canonical analysis procedure.

The mathematics of canonical analysis are most easily expressed in the notation of matrix algebra. After computation of the submatrices R_{AA}, R_{AB} and R_{BB}, a product matrix is formed to express the relationship pattern between the two sets of original variables:

$$R_{BB}^{-1} R'_{BA} R_{AA}^{-1} R_{AB}$$

This matrix is square but asymmetric, and Subroutine AEVS is therefore employed to extract its roots and vectors. If we assume that the input has been arranged so that the larger set of variables is entered first as set A then there will be C = B roots available from the factoring of the product matrix above. These roots are the squares of the canonical correlations between the independent composites on the A and B sides of the problem. They express directly the proportions of the total interset relationship pattern which are accounted for by the various independent canonical functions.

The vectors obtained from Subroutine AEVS are the weights for the B-side variables. Weights for the A set may be computed from:

$$V_{AC} = R_{AA}^{-1} R_{AB} W_{BC}$$

where C = number of canonical functions
V_{AC} = weights for the A side
W_{BC} = weights for the B side

These weight matrices are normalized by columns to maintain comparability and to simplify later computations. By applying the normalized weights V and W to their respective vectors of z-scaled raw scores, we may obtain two composite canonical scores for each of the N subjects in the sample:

$$P_{NC} = Z_{NA} V_{AC}$$
$$Q_{NC} = Z_{NB} W_{BC}$$

If we now intercorrelated the 2C columns of the P and Q matrices, we would find that the composites intercorrelate zero within each set ($I_{\Delta C}$) and that the submatrix of cross-set correlations is $E_{\Delta C}^{1/2}$, the square roots of the eigenvalues of $R_{BB}^{-1} R'_{BA} R_{AA}^{-1} R_{AB}$, which are the canonical correlation coefficients.

We have used the letter C for the number of roots in the preceding equations, since fewer than all possible (B) are usually "important." A chi-square test is available with which we may estimate the statistical significance of each of the canonical functions extracted (Cooley and Lohnes, p. 37).

Canonical Correlation Analysis

Again let us consider the special case of a single variable on the B side. The results should be the same as those yielded by the usual multiple correlation methods. Since $R_{BB} = 1.0$ and R_{AB} is a vector, the basic product matrix reduces to $R'_A R_{AA}^{-1} R_A$. This product is a scalar, which is itself the root, with an associated normalized vector (W) of 1.0. Thus, the product $R'_A R_{AA}^{-1} R_A$ should be the square of the multiple correlation coefficient.

In multiple-regression terminology, correlations between the criterion variable (B) and the predictor variables are known as "validities," and the weights for the predictor variables ("beta weights") are defined by $\beta_A = R_{AA}^{-1} R_A$, where R_{AA}^{-1} is the inverse of the predictor intercorrelations, and R_A is the vector of validities.

The inner product of the validity and beta-weight vectors defines the square of the multiple correlation coefficient, which is consistent with the earlier reduction we obtained from the canonical analysis equation:

$$M^2 = R'_A \beta_A = R'_A R_{AA}^{-1} R_A$$

Using the formula given earlier for obtaining the weights for the A (predictor) variables, we obtain the definition of beta weights before normalization:

$$R_{AA}^{-1} R_A \, 1.0 = \beta_A$$

Although the canonical analysis program (CANONA) could be used for multiple-regression problems, a quite different procedure will be presented later in this chapter which provides greater efficiency of computation and more flexibility of application to problems involving single criteria. That regression procedure will allow the use of a singular predictor matrix also, while the canonical analysis method is restricted to cases where both R_{AA} and R_{BB} are nonsingular matrices.

Interpretation of Canonical Functions. Although the vectors of weights yielded by the previous computational formulas do indicate the relative contribution of each of the original variables to the *computation* of the composite canonical scores, interpretation of these weights as indicators of the *nature* of the canonical relationships concerned may be quite misleading. What we need for this purpose are correlations between the original variables and the canonical variables on each side. In the multiple regression model these correlations are the validities since the B-side weight is 1.0. In the canonical-correlation model, however, the validity matrix R_{AB} reflects only the relationships between pairings of the original variables. We could compute canonical scores and then directly obtain the correlations we seek. As in the case of multiple discriminant analysis, however, it is more economical from a programming standpoint to compute these coefficients internally. The formulas for accomplishing this are as follows:

$$R_{AC} = R_{AA} V_{AC} (V'_{CA} R_{AA} V_{AC})_{\Delta C}^{-1/2}$$
$$R_{BC} = R_{BB} W_{BC} (W'_{CB} R_{BB} W_{BC})_{\Delta C}^{-1/2}$$

PROGRAM CANONA

Program CANONA is written to accommodate up to 50 variables on eac[h] side of the problem, but this limit could be extended easily by using mor[e] tape units for temporary storage.

Correlation matrix R_{AA} is computed first by the CORS Subroutine, an[d] then a second data-card format is read, replacing the one that followed th[e] Parameter Control Card. Subroutine CORS is again called to comput[e] correlation matrix R_{BB}. Scratch tapes 2 and 3 are used to hold the raw dat[a] for the two sets of variables. After rewinding these scratch tapes, the ra[w] data are read back into memory one subject at a time to compute th[e] cross-correlation matrix R_{AB}.

The basic relationships matrix $R_{BB}^{-1} R'_{BA} R_{AA}^{-1} R_{AB}$ is computed next an[d] submitted to Subroutine AEVS for extraction of roots and vectors, since [it] is an asymmetric matrix. The vectors returned from Subroutine AEVS ar[e] normalized to form the B-side weights, and are then used with $R_{AA}^{-1} R_{AB}$ t[o] obtain the A-side weights, which are subsequently normalized also. Co[r]relations between the canonical functions and the original variables on eac[h] side are computed in the next section.

Chi-square tests are computed next for each of the B canonical roots. A[ll] roots (squared canonical correlations), chi-square values, degrees of fre[e]dom, and chance-probability values are printed. A test is made of eac[h] successive probability value against a minimum value designated on th[e] Parameter Control Card to determine the number of "significant" canonic[al] functions. The number of functions which exceed this value will be use[d] subsequently in output of weights and the computation of canonical score[s] for individual subjects. If all functions are desired regardless of the[ir] probability values, set the cut-off field on the Parameter Control Card [at] 1.0 (10000). Canonical scores for individual subjects are punched on sep[a]rate cards for each side of the problem, C scores per card, if selected b[y] the Parameter Control Card option (Figure 11-2).

EXAMPLE PROBLEM

To illustrate the operation of this program, we will compare variables [1] through 5 as set A with varibles 6 through 8 as set B, entering the smalle[r] set B second, as required by the program. Note that we use two identic[al] data decks here, selecting the appropriate score fields with the data-car[d] formats.

Since there are three variables in the smaller set B, a maximum of thre[e] canonical relationships between the two sets of variables may be define[d]. The probabilities shown indicate that none of them reach the usual leve[l] for statistical significance, but we set the cutoff at 1.0 on the Paramete[r] Control Card in order to obtain a complete set of canonical weights an[d] scores for demonstration purposes.

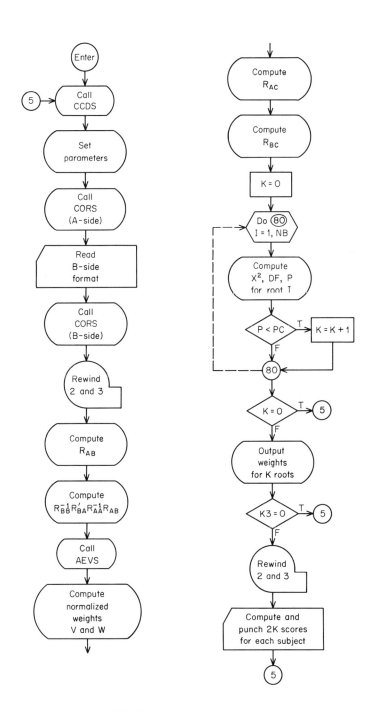

FIGURE 11-2. Program CANONA flow chart.

The *number* of multivariate relationships between the two sets of variables is suggested by the number of significant canonical correlations obtained. The *strengths* of these relationships are indicated by the squares of the canonical correlations (roots of $R_{BB}^{-1}R'_{BA}R_{AA}^{-1}R_{AB}$). Finally the *nature* of these canonical relationships may be derived from an examination of the correlation coefficients between the original variables and the canonical variables; large coefficients for a particular canonical function (column of A–CA or B–CB) can be interpreted like factor loadings, in terms of the names of the original variables, as suggesting the content of the composite dimension.

```
C     PROGRAM CANONA
C
C  MULTIPLE CANONICAL ANALYSIS CONTROL PROGRAM.
C  PARAMETER CONTROL-CARD FIELDS.
C     COL 1-5. NUMBER OF VARIABLES IN SET A (FIRST DECK) (MAX = 50).
C     COL 6-10. NUMBER OF VARIABLES IN SET B (SECOND DECK) (MAX = 50).
C     COL 11-15. NUMBER OF SUBJECTS.
C     COL 16-20. PROBABILITY CUTOFF FOR SIGNIFICANT ROOTS (F5.4 W/O DECIM
C     COL 21. 1 = PRINT SET A AND SET B MEANS, SIGMAS, INTERCORRELATIONS
C     COL 22. 1 = PUNCH WEIGHT VECTORS FOR SIGNIFICANT ROOTS.
C     COL 23. 1 = PUNCH CANONICAL SCORES FOR SIGNIFICANT ROOTS.
C  IF FIRST AND SECOND SETS HAVE UNEQUAL NUMBERS OF VARIABLES, ENTER LAR
C     SET FIRST.
C  A FORMAT CONTROL CARD MUST PRECEDE EACH SET OF DATA CARDS.
C  SUBJECTS MUST BE ENTERED IN SAME ORDER IN BOTH DATA DECKS.
C  TAPE UNITS 2 AND 3 ARE USED FOR TEMPORARY STORAGE.
C  SUBPROGRAMS REQUIRED ARE SUMF, SCPF, PRBF, CCDS, PRTS, PCDS, SUBS,
C     AXBS, INVS, CORS, AEVS.
C
    0 DIMENSION RA(50,50), RB(50,50), A(50,50), B(50,50), C(50,50),
    1 D(50,50), AM(50), AS(50), BM(50), BS(50), E(50), X(50), Y(50),
    2 Z(50), KF(16)
      ND = 50
    5 CALL CCDS (KF, NA, NB, NS, KC, KP)
C  SET PARAMETERS. COMPUTE CORRELATIONS ON A AND B SIDES.
      PC = KC
      PC = PC / 10000.0
      K1 = KP / 10000
      K2 = MOD(KP / 1000, 10)
      K3 = MOD(KP / 100, 10)
      CALL CORS (NS, NA, RA, AM, AS, KF, 2, ND)
      IF (K1 .EQ. 0) GO TO 10
      CALL PRTS (AM, NA, 1, 6HA MEAN, ND)
      CALL PRTS (AS, NA, 1, 5HA SIG, ND)
      CALL PRTS (RA, NA, NA, 6HA RMAT, ND)
   10 READ 15, KF
   15 FORMAT (16A5)
      PRINT 20, KF
   20 FORMAT (// 15H DATA FORMAT = , 16A5)
      CALL CORS (NS, NB, RB, BM, BS, KF, 3, ND)
      IF (K1 .EQ. 0) GO TO 25
      CALL PRTS (BM, NB, 1, 6HB MEAN, ND)
      CALL PRTS (BS, NB, 1, 5HB SIG, ND)
      CALL PRTS (RB, NB, NB, 6HB RMAT, ND)
C  COMPUTE CROSS-SET CORRELATIONS USING TAPED DATA.
   25 REWIND 2
      REWIND 3
      DO 30 I = 1,NA
      DO 30 J = 1,NB
```

```
   30 C(I,J) = 0.0
      DO 35 N = 1,NS
      READ (2) ID, (X(I), I = 1,NA)
      READ (3) ID, (Y(I), I = 1, NB)
      DO 35 I = 1,NA
      DO 35 J = 1,NB
   35 C(I,J) = C(I,J) + X(I) * Y(J)
      T = NS
      DO 40 I = 1,NA
      DO 40 J = 1,NB
   40 C(I,J) = (C(I,J) / T - AM(I) * BM(J)) / (AS(I) * BS(J))
      CALL PRTS (C, NA, NB, 4HR AB, ND)
C COMPUTE THE BASIC RELATIONSHIP MATRIX AND EXTRACT FACTORS.
      DO 45 I = 1,NA
      DO 45 J = 1,NA
   45 D(I,J) = RA(I,J)
      CALL INVS (NA, D, X, Y, Z, ND)
      CALL AXBS (D, C, A, NA, NB, NA, ND)
      DO 50 I = 1,NB
      DO 50 J = 1,NB
   50 D(I,J) = RB(I,J)
      CALL INVS (NB, D, X, Y, Z, ND)
      CALL AXBS (D, C, B, NB, -NA, NB, ND)
      CALL AXBS (B, A, C, NB, NB, NA, ND)
      CALL AEVS (NB, NB, 0.0, C, D, E, X, Y, Z, ND)
C NORMALIZE B-SIDE WEIGHTS AND COMPUTE A-SIDE WEIGHTS.
      DO 55 J = 1,NB
      Q = 1.0 / SQRT(E(J))
      DO 55 I = 1,NB
   55 D(I,J) = D(I,J) * Q
      CALL AXBS (A, D, C, NA, NB, NB, ND)
      DO 60 J = 1,NB
      Q = 1.0 / SQRT(SUMF(C, J, -NA, ND))
      DO 60 I = 1,NA
   60 C(I,J) = C(I,J) * Q
C COMPUTE CORRELATIONS OF RAW AND CANONICAL VARIABLES.
      CALL AXBS (RA, C, A, NA, NB, NA, ND)
      DO 65 J = 1,NB
      Q = 1.0 / SQRT(SCPF(C, A, J, J, NA, ND))
      DO 65 I = 1,NA
   65 A(I,J) = A(I,J) * Q
      CALL PRTS (A, NA, NB, 6HR A-CA, ND)
      CALL AXBS (RB, D, B, NB, NB, NB, ND)
      DO 70 J = 1,NB
      Q = 1.0 / SQRT(SCPF(D, B, J, J, NB, ND))
      DO 70 I = 1,NB
   70 B(I,J) = B(I,J) * Q
      CALL PRTS (B, NB, NB, 6HR B-CB, ND)
C COMPUTE STATISTICAL TESTS OF INDIVIDUAL ROOTS.
      Q = NA + NB + 1
      Q = Q / 2.0 - T
      W = 1.0
      DO 75 I = 1,NB
   75 W = W * (1.0 - E(I))
      CS = Q * ALOG(W)
      KDF = NA * NB
      K = 0
      DO 80 I = 1,NB
      W = W / (1.0 - E(I))
      X(I) = CS - Q * ALOG(W)
      Y(I) = KDF - (NA - I) * (NB - I)
      Z(I) = PRBF(Y(I), 1000.0, X(I) / Y(I))
      IF (Z(I) .LT. PC) K = K + 1
      KDF = (NA - I) * (NB - I)
   80 CS = CS - X(I)
```

```
      CALL PRTS (E, NB, 1, 5HROOTS, ND)
      CALL PRTS (X, NB, 1, 6HCHI SQ, ND)
      CALL PRTS (Y, NB, 1, 4HD.F., ND)
      CALL PRTS (Z, NB, 1, 5HPROB., ND)
      IF (K .EQ. 0) GO TO 5
      PRINT 85, K, PC
   85 FORMAT (// 16H WEIGHTS FOR THE, I3, 18H ROOTS WITH P .LT., F7.4)
      CALL PRTS (C, NA, K, 6HA SIDE, ND)
      CALL PRTS (D, NB, K, 6HB SIDE, ND)
      IF (K2 .EQ. 0) GO TO 90
      CALL PCDS (AM, NA, 1, 5HAMEAN, ND)
      CALL PCDS (AS, NA, 1, 5HA SIG, ND)
      CALL PCDS (C, NA, K, 5HA WTS, ND)
      CALL PCDS (BM, NB, 1, 5HBMEAN, ND)
      CALL PCDS (BS, NB, 1, 5HB SIG, ND)
      CALL PCDS (D, NB, K, 5HB WTS, ND)
   90 IF (K3 .EQ. 0) GO TO 5
C  COMPUTE AND PUNCH SETS OF CANONICAL SCORES FOR ALL SUBJECTS.
      REWIND 2
      REWIND 3
      DO 115 N = 1,NS
      READ (2) ID, (X(I), I = 1,NA)
      DO 95 I = 1,NA
   95 X(I) = (X(I) - AM(I)) / AS(I)
      DO 100 I = 1,K
  100 Y(I) = SCPF(X, C, 1, I, NA, ND)
      CALL SUBS (Y, K, 2HCA, ID)
      READ (3) ID, (X(I), I = 1, NB)
      DO 105 I = 1,NB
  105 X(I) = (X(I) - BM(I)) / BS(I)
      DO 110 I = 1,K
  110 Y(I) = SCPF(X, D, 1, I, NB, ND)
  115 CALL SUBS (Y, K, 2HCB, ID)
      GO TO 5
      END


      *** INPUT DATA DECK ***

CANONA EXAMPLE PROBLEM. VARIABLES 1-5 VS. 6-8.
000050000300016100000111
(A6, 4X, 5F7.0)
S01SRI QS     25.    21.    22.    20.    26.    26.    19.    23.    18
S02SRI QS     26.    30.    30.    26.    28.    20.    24.    28.    21
S03SRI QS     20.    25.    20.    23.    18.    24.    21.    29.    18
S04SRI QS     30.    28.    29.    29.    28.    23.    28.    30.    22
S05SRI QS     23.    25.    29.    19.    20.    27.    28.    28.    19
S06SRI QS     28.    27.    30.    22.    19.    25.    30.    26.    20
S07SRI QS     28.    24.    27.    27.    17.    21.    30.    26.    20
S08SRI QS     25.    29.    29.    27.    26.    25.    26.    25.    21
S09SRI QS     26.    30.    30.    24.    29.    24.    14.    29.    20
S10SRI QS     28.    29.    30.    26.    25.    28.    30.    28.    22
S11SRI QS     24.    28.    30.    29.    27.    23.    21.    28.    21
S12SRI QS     26.    29.    26.    27.    28.    19.    30.    27.    21
S13SRI QS     30.    27.    26.    24.    25.    21.    28.    25.    20
S14SRI QS     29.    29.    29.    28.    25.    19.    30.    27.    21
S15SRI QS     29.    25.    28.    26.    24.    21.    30.    29.    21
S16SRI QS     29.    26.    30.    20.    25.    20.    30.    28.    20
(A6, 39X, 3F7.0)
S01SRI QS     25.    21.    22.    20.    26.    26.    19.    23.    18
S02SRI QS     26.    30.    30.    26.    28.    20.    24.    28.    21
S03SRI QS     20.    25.    20.    23.    18.    24.    21.    29.    18
S04SRI QS     30.    28.    29.    29.    28.    23.    28.    30.    22
S05SRI QS     23.    25.    29.    19.    20.    27.    28.    28.    19
S06SRI QS     28.    27.    30.    22.    19.    25.    30.    26.    20
```

SRI QS	28.	24.	27.	27.	17.	21.	30.	26.	200.
SRI QS	25.	29.	29.	27.	26.	25.	26.	25.	212.
SRI QS	26.	30.	30.	24.	29.	24.	14.	29.	206.
SRI QS	28.	29.	30.	26.	25.	28.	30.	28.	224.
SRI QS	24.	28.	30.	29.	27.	23.	21.	28.	210.
SRI QS	26.	29.	26.	27.	28.	19.	30.	27.	212.
SRI QS	30.	27.	26.	24.	25.	21.	28.	25.	206.
SRI QS	29.	29.	29.	28.	25.	19.	30.	27.	216.
SRI QS	29.	25.	28.	26.	24.	21.	30.	29.	212.
SRI QS	29.	26.	30.	20.	25.	20.	30.	28.	208.

*** PUNCHED OUTPUT ***

```
MEAN   1 1    26.6250    27.0000    27.8125    24.8125    24.3750
 SIG   1 1     2.6897     2.4238     2.9202     3.1269     3.6891
 WTS   1 1     0.7381    -0.4587    -0.4158
 WTS   2 1     0.1850    -0.1692     0.7118
 WTS   3 1     0.0228     0.7392     0.3649
 WTS   4 1     0.1312    -0.2044     0.4217
 WTS   5 1    -0.6350    -0.4157    -0.0978
MEAN   1 1    22.8750    26.1875    27.2500
 SIG   1 1     2.7585     4.8117     1.7854
 WTS   1 1    -0.1196     0.8968    -0.2123
 WTS   2 1     0.9923     0.3426    -0.1128
 WTS   3 1     0.0311     0.2800     0.9707
01SRICA 1    -1.4308    -0.6439    -2.9290
01SRICB 1    -1.6918    -0.1623    -2.3827
02SRICA 1    -0.4997    -0.0353     1.3150
02SRICB 1    -0.3134    -0.9728     0.6803
03SRICA 1    -1.0105     0.1288    -0.6147
03SRICB 1    -1.0882     0.2708     0.9865
04SRICA 1     0.5634    -1.0270     0.3889
04SRICB 1     0.4163     0.6009     1.4430
05SRICA 1    -0.6289     1.9313    -0.5464
05SRICB 1     0.2080     1.5877     0.0478
06SRICA 1     1.2017     1.1088    -0.1760
06SRICB 1     0.6724     0.7663    -0.9325
07SRICA 1     1.5033     0.4574    -0.7046
07SRICB 1     0.8458    -0.5341    -0.6247
08SRICA 1    -0.4720     0.1120     1.2388
08SRICB 1    -0.1700     0.3246    -1.3824
09SRICA 1    -0.7557    -0.0172     1.0187
09SRICB 1    -2.5318    -0.2276     1.1506
10SRICA 1     0.4893     0.0316     0.7916
10SRICB 1     0.5771     2.0552    -0.0760
11SRICA 1    -0.9032     0.3621     1.4679
11SRICB 1    -1.0622    -0.2111     0.5197
12SRICA 1    -0.5653    -1.0433     0.6564
12SRICB 1     0.9499    -1.0275     0.0729
13SRICA 1     0.7704    -1.0517    -0.8743
13SRICB 1     0.4159    -0.8334    -1.1215
14SRICA 1     0.8398    -0.5228     0.7818
14SRICB 1     0.9499    -1.0275     0.0729
15SRICA 1     0.6150    -0.2533    -0.7610
15SRICB 1     0.8980    -0.0637     1.0064
16SRICA 1     0.2831     0.4626    -1.0530
16SRICB 1     0.9240    -0.5456     0.5397
```

*** PRINTED OUTPUT ***

CANONA EXAMPLE PROBLEM. VARIABLES 1-5 VS. 6-8.

REGRESSION ANALYSIS

```
PARAMETERS
COL  1- 5 =     5
COL  6-10 =     3
COL 11-15 =    16
COL 16-20 = 10000
COL 21-25 = 11100

DATA FORMAT = (A6, 4X, 5F7.0)
```

INTERCORRELATION ANALYSIS.

A MEAN	1	2	3	4	5
	26.6250	27.0000	27.8125	24.8125	24.3750

A SIG	1	2	3	4	5
	2.6897	2.4238	2.9202	3.1269	3.6891

A RMAT	1	2	3	4	5
1	1.0000	.1821	.4685	.2666	.2409
2	.1821	1.0000	.6181	.5525	.5452
3	.4685	.6181	1.0000	.2631	.3198
4	.2666	.5525	.2631	1.0000	.3529
5	.2409	.5452	.3198	.3529	1.0000

```
DATA FORMAT = (A6, 39X, 3F7.0)
```

INTERCORRELATION ANALYSIS.

B MEAN	1	2	3
	22.8750	26.1875	27.2500

B SIG	1	2	3
	2.7585	4.8117	1.7854

B RMAT	1	2	3
1	1.0000	-.2808	-.1079
2	-.2808	1.0000	-.0127
3	-.1079	-.0127	1.0000

R AB	1	2	3
1	-.3938	.5560	-.0325
2	-.2150	.0161	.3900
3	-.0495	.2694	.3087

Example Problem   293

4	-.3723	.1394	.2547
5	-.2104	-.3032	.1091

PRINCIPAL AXIS ANALYSIS (ASYMMETRIC MATRIX).

TRACE =   1.0145

100.00 PCT. OF TRACE WAS EXTRACTED BY 3 ROOTS.

R A-CA	1	2	3
1	.7784	-.3856	-.0233
2	.0700	-.1753	.9196
3	.3683	.3016	.6091
4	.2484	-.4820	.6761
5	-.3546	-.5880	.4024

R B-CB	1	2	3
1	-.3888	.8775	-.2806
2	.9930	.0994	-.0645
3	.0303	.2037	.9786

ROOTS	1	2	3
	.5530	.2575	.2040

CHI SQ	1	2	3
	9.2592	3.4237	2.6242

D.F.	1	2	3
	7.0000	5.0000	3.0000

PROB.	1	2	3
	.2350	.6377	.5439

WEIGHTS FOR THE 3 ROOTS WITH P .LT. 1.0000

A SIDE	1	2	3
1	.7381	-.4587	-.4158
2	.1850	-.1692	.7118
3	.0228	.7392	.3649
4	.1312	-.2044	.4217
5	-.6350	-.4157	-.0978

B SIDE	1	2	3
1	−.1196	.8968	−.2123
2	.9923	.3426	−.1128
3	.0311	.2800	.9707

MULTIPLE REGRESSION ANALYSIS

Multiple correlation may be considered a special case of the more general canonical correlation model, with multiple predictors on one side and a single criterion on the other. The analytic procedure determines a set of weights for the predictor variables (X_i) which will yield a composite variable ($\hat{Y}$) that correlates maximally with the criterion variable (Y). Multiple regression analysis may be considered a general model for testing any hypothesis cast in the form of predicting a criterion from particular sources of information. Especially important is the fact that the predictor information may be in the form of dichotomous scores reflecting group membership, or may consist of scores on continuously distributed variables. Both kinds of predictor variables may be included in the same equation.

Group-Membership Coding. As an example of group-membership variables, consider the case of three mutually exclusive groups. We could assume that the groups represent points on a linear scale and code each subject as "1," "2," or "3" on a single variable. This might be suitable for a variable such as *social class*. However, we could actually express more *information* about the subjects by using three variables instead of one to represent social class—one variable for each class, as shown in the following table. Note that for each variable, a subject is coded 1 if he is a member of the group and zero otherwise.

Subject	Continuous Variable	Dichotomous Variables		
		I	II	III
1	3	0	0	1
2	1	1	0	0
3	1	1	0	0
4	3	0	0	1
5	2	0	1	0

Mathematical Formulation. The mathematics of multiple regression are easily expressed in matrix algebra. The problem is to find the set of "beta" weights (B_P) that will produce composite predicted scores ($\hat{Y}_N$) which will maximally correlate with a criterion variable (Y_N). Given a matrix of intercorrelations of the predictor variables (R_{PP}) and a vector of correlations of *each* predictor with the criterion called "validities" (V_P), the needed beta weights may be defined by $B_P = R_{PP}^{-1} V_P$.

If desired, standardized predicted criterion scores ($\hat{Y}_N$) could be computed from the z-scaled predictor scores by means of $\hat{Y}_N = Z_{NP}B_P$. The correlation of $\hat{Y}_N$ and Y_N will be the multiple correlation between the predictor *set* and the criterion variable. This coefficient can be defined without computation of $\hat{Y}$ scores, however, by means of $M^2 = B'_P V_P$, where M^2 is the square of the multiple correlation, which is the proportion of the criterion variance "explained" by the set of P predictor variables.

The computational procedure used in Program REGRAN avoids the necessity of obtaining the inverse of the R_{PP} matrix. This is accomplished by an iterative procedure which "builds" a regression equation by adding variables to the predictor set, or by adjusting the weights of variables already in the set in such a way as to maximize the increase in M^2 at each step. Provision is made to designate only certain variables as available for inclusion in the predictor set for a given problem. This method of determining the beta weights avoids restrictions concerning the possible singularity of the R_{PP} matrix, and also results in a much faster computer program.

PROGRAM REGRAN

Program REGRAN begins by computing an intercorrelation matrix with Subroutine CORS, or by reading from cards an already computed correlation matrix as punched by Subroutine PTMS. The data entered may consist of any kind of numerical scores; dichotomous scores are conventionally punched as ones and zeros. The program is designed to permit sequential solution of a series of different regression problems, selecting the criterion and potential predictors independently for each problem. The set of variables entered must therefore contain all of the criteria and predictors to be used in any of the "models" to be designated (Figure 11-3).

Each regression problem to be solved is defined by means of a Model Control Card which designates the criterion variable and the potential predictor variables, as well as certain output options. The variable numbers used on these control cards refer to the order of input—the index positions in the total correlation matrix. The M^2 coefficients for each regression problem are retained as the processing continues. When all regression equations have been determined, the program will compare selected pairs of models and compute F tests of the differences between the M^2 coefficients. It is also possible to test the difference between a single model's M^2 and zero predictive efficiency. Comparing the models, where one includes only a subset of the predictors in the other model, is a very powerful way of answering questions about the "importance" of a given predictor or group of predictors within a context of other information, and with regard to a particular criterion.

Iterative Multiple Correlation. The technique used in iterative multiple correlation was developed by Greenberger and Ward (1956). An iteration-

296 REGRESSION ANALYSIS

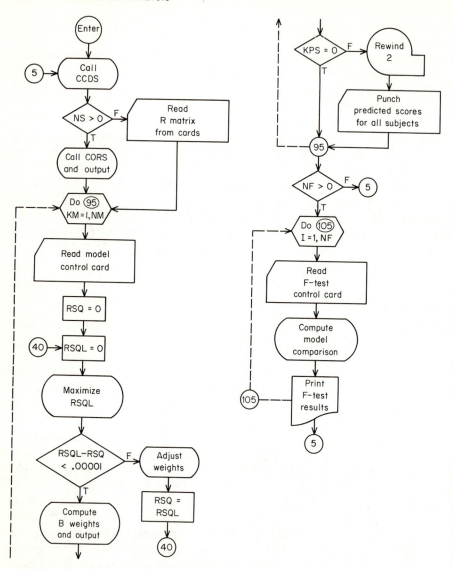

FIGURE 11-3. Program REGRAN flow chart.

stop criterion of .00001 for the increase in M^2 is used, but iteration is arbitrarily halted at 1000 if the criterion has not been reached. The iteration process begins by selecting the variable with the highest validity from those available as predictors. Available predictors as well as the criterion variable are designated for each problem by a Model Control Card. The second iteration selects the variable which will maximally increase M^2 when used together with the first variable to form a set of two predictors.

On each subsequent iteration, either another variable will be added to the predictor set or the weight assigned to one of the variables already in the set will be adjusted. In all cases the decision rests on the maximal increase in M^2. When no additions of variables or adjustments are possible which will increase M^2 more than .00001, the process is terminated and the obtained M^2 and weights are output.

One of the options on the Model Control Card permits printing of M^2 and the variable added or adjusted at each step of the iteration sequence. Such printing ceases arbitrarily after 50 iterations, even though more may be required to reach the stop criterion. The information provided by the iteration sequence may be very useful in certain research problems where one wishes to select the smallest test or item battery with maximum predictive efficiency.

Another option on the Model Control Card yields punched output of the beta weights obtained for the regression equation concerned. These weights may be used in cross-validation studies to obtain predicted scores from a new sample of subjects with the same variables. Predictor variables designated on the Model Control Card which were not added to the equation are automatically assigned zero beta weights.

The third output option on the Model Control Card results in the punching of a predicted criterion score (raw-score scaled) for every subject in the sample. In some research situations these predicted scores may be compared to the actual criterion scores of the subjects to identify individuals for whom the regression equation fails.

F Tests. Comparisons of particular pairs of models are computed according to instructions contained in F Ratio Control Cards, which may be added after the Model Control Cards in the input deck sequence. The F ratios are computed with the following formula, where A and B refer to the two models being compared:

$$F = \frac{(M_A^2 - M_B^2) \;/\; (K_A - K_B)}{(1 - M_A^2) \;/\; (N - K_A)}$$

where M^2 is a squared multiple correlation
K is the number of independent predictors in a model
N is the number of subjects in the sample

The A and B models are always chosen so that Model A is the larger of the two (the one with the greater degrees of freedom), while Model B consists of a subset of the predictor variables in Model A against the same criterion. When M_B^2 is set to zero, by using zero for the second model number on the F Ratio Control Card, K_B is assumed to be *one*. $(K_A - K_B)$ is the difference between the numbers of independent predictors in the A and B models, and defines the degrees of freedom for the numerator of the F ratio. The degrees of freedom for the denominator are $(N - K_A)$, the number of subjects minus the number of *independent predictors* in the larger model. The term "independent" associated with a predictor means that it cannot be accounted for completely by a linear combination of the other predictors. For example, there is a total of three independent predictors among three dichotomous vectors representing membership in three mutually exclusive groups. Given two of the three dichotomous vectors and the *unit vector* which is always implicitly present in the predictor set, the scores of the third dichotomous vector are perfectly predictable: $D_3 = U - D_1 - D_2$. When counting predictors to determine the degrees of freedom for F tests, the unit vector is always considered as one independent predictor. This is why K_B is assumed to be one when M_B^2 is set to zero for an F test of the significance of a single multiple correlation. Note that the unit vector *need not* be punched on the data cards as one of the predictor variables; it is implicitly present in the predictor set for any model computed with this program.

As an example of the computation of degrees of freedom, consider the problem of predicting performance in graduate school from the verbal and quantitative scores of the *Graduate Record Examination* (GRE). The equation for the first (larger) model employs three independent predictors: GRE(V), GRE(Q), and U. To test the significance (from zero) of the multiple correlation, the second (smaller) model number would be designated as zero. $K_A = 3$ and $K_B = 1$ (for U). Therefore $K_A - K_B = 2$ degrees of freedom for the numerator of the F ratio. The degrees of freedom for the denominator are the number of students in the sample minus the number of independent predictors in the full model: $N - 3$.

EXAMPLE PROBLEM

Four regression problems (models) and two F tests will be used to illustrate a few of the applications of this program. The SRI score cards will again be employed as data, but with the addition of a dichotomous group-membership score in columns 79–80. This score indicates whether the subject is among the first eight (1.) or the second eight (0.) of the 16 subjects in the sample. As indicated on the Model Control Cards, the first model uses the SRI total score (9) as the criterion, while the other three models attempt to predict variable one from other variables in the set.

Model One. Here we have used all eight subscales to predict the total score. Since the total is a linear combination (sum) of the eight part scores, it should be perfectly predictable from them, and this is confirmed by the 1.0 multiple correlation. Examination of the iteration sequence which was printed for this example shows that variable 3 is the best single predictor, as indicated in column nine of the correlation matrix. Variable four yields the greatest increase in M^2 when combined with variable three on the second iteration, despite the fact that variable two has the second highest validity. The best set of three predictors would be variables 1, 3, and 4, as indicated by the third iteration, which produced an M^2 of .8632. One could select a minimum battery of the most efficient predictors at any stage of this process.

The beta weights (standard partial regression weights) printed after the iteration sequence indicate the extent to which each variable is utilized in the regression equation, while the B-weight vector (with the additive *regression constant* or unit-vector weight) gives this information scaled in terms of the raw scores of the predictor variables. You may wish to demonstrate to yourself that a single subject's criterion score (variable 9) is exactly computed by

$$\hat{Y} = B_1X_1 + B_2X_2 + \cdots + B_8X_8 + RC$$

where $\hat{Y} = Y =$ predicted (and actual) criterion score
$B_i =$ raw-score weight
$X_i =$ raw score for a predictor variable
$RC =$ regression constant

Prediction is perfect in this special case because $M^2 = 1.0$, and no prediction error is involved.

If the iteration sequence had been used to select a subset of the eight predictors for a minimum battery, it would be necessary to run another model designating only the selected predictor variables in order to get appropriate weights for the reduced equation.

Model Two. Here we have used variable one as the criterion, and have predicted it from variables two and ten (the dichotomy). Only two iterations were necessary to maximize M^2 in this case. The M^2 of .1409 indicates considerably less than perfect prediction. Beta weights were punched for this model; note that only the second and the tenth elements (the predictors) of the weight vector contain nonzero values.

Model Three. This model employs only variable two to predict variable one. The result is a single "iteration" and the "multiple" correlation is simply the validity—the correlation of variables one and two. We will use this model and the second one later to demonstrate analysis of covariance.

Model Four. Here again we have used only a single predictor, which requires only one "iteration." The dichotomous predictor variable (10) represents membership in one or the other of two subject groups (1–8 and 9–16). This same classification of subjects was employed in Chapter 10 for the single-classification analysis of variance example problem. As you will see shortly, the regression technique yields the same answer to what is essentially the same question. In analysis of variance and in this regression model we are trying to determine the extent to which information about group membership is related to scores on variable one. If you will look back at the printed output for the analysis of variance problem, you will see that the regression constant (27.625) is equal to the mean for the B group (subjects 9–16), while the sum of this value and the single B weight is the same as the mean for the A group (subjects 1-9). The option for punching predicted criterion scores for each subject was also selected for this model, and examination of these scores reveals that they are the appropriate group means in all cases. This is to be expected since the group mean is the best prediction one can make when the only predictor information available describes group membership.

F Test One. This test concerns the significance of the prediction obtained in Model Four. The reduced or restricted model is designated as number zero. Therefore, the M^2 difference to be evaluated is the same as the M^2 for the Model Four. Comparison of the results of this test with those obtained for the comparable analysis of variance problem mentioned earlier shows that the two methods yield identical degrees of freedom, F ratios, and probability values.

The M^2 coefficient obtained from this type of model provides important information in addition to that given by the probability value. Too often research workers report the *statistical* significance of differences they obtain as if the associated probabilities were direct evidence of the *practical* significance of the results. If the sample is large enough, an infinitesimal difference might well be statistically significant—and be of no practical importance at all. The M^2 coefficient provides a check on this aspect of the statistical analysis; it may be directly interpreted as the proportion of the criterion variance which has been explained by predictor information. Another kind of caution is necessary here, however. The *smaller* the sample, the more inflated this M^2 value will be, and the more "shrinkage" may be expected upon cross-validation with a new sample using the same weights. This inflation reaches a maximum when the number of predictor variables is equal to (or greater than) the number of subjects in the sample. M^2 will always be 1.0 under this condition, but the probability value will also be 1.0. The two kinds of information provided by the M^2 and the probability should be used *together* to evaluate the results of any statistical analysis in which they are both available.

F Test Two. This comparison illustrates analysis of covariance. The question answered here is, "To what extent does variable ten predict variable one when the relationship of variable two to the criterion is held constant?" Another way of stating the question is, "How much of the predictive efficiency of variable ten is *independent*, in that it does not overlap with the prediction afforded by variable two?" Or, "How much predictive efficiency is gained by adding variable ten to variable two in the equation?" Still another way of stating the question is, "For subjects having identical scores on variable two, how well does variable ten predict variable one?" All of these questions are alternative ways of verbalizing the F test of the difference between Model 2, which contains variables two and ten, and Model 3, which contains only variable ten. The difference between the M^2 coefficients from the two models may be interpreted as the proportion of criterion variation explained by the *independent* contribution of variable ten in the presence of variable two.

In this example we find that variable ten by itself explains 14 percent of the criterion variance (M^2 from model 4 times 100), but that when the contribution of variable two is held constant (difference between models 2 and 3) it only explains 11 percent of the variance of this criterion (variable one). Holding constant the contribution of another variable does not always yield less predictive efficiency for the predictor concerned. In some situations the addition of such a variable has a *suppressor* effect, cancelling out a component of the predictor's variation that interferes with its predictive efficiency. Suppressor variables usually have very low correlations with the criterion, but are substantially related to the predictor variable in question.

The few examples in this chapter cannot begin to illustrate the tremendous versatility of the multiple linear regression approach to research problems. Any traditional analysis of variance or covariance can be duplicated by appropriate combinations of models such as those just described. Certain chi-square analyses can also be computed using a dichotomous criterion and sets of dichotomous predictors, and many other seemingly "different" statistical techniques prove to be only special cases of this general analytic procedure. More significant than the fact that traditional methods may be duplicated, however, is the facility it provides the researcher for expressing precisely the hypotheses he wishes to test. This flexibility is more demanding in the sense that he must define his purposes with more than typical precision. Many users report that this effect on their research is beneficial in itself; they are forced to think through the meaning of their questions rather than to simply dump their data into one of the ordinary analysis of variance procedures hoping that something significant will emerge. The use of this general approach to quantitative research problems will almost certainly increase in the future as machine techniques become more widely used and understood.

```
C      PROGRAM REGRAN
C
C      ITERATIVE MULTIPLE REGRESSION ANALYSIS CONTROL PROGRAM.
C      PARAMETER CONTROL-CARD FIELDS.
C          COL 1-5. NUMBER OF VARIABLES (ALL PREDICTORS
C              AND CRITERIA, MAX = 100).
C          COL 6-10. NUMBER OF SUBJECTS. SET = 0 IF R MATRIX IS TO BE
C              READ FROM CARDS, AS PUNCHED BY SUBROUTINE PTMS.
C          COL 11-15. NUMBER OF MODEL CONTROL CARDS TO BE READ (EQUATIONS
C              TO BE COMPUTED, MAX = 50).
C          COL 16-20. NUMBER OF F-TEST CONTROL CARDS TO BE READ.
C          COL 25. R MATRIX OUTPUT (0 = NONE, 1 = PRINT, 2 = PUNCH, 3 = BOTH).
C      FORMAT CONTROL CARD MUST SPECIFY A-MODE FIELD FOR SUBJECT ID
C          BEFORE SCORE-FIELD SPECIFICATIONS.
C      MODEL CONTROL CARD FIELDS.
C          COL 1-2. MODEL NUMBER (MAY BE ALPHABETIC).
C          COL 3-4. NUMBER OF CRITERION VARIABLE (IN SERIAL ORDER OF INPUT).
C          COL 5. 1 = PRINT ITERATION SEQUENCE.
```

302   REGRESSION ANALYSIS

```
C     COL 6. 1 = PUNCH VECTOR OF BETA WEIGHTS.
C     COL 7. 1 = PUNCH PREDICTED RAW SCORES FOR ALL SUBJECTS.
C     COL 9-10. NUMBER OF PREDICTOR-GROUP SPECIFICATIONS
C        TO FOLLOW (MAX = 14).
C     COL 12-15, 17-20, ETC. PREDICTOR-GROUP SPECIFICATIONS. FIRST TWO
C        DIGITS DESIGNATE FIRST VARIABLE, LAST TWO DIGITS DESIGNATE
C        LAST VARIABLE IN GROUP. SINGLE-VARIABLE GROUP INDICATED BY
C        SAME NUMBER REPEATED. USE SERIAL-ORDER NUMBERS OF VARIABLES
C        AS INPUT FROM DATA CARD(S).
C     F-TEST CONTROL-CARD FIELDS.
C        MODEL NUMBERS HERE REFER TO SERIAL ORDER OF MODEL CARDS AS INPUT.
C        COL 1-5. MODEL NUMBER OF LARGER EQUATION.
C        COL 6-10. MODEL NUMBER OF SMALLER EQUATION.
C        COL 11-15. DEGREES OF FREEDOM FOR NUMERATOR.
C        COL 16-20. DEGREES OF FREEDOM FOR DENOMINATOR.
C        COL 21-80. ALPHAMERIC LABEL (PRINTED ON OUTPUT).
C        TO TEST A MODEL AGAINST ZERO, LEAVE COL 6-10 BLANK.
C     TAPE UNIT 2 IS USED FOR TEMPORARY STORAGE (SCRATCH).
C     ORDER OF INPUT DECK AFTER FORMAT CARD IS
C        DATA CARDS, MODEL CARDS, F-TEST CARDS.
C     SUBPROGRAMS REQUIRED ARE SCPF, PRBF, CCDS, PRTS, PCDS, PTMS, SUBS, CORS.
C
      ODIMENSION R(100,100), A(100), S(100), W(100), B(100), RM(50),
     1 KF(16), KA(14), KB(14)
      ND = 100
    5 CALL CCDS (KF, NV, NS, NM, NF, KP)
      IF (NS .GT. 0) GO TO 15
C     READ R MATRIX FROM CARDS AND REFLECT.
      READ KF, ((R(I,J), J = 1,NV), I = 1,NV)
      DO 10 I = 1,NV
      S(I) = 0.0
      DO 10 J = I,NV
   10 R(J,I) = R(I,J)
      GO TO 20
C     COMPUTE AND OUTPUT MEANS, SIGMAS AND R MATRIX FROM CARDS.
   15 CALL CORS (NS, NV, R, A, S, KF, 2, ND)
      CALL PRTS (A, NV, 1, 5HMEANS, ND)
      CALL PRTS (S, NV, 1, 6HSIGMAS, ND)
      IF (KP .LT. 2) GO TO 20
      CALL PCDS (A, NV, 1, 5HMEANS, ND)
      CALL PCDS (S, NV, 1, 5HSIGMA, ND)
      CALL PTMS (R, NV, 5HR MAT, ND)
   20 IF (KP .EQ. 1 .OR. KP .EQ. 3) CALL PRTS (R, NV, NV, 5HR MAT, ND)
C     BEGIN MODEL COMPUTATION.
      DO 95 KM = 1,NM
      READ 25, KMN, KC, KIP, KBW, KPS, NG, (KA(I), KB(I), I = 1,NG)
   25 FORMAT (A2, I2, 3I1, 1X, I2, 14(1X, 2I2))
      PRINT 30, KM, KC, (KA(I), KB(I), I = 1,NG)
   30 FORMAT (/// 6H MODEL, I3, 5X, 11HCRITERION =, I3 //
     1 13H PREDICTORS =, 14(I3, 1H-, I2))
      DO 35 I = 1,NV
      W(I) = 0.0
   35 B(I) = 0.0
      SS = 0.0
      SIG2 = 0.0
      RSQ = 0.0
      DEL = 0.0
      ITER = 0
      KD = 1
C     BEGIN ITERATION SEQUENCE.
   40 RSQL = 0.0
      DO 55 I = 1,NG
      K = KA(I)
      L = KB(I)
      DO 55 J = K,L
      B(J) = B(J) + DEL * R(J,KD)
```

```
      DEN = SS - B(J) * R(J,KC)
      IF (DEN .NE. 0.0) GO TO 45
      DELT = R(J,KC)
      STEST = DELT**2
      SIG2T = STEST
      RSQT = STEST
      GO TO 50
   45 DELT = (SIG2 * R(J,KC) - SS * B(J)) / DEN
      STEST = SS + DELT * R(J,KC)
      SIG2T = SIG2 + 2.0 * B(J) * DELT + DELT**2
      RSQT = STEST**2 / SIG2T
   50 IF (RSQL .GE. RSQT) GO TO 55
      SLAR = STEST
      SIG2L = SIG2T
      RSQL = RSQT
      DELTL = DELT
      KDLAR = J
   55 CONTINUE
C  COMPARE INCREASE IN R2 AGAINST STOP CRITERION.
      IF (RSQL - RSQ .LT. 0.00001) GO TO 62
      SS = SLAR
      SIG2 = SIG2L
      RSQ = RSQL
      DEL = DELTL
      ITER = ITER + 1
      KD = KDLAR
      W(KD) = W(KD) + DEL
      IF (KIP .EQ. 1 .AND. ITER .LE. 50) PRINT 60, KD, RSQ
   60 FORMAT (4H P =, I3, 3X, 5HRSQ =, F7.4)
      IF (ITER .LT. 1000) GO TO 40
C  COMPUTE AND OUTPUT RESULTS FOR MODEL.
   62 SDS2 = SS / SIG2
      RR = SQRT(RSQ)
      PRINT 65, RR, RSQ, ITER
   65 FORMAT (/ 4H R =, F7.4, 5X, 5HRSQ =, F7.4, I10, 12H ITERATIONS.)
      PRINT 70
   70 FORMAT (/ 3X, 1HV, 6X, 4HBETA, 7X, 1HB)
      RC = 0.0
      DO 75 I = 1,NG
      K = KA(I)
      L = KB(I)
      DO 75 J = K,L
      B(J) = W(J) * SDS2
      W(J) = 0.0
      IF (S(J) .EQ. 0.0) GO TO 75
      W(J) = B(J) * (S(KC) / S(J))
      RC = RC + B(J) * (A(J) / S(J))
   75 PRINT 80, J, B(J), W(J)
   80 FORMAT (I4, 2F10.4)
      RC = A(KC) - S(KC) * RC
      PRINT 85, RC
   85 FORMAT (14H REG. CONST. =, F10.4)
      RM(KM) = RSQ
      IF (KBW .EQ. 1) CALL PCDS (B, NV, 1, KMN, ND)
      IF (KPS .EQ. 0) GO TO 95
C  COMPUTE PREDICTED SCORES FOR ALL SUBJECTS.
      REWIND 2
      DO 90 I = 1,NS
      READ (2) ID, (B(J), J = 1,NV)
      Y = SCPF(B, W, 1, 1, NV, ND) + RC
   90 CALL SUBS (Y, 1, 2HPY, ID)
   95 CONTINUE
      IF (NF .EQ. 0) GO TO 5
C  COMPUTE F TESTS OF MODEL COMPARISONS.
      DO 105 I = 1,NF
      READ 100, J, K, DN, DD, (KF(L), L = 1,10)
```

304 REGRESSION ANALYSIS

```
  100 FORMAT (2I5, 2F5.0, 10A6)
      RMK = 0.0
      IF (K .GT. 0) RMK = RM(K)
      D = RM(J) - RMK
      F = (D * DD) / ((1.0 - RM(J)) * DN)
      P = PRBF(DN, DD, F)
  105 PRINT 110, I, (KF(L), L = 1,10), RM(J), J, RMK, K, D, DN, DD, F, P
 1100 FORMAT (// 7H F-TEST, I3, 3X, 10A6 / 11H RSQ FULL =,
     1 F10.4, 5X, 5HMODEL, I3 / 14H RSQ REDUCED =, F7.4,
     2 5X, 5HMODEL, I3 / 13H DIFFERENCE =, F8.4 /
     3 6H DFN =, F4.0, 5X, 5HDFD =, F6.0, 5X, 9HF-RATIO =,
     4 F8.3, 3X, 3HP =, F7.4)
      GO TO 5
      END
```


*** INPUT DATA DECK ***

```
REGRAN EXAMPLE PROBLEM
000100001600004000020000l
(A6, 4X, 10F7.0)
S01SRI QS      25.     21.     22.     20.     26.     26.     19.     23.     182.    1.
S02SRI QS      26.     30.     30.     26.     28.     20.     24.     28.     212.    1.
S03SRI QS      20.     25.     20.     23.     18.     24.     21.     29.     180.    1.
S04SRI QS      30.     28.     29.     29.     28.     23.     28.     30.     225.    1.
S05SRI QS      23.     25.     29.     19.     20.     27.     28.     28.     199.    1.
S06SRI QS      28.     27.     30.     22.     19.     25.     30.     26.     207.    1.
S07SRI QS      28.     24.     27.     27.     17.     21.     30.     26.     200.    1.
S08SRI QS      25.     29.     29.     27.     26.     25.     26.     25.     212.    1.
S09SRI QS      26.     30.     30.     24.     29.     24.     14.     29.     206.    0.
S10SRI QS      28.     29.     30.     26.     25.     28.     30.     28.     224.    0.
S11SRI QS      24.     28.     30.     29.     27.     23.     21.     28.     210.    0.
S12SRI QS      26.     29.     26.     27.     28.     19.     30.     27.     212.    0.
S13SRI QS      30.     27.     26.     24.     25.     21.     28.     25.     206.    0.
S14SRI QS      29.     29.     29.     28.     25.     19.     30.     27.     216.    0.
S15SRI QS      29.     25.     28.     26.     24.     21.     30.     29.     212.    0.
S16SRI QS      29.     26.     30.     20.     25.     20.     30.     28.     208.    0.
M109100 01 0108
M201010 02 0202 1010
M301000 01 0202
M401001 01 1010
00004000000000100014  ANOVAR ANALOG
00002000030000100013  COVARIANCE ANALOG
```


*** PUNCHED OUTPUT ***

```
M2       1 1    0.0000    0.0551    0.0000    0.0000    0.0000    0.0000    0.0000
M2       1 2    0.0000    0.0000   -0.3519
S01SRIPY 1     25.6250
S02SRIPY 1     25.6250
S03SRIPY 1     25.6250
S04SRIPY 1     25.6250
S05SRIPY 1     25.6250
S06SRIPY 1     25.6250
S07SRIPY 1     25.6250
S08SRIPY 1     25.6250
S09SRIPY 1     27.6250
S10SRIPY 1     27.6250
S11SRIPY 1     27.6250
S12SRIPY 1     27.6250
S13SRIPY 1     27.6250
S14SRIPY 1     27.6250
S15SRIPY 1     27.6250
S16SRIPY 1     27.6250
```

*** PRINTED OUTPUT ***

1REGRAN EXAMPLE PROBLEM

```
PARAMETERS
COL  1- 5 =    10
COL  6-10 =    16
COL 11-15 =     4
COL 16-20 =     2
COL 21-25 =     1
```

DATA FORMAT = (A6, 4X, 10F7.0)

INTERCORRELATION ANALYSIS.

	1	2	3	4	5	6	7	8	9	10
MEANS	26.6250	27.0000	27.8125	24.8125	24.3750	22.8750	26.1875	27.2500	206.9375	.5000

	1	2	3	4	5	6	7	8	9	10
SIGMAS	2.6897	2.4238	2.9202	3.1269	3.6891	2.7585	4.8117	1.7854	11.9188	.5000

R MAT

	1	2	3	4	5	6	7	8	9	10
1	1.0000	.1821	.4685	.2666	.2409	-.3938	.5560	-.0325	.6504	-.3718
2	.1821	1.0000	.6181	.5525	.5452	-.2150	.0161	.3900	.7247	-.3610
3	.4685	.6181	1.0000	.2631	.3198	-.0495	.2694	.3087	.7880	-.2782
4	.2666	.5525	.2631	1.0000	.3529	-.3723	.1394	.2547	.6168	-.2199
5	.2409	.5452	.3198	.3529	1.0000	-.2104	-.3032	.1091	.4909	-.4405
6	-.3938	-.2150	-.0495	-.3723	-.2104	1.0000	-.2808	-.1079	-.2055	.3625
7	.5560	.0161	.2694	.1394	-.3032	-.2808	1.0000	-.0127	.4743	-.0909
8	-.0325	.3900	.3087	.2547	.1091	-.1079	-.0127	1.0000	.3679	-.2100
9	.6504	.7247	.7880	.6168	.4909	-.2055	.4743	.3679	1.0000	-.4038
10	-.3718	-.3610	-.2782	-.2199	-.4405	.3625	-.0909	-.2100	-.4038	1.0000

306 REGRESSION ANALYSIS

```
MODEL   1      CRITERION =   9

PREDICTORS =   1- 8
P =   3     RSQ =    .6209
P =   4     RSQ =    .8011
P =   1     RSQ =    .8632
P =   2     RSQ =    .8866
P =   7     RSQ =    .9152
P =   5     RSQ =    .9365
P =   6     RSQ =    .9537
P =   3     RSQ =    .9648
P =   8     RSQ =    .9757
P =   7     RSQ =    .9866
P =   6     RSQ =    .9896
P =   5     RSQ =    .9925
P =   7     RSQ =    .9944
P =   4     RSQ =    .9955
P =   8     RSQ =    .9966
P =   3     RSQ =    .9978
P =   5     RSQ =    .9987
P =   4     RSQ =    .9992
P =   1     RSQ =    .9995
P =   2     RSQ =    .9996
P =   3     RSQ =    .9997
P =   1     RSQ =    .9998
P =   4     RSQ =    .9999
P =   3     RSQ =    .9999
P =   8     RSQ =    .9999
P =   1     RSQ =   1.0000
P =   7     RSQ =   1.0000

R = 1.0000      RSQ = 1.0000        27 ITERATIONS.

    V       BETA         B
    1       .2308      1.0227
    2       .2070      1.0180
    3       .2432       .9924
    4       .2643      1.0075
    5       .3023       .9767
    6       .2309       .9977
    7       .3987       .9876
    8       .1499      1.0006
REG. CONST. =     -.1397


MODEL   2      CRITERION =   1

PREDICTORS =   2- 2 10-10

R =  .3753      RSQ =  .1409         2 ITERATIONS.

    V       BETA         B
    2       .0551       .0612
   10      -.3519     -1.8930
REG. CONST. =    25.9201


MODEL   3      CRITERION =   1

PREDICTORS =   2- 2

R =  .1821      RSQ =  .0332         1 ITERATIONS.
```

```
V        BETA       B
2        .1821     .2021
REG. CONST. =    21.1676



MODEL   4      CRITERION =  1

PREDICTORS = 10-10

R =  .3718     RSQ =  .1382         1 ITERATIONS.

V        BETA       B
10      -.3718    -2.0000
REG. CONST. =    27.6250


F-TEST  1        ANOVAR ANALOG
RSQ FULL  =       .1382      MODEL  4
RSQ REDUCED =     .0000      MODEL  0
DIFFERENCE =      .1382
DFN = 1.         DFD =   14.      F-RATIO =    2.246     P =  .1534


F-TEST  2        COVARIANCE ANALOG
RSQ FULL  =       .1409      MODEL  2
RSQ REDUCED =     .0332      MODEL  3
DIFFERENCE =      .1077
DFN = 1.         DFD =   13.      F-RATIO =    1.630     P =  .2224
```

Review Exercises

1. In terms of the correlations between raw-score variables and the canonical axis, what is the *nature* of the first canonical function? What is the *strength* of this first multivariate relationship between sides A and B?
2. Run a canonical analysis using variables 1 through 8 as the A-side set, and variable 9 (total score) as the B-side set. Why are the A-side weights not the same as the beta weights obtained in example problem 1 for Program REGRAN?
3. Suppose that we wished to select variables 1, 3, and 4 as a test battery for predicting the total score, as suggested in the description of example problem 1. Run a regression model selecting only these three variables as predictors and variable 9 as the criterion. Compare the weights with those obtained in example problem 1.
4. Modify Program REGRAN so that it will punch raw-score weights and the regression constant instead of beta weights when the option in column 6 of the Model Control Card is selected.

12 / miscellaneous statistical methods

The techniques to be described in this chapter were chosen because of their usefulness in behavioral research, and because they represent common types of programming problems. Our selections are inevitably arbitrary, since the list of quantitative methods is virtually endless. We have tried to illustrate the most useful problem-solving approaches in our choice of functions, subroutines, and programs for this book. It is important to realize, however, that most computer programs are constructed specifically for data-processing jobs that will never again occur in exactly the same form. Acquiring the level of skill necessary for this kind of programming is largely a matter of experience in applying the basic language and idioms.

The first section of the chapter covers Hierarchical Grouping, one of a variety of clustering techniques. The purpose of the program is to compare a series of score profiles (over a series of variables), and to progressively associate them into groupings in such a way as to minimize an overall estimate of variation within clusters. The second section concerns Thurstone's Successive Intervals method of obtaining scale values for a series of items. Like other scaling procedures, this method involves a great deal of tedious tabulation which is easily adapted to machine processing. The last section deals with the problem of compiling contingency tables for pairings of categorical variables, and the analysis of such frequency tables with the chi-square technique. These methods are especially useful in sociological and social psychological research.

HIERARCHICAL GROUPING ANALYSIS

Given a set of N objects (persons, test items, and so forth), each measured on K different variables, one may ask to what extent there exist natural groups among the N objects—groups which are similar in their scores on the K variables used to describe them. Theoretically, an *optimum* grouping of the objects can be defined for each particular number of groups from 2 to N-1. (One group and N groups of one each are limiting cases.) Such an optimum grouping should maximize the average *inter*-group distance while minimizing the average *intra*-group distance. Unfortunately, the computational burden involved with four groups and 20 objects—a relatively small problem—is prohibitive even with the aid of a computer, since *every* possible grouping of the 20 objects into four sets would have to be used as a basis for calculating an index of cluster separation.

Ward (1963) has provided a compromise approach to the goal of determining optimum groupings. The method begins by defining each original object as a "group." These N groups are then reduced in number by a series of step-decisions until all N persons have been classified into one or the other of two groups. At each step some pair of groups is combined, thus reducing the number of groups by one. The decision regarding the particular pair to be combined at any stage is made on the basis of some particular "value-reflecting" function. The HGROUP Program is designed to deal with the problem of profile similarity, and utilizes the total within-groups variation as the function to be *minimally* increased at each step in the process.

This procedure is a compromise with the theoretical ideal of optimum grouping described earlier, since at each stage of the process the previous grouping is accepted as the basis for determining the next reduction. One can imagine this process leading gradually to a solution which is not optimum, but only under circumstances where the "natural" clustering of the object's profiles is quite weak.

A Simple Example. As an illustration of the process, consider this case of four objects, described by scores on three variables:

Object	Variable 1	Variable 2	Variable 3
A	5	4	5
B	4	5	4
C	3	2	3
D	2	3	2

It is interesting to note that a (transposed) factor analysis of these four objects would yield two groups of profiles with identical *shapes* (A−C and B−D), since the means and sigmas of the objects would be implicitly equated by the intercorrelation process. The hierarchical grouping method to be described, however, is sensitive to the absolute *distances* among the object's score profiles, and leads to a grouping of the "closest" pairs (A−B and C−D).

At the beginning of the process we have four "groups" of one object each, and the "error within" each group is therefore zero. As the number of objects within a group increases, its error will increase also. The first stage of the process is to compute a matrix of potential error terms for each pair of objects. This error index is the sum of the squared differences between corresponding scores in the profiles, divided by the number of objects in the potential group (two, at this point).

Object	A	B	C	D
A	0	1.5	6.0	9.5
B		0	5.5	6.0
C			0	1.5
D				0

Since two of the potential groups have the same minimum error (1.5), we could pair either A with B or C with D at this first stage. We will form a single group from objects A and B, leaving a total of three groups. The new group will retain the label "A" and the error measure will be moved to its diagonal element. The other elements reflecting potential error for combination with this group must now be modified also. The correction process is exemplified for one cell (AC) by the following formula:

$$E_{AC} = [E_{AC}(N_A + N_C) + E_{BC}(N_B + N_C) + E_{AB}(N_A + N_B) - E_{AA}(N_A)$$
$$- E_{BB}(N_B) - E_{CC}(N_C)] \ / \ (N_A + N_B + N_C)$$
$$E_{AC} = [6.0(2) + 5.5(2) + 1.5(2) - 0(1) - 0(1) - 0(1)] \ / \ (1 + 1 + 1)$$

$$E_{AC} = 12.0$$

E represents an estimate of potential error for combining two groups. N represents the number of cases in a particular group.

After the first reduction, the error matrix will hold the necessary information for selecting the second pairing of groups. This decision is always made by determining the cell which, when its corresponding diagonal-cell values have been subtracted, yields the smallest value: $X = E_{IJ} - E_{II} - E_{JJ}$. All elements pertaining to the "absorbed" object B are indicated by dashes, and will be ignored in all later decisions about grouping. (This is accomplished with a signal vector in Program HGROUP.)

Object	A	B	C	D
A	1.5	–	12.0	11.3
B		–	–	–
C			0	1.5
D				0

The next stage of the process will put together objects C and D, since the criterion value is by far the smallest for this combination. Again, the error associated with the pairing will be 1.5. The resulting error matrix is shown here. After completing this reduction to two groups, an error of 17.5 remains in the matrix, indicating the "cost" of collapsing the two pairs into a single group of four objects. This value, even after subtracting the diagonal elements (17.5 − 1.5 − 1.5 = 14.5), is still substantially larger than the error associated with either of the first two reductions. Examination of the errors associated with successive stages of the grouping process will usually reveal a particular level (number of groups) that is especially worthy of study, since reduction to the next stage would involve a substantially larger increase in error than had been associated with previous reductions.

Object	A	B	C	D
A	1.5	–	17.5	–
B		–	–	–
C			1.5	–
D				–

A number of important considerations must be mentioned before we present Program HGROUP. First of all, it should be noted that each of the variables constituting the profiles is equally important in determining the single distance index between pairs of groups. Equally important *kinds* of variables should be represented by equal *numbers* of variables in the profile. Factor analytic methods may help to avoid overweighting particular sources of variation through the use of factor scores rather than original variables.

Another important consideration is the fact that variables with smaller variabilities will contribute less to the index of group distance than will variables which are scaled with larger variances. An option in Program HGROUP provides a means of avoiding this kind of distortion by prestandardizing the raw data matrix by columns (variables) before computation of the initial error matrix.

Finally, we want to emphasize the fact that this method is primarily descriptive of the data in a particular sample, and provides no statistical basis for inferring the stability of results to other samples. Caution should be exercised in cases where no clear clustering of objects emerges from application of the technique. One can, of course, carry out analyses of variance or discriminant analysis to check characteristics of the groups produced, but the F tests computed for the variables of the profile will be artificially (and unreliably) significant.

PROGRAM HGROUP

Program HGROUP utilizes a generalized distance function based on the concept of error sum of squares — within-group variance — the sum of squared deviations from group means. During the grouping process, each of the values in matrix D reflects the potential error increase which would result from combining the objects indexed by the row and column of the cell concerned.

All raw scores are read into the matrix D at the beginning of the program; rows represent subjects and columns represent the variables which make up the profiles. If optioned, each column of the matrix is standardized to z-score form next. After this stage, an option is provided to transpose the data matrix within array D to permit grouping of variables rather than subjects. If this option is taken, the values of NS and NV are reversed.

The next phase of the routine converts the raw-data profiles stored as rows in D into a matrix of error potentials for all pairings of these NS profiles. Vector W is used for temporary storage in this process. Only the above-diagonal cells are needed for this purpose; the cells below the diagonal are zeroed to simplify computation later in the program.

The vector KG is initialized next. Its cells will contain the group number to which each of the original objects is assigned during the process. The vector W is also set to contain the number of subjects in each group. The next section of the program locates the combination of objects involving the least increase in error. Only combinations representing still unabsorbed objects or groups are considered. The result of this decision process is printed, and the necessary modifications of KG, W, and D are carried out. If the number of groups at this stage is less than the parameter-card option value, the original code numbers of subjects (or index numbers of variables) will be printed for each group. Control then returns to statement 65 to begin the next reduction (Figure 12-1).

EXAMPLE PROBLEMS

The first problem for this program uses the basic deck of 16 subjects, and a profile of eight variables. The total score is not included since it would bias the grouping decision. The standardization option is taken to equalize the variances, and hence the contributions to the criterion of the eight variables. The results from this analysis at the three-group stage were used earlier to demonstrate Program DSCRIM (Chapter 10), but it is apparent from the error terms printed here that the five-group stage might have been a better choice as far as "natural" clustering is concerned. The largest error increase occurs in going from five to four groups.

The second example problem utilizes the same data as the first problem, but the transposition option has been taken, resulting in the grouping of the eight variables rather than the 16 subjects. The results suggest that variables 1, 6 and 7 — particularly number 6 — are distinctly different from the other variables in the reactions they elicit from these subjects. It is interesting to compare these results with the rotated factor loadings for example

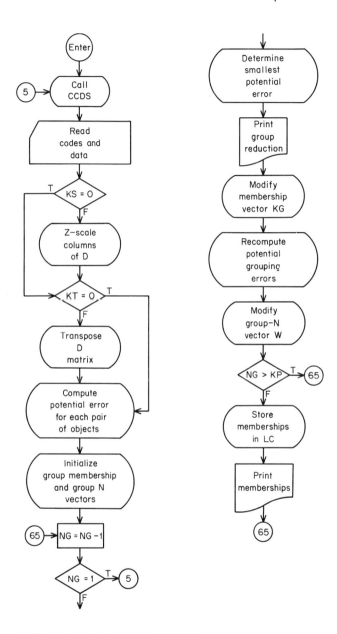

FIGURE 12-1. Flow chart for Program HGROUP.

problem one for Program FACTOR (Chapter 9). In that matrix, variables 1 and 7 appear to define the second factor, although the other two factors do not correspond directly with the three-group stage of the grouping analysis.

MISCELLANEOUS STATISTICAL METHODS

```
C     PROGRAM HGROUP
C
C  HIERARCHICAL PROFILE-GROUPING ANALYSIS.
C  PARAMETER CONTROL-CARD FIELDS.
C     COL 1-5. NUMBER OF VARIABLES (MAX = 100).
C     COL 6-10. NUMBER OF SUBJECTS (MAX = 100).
C     COL 11-15. LEVEL OF GROUPING TO BEGIN GROUP-MEMBERSHIP PRINTING.
C     COL 20. 1 = STANDARDIZE DATA ON EACH VARIABLE BEFORE GROUPING.
C     COL 25. 1 = TRANSPOSE DATA MATRIX IN ORDER TO GROUP VARIABLES.
C  FORMAT MUST SPECIFY AN ALPHAMERIC SUBJECT-CODE FIELD, FOLLOWED BY
C     NV SCORE FIELDS. IF DATA MATRIX IS TRANSPOSED (COL 25 = 1),
C     GROUP-MEMBERSHIP CODES WILL BE SERIAL NUMBERS OF VARIABLES.
C  SUBPROGRAMS REQUIRED ARE SUMF AND CCDS.
C
      DIMENSION D(100,100), KG(100), W(100), KC(100), LC(100), KF(16)
      ND = 100
    5 CALL CCDS (KF, NV, NS, KP, KS, KT)
      T = NS
C  READ ALL DATA CARDS AND STANDARDIZE COLUMNS (VARIABLES), IF OPTIONED.
      DO 10 I = 1,NS
   10 READ KF, KC(I), (D(I,J), J = 1,NV)
      IF (KS .EQ. 0) GO TO 20
      DO 15 J = 1,NV
      A = SUMF(D, J, NS, ND) / T
      S = SQRT(SUMF(D, J, -NS, ND) / T - A * A)
      DO 15 I = 1,NS
   15 D(I,J) = (D(I,J) - A) / S
   20 IF (KT .EQ. 0) GO TO 30
C  TRANSPOSE DATA MATRIX, IF OPTIONED.
      N = MAX0(NS, NV)
      DO 25 I = 1,N
      DO 25 J = I,N
      X = D(I,J)
      D(I,J) = D(J,I)
   25 D(J,I) = X
      NS = NV
      NV = T
C  CONVERT DATA MATRIX TO INITIAL MATRIX OF ERROR POTENTIALS.
   30 DO 45 I = 1,NS
      DO 35 J = 1,NV
   35 W(J) = D(I,J)
      DO 45 J = I,NS
      D(I,J) = 0.0
      DO 40 K = 1,NV
   40 D(I,J) = D(I,J) + (D(J,K) - W(K))**2
   45 D(I,J) = D(I,J) / 2.0
      DO 55 I = 1,NS
      DO 55 J = I,NS
   55 D(J,I) = 0.0
      NG = NS
C  INITIALIZE GROUP-MEMBERSHIP AND GROUP-N VECTORS.
      DO 60 I = 1,NS
      KG(I) = I
   60 W(I) = 1.0
C  LOCATE OPTIMAL COMBINATION, IF MORE THAN 2 GROUPS REMAIN.
   65 NG = NG - 1
      IF (NG .EQ. 1) GO TO 5
      X = 10.0**10
      DO 75 I = 1,NS
      IF (KG(I) .NE. I) GO TO 75
      DO 70 J = I,NS
      IF (I .EQ. J .OR. KG(J) .NE. J) GO TO 70
      DX = D(I,J) - D(I,I) - D(J,J)
      IF (DX .GE. X) GO TO 70
      X = DX
```

```
      L = I
      M = J
   70 CONTINUE
   75 CONTINUE
      NL = W(L)
      NM = W(M)
      PRINT 80, NG, L, NL, M, NM, X
  800 FORMAT (/ I4, 25H GROUPS AFTER COMBINING G, I3,
     1 4H (N=, I3, 7H) AND G, I3, 4H (N=, I3, 10H). ERROR =, F10.4)
C     MODIFY GROUP-MEMBERSHIP AND GROUP-N VECTORS, AND ERROR POTENTIALS.
      WS = W(L) + W(M)
      X = D(L,M) * WS
      Y = D(L,L) * W(L) + D(M,M) * W(M)
      D(L,L) = D(L,M)
      DO 85 I = 1,NS
      IF (KG(I) .EQ. M) KG(I) = L
   85 CONTINUE
      DO 95 I = 1,NS
      IF (I .EQ. L .OR. KG(I) .NE. I) GO TO 95
      IF (I .GT. L) GO TO 90
      OD(I,L) = (D(I,L) * (W(I) + W(L)) + D(I,M) * (W(I) + W(M))
     1 + X - Y - D(I,I) * W(I)) / (W(I) + WS)
      GO TO 95
  900 D(L,I) = (D(L,I) * (W(L) + W(.I)) + (D(M,I) + D(I,M))
     1 * (W(M) + W(I)) + X - Y - D(I,I) * W(I)) / (W(I) + WS)
   95 CONTINUE
      W(L) = WS
      IF (NG .GT. KP) GO TO 65
C     PRINT GROUP MEMBERSHIPS OF ALL OBJECTS, IF OPTIONED.
      DO 115 I = 1,NS
      IF (KG(I) .NE. I) GO TO 115
      L = 0
      DO 100 J = I,NS
      IF (KG(J) .NE. I) GO TO 100
      L = L + 1
      LC(L) = KC(J)
      IF (KT .EQ. 1) LC(L) = J
  100 CONTINUE
      IF (KT .EQ. 1) PRINT 105, I, L, (LC(J), J = 1,L)
  105 FORMAT (2H G, I3, 4H (N=, I3, 2H) , 25I4 / (14X, 25I4))
      IF (KT .EQ. 0) PRINT 110, I, L, (LC(J), J = 1,L)
  110 FORMAT (2H G, I3, 4H (N=, I3, 2H) , 15A7 / (14X, 15A7))
  115 CONTINUE
      GO TO 65
      END


*** INPUT DATA DECK ***

GROUP EXAMPLE PROBLEM 1. SUBJECTS.
0008000160000500001
A6, 4X, 8F7.0)
01SRI QS    25.   21.   22.   20.   26.   26.   19.   23.   182.
02SRI QS    26.   30.   30.   26.   28.   20.   24.   28.   212.
03SRI QS    20.   25.   20.   23.   18.   24.   21.   29.   180.
04SRI QS    30.   28.   29.   29.   28.   23.   28.   30.   225.
05SRI QS    23.   25.   29.   19.   20.   27.   28.   28.   199.
06SRI QS    28.   27.   30.   22.   19.   25.   30.   26.   207.
07SRI QS    28.   24.   27.   27.   17.   21.   30.   26.   200.
08SRI QS    25.   29.   29.   27.   26.   25.   26.   25.   212.
09SRI QS    26.   30.   30.   24.   29.   24.   14.   29.   206.
10SRI QS    28.   29.   30.   26.   25.   28.   30.   28.   224.
11SRI QS    24.   28.   30.   29.   27.   23.   21.   28.   210.
12SRI QS    26.   29.   26.   27.   28.   19.   30.   27.   212.
13SRI QS    30.   27.   26.   24.   25.   21.   28.   25.   206.
```

316   MISCELLANEOUS STATISTICAL METHODS

```
S14SRI QS      29.    29.    29.    28.    25.    19.    30.    27.    216.
S15SRI QS      29.    25.    28.    26.    24.    21.    30.    29.    212.
S16SRI QS      29.    26.    30.    20.    25.    20.    30.    28.    208.
HGROUP EXAMPLE PROBLEM 2. VARIABLES.
00008000160000700001000O1
(A6, 4X, 8F7.0)
S01SRI QS      25.    21.    22.    20.    26.    26.    19.    23.    182.
S02SRI QS      26.    30.    30.    26.    28.    20.    24.    28.    212.
S03SRI QS      20.    25.    20.    23.    18.    24.    21.    29.    180.
S04SRI QS      30.    28.    29.    29.    28.    23.    28.    30.    225.
S05SRI QS      23.    25.    29.    19.    20.    27.    28.    28.    199.
S06SRI QS      28.    27.    30.    22.    19.    25.    30.    26.    207.
S07SRI QS      28.    24.    27.    27.    17.    21.    30.    26.    200.
S08SRI QS      25.    29.    29.    27.    26.    25.    26.    25.    212.
S09SRI QS      26.    30.    30.    24.    29.    24.    14.    29.    206.
S10SRI QS      28.    29.    30.    26.    25.    28.    30.    28.    224.
S11SRI QS      24.    28.    30.    29.    27.    23.    21.    28.    210.
S12SRI QS      26.    29.    26.    27.    28.    19.    30.    27.    212.
S13SRI QS      30.    27.    26.    24.    25.    21.    28.    25.    206.
S14SRI QS      29.    29.    29.    28.    25.    19.    30.    27.    216.
S15SRI QS      29.    25.    28.    26.    24.    21.    30.    29.    212.
S16SRI QS      29.    26.    30.    20.    25.    20.    30.    28.    208.
```

*** PRINTED OUTPUT ***

1HGROUP EXAMPLE PROBLEM 1. SUBJECTS.

```
PARAMETERS
COL  1- 5 =       8
COL  6-10 =      16
COL 11-15 =       5
COL 16-20 =       1
COL 21-25 =       0

DATA FORMAT = (A6, 4X, 8F7.0)

   15 GROUPS AFTER COMBINING G 12 (N=  1) AND G 14 (N=  1). ERROR =     1.531
   14 GROUPS AFTER COMBINING G  2 (N=  1) AND G 11 (N=  1). ERROR =     1.899
   13 GROUPS AFTER COMBINING G 15 (N=  1) AND G 16 (N=  1). ERROR =     2.419
   12 GROUPS AFTER COMBINING G  8 (N=  1) AND G 10 (N=  1). ERROR =     3.117
   11 GROUPS AFTER COMBINING G 12 (N=  2) AND G 13 (N=  1). ERROR =     3.453
   10 GROUPS AFTER COMBINING G  5 (N=  1) AND G  6 (N=  1). ERROR =     3.600
    9 GROUPS AFTER COMBINING G  2 (N=  2) AND G  9 (N=  1). ERROR =     3.988
    8 GROUPS AFTER COMBINING G  4 (N=  1) AND G 15 (N=  2). ERROR =     4.989
    7 GROUPS AFTER COMBINING G  4 (N=  3) AND G 12 (N=  3). ERROR =     6.111
    6 GROUPS AFTER COMBINING G  5 (N=  2) AND G  7 (N=  1). ERROR =     7.133
    5 GROUPS AFTER COMBINING G  2 (N=  3) AND G  8 (N=  2). ERROR =     8.440
G  1 (N=  1) S01SRI
G  2 (N=  5) S02SRI S08SRI S09SRI S10SRI S11SRI
G  3 (N=  1) S03SRI
G  4 (N=  6) S04SRI S12SRI S13SRI S14SRI S15SRI S16SRI
G  5 (N=  3) S05SRI S06SRI S07SRI
```

Example Problems 317

```
4 GROUPS AFTER COMBINING G   1 (N=   1) AND G   3 (N=   1). ERROR =    12.1319
  1 (N=   2) S01SRI S03SRI
  2 (N=   5) S02SRI S08SRI S09SRI S10SRI S11SRI
  4 (N=   6) S04SRI S12SRI S13SRI S14SRI S15SRI S16SRI
  5 (N=   3) S05SRI S06SRI S07SRI

3 GROUPS AFTER COMBINING G   2 (N=   5) AND G   4 (N=   6). ERROR =    15.6645
  1 (N=   2) S01SRI S03SRI
  2 (N=  11) S02SRI S04SRI S08SRI S09SRI S10SRI S11SRI S12SRI S13SRI S14SRI
             S15SRI S16SRI
  5 (N=   3) S05SRI S06SRI S07SRI

2 GROUPS AFTER COMBINING G   1 (N=   2) AND G   5 (N=   3). ERROR =    17.7201
  1 (N=   5) S01SRI S03SRI S05SRI S06SRI S07SRI
  2 (N=  11) S02SRI S04SRI S08SRI S09SRI S10SRI S11SRI S12SRI S13SRI S14SRI
             S15SRI S16SRI
```

GROUP EXAMPLE PROBLEM 2. VARIABLES.

PARAMETERS
```
L  1- 5 =      8
L  6-10 =     16
L 11-15 =      7
L 16-20 =      1
L 21-25 =      1
```

DATA FORMAT = (A6, 4X, 8F7.0)

```
7 GROUPS AFTER COMBINING G   2 (N=   1) AND G   3 (N=   1). ERROR =     6.1102
  1 (N=   1)   1
  2 (N=   2)   2   3
  4 (N=   1)   4
  5 (N=   1)   5
  6 (N=   1)   6
  7 (N=   1)   7
  8 (N=   1)   8

6 GROUPS AFTER COMBINING G   1 (N=   1) AND G   7 (N=   1). ERROR =     7.1045
  1 (N=   2)   1   7
  2 (N=   2)   2   3
  4 (N=   1)   4
  5 (N=   1)   5
  6 (N=   1)   6
  8 (N=   1)   8

5 GROUPS AFTER COMBINING G   2 (N=   2) AND G   5 (N=   1). ERROR =    10.0698
  1 (N=   2)   1   7
  2 (N=   3)   2   3   5
  4 (N=   1)   4
  6 (N=   1)   6
  8 (N=   1)   8

4 GROUPS AFTER COMBINING G   2 (N=   3) AND G   4 (N=   1). ERROR =    10.6073
  1 (N=   2)   1   7
  2 (N=   4)   2   3   4   5
  6 (N=   1)   6
  8 (N=   1)   8

3 GROUPS AFTER COMBINING G   2 (N=   4) AND G   8 (N=   1). ERROR =    13.4427
  1 (N=   2)   1   7
  2 (N=   5)   2   3   4   5   8
  6 (N=   1)   6

2 GROUPS AFTER COMBINING G   1 (N=   2) AND G   2 (N=   5). ERROR =    23.5017
  1 (N=   7)   1   2   3   4   5   7   8
  6 (N=   1)   6
```

SUCCESSIVE INTERVALS SCALING[1]

Social scientists have developed a wide variety of methods for obtaining quantitative measurements of attitudes. Green (1954) reviews a number of these methods, and provides formulas for the particular method we have chosen to use here as an example of scaling procedures. The *successive intervals* method is one of the variants of the *judgment method* due to Thurstone (Thurstone and Chave, 1929). The purpose of these methods is to determine mathematically a scale value on an attitude dimension for each of a set of item-statements by analyzing the way in which a group of judges rate the items with regard to their favorableness. Once scale values have been computed for each item, the item set can be administered as a questionnaire and a composite score may be computed for each subject, using the previously determined scale values as weights. Note that the "judges" here do not respond to the items with their own attitudes, but with their opinions as to the favorableness of the items in regard to the attitude being measured.

Suppose we wished to measure attitude toward Negroes. An item with a positive scale value (favorable) would be, *"Members of the Negro race have made valuable contributions to the American culture."* When a group of items is analyzed in terms of actual judgmental behavior, some items may manifest unusually large variabilities, suggesting ambiguity of implication with respect to the attitude. An example in measuring attitude toward Negroes might be, *"All Negroes have an excellent sense of rhythm."* To some judges, agreement with this old myth might signify a prejudicial (unfavorable) attitude toward the race. Other items may turn out to be irrelevant to the attitude being measured, but these items are not so easily located. Any item which has a disproportionate number of placements at the center of the favorableness continuum would be open to suspicion, but such an item could also be simply a good one for measuring neutral attitudes. Because of the mathematics of the procedure for determining scale values, the investigator should eliminate ambiguous or irrelevant items before proceeding with the calculation of scale values.

When the number of items to be judged is small, the method of *paired comparisons* can be used effectively to determine scale values. This involves the pairing of each item with every other for a choice as to the more favorable of the two. As the number of items in the set increases, this method rapidly becomes unwieldy due to the fact that $K(K-1)/2$ item pairs must be judged, where K is the number of items. For example, 300 pairs are possible among 25 items.

The method of *equal-appearing intervals* is the most widely used judgmental method. Each judge is asked to sort the items into a certain

---

[1] The author wishes to thank Dr. Richard Purnell for providing the original version of the successive intervals program (Purnell, in press) from which Program TSCALE was derived.

number of categories, usually an odd number such as 7 or 9 to provide a center category. The judges are asked to assume that the categories are equally spaced along a scale of favorableness.

Since the assumption of equal intervals does not usually square with the judges' actual behavior, Thurstone designed the method of *successive intervals* to handle this problem, while retaining the advantage of requiring each judge to place each item only once. Categories are used as in the method of equal-appearing intervals, but the judges are only instructed to consider the categories as being arranged in rank order, with the "widths" of the categories left undefined.

The mathematical treatment of the judgmental data begins with a complied frequency table—items by categories. The model assumes normality of the distributions of judgments for each item. The steps in the determination of scale values for the items will be outlined when we describe Program TSCALE.

The metric of the scale produced by this method is essentially equal-interval in nature. Interestingly, the degree of confusion in the judgments —disagreement among the judges—is the basis for determining the scale values. If all judges agreed on all items, the method would be totally unworkable. In practice, this seldom happens.

It would be a mistake to assume that attitude measurement *requires* the use of a judgmental analysis to obtain scale values for the items. The Likert (1932) method, sometimes called the method of *summated ratings,* is probably the most widely used method of attitude measurement. Each item is simply rated by the subject on a five-point scale of agreement, and these scale-point values are summed over all items to yield a total score. The SRI instrument described in Chapter 8 is scored in this manner. Most studies comparing various scaling techniques have demonstrated very high correlations between the Likert technique and other methods. See also Stevens (1966) for a comparison of Thurstone's "confusion" methods with the more recent "direct estimation" methods of scale construction.

PROGRAM TSCALE

Program TSCALE will accept up to 200 items judged with up to 11 categories. Category numbers for the items are punched across one or more cards per judge. If any item judgments are missing from the data, the corresponding card columns may be left blank or punched with zeros.

The program begins by reading a series of constants from two "key" cards which are always inserted *before* the Title Control Card of the first problem deck whenever the program is used. These constants are employed to build a vector a z-score equivalents, which is referenced later in conjunction with a vector of proportion values ranging from .025 to .975 by steps of .01, which is also initialized at the beginning of the program.

Subroutine CCDS is then called for the parameter information for the

320 MISCELLANEOUS STATISTICAL METHODS

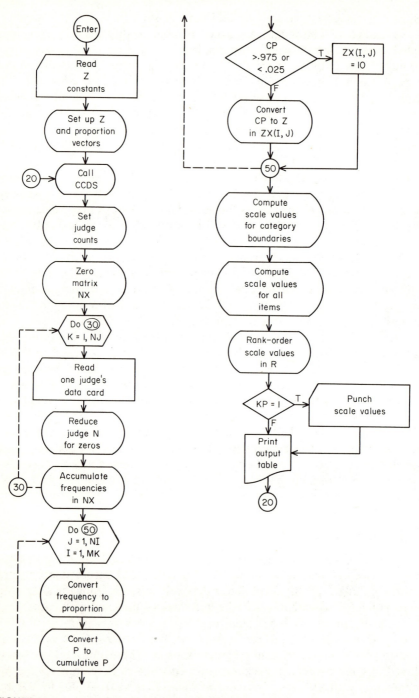

FIGURE 12-2. Flow chart for Program TSCALE.

first problem. The total number of judges is stored in each element of vector KI, and the frequency-distribution matrix NX is zeroed. Data cards are then read and frequencies of category use are accumulated in matrix NX. If a judgment-category score of zero is encountered, the element of KI for that item is reduced by 1. (See Figure 12-2.)

The next section of the program converts the frequency distribution matrix NX into cumulative proportions (over categories for each item) in matrix ZX, and then converts these proportion values to z scores through the use of the vectors of constants set up at the start of the program. If the cumulative proportion for a category is outside the range .025 – .975, the corresponding z value is set = 10, as a signal. Later in the process, such values will be ignored in order to avoid distortion in the calculation of z values for category boundaries. It should be noted that the beginning of this section involved the computation of raw proportions for each item-category combination. This is carried out using only the valid (nonzero) responses, adjusting for missing scores separately for each item as necessary.

The next section of the program computes scale values for the boundaries between adjacent categories, adjusting these computations to take account of any rejected (coded 10) z values. The scale values are then determined for each item by computing the average of the differences between category-boundary values and the valid z values in a row of matrix ZX. Index numbers of the items are also established in vector KI and the scale values stored in vector V are duplicated in vector R during this process.

The scale values stored in R, along with their index numbers, are arranged in rank order in the final section of the program, and a single table containing the scale values in item and rank order is printed, along with the item-category frequency distributions from matrix NX. At option, the scale values may also be punched for use with another program to compute attitude scores for subjects who are asked to respond to the items.

EXAMPLE PROBLEM

To illustrate the operation of this program we have utilized the raw data cards for the 16 subjects who responded to the SRI instrument. These cards, you will recall, were used in Chapter 8 in connection with the scoring Program TESTAT. Their use in the present context is inappropriate since the 16 subjects were not judging the favorableness of the 48 items with regard to any specific attitude scale, but were responding to the content of the items in order to reflect their own feelings. These data, however, will serve to illustrate the operation of the TSCALE Program if we assume that the 16 data cards contain numbers reflecting the category placements made by each of 16 judges who were presented with the 48 items and asked to sort them.

322 MISCELLANEOUS STATISTICAL METHODS

It is important to recognize that a *zero* scale value may mean one of two things. Either the item had no variability (all judges put it in the same category) or the item is actually appropriate at this scale point. Note also that the final scaling is arbitrary in that the center of the middle category is not necessarily equal to a scale value of zero. It is a good idea to scan the frequency distributions of the items to locate those which are so variable as to suggest ambiguity of meaning. Such items should be eliminated and the problem rerun to obtain a less distorted scaling of the other items in the set.

```
C     PROGRAM TSCALE
C
C     THURSTONIAN SUCCESSIVE-INTERVALS SCALE CONSTRUCTION.
C     PARAMETER CONTROL-CARD FIELDS.
C        COL 1-5  = NUMBER OF ITEMS (MAX = 200).
C        COL 6-10 = NUMBER OF JUDGES.
C        COL 11-15 = NUMBER OF JUDGEMENT CATEGORIES (MAX = 11).
C        COL 20.  1 = PUNCH SCALE VALUES FOR ALL ITEMS.
C     FORMAT CONTROL-CARD SPECIFIES FIELDS FOR ITEM JUDGEMENTS.
C        EACH JUDGE BEGINS A NEW DATA CARD (SERIES).
C     TWO KEY CARDS (SHOWN WITH EXAMPLE-PROBLEM DECK) ARE REQUIRED
C        AS INPUT BEFORE TITLE CONTROL CARD OF FIRST PROBLEM.
C     SUBPROGRAMS REQUIRED ARE CCDS AND PCDS.
C
      DIMENSION KF(16), Z(97), C(97), NX(11,200), ZX(10,200), KI(200),
     1 V(200), R(200), B(10)
C     READ Z-CONSTANTS. SET UP Z AND PROPORTION VECTORS.
      READ 5, (Z(I), I = 1,48)
    5 FORMAT (14F3.0 / 31F2.0, 3F1.0)
      DO 10 I = 1,48
      J = 98 - I
      Z(J) = Z(I) / 100.0
   10 Z(I) = -Z(J)
      Z(49) = 0.0
      C(1) = 0.025
      DO 15 I = 2,96
      C(I) = I + 1
   15 C(I) = C(I) / 100.0
      C(97) = 0.975
C     BEGIN PROBLEM INPUT. READ DATA, COMPUTE FREQUENCY DISTRIBUTIONS.
   20 CALL CCDS (KF, NI, NJ, NK, KP, I)
      DO 25 J = 1,NI
      KI(J) = NJ
      DO 25 I = 1,NK
   25 NX(I,J) = 0
      DO 30 K = 1,NJ
      READ KF, (V(J), J = 1,NI)
      DO 30 J = 1,NI
      I = V(J)
      IF (I .EQ. 0) KI(J) = KI(J) - 1
      IF (I .GT. 0) NX(I,J) = NX(I,J) + 1
   30 CONTINUE
C     CONVERT FREQUENCIES TO CUMULATIVE PROPORTIONS, AND THEN TO Z-SCORES.
      MK = NK - 1
      DO 50 J = 1,NI
      TJ = KI(J)
```

Example Problem

```
      CP = 0.0
      DO 50 I = 1,MK
      FX = NX(I,J)
      CP = CP + FX / TJ
      IF (CP .GT. 0.975 .OR. CP .LT. 0.025) GO TO 40
      DO 35 K = 1,97
      IF (CP .LE. C(K)) GO TO 45
   35 CONTINUE
   40 ZX(I,J) = 10.0
      GO TO 50
   45 IF (C(K) - CP .GT. 0.005) K = K - 1
      ZX(I,J) = Z(K)
   50 CONTINUE
      LK = MK - 1
C COMPUTE WEIGHTS FOR CATEGORY BOUNDARIES.
      B(1) = 0.0
      DO 65 I = 1,LK
      B(I+1) = 0.0
      TN = 0.0
      DO 60 J = 1,NI
      D = 0.0
      IF (ZX(I,J) .EQ. 10.0 .OR. ZX(I+1,J) .EQ. 10.0) GO TO 55
      D = ZX(I+1,J) - ZX(I,J)
   55 IF (D .NE. 0.0) TN = TN + 1.0
   60 B(I+1) = B(I+1) + D
   65 B(I+1) = B(I+1) / TN + B(I)
C COMPUTE SCALE VALUES.
      DO 75 J = 1,NI
      S = 0.0
      X = 0.0
      DO 70 I = 1,MK
      IF (ZX(I,J) .EQ. 10.0) GO TO 70
      X = X + 1.0
      S = S + B(I) - ZX(I,J)
   70 CONTINUE
      KI(J) = J
      V(J) = S / X
   75 R(J) = V(J)
C RANK-ORDER SCALE VALUES.
      DO 85 I = 1,NI
      K = I
      DO 80 J = I,NI
      IF (R(K) .LT. R(J)) K = J
   80 CONTINUE
      IF (K .EQ. I) GO TO 85
      KX = KI(K)
      KI(K) = KI(I)
      KI(I) = KX
      X = R(K)
      R(K) = R(I)
      R(I) = X
   85 CONTINUE
C OUTPUT TABLE OF SCALE VALUES AND FREQUENCIES.
      IF (KP .EQ. 1) CALL PCDS (V, NI, 1, 4HIVAL, 200)
      PRINT 90, (I, I = 1,NK)
   90 FORMAT (// 4X, 22HS C A L E   V A L U E S, 5X,
     1 21HF R E Q U E N C I E S // 28H RANK-ORDERED    ITEM-ORDERED,11I5)
      DO 95 I = 1,NI
   95 PRINT 100, KI(I), R(I), I, V(I), (NX(J,I), J = 1,NK)
  100 FORMAT (/ I5, F8.2, I7, F8.2, 11I5)
      GO TO 20
      END
```

```
*** INPUT DATA DECK ***

1961881751641551481411341281222118131081O4                              KEY CARD 1
9995928884817774716764615855525047444139363312825232017151310853        KEY CARD 2
TSCALE EXAMPLE PROBLEM.
0004800016000050000l
(10X, 48F1.0)
S01SRI  242424241423153541523 3423514253413331333312541333l
S02SRI  1522 141514231513151411115251515 1511141515151
S03SRI  2121525225154114523541242324 44153255512221525251
S04SRI  1411541415152524515141151441525152514111515151
S05SRI  11221142415151534515 12415142 1 45454211 151121
S06SRI  11124151415251515515515251115331123555111515121
S07SRI  121251514525153543432135151434151451422141511512
S08SRI  141241414232415335231412522551524225421152511251
S09SRI  14113152512115153251425151521153141513521341415Ll
S10SRI  23115141515151535155251251535l 1425 5511151515151
S11SRI  1521514251315115125114151253514252242542134251252
S12SRI  141251435151545525523231251525142425135111525114Ll
S13SRI  14125252414242544525322255152525225224422152552513
S14SRI  1412515 5151525253151212151514151425 25111514114Ll
S15SRI  241415441525255514231251513251524252111151411512
S16SRI  24113151425131515153112525341215152331115141515Ll

*** PUNCHED OUTPUT ***

IVAL  1  1   -0.5000    1.3072   -0.5000    0.1500    2.0597   -0.8800    2.2648
IVAL  1  2    0.1180    2.0348   -0.4520    2.0463   -0.3300    2.6501    0.0114
IVAL  1  3    2.6397    0.5780    1.6272    3.0901   -0.5107    2.0701    0.3497
IVAL  1  4    1.4097   -1.1800    0.1743    3.2448   -0.5107    2.3147   -0.0107
IVAL  1  5    2.3551   -0.0620    1.8622   -0.5000    2.2751    0.2314    2.5696
IVAL  1  6    0.7797    1.5922    2.2630   -0.4207   -0.8800   -0.4957    2.5863
IVAL  1  7   -0.4520    2.3772   -0.7857   -0.1478    2.2896   -0.5957
```

*** PRINTED OUTPUT ***

1TSCALE EXAMPLE PROBLEM.

```
PARAMETERS
COL  1- 5 =    48
COL  6-10 =    16
COL 11-15 =     5
COL 16-20 =     1
COL 21-25 =     0
```

DATA FORMAT = (10X, 48F1.0)

SCALE VALUES				FREQUENCIES				
RANK-ORDERED		ITEM-ORDERED		1	2	3	4	5
25	3.24	1	-.50	11	5	0	0	0
18	3.09	2	1.31	3	1	1	9	2
13	2.65	3	-.50	11	5	0	0	0
15	2.64	4	.15	7	9	0	0	0
42	2.59	5	2.06	1	0	2	4	8
35	2.57	6	-.88	13	3	0	0	0
44	2.38	7	2.26	0	0	0	7	9
29	2.36	8	.12	7	5	1	2	0
27	2.31	9	2.03	0	0	0	8	7
47	2.29	10	-.45	11	4	0	1	0
33	2.28	11	2.05	0	2	3	2	9
7	2.26	12	-.33	10	6	0	0	0
38	2.26	13	2.65	0	0	2	2	12
20	2.07	14	.01	9	4	1	2	0
5	2.06	15	2.64	1	0	0	0	15
11	2.05	16	.58	4	4	6	2	0
9	2.03	17	1.63	2	2	1	4	7
31	1.86	18	3.09	0	0	1	1	14
17	1.63	19	-.51	10	5	1	0	0
37	1.59	20	2.07	0	0	3	5	6
22	1.41	21	.35	5	5	4	0	1
2	1.31	22	1.41	2	3	2	4	5
36	.78	23	-1.18	14	2	0	0	0

16	.58	24	.17	4	10	2	0	0
21	.35	25	3.24	0	0	0	2	14
34	.23	26	-.51	10	5	1	0	0
24	.17	27	2.31	1	0	1	2	12
4	.15	28	-.01	8	5	3	0	0
8	.12	29	2.36	0	0	2	5	8
14	.01	30	-.06	8	5	2	1	0
28	-.01	31	1.86	1	1	1	4	6
30	-.06	32	-.50	11	5	0	0	0
46	-.15	33	2.28	0	0	2	6	7
12	-.33	34	.23	4	8	3	1	0
39	-.42	35	2.57	0	1	1	2	12
43	-.45	36	.78	4	5	0	1	3
10	-.45	37	1.59	2	1	4	2	7
41	-.50	38	2.26	0	1	2	5	8
3	-.50	39	-.42	9	6	1	0	0
1	-.50	40	-.88	13	3	0	0	0
32	-.50	41	-.50	12	2	2	0	0
26	-.51	42	2.59	0	1	0	4	10
19	-.51	43	-.45	11	4	0	1	0
48	-.60	44	2.38	1	0	0	4	11
45	-.79	45	-.79	13	2	1	0	0
6	-.88	46	-.15	12	2	1	0	1
40	-.88	47	2.29	0	2	1	2	11
23	-1.18	48	-.60	11	4	1	0	0

CONTINGENCY TABLE CONSTRUCTION

In Chapter 8 a program (DISTAT) was discussed which provided frequency distributions for each of a series of numeric variables. In the next chapter we will describe methods for tabulating frequencies of occurrence for alphameric variables. Both of these programs are one-dimensional in that they tabulate frequencies only for one variable at a time. In order to answer many important research questions we need a technique which will yield a two-dimensional table of frequencies, often called a *cross-plot* or *contingency table*. We would also prefer that this program accept all legitimate key-punch characters as code symbols, in addition to the numerals 0–9. Further, it would be convenient to have a program which would accept data cards containing symbol codes for a series of variables, which could be paired in all possible combinations, yielding a contingency table for each pairing of variables.

Contingency tables are most familiar in the context of chi-square analysis, where the purpose is to obtain a statistical index of association between two variables which are schemes for classifying subjects. For instance, suppose we wish to determine the degree to which political affiliation is associated with opinion on a certain controversial issue. We could code political affiliation as D = Democrat, R = Republican, and I = Independent. Opinions on the issue in question might be coded Y = Yes, N = No, and U = Undecided. Tabulation of the responses of a random sample of 500 subjects might yield the following contingency table:

		Opinion			
		Y	N	U	Totals
Political Affiliation	D	150	105	5	260
	R	30	100	5	135
	I	20	45	40	105
	Totals	200	250	50	500

Usually the researcher will obtain such data on a series of questions, and will also attempt to measure other background characteristics of the respondents at the same time. Although not all pairings of variables may be important, many interesting combinations are often ignored in such studies because of the cost and tedium of tabulating the necessary contingency tables.

PROGRAM CONTAB

Program CONTAB will accept data cards containing single-character alphameric codes for a series of variables and will compute contingency tables for all possible pairs or for selected combinations of the variables.

If only selected combinations are to be tabled, a matrix of signals is read from a special control-card deck which precedes the data deck. This selection deck contains one card per variable, punched with ones (compute table) or zeros (ignore) in columns corresponding also to the variable numbers. This card series defines the contents of a square matrix, the diagonal of which is ignored since it designates combinations of variables with themselves. The program examines both of the corresponding cells for each off-diagonal combination during processing and compiles a contingency table if either cell in the selection matrix contains a one.

After reading the optional selection matrix, all data cards are read and

328 MISCELLANEOUS STATISTICAL METHODS

stored on tape in binary form. This tape will be rewound and read once for each combination of variables to be tabled. The tables for all or selected combinations of variables are computed and output in the remainder of the program.

The process used here for each pair of variables develops a list of all different symbols used for the row variable in KR and for the column variable in KC. Frequencies of the use of various symbol combinations are accumulated in matrix KT, using the indexes of the cells in KR and KC which contain the matching symbols for each subject's data. The list of symbols in KR is developed only once for each variable, and is retained for all combinations with other variables, but the series of symbols in KC must be recompiled for each combination. Rezeroing of the table is carried out only as necessary, by zeroing a column of KT whenever a code symbol is added to the KC list.

When all subjects have been processed for a particular combination of variables, the contents of the KT matrix are printed, bordered by the appropriate symbols used for the two variables concerned (Figure 12-3).

EXAMPLE PROBLEM

A set of 20 data cards containing a code number and four alphameric "scores" for each subject was used, along with a selection matrix which designated tabling of combinations 1−2, 1−3, 1−4, and 2−3 with omission of all other pairings. We could have left the below-diagonal elements of this matrix as zeros, since a variable will be selected if a 1 appears for a given combination either above or below the diagonal of this matrix.

Variable one consists of the symbols −, 0, and +; variable two has five symbols A, B, C, D, and F; while variable three consists of the two symbols M and F. Variable four is not really variable, since all subjects have the symbol 1; it was included to demonstrate a method of obtaining simple frequency distributions for single variables.

```
C      PROGRAM CONTAB
C
C   COMPUTE CONTINGENCY TABLES FOR PAIRS OF ALPHAMERIC-CODED VARIABLES.
C   PARAMETER CONTROL-CARD FIELDS.
C      COL 1-5 = NUMBER OF VARIABLES (MAX = 75).
C      COL 6-10 = NUMBER OF SUBJECTS.
C      COL 15 = 1 IF SELECTION MATRIX IS TO BE READ,0 = NO SELECTION MAT
C   IF NO SELECTION MATRIX, ALL POSSIBLE PAIRS OF VARIABLES WILL BE TABL
C   SELECTION MATRIX IS INPUT AS SQUARE MATRIX OF 1 AND 0 DIGITS.
C      EACH VARIABLE BEGINS A NEW CARD. ON EACH CARD, COLUMNS = VARIABLE
C      IF DIGIT ABOVE OR BELOW DIAGONAL = 1, TABLE WILL BE COMPUTED FOR
C         PAIRING OF VARIABLES.
C      IF BOTH ARE ZERO, TABLE WILL BE OMITTED.
C   DATA-CARD FORMAT MUST SPECIFY A SINGLE-COLUMN A-MODE FIELD
C      FOR EACH VARIABLE. DATA SYMBOLS MAY BE ANY KEY-PUNCH CHARACTER.
C   SELECTION MATRIX PRECEDES DATA CARDS IN INPUT DECK.
C   TAPE UNIT 2 IS USED FOR TEMPORARY STORAGE.
```

Example Problem   329

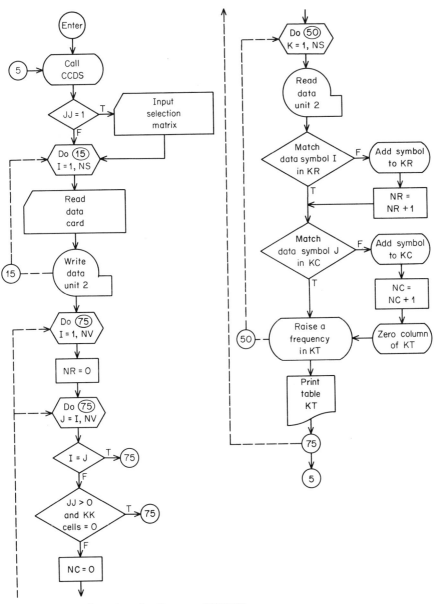

FIGURE 12-3. Flow chart for Program CONTAB.

```
C    SUBROUTINE CCDS IS REQUIRED.
C
     DIMENSION KF(16), KK(75,75), KT(50,50), KR(50), KC(50), KD(50)
   5 CALL CCDS (KF, NV, NS, JJ, I, J)
C    READ SELECTION MATRIX IF COLUMN 15 OPTION = 1.
     IF (JJ .EQ. 1) READ 10, ((KK(I,J), J = 1,75), I = 1,NV)
  10 FORMAT (75I1)
```

MISCELLANEOUS STATISTICAL METHODS

```
C     STORE ALL DATA ON TAPE IN BINARY FORM.
      REWIND 2
      DO 15 I = 1,NS
      READ KF, (KD(J), J = 1,NV)
   15 WRITE (2) (KD(J), J = 1,NV)
C     BEGIN TABULATION OF VARIABLE PAIRINGS.
      DO 75 I = 1,NV
      NR = 0
      DO 75 J = I,NV
      IF (I .EQ. J) GO TO 75
      IF (JJ .GT. 0 .AND. KK(I,J) + KK(J,I) .EQ. 0) GO TO 75
C     ACCUMULATE CODES USED IN KR AND KC, AND FREQUENCIES IN KT. NR AND NC A
C     NUMBERS OF DIFFERENT CODES USED FOR ROW AND COLUMN VARIABLES.
      REWIND 2
      NC = 0
      DO 50 K = 1,NS
      READ (2) (KD(L), L = 1,NV)
      IF (NR .EQ. 0) GO TO 25
C     LOCATE A MATCHING CODE SYMBOL IN KR, IF ANY.
      DO 20 L = 1,NR
      IF (KD(I) .EQ. KR(L)) GO TO 30
   20 CONTINUE
C     ADD A CODE SYMBOL TO THE LIST IN KR.
   25 NR = NR + 1
      KR(NR) = KD(I)
      L = NR
   30 IF (NC .EQ. 0) GO TO 40
C     LOCATE A MATCHING CODE SYMBOL IN KC, IF ANY.
      DO 35 M = 1,NC
      IF (KD(J) .EQ. KC(M)) GO TO 50
   35 CONTINUE
C     ZERO A COLUMN OF THE KT TABLE, AND ADD A CODE SYMBOL TO THE LIST IN KC
   40 NC = NC + 1
      DO 45 M = 1,50
   45 KT(M,NC) = 0
      KC(NC) = KD(J)
      M = NC
C     RAISE FREQUENCY IN A CELL OF THE KT TABLE.
   50 KT(L,M) = KT(L,M) + 1
      PRINT 55, I, J
   55 FORMAT ( // 12H ROWS = ITEM, I3, 5X, 14HCOLUMNS = ITEM, I3)
C     PRINT A CONTINGENCY TABLE, BORDERED BY APPROPRIATE CODE SYMBOLS.
      DO 65 K = 1,NC,20
      L = MIN0(NC, K + 19)
      PRINT 60, (KC(M), M = K,L)
   60 FORMAT ( / 6H  CODE, 4X, 20A5)
      DO 65 N = 1,NR
   65 PRINT 70, KR(N), (KT(N,M), M = K,L)
   70 FORMAT (/ 4X, A2, 20I5)
   75 CONTINUE
      GO TO 5
      END


      *** INPUT DATA DECK ***


CONTAB EXAMPLE PROBLEM
000040002000001
(4X,4A1)
0111                                                                    SMV
1010                                                                    SMV
1100                                                                    SMV
1000                                                                    SMV
S01 +AM1
```

S02 OCM1
S03 -DF1
S04 +BM1
S05 OCF1
S06 +AM1
S07 ODM1
S08 -FF1
S09 +AF1
S10 +CM1
S11 -FM1
S12 -DM1
S13 -CF1
S14 +BM1
S15 +BF1
S16 -CF1
S17 -FM1
S18 ODF1
S19 OCF1
S20 OBF1

*** PRINTED OUTPUT ***

1CONTAB EXAMPLE PROBLEM

PARAMETERS
COL   1- 5 =   4
COL   6-10 =   20
COL 11-15 =   1
COL 16-20 =   0
COL 21-25 =   0

DATA FORMAT = (4X,4A1)

ROWS = ITEM 1   COLUMNS = ITEM 2

CODE	A	C	D	B	F
+	3	1	0	3	0
0	0	3	2	1	0
-	0	2	2	0	3

ROWS = ITEM 1   COLUMNS = ITEM 3

CODE	M	F
+	5	2
0	2	4
-	3	4

ROWS = ITEM 1   COLUMNS = ITEM 4

CODE	1
+	7
0	6
-	7

332 MISCELLANEOUS STATISTICAL METHODS

```
ROWS = ITEM  2        COLUMNS = ITEM  3
CODE      M      F
  A       2      1
  C       2      4
  D       2      2
  B       2      2
  F       2      1
```

CHI-SQUARE ANALYSIS

The familiar statistical method of chi-square analysis is almost impossible to incorporate satisfactorily into a general-purpose computer program which computes contingency tables. The reason is that in any practical application the researcher almost inevitably wishes to adjust the contingency tables produced by tabulation such as that carried out by Program CONTAB. To meet the assumptions of the method, each expected frequency should be greater than 1, and no more than 20 percent of the cells should have expected frequencies of less than 5 (Siegel, 1956). This very often forces the researcher to combine or drop categories in order to carry out an analysis. One could write a routine which would allow designation of such modifications through the use of special control cards, but in most cases two passes through such a program would be needed—one to identify the necessary modifications and one to compute the analysis.

We have adopted a different viewpoint on this problem by providing separate programs for tabulation of contingency tables and for chi-square analysis of frequencies. Program CONTAB serves the former purpose, while Program CHICHI carries out the latter.

PROGRAM CHICHI

Subroutine CCDS is not used in Program CHICHI since the first fields of the data cards themselves define all of the necessary parameters. For most problems a single data card will be sufficient, although large contingency tables may require multiple cards. A blank card at the end of the data deck serves to terminate processing.

The data cards are punched according to a fixed format which is incorporated in the program. As specified in the program listing on a following page, the first ten columns of each card contain an alphameric label and the numbers of rows and columns in the contingency table to be analyzed. These columns are ignored on any "continuation" cards required. Column 11 is also ignored, but may be used to hold the card number when more than one data card is required by the problem. Beginning in column 12, up to 23 cell frequencies are recorded in order across the rows of the contingency table, as illustrated by the example problems for this program. These frequencies are always punched as three-digit integers.

A number of options have been incorporated into this routine to permit important variations in the use of the chi-square technique. First of all, Yates correction for continuity (Siegel, 1956) is automatically applied to any problem involving a single degree of freedom for chi-square.

Two options are provided for chi-square tests of frequency lists (contingency tables with one row or column). If columns 9–10 are set = 01, the list of frequencies entered from the data card will be tested against an hypothesis of equal frequencies. (All expected frequencies will be equal proportions of the total number of cases.) If columns 7–8 are set = 01, however, the observed frequencies read from the usual data card will be tested against a list of expected frequencies read from a special data card which is expected to follow immediately in the data deck. A special format is used in this case to permit fractional expectations to be represented.

When multiple rows and columns are involved, as is the case for the well-known chi-square test of association between two variables, the expected frequencies for each cell are computed from marginal totals for the appropriate row and column; their product is divided by the table total to yield the expected frequency.

The output from the program for each problem is the alphameric problem label, the chi-square value with its associated chance probability, the degrees of freedom, and the total frequency of all cells. This is followed by printing of the observed frequencies, the marginal totals, and the expected frequencies (Figure 12-4).

EXAMPLE PROBLEMS

Four problems have been concocted to illustrate the different applications of this program. The first problem tests the three observed frequencies 231, 86, and 283 against the hypothesis that the population contains equal frequencies (200, 200, 200). Printing of these expected frequencies is omitted by the program.

The second problem tests the five observed frequencies, 5, 17, 50, 22, and 6, against the specific expected frequencies, 10, 20, 40, 20, and 10, which are entered from a separate card.

Problem three is a 2-by-2 chi-square problem, which automatically invokes the continuity correction.

Problem four exemplifies a larger contingency table, with three levels on one dimension and four on the other. This and the previous problem might well have been set up from information contained in output from Program CONTAB, although this was not actually the case.

334 MISCELLANEOUS STATISTICAL METHODS

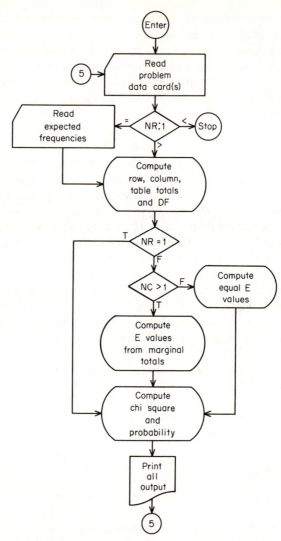

FIGURE 12-4. Flow chart for Program CHICHI.

```
C      PROGRAM CHICHI
C
C   COMPUTE CHI-SQUARE ANALYSES OF FREQUENCY TABLES.
C   PROGRAM REQUIRES NO CONTROL CARDS. DATA CARDS CONTAIN OBSERVED
C      FREQUENCIES COMPILED BY HAND COUNT OR ANOTHER PROGRAM.
C   DATA-CARD FORMAT.
C      COL 1-6 = ALPHAMERIC LABEL FOR PROBLEM.
C      COL 7-8 = NUMBER OF ROWS IN FREQUENCY TABLE. (MAX = 20)
C      COL 9-10 = NUMBER OF COLUMNS IN FREQUENCY TABLE. (MAX = 99)
C      COL 11 = CARD NUMBER IN SERIES, IF NECESSARY.
C      COL 12-80 = UP TO 23 THREE-DIGIT FREQUENCIES, IN ORDER
C         ACROSS ROWS OF THE TABLE, AS A CONTINUOUS SERIES.
```

Example Problems

ADDITIONAL CARDS WITH THE SAME FORMAT ARE USED WHEN THE TABLE
CONTAINS MORE THAN 23 CELLS.
WHEN THE TABLE HAS ONLY ONE ROW, AND THE TEST IS TO BE AGAINST THE
  HYPOTHESIS OF EQUAL FREQUENCIES FOR ALL CELLS, SET COL 9-10 = 1.
TO TEST A SINGLE-ROW TABLE AGAINST A PARTICULAR HYPOTHETICAL
  DISTRIBUTION, SET COL 7-8 = 1 AND ENTER THE LIST OF HYPOTHETICAL
  FREQUENCIES FROM CARDS FOLLOWING THE OBSERVED FREQUENCIES,
  USING THE FORMAT (5X, 15F5.2).
A BLANK CARD FOLLOWS THE LAST PROBLEM-CARD (SERIES).
YATES CORRECTION FOR CONTINUITY IS AUTOMATICALLY APPLIED WHEN
  THE TEST IS BASED ON ONE DEGREE OF FREEDOM.
SUBPROGRAMS REQUIRED ARE SUMF, PRBF, AND PRTS.

```
      DIMENSION O(20,99), E(20,99), R(20), C(99)
      ND = 20
READ LABEL, TABLE DIMENSIONS, AND OBSERVED FREQUENCIES.
    5 READ 10, KH, NR, NC, ((O(I,J), J = 1,NC), I = 1,NR)
   10 FORMAT (A6, 2I2, 1X, 23F3.0 / (11X, 23F3.0))
      IF (NR - 1) 15, 20, 30
   15 STOP
READ EXPECTED FREQUENCY LIST IF NR = 1.
   20 READ 25, (E(1,I), I = 1,NC)
   25 FORMAT (5X, 15F5.2)
COMPUTE COLUMN, ROW, AND TABLE TOTALS FROM OBSERVED FREQUENCIES.
   30 DO 35 I = 1,NC
   35 C(I) = SUMF(O, I, NR, ND)
      DO 40 I = 1,NR
   40 R(I) = SUMF(O, -I, NC, ND)
      T = SUMF(R, 1, NR, ND)
      DF = MAX0(1, NR - 1) * MAX0(1, NC - 1)
      IF (NR .EQ. 1) GO TO 60
      IF (NC .GT. 1) GO TO 50
      RN = NR
COMPUTE EQUAL EXPECTED FREQUENCIES IF NC = 1.
      DO 45 I = 1,NR
      O(1,I) = O(I,1)
   45 E(I,1) = T / RN
      GO TO 60
COMPUTE EXPECTED FREQUENCIES FROM MARGINAL TOTALS IF NR AND NC EXCEED 1.
   50 DO 55 I = 1,NR
      DO 55 J = 1,NC
   55 E(I,J) = R(I) * C(J) / T
COMPUTE CHI-SQUARE (CORRECTED IF NECESSARY) AND PROBABILITY.
   60 CS = 0.0
      DO 65 I = 1,NR
      DO 65 J = 1,NC
      D = ABS(O(I,J) - E(I,J))
      IF (DF .EQ. 1.0) D = D - 0.5
   65 CS = CS + D * D / E(I,J)
      P = PRBF(DF, 1000.0, CS / DF)
      PRINT 70, KH, T, P, CS, DF
   70 FORMAT (1H1PROBLEM = , A6, 5X, 3HN =, F7.0 // 4H P =, F7.4,
     1 17H FOR CHI-SQUARE =, F8.3, 12H WITH D.F. =, F5.0)
      IF (NR .GT. 1 .AND. NC .GT. 1) CALL PRTS (R, NR, 1, 5HROW T, ND)
      CALL PRTS (O, NR, NC, 5HOBS F, ND)
      IF (NR .GT. 1 .AND. NC .GT. 1) CALL PRTS (C, NC, 1, 5HCOL T, ND)
      IF (NC .GT. 1) CALL PRTS (E, NR, NC, 5HEXP F, ND)
      GO TO 5
      END
```

*** INPUT DATA DECK ***

E   0301 231086283

336 MISCELLANEOUS STATISTICAL METHODS

```
TWO     0105  005017050022006
TWO E         10000200004000020000100
THREE   0202  021004019036
FOUR    0304  010025044016023198210023235032030242
```

*** PRINTED OUTPUT ***

1PROBLEM = ONE   N =   600.

P =   .0000 FOR CHI-SQUARE = 104.230 WITH D.F. =   2.

OBS F   1   2   3
              231.0000   86.0000   283.0000

1PROBLEM = TWO   N =   100.

P =   .1230 FOR CHI-SQUARE =   7.250 WITH D.F. =   4.

OBS F   1   2   3   4   5

  1   5.0000   17.0000   50.0000   22.0000   6.0000

EXP F   1   2   3   4   5

  1   10.0000   20.0000   40.0000   20.0000   10.0000

1PROBLEM = THREE   N =   80.

P =   .0003 FOR CHI-SQUARE =   14.895 WITH D.F. =   1.

ROW T   1   2
              25.0000   55.0000

OBS F   1   2

  1   21.0000   4.0000

  2   19.0000   36.0000

COL T   1   2
              40.0000   40.0000

EXP F   1   2

  1   12.5000   12.5000

  2   27.5000   27.5000

1PROBLEM = FOUR   N =   1088.

P =   .0000 FOR CHI-SQUARE = 633.801 WITH D.F. =   6.

ROW	T	1	2	3	
		95.0000	454.0000	539.0000	

OBS	F	1	2	3	4
1		10.0000	25.0000	44.0000	16.0000
2		23.0000	198.0000	210.0000	23.0000
3		235.0000	32.0000	30.0000	242.0000

COL	T	1	2	3	4
		268.0000	255.0000	284.0000	281.0000

EXP	F	1	2	3	4
1		23.4007	22.2656	24.7978	24.5358
2		111.8309	106.4063	118.5074	117.2555
3		132.7684	126.3281	140.6949	139.2086

Review Exercises

1. Run the four-object, three-variable problem presented as an example in the text on Program HGROUP with and also without prestandardization of the variables. Explain the results obtained.
2. Modify Program TSCALE to include the computation and printing of item means and variances before calculation of scale values.
3. Write down the names of 20 of your acquaintances — 10 that you like and 10 that you dislike. Now develop a code system (1 character per variable) for like-dislike, sex, age, taller-shorter (than yourself), and estimated intelligence (higher-lower than yourself). Punch a card for each person and run the deck on Program CONTAB for all combinations of the five variables. Interesting, isn't it?
4. Run the CHICHI Program using the 3-by-3 example problem for Program CONTAB in the text.

13 / compilation and analysis of verbal data

A modern digital computer is basically a symbol-manipulating device capable of processing verbal as well as numerical data. The major part of this book has been devoted to statistical techniques for quantitative data because this is the nature of most analytic research in the behavioral sciences. The present chapter will introduce a few of the ways in which the computer can be used to prepare verbal data for quantification. The availability of these techniques can greatly extend the practical limits of research in certain fields.

A considerable amount of behavioral research involves analysis of data which we will call *constructed responses* to various kinds of standard stimuli. Examples of such data are sentence-completion responses, *Thematic Apperception Test* stories, Rorschach responses, and replies to open-end questionnaires. In contrast, standard personality questionnaires such as the *Minnesota Multiphasic Personality Inventory* and the *California Psychological Inventory* require that the subject make what we will call *choice responses,* selecting an answer from a series of supplied alternatives. Rating scales, ranking tasks, and the Q-sort technique also would fall into this second category.

Many psychologists believe that constructed-response data-gathering devices provide more useful information about personality characteristics and behavioral tendencies, since the subject must fall back upon his natural response modes to a greater degree when he is not supplied with ready-made answers to the problems posed by the stimuli. The primary difficulty with open-end questions, however, is the variety of responses they elicit. While this variety is highly valued by clinicians, it is a major source of difficulty for the researcher who must quantify the data in order to conduct objective analyses. The techniques in this chapter go a long way toward bringing these difficulties under control, making the use of open-end questions a feasible method in many situations where it once would have been prohibitively expensive.

SOME RECENT RESEARCH WITH VERBAL DATA

One of the most extensive programs employing the computer to process verbal data has grown out of the development of the *General Inquirer* system at Harvard University (Stone, *et al.*, 1962). This basic technique permits automatic analysis of the content of any type of verbal material. The method may include an extensive precoding of the raw data for parts of speech, referents of adjectives, and so forth. The content analysis is accomplished by reference to a particular "dictionary" of terms organized according to a predetermined system of concepts. Many different dictionaries have been compiled for various purposes. Political scientists at Stanford University (Holsti, 1964), for example, have constructed a *General Inquirer* dictionary oriented toward their own field, in which all terms are coded for Osgood's (1957) three factors of meaning. The output from such a system is a series of quantitative indices of usage of the various concepts concerned. Hypotheses are tested by comparing selected samples of verbal data.

At the University of California, J. A. Starkweather (1964) has used a computer to compile the word-usage characteristics of interview transcripts prior to intensive analysis of content. A more recent report (1965) concerns the use of the computer as the interviewer, communicating with the subject through a typewriter. Such procedures are currently only in the experimental stages, but their use will undoubtedly expand rapidly, along with the development of hardware for computer-assisted instruction.

E. C. Moseley and D. Gorham (1963) of the Veterans Administration have developed a computer-based system for automatic scoring of the *Holtzman Inkblot Test,* asking for three-word responses to each of the blots. Using a single massive dictionary of individual words precoded for most of the original 22 scoring categories, they have achieved very close agreement between computer output and hand scoring of the same protocols. The advantages of such an automated system of scoring group-administered tests in mass screening programs are obvious. Less obvious, but perhaps more significant, is the fact that such a system is completely objective, allowing careful checking of the coding system and gradual improvement of its accuracy. Human judges vary in their objectivity from day to day, and even their systematic errors are difficult to locate. Such "dehumanized" scoring systems cannot cover the range of constructs which a clinician can assess, but the trade-off with objectivity may be advantageous for many purposes.

At the University of Texas, R. F. Peck, Shirley Menaker, and the author are currently engaged in a long-term project aimed at development of a computer-based system for personality assessment, using sentence completion data (Peck and Veldman, 1962). Single-word responses to the sentence blanks have been compiled and reduced to word roots. The output of an automated system of this type may in some applications be no more than a probability statement regarding the subject's predicted behavior in a particular situation, or it may be a general descriptive analysis of his verbal behavior in normative terms. In any case, a complete trace of the chain of programmed inferences which led to the output can be obtained from the computer. Thus, the computer program may be considered to be a theory of assessment defined entirely in operational terms.

If one were to examine the actual computer programs employed in the researches just described, a number of points would be immediately apparent. First of all, not all programs for processing verbal data are written in the Fortran language; specialized languages have been developed for certain kinds of applications. An outstanding example is IPL-V (*Information Processing Language*-version 5; Newell, 1961), which is especially suited to the manipulation of lists and list structures. This is not to say that Fortran is unsuited to such applications, or that some operations upon lists cannot be specified in the Fortran language. The choice among language vehicles is mostly a matter of convenience for the programmer, and an estimate of convenience should include the time and effort required to master the languages involved. We believe that a thorough command of a single language is preferable to a partial understanding of a number of different languages. Most behavioral scientists have neither the time nor interest to invest in acquiring genuine fluency in more than one computer language. We recommend Fortran because it is so widely used and because it has a surprising flexibility of application to many types of programming problems. In fact, through the use of subprograms, Fortran control programs can be written which are as convenient and almost as efficient as specialized routines written directly in a special-purpose language.

NUMBER SYSTEMS AND ALPHAMERIC DATA

Before we can begin discussing procedures for processing verbal data, we will have to add some depth to our earlier coverage of data storage and conversion. You will recall that a computer's memory is organized in terms of *words* of storage, and that a common memory size for large general-purpose computers, such as the CDC 1604 and the IBM 7094, is 32,768 words of memory. The main memory of a modern computer is often called "core" storage, because each word consists physically of a series of tiny iron rings called *cores*. The number of cores per word of storage varies among computers. Our examples in this chapter will assume a word size of 36 cores, since this is currently the most common. As we will see later, the discussion would apply with little or no change to computers with 48 or even 60 cores per word. Readers who have access to an IBM System/360 machine may find that the methods described here, although workable, are less efficient than others that could be developed to take advantage of the atypical memory organization and extended character set available to them.

The individual cores in a word of memory are sometimes called *bits,* which is an abbreviation for *binary digit*. Thus, a word of memory is said to be 36 bits long. A core can register one of two states at any given instant; it can be magnetized in one direction or the other. Wires passing through the individual cores carry current which can change the magnetic state of the cores thousands of times every second if necessary. At any given instant, the magnetic states of the 36 cores in a word of memory constitute the *contents* of the memory cell. (We will use the terms *word, cell,* and *location* interchangeably.) These 36 cores or bits represent a single *binary number*; all data stored in the computer memory are coded as binary numbers. Once data have been stored in the computer's memory, there is no way of distinguishing whether they had been converted from real numbers, integer numbers, or alphameric characters. Different coding conventions are employed to convert these kinds of data to binary numbers, but once they have been converted they are all alike in that they are strings of binary digits.

Number Systems. An understanding of number systems is essential to the material which follows, and therefore deserves careful study. First let us note that there is nothing "special" about the *decimal* number system, except that it is so common that many college students do not realize there are others. Decimal numbers have a *base* of ten, which for our purposes means only that there are ten *numerals* in the set used to describe a particular *number* quantity in this system. Note the very important distinction between the terms "numeral" and "number." The ten decimal numerals are 0, 1, 2, 3, 4, 5, 6, 7, 8, 9. If we want to express the number which is the base of the system we must use the two numerals, 10. This is true of all number systems.

Any number may serve as the base of a number system. Let us consider next *binary* numbers. Here there are only two numerals available to express number quantities. The base of the system (two) requires two digits (bits): 10. Thus, the significance of the numerals used to express a number quantity depends on the base of the number system concerned. In contexts such as this where we are discussing numbers expressed in various systems, a subscript for the base of the system is often appended to each numeral set. So, $10_2 = 2_{10}$. To be sure that you have this notion clearly in mind, study the following table of binary-decimal equivalents and fill in the blanks.

Decimal	Binary	Decimal	Binary
1	1	7	111
2		8	
3	11	9	1001
4	100	10	1010
5	101	11	
6	110	12	1100

Note that each time an additional place or numeral is needed to express a number in an increasing series, the number concerned is a *power* of the base equal to the number of zero numerals. Thus:

$$10_{10} = 10_{10}{}^1 \qquad 10_2 = 2_{10}{}^1$$
$$100_{10} = 10_{10}{}^2 \qquad 100_2 = 2_{10}{}^2$$
$$1000_{10} = 10_{10}{}^3 \qquad 1000_2 = 2_{10}{}^3$$

All data are represented in the computer memory as binary numbers, and for this reason an understanding of the binary number system is very important. There is another number system which is also useful to programmers, called the *octal* system (base 8). It offers a convenient shorthand for expressing binary numbers. Each digit in an octal number translates directly to three binary digits, and vice versa. In the table that follows we have grouped sets of three digits in the binary number columns to emphasize this fact.

Decimal	Octal	Binary	Decimal	Octal	Binary
0	0	000	6	6	110
1	1	001	7	7	111
2	2	010	8	10	001 000
3	3	011	9	11	001 001
4	4	100	10	12	001 010
5	5	101	11	13	001 011

Note that there are no such numerals as 8 and 9 in the octal system; the number eight is the first power of the base (eight) and therefore is the numeral-pair 10. Predictably, the second power of the base $64_{10} = 100_8$.

The only importance of the octal system from our viewpoint is the convenience it affords for representing the binary numbers corresponding to alphameric characters. You will recall from our discussion of A-mode data in Chapter 4 that a total of six characters may be stored in a single word of memory. If each word contains 36 bits, then each character must require six bits. If three bits convert directly to a single octal digit, then each alphameric character can be represented conveniently by two octal digits instead of six binary digits. The next table shows the octal-number equivalents for each of the letters, numbers, and special characters, according to the most widely used (BCD) coding system. Some computer systems operate with this coding for external tapes, but use a somewhat different set of codes for central storage, while other computers use this coding consistently. Such differences in coding procedures are of no significance for most of the techniques to be described later in this chapter, but may affect more complex procedures for handling verbal data.

OCTAL CODES FOR BCD CHARACTERS

Character	Code	Character	Code	Character	Code
A	61	Q	50	7	07
B	62	R	51	8	10
C	63	S	22	9	11
D	64	T	23	0	12
E	65	U	24	=	13
F	66	V	25	Δ	20
G	67	W	26	/	21
H	70	X	27	,	33
I	71	Y	30	(	34
J	41	Z	31	-	40
K	42	1	01	$	53
L	43	2	02	*	54
M	44	3	03	+	60
N	45	4	04	.	73
O	46	5	05	)	74
P	47	6	06		

Character Conversion and Storage. There are BCD equivalents for all of the numerals and special characters, as well as the letters of the alphabet. To be sure that you understand the fact that the same numeral symbol read with an A-mode (BCD) format specification will be coded differently than if read with an I-mode format specification, let us consider a few examples. Suppose that card columns 1–6 contain the following symbols: ΔΔΔΔ43. If we read this field with the format specification A6, each of the six symbols would be translated to a set of binary digits as follows:

Symbol	Column	Binary		Octal
Δ	1	010	000	20
Δ	2	010	000	20
Δ	3	010	000	20
Δ	4	010	000	20
4	5	000	100	04
3	6	000	011	03

Thus, the complete 36-bit storage location would hold the binary number
    010 000 010 000 010 000 010 000 000 100 000 011 (base 2)
which also may be written
    202020200403 (base 8)

Now let us suppose that this same six-character field had been read with the format specification I6. Rather than a character-by-character BCD conversion, the entire field would be treated as a single number quantity to be converted from base 10 to base 2. The storage location in this case would hold the bit string

000 000 000 000 000 000 000 000 000 000 101 011 (base 2)

which is the same as

000000000053 (base 8)

Once the data have been stored in the memory location, we can manipulate it in any consistent manner which suits our purposes; the computer does not remember how it was translated on input. Therefore, the contents 202020200403_8 which resulted from the BCD coding *could* be treated in the program as an integer number to be compared with the contents of other memory locations — even though it was not a number on the data card from which it was input.

In the previous example we read a six-character field, which completely filled a memory location. If we had read only the two nonblank characters with the specifications 4X, A2, the contents of the referenced storage location would have been 040320202020_8, since the characters are stored left-justified in the computer word and all unused character spaces to the right are automatically filled with blank-codes (20_8). If interpreted as an integer number, this memory location obviously is unequal to the previous example. In contrast, if we had read the data card with the format specifications 4X, I2, the contents of the referenced memory location would be identical to those obtained by using I6 in the format, since the number value of the field would be the same.

Since we can *interpret* the contents of any storage location in the program as representing an integer number no matter which mode of data conversion was employed to set the bits of the location, we can use ordinary IF statements to compare the contents of pairs of storage locations for identity. If two locations KA and KB were filled by means of A-mode format specifications from cards holding the same character strings, then the statement IF (KA .EQ. KB) will be true. Note that the two inputs need not be identical, as long as the resulting BCD codes are the same. For example, the first six columns of a card might hold ABΔΔΔΔ. Either format specification A6 or A2 would result in the same stored binary number, since incomplete fields are filled to the right with blank-codes during translation into a memory cell.

We will discuss the use of IF statements to compare locations for equality and even for "size" later in this chapter. The important thing to remember is that the content of a memory location is always a string of binary digits, interpretable as an integer number, even when A-mode format specifications were used to fill it.

AN EXAMPLE PROBLEM

The problem outlined next exemplifies many common aspects of research employing open-end questions. We will use the same set of data to illustrate procedures for compiling, reducing, and analyzing verbal responses. The task described here is artificially restricted in scope in order to allow concentration on the methods used, and does not begin to represent the immense volume of data that is normally processed in practical applications of these techniques.

Let us suppose that we have asked each of 100 male and 100 female college students to write down a single word to answer the question, "What do you like most in a woman?" The first step in processing these data would be to punch the answers into tab cards, one card per subject, containing his or her response word. We will use the following card format:

Cols. 1-3: subject code number (1-100)
Col. 5: subject sex (1 = male, 2 = female)
Cols. 7-18: response word.

Our reason for coding subject sex as 1-2 rather than 1-0 will be apparent later when we reach the problem of comparing responses from the male and female subsamples. We have allotted 12 card columns to the subject's response, which will completely fill two 36-bit (six character) storage locations when read into the computer memory in A mode.

Instructions to the key-punch operator for these data were to ignore any leading articles (a, an, the) and to ignore spaces and hyphens in multiword responses, punching all alphabetic characters as a continuous string up to the 12-character limit. She was also instructed to correct any misspellings encountered. Although variant spelling is usually standardized in verbal-data processing problems such as this, the information contained in the subject's spelling accuracy is often of considerable interest and could be recorded as a separate datum when the original protocols are transferred to punch cards.

The remainder of this chapter will concern techniques for processing the information in this basic data deck. We will first compile a list of all *different* responses and their frequencies of occurrence in the sample. We will then reorder this list according to the frequencies, and then reorder the list again in terms of the alphabetic similarity of the responses themselves. The next section of the chapter will concern an alternate procedure for organizing a response list which, although more complex than the straightforward method to be discussed first, is far more efficient with the large samples of data which are processed in most practical research applications. The final section of the chapter will concern response grouping and comparison of subsamples.

The example dealing with males and females is artificially small in order

346 COMPILATION AND ANALYSIS OF VERBAL DATA

to simplify presentation of the processing methods. The processing programs are also artificially simple, in that they were written only for this particular problem. The methods used are our prime concern; the programs are not intended to be general-purpose routines for a program library like the statistical programs discussed in earlier chapters. Research with verbal data is so varied that any attempt to construct a comprehensive and efficient set of general-purpose programs would be futile. A thorough understanding of the principles outlined in this chapter should allow you to develop your own programs as needed for this kind of research.

The complete data deck of 200 cards is printed here for your use in checking the programs in this chapter, or programs of this type. (Each line of this listing contains the contents of two nonconsecutive cards in the data deck.)

```
                  *** INPUT DATA DECK ***
          001  1  PERSONALITY       046  1  SERIOUSNESS
          002  1  CONGENIALITY      047  1  FRIENDLINESS
          003  1  NEAT              048  1  BEAUTY
          004  1  CUTE              049  1  LOOKS
          005  1  HONEST            050  1  INTELLIGENCE
          006  1  NEATNESS          051  1  PERSONALITY
          007  1  LOOKS             052  1  NEATNESS
          008  1  VIVACIOUS         053  1  HONEST
          009  1  PERSONALITY       054  1  FAITHFULNESS
          010  1  GOODLOOKING       055  1  HONESTY
          011  1  HONESTY           056  1  INTELLIGENT
          012  1  BEAUTY            057  1  ABILITY
          013  1  HONESTY           058  1  PERSONALITY
          014  1  ATTRACTIVENE      059  1  PERSONALITY
          015  1  TRUTH             060  1  APPEARANCE
          016  1  LOVE              061  1  NEAT
          017  1  UNDERSTANDAB      062  1  ATTRACTIVE
          018  1  PERSONALITY       063  1  PERSONALITY
          019  1  PRETTY            064  1  BEAUTY
          020  1  BEAUTY            065  1  NEATNESS
          021  1  THRIFT            066  1  LOOKS
          022  1  APPEARANCES       067  1  FRIENDLINESS
          023  1  PRETTY            068  1  PERSONALITY
          024  1  INTELLIGENT       069  1  CONSIDERATIO
          025  1  LOOKS             070  1  DEPENDABILIT
          026  1  POLITENESS        071  1  BEAUTIFUL
          027  1  TALL              072  1  APPEARANCE
          028  1  RESPECT           073  1  KINDNESS
          029  1  CONSIDERATIO      074  1  MANNERED
          030  1  GENTLENESS        075  1  SOFTNESS
          031  1  ATTRACTIVE        076  1  BEAUTY
          032  1  WARMTH            077  1  PERSONALITY
          033  1  GROOMING          078  1  KIND
          034  1  GENIAL            079  1  FRIENDLY
          035  1  CUTE              080  1  EYES
          036  1  NEATNESS          081  1  BEAUTY
          037  1  SPIRITUAL         082  1  HONESTY
          038  1  PERSONALITY       083  1  BEAUTY
          039  1  MATURITY          084  1  PERSONALITY
          040  1  TOLERANCE         085  1  BEAUTY
          041  1  FRIENDLINESS      086  1  PLEASANT
          042  1  LOVABLE           087  1  ATTRACTIVENE
          043  1  INTELLIGENCE      088  1  HUMOR
          044  1  LOVABLENESS       089  1  HONESTY
          045  1  PERSONALITY       090  1  CLOTHING
```

091	1	BEAUTY		046	2	PERSONALITY
092	1	KIND		047	2	HONESTY
093	1	HONEST		048	2	COURTEOUS
094	1	NEATNESS		049	2	GRACEFULNESS
095	1	APPEARANCE		050	2	KINDNESS
096	1	LOOK		051	2	THOUGHTFUL
097	1	WIT		052	2	SINCERITY
098	1	INTELLIGENCE		053	2	NEATNESS
099	1	VIRTUE		054	2	NEATNESS
100	1	INTEGRITY		055	2	CHARM
001	2	FRIENDLINESS		056	2	CLEANLINESS
002	2	CLEANLINESS		057	2	KINDNESS
003	2	HONESTY		058	2	NEATNESS
004	2	CHARM		059	2	WOMANLINESS
005	2	HONESTY		060	2	PRETTY
006	2	SINCERE		061	2	SINCERITY
007	2	FRIENDLY		062	2	FRIENDLINESS
008	2	NEATNESS		063	2	PERSONALITY
009	2	HONESTY		064	2	SINCERITY
010	2	CLEANLINESS		065	2	HONESTY
011	2	CHEERFULNESS		066	2	NEATNESS
012	2	HONESTY		067	2	LOOKS
013	2	POISE		068	2	HONESTY
014	2	FRIENDLINESS		069	2	FRIENDLINESS
015	2	POLITE		070	2	NEATNESS
016	2	SINCERITY		071	2	FRIENDLINESS
017	2	LOYALTY		072	2	FRIENDLINESS
018	2	NEATNESS		073	2	HONESTY
019	2	SINCERITY		074	2	SINCERITY
020	2	PUNCTUALITY		075	2	HONESTY
021	2	NEATNESS		076	2	HONESTY
022	2	POISE		077	2	PERSONALITY
023	2	NEAT		078	2	BEAUTY
024	2	CLEANLINESS		079	2	FEMININE
025	2	MODESTY		080	2	NEATNESS
026	2	CHARMING		081	2	KINDNESS
027	2	ATTRACTIVE		082	2	KINDNESS
028	2	NEATNESS		083	2	CHEERFULNESS
029	2	NEATNESS		084	2	SINCERITY
030	2	FRIENDLINESS		085	2	VIRTUE
031	2	HUMOR		086	2	STEADFASTNESS
032	2	GOODATTITUDE		087	2	INTEGRITY
033	2	CHEEFULNESS		088	2	UNDERSTANDIN
034	2	LOYALTY		089	2	PERSONALITY
035	2	TALKATIVE		090	2	SINCERE
036	2	SIMPLICITY		091	2	SINCERITY
037	2	POLITE		092	2	KINDNESS
038	2	HUMOR		093	2	KIND
039	2	ATTRACTIVE		094	2	MANNERS
040	2	HONESTY		095	2	FRIENDLY
041	2	GENTLENESS		096	2	INTEGRITY
042	2	CHARMING		097	2	FRIENDLY
043	2	KIND		098	2	FEMININE
044	2	GRACE		099	2	QUIETNESS
045	2	FUN		100	2	SINCERITY

COMPILATION OF A RESPONSE LIST

Program LISTA, which was written specifically for the sample of 200 data cards accomplishes three things: (1) it compiles a list of all different responses occurring in the sample along with their frequencies of occurrence; (2) it orders this response list in terms of the frequencies; and (3) it reorders the list according to the alphabetic similarity of the responses themselves. After each of these three stages, the program prints the complete list of responses and frequencies. The first-stage list is printed here only for illustrative purposes, but the lists yielded by stages two and three are useful to the researcher, particularly in the preparation of response categories. Stage one is included in the main body of Program LISTA. Stages two and three are written as subroutines which are called into operation by this main program.

STAGE ONE: LIST COMPILATION

Since data are ultimately converted to strings of binary digits before storage in the computer memory no matter which conversion system is used, we can operate upon the contents of memory locations holding alphabetic character codes as if they represent integer numbers. The key statement in Program LISTA is the logical IF before statement 10 which compares the two halves of the incoming response with a particular response in the compiled list. The question implied by the operator .EQ. is actually answered by integer subtraction even though the contents of both locations were originally stored by A-mode conversion (FORMAT 5).

The flow chart for this program reveals the essential simplicity of the compiling procedure. A list of responses and their frequencies is gradually built up in matrix LX; the index variable L indicates the length of the list—the number of significant rows in the matrix. Each subject's response is read in turn into KA and KB and is compared to each of the significant rows in the matrix. If an exact match is found in the list (columns two and three), the counter in column one is incremented. If none of the L responses in the list match KA and KB, the new response is added to the end of the list, incrementing L. After all subjects have been processed, the contents of the first L rows of LX are printed. Subroutine FORD is then called to reorder the list according to the response frequencies (column one of LX) and the list is again printed. Subroutine CORD is then called to reorder the list again according to the alphabetic content of the responses, and the list is printed once more. The final step in the program is the punching of the rows of LX, one per card, for later use in reducing the responses to word roots and group coding (Figure 13-1).

Since the data to be output are partially alphabetic, Subroutine PRTS cannot be used for this printing: the frequencies are integer mode anyway. To obtain a compact table we would like to output multiple columns, but for ease of reading we would like successive rows of LX to be arranged below one another in each column. After determining that we can print six columns of responses and their frequencies across the page, we need to compute the number of rows that will be necessary for a table of L responses. This turns out to be L/6 if L is exactly divisible by 6, and one more if it is not. It will be worthwhile to study the indexing of the DO loop and PRINT statement (30) which accomplishes the output of this table. The

Stage One: List Compilation 349

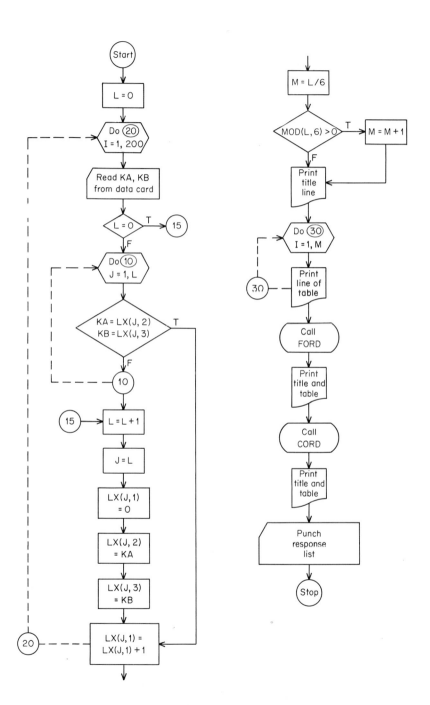

FIGURE 13-1. Flow chart for Program LISTA.

procedure is general in that it can be used for any multiple-column output problem of this type. Note that the output of the list in LX is accomplished by identical statements after frequency ordering and after content ordering, so a subroutine could have been written for this purpose.

Although all of the output from Program LISTA is, of course, printed continuously, we have included only the stage one table here. The frequency-ordered and content-ordered output lists will be included later with the descriptions of the subroutines that produced them. We have omitted the punched output listing, but the use of this card deck will be described later in this chapter.

```
C     PROGRAM LISTA
C
C     COMPILES LISTS OF RESPONSES AND FREQUENCIES. PRINTS LIST UNORDERED,
C       FREQUENCY-ORDERED, AND CONTENT-ORDERED, AND PUNCHES ONE PER CARD.
C     SUBROUTINE CCDS IS NOT USED IN THIS SPECIAL-PURPOSE PROGRAM, WHICH
C       WAS WRITTEN SPECIFICALLY FOR 200 SUBJECTS, ONE RESPONSE EACH, USI
C       THE DATA FORMAT GIVEN IN STATEMENT 5.
C     LX COL 1 = FREQUENCIES, COL 2-3 = TWO 6-CHARACTER RESPONSE PARTS.
C     L = NUMBER OF DIFFERENT RESPONSES IN COMPILED LIST (ROWS OF LX).
C
      DIMENSION LX(100,3)
      L = 0
C     BEGIN DATA INPUT.
      DO 20 I = 1,200
      READ 5, KA, KB
    5 FORMAT (6X, 2A6)
      IF (L .EQ. 0) GO TO 15
C     SEARCH LIST FOR MATCHING RESPONSE. IF NONE, ADD NEW RESPONSE TO LIST
      DO 10 J = 1,L
      IF (KA .EQ. LX(J,2) .AND. KB .EQ. LX(J,3)) GO TO 20
   10 CONTINUE
   15 L = L + 1
      J = L
      LX(J,1) = 0
      LX(J,2) = KA
      LX(J,3) = KB
C     RAISE FREQUENCY COUNTER FOR THE RESPONSE.
   20 LX(J,1) = LX(J,1) + 1
C     DETERMINE ROWS NEEDED FOR 6-COLUMN PRINTED LISTING OF LX.
      M = L / 6
      IF (MOD(L, 6) .GT. 0) M = M + 1
      PRINT 25, L
   25 FORMAT (18H1UNORDERED LIST OF, I3, 11H RESPONSES.)
      DO 30 I = 1,M
   30 PRINT 35, ((LX(J,K), K = 1,3), J = I,L,M)
   35 FORMAT (/ 6(I5, 1X, 2A6))
C     REORDER ROWS OF LX ACCORDING TO FREQUENCIES (COL 1).
      CALL FORD (LX, L)
      PRINT 40
   40 FORMAT (/// 24H1FREQUENCY-ORDERED LIST.)
      DO 45 I = 1,M
   45 PRINT 35, ((LX(J,K), K = 1,3), J = I,L,M)
C     REORDER ROWS OF LX ACCORDING TO ALPHABETIC CONTENT OF RESPONSES.
      CALL CORD (LX, L)
      PRINT 50
   50 FORMAT (/// 22H1CONTENT-ORDERED LIST.)
      DO 55 I = 1,M
   55 PRINT 35, ((LX(J,K), K = 1,3), J = I,L,M)
C     PUNCH RESPONSES ON SEPARATE CARDS FOR ROOT REDUCTION.
      PUNCH 60, ((LX(I,J), J = 1,3), I = 1,L)
   60 FORMAT (I5, 1X, 2A6)
      END
```

Stage One: List Compilation

```
*** PRINTED OUTPUT ***

1 UNORDERED LIST OF 80 RESPONSES.

16 PERSONALITY      1 UNDERSTANDAB    1 SPIRITUAL       1 MANNERED     2 SINCERE         1 FUN
 1 CONGENIALITY     3 PRETTY          1 MATURITY        1 SOFTNESS     2 CHEERFULNESS    1 COURTEOUS
 3 NEAT             1 THRIFT          1 TOLERANCE       4 KIND         2 POISE           1 GRACEFULNESS
 2 CUTE             1 APPEARANCES    10 FRIENDLINESS    4 FRIENDLY     2 POLITE          1 THOUGHTFUL
 3 HONEST           2 INTELLIGENT     1 LOVABLE         1 EYES         9 SINCERITY       1 WOMANLINESS
16 NEATNESS         1 POLITENESS      3 INTELLIGENCE    1 PLEASANT     2 LOYALTY         2 FEMININE
 5 LOOKS            1 TALL            1 LOVABLENESS     3 HUMOR        1 PUNCTUALITY     1 STEADFASTNES
 1 VIVACIOUS        1 RESPECT         1 SERIOUSNESS     1 CLOTHING     1 MODESTY         1 UNDERSTANDIN
 1 GOODLOOKING      2 CONSIDERATIO    1 FAITHFULNESS    1 LOOK         2 CHARMING        1 MANNERS
16 HONESTY          2 GENTLENESS      1 ABILITY         1 WIT          1 GOODATTITUDE    1 QUIETNESS
10 BEAUTY           4 ATTRACTIVE      3 APPEARANCE      2 VIRTUE       1 CHEEFULNESS
 2 ATTRACTIVENE     1 WARMTH          1 DEPENDABILIT    3 INTEGRITY    1 TALKATIVE
 1 TRUTH            1 GROOMING        1 BEAUTIFUL       4 CLEANLINESS  1 SIMPLICITY
 1 LOVE             1 GENIAL          6 KINDNESS        2 CHARM        1 GRACE
```

STAGE TWO: FREQUENCY ORDERING

Subroutine FORD is written in the simplest form possible to aid understanding of the method used. Many modifications could be made to increase its flexibility of application. For instance, addition of a variable-dimension argument would permit variations in the maximum length of the list stored in matrix LX. We arbitrarily set this at 100 here to suit the 200-subject problem we chose as an example. (As it happened, there were only 80 significant rows in LX.)

The two arguments to this subroutine are the name of the storage matrix (LX) and the number of significant rows (L). It is assumed that columns two and three contain the two halves of the 12-character alphabetic response

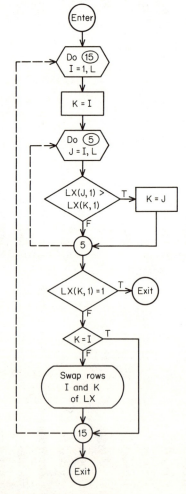

FIGURE 13-2. Flow chart for Subroutine FORD.

Stage Three: Alphabetic Content Ordering

field, while the frequencies of these responses are held in corresponding cells of column one in the LX matrix.

The frequency-ordering process is described graphically in Figure 13-2 and is summarized verbally as follows:

(1) set index variable I = 1
(2) find the highest frequency (cell K) in column one from cell I to L
(3) if the highest frequency is one, ordering is complete
(4) if the highest frequency is the same as that for response I, go to step (6)
(5) since the frequency of response K exceeds that of response I, *swap* the responses and frequencies in these two rows of LX
(6) raise index variable I and go to step (2)

Note that exit from the ordering process will occur whenever the remaining frequencies (from row I to row L) are all equal to one, since every response in the list must have a frequency of at least one. If no responses have a frequency of one, exit occurs when the DO 15 loop is satisfied.

STAGE THREE: ALPHABETIC CONTENT ORDERING

Subroutine CORD accomplishes this purpose with a procedure almost identical in general form to that of Subroutine FORD. There are certain crucial differences, however, that should be fully understood (Figure 13-3).

This procedure seeks to order the responses according to the similarity of their alphabetic content. The ordering achieved is less restrictive than alphabetization, but we are not really interested in that particular content order. We only want to obtain an ordering which gives the left-most characters greater importance in the ordering—just as the left-most digits are more heavily weighted in the rank-ordering of numeric quantities. We can achieve this goal by treating the contents of the cells of the second column of matrix LX *as if* they were integer-number representations.

It may have already occurred to you that the content ordering obtained would be true alphabetization if the BCD characters had numeric equivalents corresponding to the order of the alphabet. This is so except for one vital characteristic of the Fortran interpretive system for integer quantities which we must take into account in programming this ordering procedure.

We stated earlier that a memory location could hold an integer value no greater than $2^{35} - 1$. The reason why this maximum is not 2^{35} is that the left-most bit postion in the 36-bit word is not considered to be a part of the number, but instead is interpreted as its sign: 1 = negative, 0 = positive. When data are stored according to the 6-bit character codes of the A-mode BCD system, this interpretation of the first bit is not relevant. Whenever we interpret such a memory location as if it represented an integer number, however, the first bit of the six corresponding to the first letter of the response will determine whether the location is understood to be a positive or a negative value. By examining the tables of octal-binary-BCD equiva-

354 COMPILATION AND ANALYSIS OF VERBAL DATA

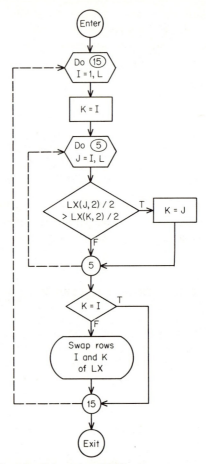

FIGURE 13-3. Flow chart for Subroutine CORD.

lents, you can see that any response beginning with a letter whose octal code is 40 or more will be treated as a negative integer value since the first bit position will contain a 1.

The reason that this complicates the content ordering process can be understood by considering what happens when two cells are interpreted as integer numbers having opposite signs. The comparison is carried out by sign-reversal and addition of the values, which will result in a value larger than the capacity of the computer for integer values. The high-order bits of this value will be lost, and half the time an incorrect decision will be made as to which of the two original cells held the larger integer number. Since the rank-ordering process depends on the accuracy of such decisions, we will not obtain the results we seek without resorting to some sleight-of-hand. We said earlier that decimal 2 = binary 10. Since division by 10 in any number system effectively *shifts* the digit string one place to the right without otherwise affecting it, we can move the contents of each cell the necessary one bit away from the sign bit by dividing it by integer 2 before making the comparison necessary to the ranking process.[1] These divisions are incorporated into the IF statement which compares contents of locations in column one of LX. In other respects this subroutine operates just as did Subroutine FORD, locating the highest value remaining in the list and swapping locations when necessary.

The alphabetic order of the final list produced by this routine depends on the computer used, since some machines employ a different system for coding alphabetic data into core storage. In any case, the ordering will be by alphabetic similarity as far as the fifth character of the response. The sixth character is not fully represented after the division by 2, which is a part of the ordering process. The ordering could be carried on into the second half of the responses, but this would complicate the procedure greatly. The interested reader might pursue this possibility.

Although not immediately apparent, the value of this content-ordering procedure far outweighs the difficulty of understanding it. With large samples of data which include many variants of common word roots, the reduction of the response list along the lines described in the last section of this chapter is greatly speeded if the list can be made available from the computer already ordered by alphabetic content. With multiple lists, each containing hundreds of responses, the sorting task is formidable, and often impractical if one must rely on the single-column card-sorting machine.

COMPILATION BY SUBLISTING

Compiling lists of different responses and their frequencies of occurrence is the most common and most expensive operation involved in quantitative analysis of verbal behavior data. For small samples of data the straightforward procedure implemented by Program LISTA is more efficient, since the simplicity of the routine compensates for the fact that the entire list of compiled responses must be searched for each new response. This method is also best for problems where the number of different responses is known to be small, even though the volume of data to be processed may be great.

As the length of the compiled list increases, the time required to search the list increases also, and in most practical applications which are large enough to require the use of a computer, the search time becomes prohibitive. The alternative procedure to be described in this section ordinarily requires additional storage locations and also involves more operations for each comparison of the new word with one from the compiled list, but huge savings in time are made possible by reducing the number of such comparisons for each new response that is processed. The basis for this method is the definition of *sublists* of responses which have some characteristic in common, such as number of characters or initial letter. The idea is to search for a match to a new word among the words in an appropriate sublist.

---

[1] This procedure will work only with computers which store data as binary numbers.

```fortran
      SUBROUTINE FORD (LX, L)
C
C     RE-ORDER ROWS OF TABLE LX ACCORDING TO FREQUENCIES (COL 1).
C
      DIMENSION LX(100,3)
      DO 15 I = 1,L
      K = I
C     LOCATE HIGHEST FREQUENCY IN COLUMN 1 OF LX.
      DO 5 J = I,L
      IF (LX(J,1) .GT. LX(K,1)) K = J
    5 CONTINUE
C     ORDERING IS COMPLETE IF HIGHEST FREQUENCY IS ONE.
      IF (LX(K,1) .EQ. 1) RETURN
      IF (K .EQ. I) GO TO 15
C     SWAP ROWS OF TABLE LX SO THAT ROW I HAS HIGHEST REMAINING FREQUENCY.
      DO 10 J = 1,3
      M = LX(I,J)
      LX(I,J) = LX(K,J)
   10 LX(K,J) = M
   15 CONTINUE
      RETURN
      END
```

*** PRINTED OUTPUT ***

1 FREQUENCY-ORDERED LIST.

16 PERSONALITY	3 INTELLIGENCE	2 POISE	1 MANNERED	1 GROOMING	1 FUN
16 NEATNESS	3 APPEARANCE	2 POLITE	1 SOFTNESS	1 GENIAL	1 COURTEOUS
16 HONESTY	3 NEAT	2 LOYALTY	1 THRIFT	1 SPIRITUAL	1 GRACEFULNESS
10 BEAUTY	3 HUMOR	2 CHARMING	1 RESPECT	1 MATURITY	1 THOUGHTFUL
10 FRIENDLINESS	3 INTEGRITY	2 FEMININE	1 EYES	1 CONGENIALITY	1 WOMANLINESS
9 SINCERITY	2 CONSIDERATIO	1 UNDERSTANDAB	1 PLEASANT	1 TOLERANCE	1 LOVABLE
6 KINDNESS	2 GENTLENESS	1 LOVABLENESS	1 APPEARANCES	1 PUNCTUALITY	1 STEADFASTNES
5 LOOKS	2 CUTE	1 SERIOUSNESS	1 CLOTHING	1 MODESTY	1 UNDERSTANDIN
4 ATTRACTIVE	2 VIRTUE	1 FAITHFULNESS	1 LOOK	1 LOVE	1 MANNERS
4 KIND	2 INTELLIGENT	1 ABILITY	1 WIT	1 GOODATTITUDE	1 QUIETNESS
4 FRIENDLY	2 ATTRACTIVENE	1 TRUTH	1 POLITENESS	1 CHEEFULNESS	
4 CLEANLINESS	2 CHARM	1 DEPENDABILIT	1 TALL	1 TALKATIVE	
3 PRETTY	2 SINCERE	1 BEAUTIFUL	1 GOODLOOKING	1 SIMPLICITY	
3 HONEST	2 CHEERFULNESS	1 VIVACIOUS	1 WARMTH	1 GRACE	

```
      SUBROUTINE CORD (LX, L)
C
C   RE-ORDER ROWS OF TABLE LX ACCORDING TO ALPHABETIC CONTENT OF RESPONSE (COL 2)
C
      DIMENSION LX(100,3)
      DO 15 I = 1,L
      K = I
C   LOCATE LARGEST INTEGER INTERPRETATION OF CONTENT IN COL 2.
C   DIVISION BY INTEGER 2 AVOIDS MISINTERPRETATION OF THE SIGN BIT.
      DO 5 J = I,L
      IF (LX(J,2) / 2 .GT. LX(K,2) / 2) K = J
    5 CONTINUE
C   SWAP ROWS OF TABLE LX, IF ROW I WORD DOES NOT HAVE HIGHEST INTEGER VALUE.
      IF (K .EQ. I) GO TO 15
      DO 10 J = 1,3
      M = LX(I,J)
      LX(I,J) = LX(K,J)
   10 LX(K,J) = M
   15 CONTINUE
      RETURN
      END
```

Subroutine CORD

```
*** PRINTED OUTPUT ***

1CONTENT-ORDERED LIST.
```

1 WIT	9 SINCERITY	1 GRACEFULNESS	2 ATTRACTIVENE	1 MATURITY
1 WARMTH	1 SIMPLICITY	1 GRACE	1 RESPECT	1 MODESTY
1 WOMANLINESS	1 SERIOUSNESS	1 GROOMING	1 CONGENIALITY	1 QUIETNESS	5 LOOKS
2 VIRTUE	1 SPIRITUAL	1 GOODATTITUDE	2 CONSIDERATIO	16 PERSONALITY	1 LOOK
1 VIVACIOUS	1 SOFTNESS	1 GOODLOOKING	1 COURTEOUS	3 PRETTY	2 LOYALTY
1 UNDERSTANDAB	1 STEADFASTNES	2 FEMININE	4 CLEANLINESS	2 POISE	1 LOVE
1 UNDERSTANDIN	3 INTEGRITY	1 FAITHFULNESS	1 CLOTHING	2 POLITE	1 LOVABLE
1 THRIFT	2 INTELLIGENT	10 FRIENDLINESS	2 CUTE	1 POLITENESS	1 LOVABLENESS
1 THOUGHTFUL	3 INTELLIGENCE	4 FRIENDLY	1 BEAUTIFUL	1 PLEASANT	6 KINDNESS
1 TALL	3 HONEST	1 FUN	10 BEAUTY	1 PUNCTUALITY	4 KIND
1 TALKATIVE	16 HONESTY	1 EYES	1 ABILITY	16 NEATNESS	
1 TRUTH	3 HUMOR	1 DEPENDABILIT	1 APPEARANCES	3 NEAT	
1 TOLERANCE	1 GENIAL	1 CHEEFULNESS	3 APPEARANCE	1 MANNERED	
2 SINCERE	2 GENTLENESS	2 CHEERFULNESS	4 ATTRACTIVE	1 MANNERS	

The procedure implemented by Program LISTB employs the initial character of the response as the basis for defining sublists. Since there are 26 possible initial characters, must we assign $\frac{1}{26}$ of the available memory to each sublist? Since the frequency of occurrence of some initial characters will be very small, and even zero for a few, so much space might be wasted that we would not have enough room for the sublists of words with the more common initial characters. We can avoid this problem altogether by borrowing a concept from the organization of list-processing languages such as IPL–V. The method in Program LISTB permits us to lengthen any sublist as it becomes necessary, while using all of the available memory.

The key to this method is the fact that responses included in a particular sublist are *not* stored in serial order in the computer memory. Rather, each response has an associated *link,* which is the location of the next word in its sublist. If the response is the last in the sublist, its link is zero. The location of the *first* response in a particular sublist is contained in one of a special set of 26 *key* cells. A key cell containing zero signifies an empty sublist. One more storage location is needed in the compilation of a set of data; this cell will hold the index value of the next available unused position in the available memory array. Every time a sublist must be lengthened to include a new response, this cell will be referenced and its value incremented.

PROGRAM LISTB

Program LISTB was written to illustrate the sublist method of compiling responses. It accomplishes the same thing as stage one of Program LISTA. The output includes the contents of the "key" cells as well as the "link" locations associated with each response in the compiled list, in addition to the responses and their frequencies of occurrence. The previous sample of 200 responses will be used to illustrate the operation of this routine.

Two arrays of storage locations are dimensioned. LX will contain the compiled response list, with responses in columns 2 and 3, frequencies in column 1, and links in column 4. The array KEY will contain the 26 possible initial alphabetic characters in column 1 and the row index numbers of the first locations of the sublists corresponding to these letters in column 2. The program begins by reading the 26 letters of the alphabet from a key card which precedes the data deck. A constant (KSF) is then defined which will result in a shift of the bit string of any memory location by 30 binary places (10 octal places or 5 characters) when it is used as a multiplier or divisor of the memory location concerned. This constant is then immediately employed to shift the single characters held in each of the 26 locations of KEY column 1 to the right ends of their respective memory cells. The corresponding cells of KEY column 2 are set at zero in this same loop. The zeroing of all sublist starting locations means simply that all sublists are empty before processing begins. The available-cell locator KX is next set at 1, indicating that the first row of matrix LX is available for lengthening a sublist with a new response (Figure 13-4).

Data input is controlled by the DO 50 loop using index variable I. The two 6-character halves of a subject's response are read into KA and KB, and the variable K is defined as KA shifted so as to isolate the first character of the response at the right end of the storage location. This location (K) is then compared with each of the cells of KEY column 1, and K is redefined as the contents of the corresponding cell in KEY column 2 when a match is found. If the initial character is not a letter of the alphabet, it is arbitrarily assigned to sublist 26 (Z).

The value K is then checked to determine whether the sublist concerned is empty (K = 0). If the sublist is empty, the appropriate cell of KEY is changed from zero to the value in KX, which will now be the first location in the sublist. Control then goes to the sequence which stores a new response. On the other hand, if K is not zero it is used as the row subscript for the cells in matrix LX which hold the first response in the appropriate sublist—the one containing responses which begin with the same character as does the new response in KA and KB. The contents of KA and KB are then compared to this response.

If this first comparison is unsuccessful, the link location LX(K, 4) is examined. If it is zero, the end of the sublist has been reached and this zero is replaced by the current value of KX, after which control goes to the sequence which stores a new response in the compiled list. If the link is not zero, K is changed to its value and another comparison of responses is carried out. If a comparison of KA and KB with a response from LX (statement 30) is successful, control goes directly to statement 50 which increments the frequency counter of the response in LX which was matched.

The sequence of steps for storage of a new response in the compiled list begins by setting K equal to the index stored in KX, which is the next available row of LX. KX is then incremented by one. The frequency counter is set at zero, the two halves of the alphabetic response are stored and the link cell is set to zero, since this is now the end of the sublist concerned. The response-frequency cell is then incremented to one, using the same statement employed after a successful match.

When all subjects have been processed, KX is reduced by one to serve as the length of the compiled list. It is interesting to note that the order of the responses in the final compiled response list will be the same with this method as with the one used in Program LISTA. This compiled list may now be reordered as before, either in terms of frequencies or of the alphabetic content of the responses.

We use the first character of the response as the basis for sublisting in this example. With a larger problems, it may be more economical to use the first *two* characters in combination. This would necessitate a KEY *matrix* of at least $26 \times 26 = 676$ cells and a somewhat more complicated method of determining the appropriate sublist for each new response. An apparent disadvantage of the sublisting method is the need for 33 percent more storage locations in the compiled-list matrix in order to accommodate the links. This drawback can be largely overcome by storing the links in the

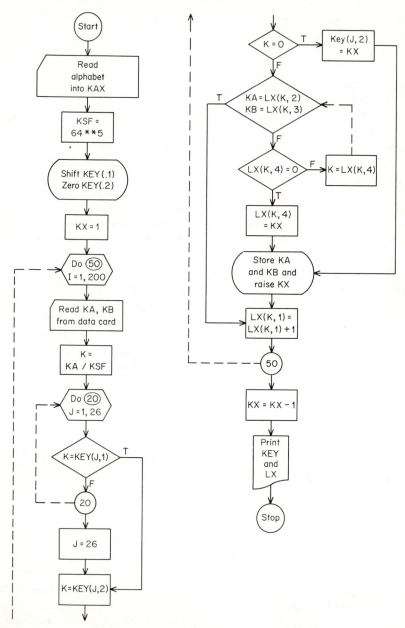

FIGURE 13-4. Flow chart for Program LISTB.

same locations used to hold the response frequencies. This may be achieved by converting the frequency and link (KF and KL) to a single value (KP) prior to storage, using the formula KP = KF(10000) + KL. The frequency would then occupy the higher-order digits in KP, while the link value would be contained in the lower-order four digits. These two values could then be decoded by the following statements wherever necessary:

$$KF = KP \ / \ 10000 \quad \text{and} \quad KL = MOD(KP, 10000)$$

Again, we want to emphasize the fact that the routines presented in this chapter are not intended to be general-purpose programs for verbal-data processing. They were written specifically for the example problem in order to facilitate understanding of the procedures. As you encounter practical research problems of this kind, you will incorporate refinements and extensions of the methods described here into your programs.

```
C     PROGRAM LISTB
C
C     LIST COMPILATION BY MEANS OF SUB-LISTING.
C     LX COL 1 = FREQUENCIES. COL 2,3 = RESPONSE HALVES. COL 4 = LINKS.
C     KAX = LETTERS OF ALPHABET, AS READ FROM KEY CARD.
C     KEY COL 1 = LETTERS OF ALPHABET, RIGHT-SHIFTED.
C         COL 2 = SUBLIST STARTING INDEX VALUES (ROWS IN LX)
C     KEY CARD CONTAINING ALPHABET IN COLUMN 1-26 IS READ BEFORE DATA DECK.
C
      DIMENSION LX(100,4), KEY(26,2), KAX(26)
      READ 5, KAX
    5 FORMAT (26A1)
      KSF = 64**5
C     SHIFT LETTERS TO RIGHT ENDS OF LOCATIONS AND ZERO KEY INDEX CELLS.
      DO 10 I = 1,26
      KEY(I,1) = KAX(I) / KSF
   10 KEY(I,2) = 0
      KX = 1
      DO 50 I = 1,200
C     READ ONE RESPONSE AND DETERMINE APPROPRIATE SUBLIST.
      READ 15, KA, KB
   15 FORMAT (6X, 2A6)
      K = KA / KSF
      DO 20 J = 1,26
      IF (K .EQ. KEY(J,1)) GO TO 25
   20 CONTINUE
      J = 26
   25 K = KEY(J,2)
C     COMPARE RESPONSES IN SUBLIST TO KA AND KB.
      IF (K .EQ. 0) GO TO 35
   30 IF (KA .EQ. LX(K,2) .AND. KB .EQ. LX(K,3)) GO TO 50
      IF (LX(K,4) .EQ. 0) GO TO 40
      K = LX(K,4)
      GO TO 30
C     RESET KEY OR LINK IF NECESSARY, AND ADD NEW RESPONSE TO LIST.
   35 KEY(J,2) = KX
      GO TO 45
   40 LX(K,4) = KX
   45 K = KX
      KX = KX + 1
      LX(K,1) = 0
      LX(K,2) = KA
      LX(K,3) = KB
      LX(K,4) = 0
C     RAISE FREQUENCY COUNTER FOR THE RESPONSE.
   50 LX(K,1) = LX(K,1) + 1
      KX = KX - 1
C     PRINT CONTENTS OF KEY AND LX.
      OPRINT 55, KX, KAX, (KEY(I,2), I = 1,26),
     1 ((LX(I,J), J = 1,4), I = 1,KX)
   55 FORMAT (1H1 / I5, 21H DIFFERENT RESPONSES. // 13H FIRST LETTER,
     1 3X, 26A3 // 14H SUBLIST START, 26I3 /// 20H FREQUENCY RESPONSE,
     2 6X, 4HLINK / 1X / (I7, 5X, 2A6, I5))
      STOP
      END
```

*** PRINTED OUTPUT ***

1 80 DIFFERENT RESPONSES.

FIRST LETTER	A	B	C	D	E	F	G	H	I	J	K	L	M	N	O	P	Q	R	S	T	U	V	W	X	Y	Z
SUBLIST START	12	11	2	40	47	32	9	5	19	0	42	7	30	3	0	1	80	22	29	13	15	8	26	0	0	0

FREQUENCY	RESPONSE	LINK
16	PERSONALITY	16
1	CONGENIALITY	4
3	NEAT	6
2	CUTE	23
3	HONEST	10
16	NEATNESS	0
5	LOOKS	14
1	VIVACIOUS	53
1	GOODLOOKING	24
16	HONESTY	49
10	BEAUTY	41
2	ATTRACTIVENE	18
1	TRUTH	17
1	LOVE	33
3	UNDERSTANDAB	78
1	PRETTY	20
1	THRIFT	21
1	APPEARANCES	25
2	INTELLIGENT	34
1	POLITENESS	48
1	TALL	31
1	RESPECT	0
2	CONSIDERATIO	50
2	GENTLENESS	27
4	ATTRACTIVE	38
1	WARMTH	52
1	GROOMING	28
1	GENIAL	66
1	SPIRITUAL	36
1	MATURITY	43
1	TOLERANCE	68
10	FRIENDLINESS	37
1	LOVABLE	35

1	FAITHFULNESS	46
1	ABILITY	39
3	APPEARANCE	0
1	DEPENDABILIT	0
1	BEAUTIFUL	0
6	KINDNESS	45
1	MANNERED	64
1	SOFTNESS	57
4	KIND	0
4	FRIENDLY	71
1	EYES	0
1	PLEASANT	59
3	HUMOR	0
1	CLOTHING	55
1	LOOK	62
1	WIT	75
1	VIRTUE	0
2	INTEGRITY	0
3	CLEANLINESS	56
4	CHARM	58
2	SINCERE	61
2	CHEERFULNESS	65
2	POISE	60
2	POLITE	63
2	SINCERITY	69
9	LOYALTY	0
2	PUNCTUALITY	79
1	MODESTY	79
1	CHARMING	67
2	GOODATTITUDE	70
1	CHEEFULNESS	72
1	TALKATIVE	74
1	SIMPLICITY	77
1	GRACE	73
1	FUN	76
1	COURTEOUS	0
1	GRACEFULNESS	0
1	THOUGHTFUL	0
1	WOMANLINESS	0
2	FEMININE	0
1	STEADFASTNES	0
1	UNDERSTANDIN	0
1	MANNERS	0
1	QUIETNESS	0

RESPONSE GROUPING

Data obtained from choice-response instruments are classified automatically by the format of the questions themselves, which restrict the subject to a set of supplied alternatives. Constructed responses, on the other hand, are much more differentiated than is appropriate for any particular research purpose, and some kind of reduction or classification system is necessary to prepare the data for quantitative analysis. Four levels of response equivalence may be identified: (1) literal, (2) syntactic, (3) semantic, and (4) pragmatic.[2]

The LISTA and LISTB Programs achieve response grouping at the *literal* level, where responses are equated only if they are identical on a character-by-character basis. Even the accidental inclusion of a misspelling (CHEEFULNESS) results in a separate entry, however, and most investigators would require more reduction than is achieved at this level of equivalence.

At the *syntactic* level of grouping, grammatical variants of the same word roots would be equated. For instance, the responses SINCERE and SINCERITY would be considered the same at this level. The problem is one of defining a set of word *roots* and a method for systematically reducing responses with variant endings to these root forms. The technique programmed as Subroutine ROOT, which will be discussed later in this chapter, accomplishes this by matching a response to various roots character by character for as many characters as are contained in the root. If a match is found, the response is considered to be a variant of the root that was matched. This method requires careful selection of word roots to permit identification of possible variants. For instance, the root word LOVE would be entered in the root dictionary as LOV so that variants such as LOVING and LOVABLE would be equated as well as such forms as LOVED and LOVES.

At the third level, *semantic* equivalence, we are concerned with the *meanings* of the various responses—specifically, with the meanings they held for the subjects who used them. At this level we might wish to consider responses such as *beauty, attractive,* and *pretty* to be equivalent in meaning—that is, equivalent in the sense that the subjects who gave these responses *probably* would consider the terms synonymous. The word "probably" is of particular importance here, since semantic equivalencing may be carried to various lengths, and the more general the categories, the more uncertainty will arise regarding the synonymity of the responses included within the categories.

The semantic equivalence of a group of responses could be established empirically by special instructions to respond with two or three synonyms

---

[2] This notion of levels of verbal similarity was suggested by the work of Charles Morris (1946). See also Osgood (1957, p. 3) for a lucid discussion of the problem of meaning.

to each question, but the cost of such studies is usually prohibitive.[3] At more conservative levels of response grouping an investigator's intuition is not likely to be far wrong, but the use of relatively broad categories may be expected to combine a considerable variety of subjects' intentions within sets of responses which are to be assumed equivalent—often leading to such heterogenity as to make subgroup differentiation quite unlikely. There is no completely satisfactory basis for deciding upon an optimum degree of grouping, except as trial and error may yield empirical evidence in particular research applications.

The fourth level is called *pragmatic* equivalence because some particular external criterion is used as the basis for decisions about the similarity of responses; in other words, responses are equated to achieve a particular purpose. As an example of this kind of response analysis, let us suppose that for each of the responses classified at a lower level we can determine the proportion of males who give that response. We could then classify each response as a "male" or "female" indicator, or we could use the porportion as an index value in order to classify the responses as *very likely male, likely male, uncertain, likely female,* or *very likely female.* In either case we can ignore the content of the responses and classify them only in terms of their empirically established significance for predicting a particular criterion (biological sex of the subject, in this example). The SCORE Program to be discussed later actually carries out an analysis yielding results of this kind.

It is worth noticing here that a clinical psychologist who says to himself in the course of interpreting a sentence-completion test, "This is a hostile kind of response," is actually making use of an implicit response-grouping system on this fourth level. The clinician's basis for considering certain responses as hostile is *not* to be found necessarily in the subject's intentions; the responses may not be synonyms at all. The clinician equates them under the heading "hostile" because his experience leads him to believe that persons who give such responses tend to be alike in a particular way—and that their behavior is predictable to some degree greater than chance.

Unique Responses. A major consideration in grouping responses is the fate of low-frequency words, especially those which are unique within a normative sample of subjects. Some of these may be identified as grammatical variants of common-response roots, or they may be equated to common responses at a relatively low level of semantic classification. Others represent virtually unique reactions to the stimulus, and demand careful consideration in the construction of an objective system of response

---

[3] Borko (1965) has reported the use of factor analysis to cluster key words extracted from titles in the psychological literature. Such procedures, however, are more nearly appropriate to what we are calling the pragmatic level of response equivalence.

grouping. The problem is that when pragmatic analysis methods are used, the low-frequency responses (or categories) will have little to contribute to the objective system since their low probabilities of occurrence make it very difficult to establish reliable weights.

We encounter here the basic distinction between art and science in psychological assessment. The clinician makes much of the truly unique responses in forming his internal analog of a subject's personality, since rare responses usually signify potent dispositions or concerns. An objective assessment system which is developed empirically, however, can do nothing with these same responses because of their very uniqueness. A promising avenue toward maximum efficiency in psychological assessment would appear to be the use of a two-stage process: the computer would be instructed to do its best with the common responses of a given subject, using empirically derived weights based on large normative samples. The machine would then return its preliminary findings to the clinician along with a list of unique responses. The clinician would fit the unique data into the tentative pattern prepared by the computer in order to construct a final summary report. In this way the computer would serve as a kind of screening device, providing the clinician with the results of a set of standard "laboratory" tests to be considered in arriving at a final diagnosis. Without some kind of man-machine interchange of this type, which combines the objectivity of automated comparisons against norms with the synthesizing ability of the human judge, the efficiency of psychological assessment is not likely to rise significantly above its present plateau.

Example of Reduction to Word Roots. On a following page is shown the content-ordered list of responses produced by Program LISTA, marked to indicate alterations which will yield a list of root forms. Note that many of the entries in this list can be eliminated entirely. The circled portions of other responses are to be removed as the root list is repunched. Many of these alterations are unnecessary as long as we intend to deal only with the present sample of 200 cases, but we have indicated the kind of root list one might wish to use with a cross-validation sample to maximize the likelihood of picking up variations not yet encountered.

Note that the misspelled word CHEEFULNESS has been eliminated from the root dictionary, even though it will not be picked up by the root CHEER. The purpose of the root dictionary is to provide a minimum list of basic response forms against which any person's protocol may be compared. As a general policy, idiosyncratic data errors in the normative sample should not be included.

The final form of the root dictionary is shown on a following page as it is entered to the SCORE Program. Since the frequencies are no longer appropriate, they were removed from the cards output by Program LISTA when those cards were revised.

We have also *added* numeric codes to the cards holding the root-word

1 CONTENT-ORDERED LIST.

9 ~~SINCERITY~~	1 ~~GRACEFULNESS~~	2 ~~CHARMING~~	2 ~~ATTRACTIVENE~~	1 MATUR(ITY)
1 WIT				
1 WARM(TH)	1 SIMPL(ICITY)	1 GRACE	2 CHARM	1 RESPECT	1 MODEST(Y)
1 WOMANLI(NESS)	1 SERIOUS(NESS)	1 GROOM(ING)	1 CONGEMIAL(ITY)	1 QUIET(NESS)	5 ~~LOOKS~~
2 VIRTU(E)	1 SPIRITUAL	1 GOODATTITUDE	2 CONSIDERAT(IO)	16 PERSONALITY	1 LOOK
1 VIVACI(OUS)	1 SOFT(NESS)	1 GOODLOOK(ING)	1 COURTE(OUS)	3 PRETT(Y)	2 LOYAL(TY)
1 UNDERSTAND(AB)	1 STEADFAST(NES)	2 FEMININ(E)	4 CLEAN(LINESS)	2 POISE	1 LOVE(E)
1 ~~UNDERSTANDIN~~	3 INTEGRITY	1 FAITHFUL(NESS)	1 CLOTH(ING)	2 POLITE	1 ~~LOVABLE~~
1 THRIFT	2 ~~INTELLIGENT~~	10 ~~FRIENDLINESS~~	2 CUTE	1 ~~POLITENESS~~	1 ~~LOVABLENESS~~
1 THOUGHTFUL	3 INTELLIGEN(CE)	4 FRIEND(LY)	1 ~~BEAUTIFUL~~	1 PLEASANT	6 ~~KINDNESS~~
1 TALL	3 HONEST	1 FUN	10 BEAUT(Y)	1 PUNCTUAL(ITY)	4 KIND
1 TALK(ATIVE)	16 ~~HONESTY~~	1 EYES	1 ABILI(TY)	16 ~~NEATNESS~~	
1 TRUTH	3 HUMOR	1 DEPENDABI(LIT)	1 ~~APPEARANCES~~	3 NEAT	
1 TOLERAN(CE)	1 GENIAL	1 ~~CHEERFULNESS~~	3 APPEARANCE	1 ~~MANNERED~~	
2 SINCER(E)	2 GENTLE(NESS)	2 CHEERFUL(NESS)	4 ATTRACT(IVE)	1 MANNER(S)	

forms. These represent categories of content based on a semantic equivalence system developed by the author. These categories were *not* a product of machine analysis, but rather represent only one of many possible classifications of the response content which could have been invented. Human judgment is unavoidable at this stage of the processing.

1. sociability
2. warmth
3. character
4. manners
5. attractiveness
6. grooming
7. capability
8. sex role

The input deck of root cards has been sorted according to their category-code numbers to assist identification of the specific contents. The output from Program SCORE refers to these eight categories only by number.

PROGRAM SCORE

Program SCORE, like Programs LISTA and LISTB, was written specifically for the 200-subject example problem, and is not intended to serve as a general routine for verbal data processing. It illustrates three important processes commonly employed in research with verbal data: (1) reduction of responses to basic root forms, (2) conversion of root-forms to semantic-level category codes, and (3) comparison of subsamples of subjects for usage of content categories.

Input to the program is a series of cards containing root-forms and the content-category codes assigned to them, followed by the original data deck containing the responses of the 200 subjects. These data cards contain criterion group numbers in column 5 (1 = male, 2 = female). This information is used by the program in compiling frequencies of usage for each criterion group of subjects for each content category.

After input of a control card holding the number of roots (NR), number of response categories (NC), and a blank field (MM), the root-form dictionary is stored in matrix LR. The two halves of each root are stored in columns 2 and 3, and the corresponding category codes are stored in column 4. The constant KK is next derived from MM; this constant is used only by Function LGTH. The lengths of each of the roots (number of characters) are then determined by calling the Function Subprogram LGTH, and are stored in the appropriate cells of column 1 of this matrix. After zeroing the category-usage counters (matrix F), input of subject data is begun (Figure 13-5).

Each subject's response is sent to Function LGTH, to determine its length and then Subroutine ROOT is called to search the root dictionary for a match, if one can be achieved. This matching is carried out for only as many characters as are contained in each root concerned.

If a match is obtained in the ROOT Subroutine, the returned index value

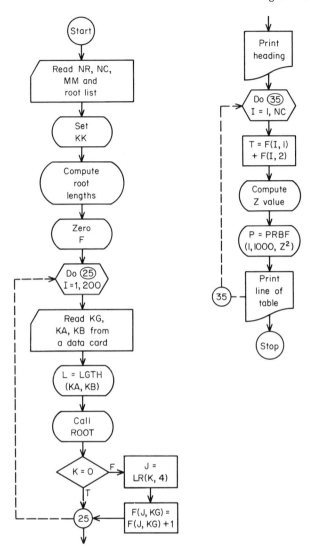

FIGURE 13-5. Flow chart for Program SCORE.

K will be nonzero and the corresponding category code for this root is picked up and used as the row index for incrementing a frequency-counter cell in matrix F. After all subjects have been processed, the frequency data are used to compute significance tests of the differences in category usage by the male and female subsamples.

Criterion Analysis. The usual goal in research employing content analysis of verbal data is the detection of particular kinds of group differences in response tendencies. The research may be exploratory, as exemplified by the problem we are using in this chapter as a demonstration, or it may involve the testing of pre-established hypotheses. Exploratory studies usually require a semantic-level grouping of responses before comparing various subsamples. Hypothesis testing, on the other hand, usually requires response grouping at the pragmatic level, in which categories are derived from theoretical considerations instead of emerging from inspection of the data.

A typical hypothesis-testing problem would be the comparison of groups of subjects who have been identified as representing opposite extremes on some continuum of interest, such as college grades or anxiety. Responses would be classified according to theoretical considerations relevant to the criterion to be predicted. If the two extreme criterion groups could be discriminated successfully by the categorized responses, the hypothesized relationship between the theory applied to the categorization of the responses and that which led to criterion-group selection would be supported.

Significance Test. The example problem of this chapter is typical of exploratory applications of content analysis. The criterion groups to be compared are males and females, represented by the first and second sets of 100 data cards, and by the first and second columns of matrix F in Program SCORE. The third stage of this program seeks to detect differences between the males and females in the frequencies with which they use each category of responses. For instance, are terms in category one (*sociability*) used more often by males or females in response to the basic question, "What do you like in a woman?"

Tests of the significance of the observed differences between frequencies in the rows of table F are computed by means of the following formula, which yields a z score, which is sent to Subroutine PRBF, which returns the probability that the observed difference occurred only by chance.

$$z = \frac{[2f_M - f_T] - 1}{\sqrt{f_T}}$$

where f_M is the frequency among males (column 1 of matrix F) and f_T is the total number of such responses (column 1 + column 2).

Before we consider the LGTH and ROOT routines, let us examine the results output by Program SCORE for the example problem, which appear after the input deck listing. Two of the eight response categories produced significant sex differences: category 5, *attractiveness,* was used 26 times by males but only five times by females. Also, category 7, *capability,* was used exclusively by males. Although significant only at the 10 percent level of confidence, categories 3, *character,* and 4, *manners,* were favored by female subjects. Note that the sum of the total frequencies is 199 rather than 200, because the misspelling CHEEFULNESS was not located in the root list.

Program SCORE

```
C     PROGRAM SCORE
C
C     CONVERT RAW DATA TO RESPONSE-CATEGORY CODES, AND DETERMINE SUB-SAMPLE
C        DIFFERENCES IN USAGE OF CATEGORIES.
C     INPUT OF WORD-ROOTS PRE-CODED FOR RESPONSE CATEGORIES (LR) IS ASSUMED.
C     OUTPUT INCLUDES CHANCE PROBABILITY OF EACH OBSERVED CATEGORY DIFFERENCE.
C     INPUT CONTROL CARD WITH NUMBER OF ROOTS, NUMBER OF CATEGORIES,
C        AND A BLANK FIELD. READ ROOTS NEXT INTO COL 2-3 OF LR AND CATEGORY
C        NUMBERS INTO COL 4. THEN READ AND PROCESS DATA CARDS.
C     REQUIRES SUBPROGRAM PRBF, IN ADDITION TO ROOT AND LGTH.
C
      DIMENSION LR(100,4), F(25,2)
      READ 5, NR, NC, MM, ((LR(I,J), J = 2,4), I = 1,NR)
    5 FORMAT (2I5, A6 / (6X, 2A6, I7))
C     STORE ROOT LENGTHS IN COL 1 OF LR, AND ZERO CATEGORY-USAGE COUNTERS.
C     COLUMNS OF F ARE FOR THE TWO SUBSAMPLES.
      KK = IABS(MOD(MM, 64))
      DO 10 I = 1,NR
   10 LR(I,1) = LGTH(LR(I,2), LR(I,3), MM, KK)
      DO 15 I = 1,NC
      F(I,1) = 0.0
   15 F(I,2) = 0.0
C     BEGIN DATA-CARD INPUT, REDUCTION, AND CATEGORY-USE COUNTING.
C     COL 5 OF DATA CARDS HOLDS GROUP NUMBER (KG).
      DO 25 I = 1,200
      READ 20, KG, KA, KB
   20 FORMAT (4X, I1, 1X, 2A6)
C     DETERMINE LENGTH OF WORD, ROOT CODE, AND CATEGORY NUMBER.
      L = LGTH(KA, KB, MM, KK)
      CALL ROOT (K, LR, NR, KA, KB, L)
      IF (K .EQ. 0) GO TO 25
      J = LR(K,4)
      F(J,KG) = F(J,KG) + 1.0
   25 CONTINUE
C     PRINT TABLE OF CATEGORY USAGE BY SUBSAMPLES, WITH
C        ASSOCIATED PROBABILITIES.
      PRINT 30
   30 FORMAT (31H1CAT.   TOTAL    GP.1    GP.2          P)
      DO 35 I = 1,NC
      T = F(I,1) + F(I,2)
      Z = AMAX1(0.0, (ABS(2.0 * F(I,1) - T) - 1.0) / SQRT(T))
      P = PRBF(1.0, 1000.0, Z * Z)
   35 PRINT 40, I, T, F(I,1), F(I,2), P
   40 FORMAT (/ I4, 2F7.0, F6.0, F9.4)
      STOP
      END
```

(Each printed line below contains content from two nonconsecutive data cards.)

*** INPUT DATA DECK ***

```
0006200008
          PERSONALITY     1        CONSIDERAT      2
          HUMOR           1        GENTLE          2
          FRIEND          1        SOFT            2
          CHARM           1        WARM            2
          CHEER           1        TOLERAN         2
          VIVACI          1        LOV             2
          PLEASANT        1        UNDERSTAND      2
          WIT             1        SIMPL           2
          GENIAL          1        THOUGHTFUL      2
          CONGENIAL       1        HONEST          3
          GOODATTITUDE    1        SINCER          3
          TALK            1        INTEGRITY       3
          FUN             1        VIRTU           3
          KIND            2        LOYAL           3
```

COMPILATION AND ANALYSIS OF VERBAL DATA

SERIOUS	3		CUTE	5
STEADFAST	3		EYES	5
FAITHFUL	3		TALL	5
TRUTH	3		NEAT	6
DEPENDAB	3		CLEAN	6
THRIFT	3		APPEARANCE	6
SPIRITUAL	3		CLOTH	6
MATUR	3		GROOM	6
PUNCTUAL	3		INTELLIGEN	7
POLITE	4		ABILIT	7
MANNER	4		FEMININ	8
RESPECT	4		WOMANL	8
MODEST	4	001 1	PERSONALITY	
COURTE	4	002 1	CONGENIALITY	
QUIET	4	003 1	NEAT	
POISE	4	004 1	CUTE	
GRACE	4	005 1	HONEST	
BEAUT	5	006 1	NEATNESS	
LOOK	5	007 1	LOOKS	
GOODLOOK	5	008 1	VIVACIOUS	
ATTRACT	5	009 1	PERSONALITY	
PRETT	5	010 1	GOODLOOKING	

*** LAST 190 DATA CARDS OMITTED ***

*** PRINTED OUTPUT ***

CAT.	TOTAL	GP.1	GP.2	P
1	47.	22.	25.	0.7680
2	24.	13.	11.	0.8327
3	46.	17.	29.	0.1010
4	13.	3.	10.	0.0923
5	31.	26.	5.	0.0006
6	29.	13.	16.	0.7119
7	6.	6.	0.	0.0389
8	3.	0.	3.	0.2469

FUNCTION LGTH (KA, KB, MM, KK)

The purpose of this routine is to determine the number of nonblank characters in the response or root sent as arguments KA and KB. Two additional arguments holding necessary constants are also sent to the routine: MM contains six blank characters, while KK holds the code for a single blank character in its rightmost six bits, which are preceded by zeros.

The routine begins by setting the maximum length LGTH as six characters and the variable KX equal to KA. KB is then compared to MM to determine whether it contains only blanks; if not, LGTH is reset to 12 and KX is equated to KB. The rest of the routine examines the characters in KX from right to left until it comes to a nonblank character. Every time a

Function LGTH 375

blank is encountered in this loop, the value of LGTH is reduced by one and KX is shifted right by one character for the next test. Thus, the comparison is always made on the rightmost six bits. When a nonblank is reached, LGTH is the needed value and control is returned to the calling routine (Figure 13-6).

In order to compare only on the last character in KK and KX, the first five characters are "masked" by the use of the absolute function IABS and the MOD function of 64_{10} ($100_8 = 1000000_2$). The *remainder* after division by this value will be the numeric equivalent of the rightmost character code. This same conversion was used in the SCORE Program to derive KK from MM. The absolute value of the remainder is required because KA or KB may sometimes hold a character in the first position which exceeds 37_8, producing a "negative sign bit" that would interfere with the comparisons.

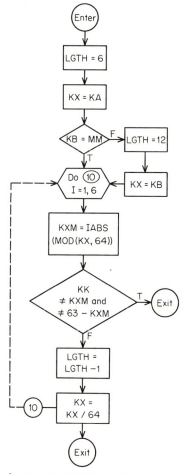

FIGURE 13-6. Flow chart for Function LGTH.

The absolute value is also obtained in deriving KK, because some computers do not code a blank as 20_g.

The second half of the major IF statement is necessary only with computers such as the CDC 1604 which store negative numbers in complement form. Other machines such as the IBM 7040 store all values in positive form, and the IABS function suffices to make the signs of KK and KXM consistent for each comparison.

```
      FUNCTION LGTH (KA, KB, MM, KK)
C
C  DETERMINE NUMBER OF LETTERS IN RESPONSE LEFT-JUSTIFIED
C     IN TWO SIX-CHARACTER LOCATIONS (KA AND KB).
C  MM = ALL BLANKS
C  KK = SINGLE BLANK IN SIXTH CHARACTER POSITION
C
      LGTH = 6
      KX = KA
      IF (KB .EQ. MM) GO TO 5
      LGTH = 12
      KX = KB
    5 DO 10 I = 1,6
      KXM = IABS(MOD(KX, 64))
      IF (KXM .NE. KK .AND. 63 - KXM .NE. KK) RETURN
      LGTH = LGTH - 1
   10 KX = KX / 64
      RETURN
      END
```

SUBROUTINE ROOT (K, LR, N, KA, KB, L)

Like the LGTH routine, this one was written specifically for the example problem of this chapter, but it could be modified easily for other problems, or incorporated into the body of another program. The location K is returned holding the row index in LR of the root matched to the input response (KA, KB). If no matching root can be located, K is returned with a zero value. Note that this routine could have been written in the form of a function subprogram instead of a subroutine, using an integer name for the routine, which would take the place of argument K.

The outside loop (20) sequences comparison of the input response with each root in matrix LR until a match is found. The first step in each comparison is to determine whether the length of the root exceeds, equals, or is less than that of the response. The length of the response is sent as argument L, while root lengths are available in column one of matrix LR. If the root is longer than the response, a match is impossible and control goes to statement 20. If the root and response are the same length, statement 5 checks for the exact match which would be required. If the response length exceeds that of the root, a character by character matching of root and response is conducted for as many characters as are contained in the *root*. Thus, if the first LR(K, 1) letters of the root and response are identical, the remaining characters of the response are ignored, and a match is assumed.

This matching process is done either in the first or second half of the response and root, depending on the root length. If the length of the root is not an exact multiple of 6, the contents of the locations to be compared are temporarily shifted to the right by integer division to allow comparison only on the required characters at the left ends of the original locations concerned (Figure 13-7).

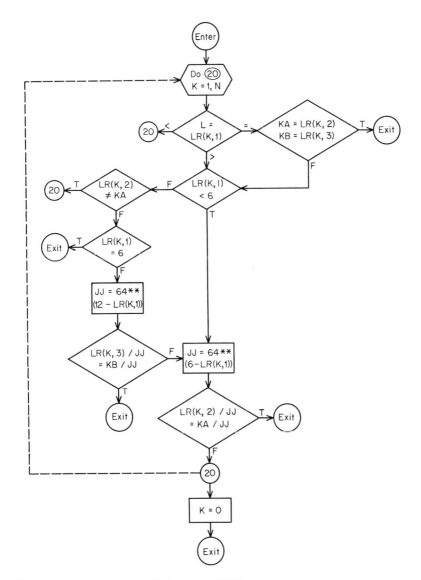

FIGURE 13-7. Flow chart for Subroutine ROOT.

378 COMPILATION AND ANALYSIS OF VERBAL DATA

```
      SUBROUTINE ROOT (K, LR, N, KA, KB, L)
C
C     DETERMINE ROW NUMBER OF MATCHING ROOT, IF ANY.
C     K = RETURNED AS ROW INDEX SOUGHT. ZERO IF NO MATCH IS FOUND.
C     LR = TABLE OF ROOTS (COL 2-3) AND THEIR LENGTHS (COL 1).
          (COL 4 IRRELEVANT)
C     N = NUMBER OF ROOTS (ROWS OF LR).
C     KA,KB = TWO 6-CHARACTER PARTS OF WORD TO BE MATCHED.
C     L = LENGTH OF WORD TO BE MATCHED.
C
      DIMENSION LR(100,4)
      DO 20 K = 1,N
C     COMPARE LENGTH OF WORD TO THAT OF ROOT K. IF LESS, DO NOT MATCH. IF
C     SAME, COMPARE DIRECTLY. IF MORE, COMPARE CHARACTERS OF ROOT ONLY.
      IF (L - LR(K,1)) 20,5,10
    5 IF (KA .EQ. LR(K,2) .AND. KB .EQ. LR(K,3)) RETURN
      GO TO 20
   10 IF (LR(K,1) .LT. 6) GO TO 15
C     COMPARE CHARACTERS OF ROOT IN FIRST PART, WHEN .GE. 6.
      IF (LR(K,2) .NE. KA) GO TO 20
      IF (LR(K,1) .EQ. 6) RETURN
C     COMPARE CHARACTERS OF ROOT IN SECOND PART, WHEN LONGER THAN 6.
      JJ = 64**(12 - LR(K,1))
      IF (LR(K,3) / JJ .EQ. KB / JJ) RETURN
      GO TO 20
C     COMPARE CHARACTERS OF ROOT IN FIRST PART, WHEN SHORTER THAN 6.
   15 JJ = 64**(6 - LR(K,1))
      IF (LR(K,2) / JJ .EQ. KA / JJ) RETURN
   20 CONTINUE
      K = 0
      RETURN
      END
```

Extensions of the Root System. The most obvious weakness of the system described here is encountered with negation endings such as *less*, which cannot be removed without radically changing the semantic import of the roots to which they are attached. Another weakness of the system is that it cannot recognize roots preceded by common prefixes such as *in*, *semi*, *un*, or words such as *be*, *to*, *very*. Here also, negation prefixes would have to be handled differently from others which do not alter the semantic significance of the roots.

Root-reduction systems have been implemented that can handle these problems, but their complexity is beyond the scope of this book. The example used in this chapter also fails to demonstrate the rather subtle difficulties one encounters in deciding upon the best root form to include in the dictionary. If too many characters are included in the root, its inclusiveness may be severely restricted. If too few characters are used, the root will be equated by the system to many semantically dissimilar responses, which then must be added to the dictionary as exceptions.

The root-form approach, then, is not a perfect answer to the problem of grammatical variants. Because of the inconsistency of the English language and the varied purposes to which verbal data may be applied, no perfect answer to these problems will ever emerge. All we can hope to achieve is automation of as much of the reduction process as can be systematized. In every problem a certain residual of decisions will have to be made by the researcher himself. It is important to remember that any systematization of observed behavior—including "objective" personality inventories—ultimately rests upon the same sort of basis in human judgment.

Review Exercise

Write a program which will accept straight narrative text punched on tab cards, break the stream of input characters into separate words, and compile a list of all different words and their frequencies for a sample of any size.

Reserve columns 1-5 on each tab card for ID coding and card number within the sample series. Use a blank character as a word separator, and assume all nonalphabetic characters have been removed from the text. Also assume that no words will be split between successive cards.

Hint: input the data in A1 format, and store the words as series of 10-location rows in a memory matrix. Provide for ignoring extra characters of words longer than 10.

answers to review exercises

Chapter 1. Introduction to Computer Systems

1. See Figure 1-1.
2. Items a–f are mentioned in the text. *Telegraph* transmission is digital in nature, since the code consists of discrete impulses of two durations. The *thermostat* is an analog-to-digital converter; when the physical state of the temperature-registering device reaches a particular breakpoint, an electrical switch is thrown from one to the other of two possible states.
3. As indicated in the section on computer history, a number of different answers are possible, depending on how the term "computer" is defined.
4. Input: a, b, c, e, g, h, l.
   Output: a, b, c, e, g, i, j, k.
   Storage: c, d, e, f.
5. See text for description and a few projections.

Chapter 2. Programming Languages and Applications

1. These concepts are discussed in the text.
2. See Figure 2-1.
3. Consider the consequences of CAI use with regard to the design of school buildings, the selection and training of teachers, the traditional grade-level structure, the development of special talents, and provision of study facilities outside the classroom—to name a few areas of impact. You can probably think of many others. Or try to imagine what "school" will be like for the student in such a system.

Answers to Review Exercises   381

Chapter 3. Punch-Card Processing

1. No. Even if only capital letters were used, the question mark could not be punched.
2. +, —, 0. The card code for each alphabetic character is a combination of a zone punch with one of the numerals 1–9.
3. The reproducer. The key-punch machine would have to be hand-fed one card at a time, and is also much slower.
4. See the text for one example. Use a research report in the literature of your field, or a research project at your institution with which you are acquainted.
5. Three digits for a subject code number (1–500), one digit for the subject's sex, and another digit for an instrument code. If any of the instruments require multiple cards, an extra column in the code block should be reserved for a card-number digit.
6. Two seven-digit fields with four decimal places, followed by four three-digit fields with two decimal places each. Omit decimal points.
7. Note that because these cards were punched by a computer program, the score fields include decimal points, and the fields are much wider than necessary. Punch the card deck as shown, however, since it will be used in Exercise 1 for Chapter 5.

Chapter 4. Fortran: Vocabulary and Grammar

1. col.1: blank, unless "C" for comment cards.
   cols. 2–5: statement number or blank.
   col. 6: continuation mark for multiple-card statements or blank.
   cols. 7–72: text of Fortran statement.
   cols. 73–80: card numbering and/or labeling or blank.
2.

	integer		real		alphameric	
constant	2	−23	3.0	−7.605	AAAAAA	NAMEAA (in memory)
variable	I	KSUM	X	SIGMA	KODE	F

3. Diagnostic Printout for Program ERRORS from an IBM 7040 Fortran System.

```
    ERROR MESSAGES
4 STATEMENT  7       ERROR 1113    ISN-1     ERRONEOUS INTEGER CONSTANT.
4 STATEMENT  7       ERROR 1103    ISN-2     ARITHMETIC OR LOGICAL SET STATEMENT
                                             OR STATEMENT DEFINITION MUST BEGIN WITH A
                                             NAME FOLLOWED BY OR =.
4 STATEMENT  7       ERROR 1152    ISN-4     INCORRECT DO STATEMENT.
4 STATEMENT  7       ERROR 1136    ISN-5     INCORRECT SUBSCRIPT FOR ARRAY X.
4 STATEMENT  7       ERROR 1158    ISN-6     TRUE TRANSFER OF LOGICAL IF
                                             STATEMENT CANNOT BE A DO OR ANOTHER
                                             LOGICAL IF.
4 STATEMENT  7       ERROR 1153    ISN-11    INCORRECT GO TO STATEMENT.
2 STATEMENT 15       ERROR 1323    ISN-3     ILLEGAL MIXED MODE ON RIGHT HAND
                                             SIDE OF ARITHMETIC STATEMENT.
2 STATEMENT 15       ERROR 1323    ISN-6     ILLEGAL MIXED MODE ON RIGHT HAND
                                             SIDE OF ARITHMETIC STATEMENT.

HIGHEST SEVERITY WAS 4.  EXECUTION DELETED.
```

ANSWERS TO REVIEW EXERCISES

4. Output format fields for real-mode data must provide a column for (1) a sign, (2) at least one integer, and (3) a decimal point, in addition to any decimal places. Thus, in F *a.b.*, *a* must exceed *b* by at least three columns. These extra columns are not required for real-mode *input* fields. If no negative signs are present in the data for an input field, its length need only accommodate the digits; the decimal point may be omitted since its placement is indicated in the field specification.

5.   READ 5, A, B, C
     5 FORMAT (1X, F3.1, 1X, F3.2, 1X, F3.0)
       PUNCH 10, A, B, C
   10 FORMAT (F4.1, F7.3, F6.0)

6.

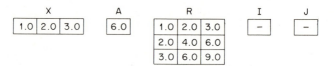

Note that, although dimensioned, cells X(1, 3) and X(2, 3) are not referenced in the indexing of the READ statement.

7. zero
8. three
9.

X				A		R			I	J
1.0	2.0	3.0		6.0		1.0	2.0	3.0	–	–
						2.0	4.0	6.0		
						3.0	6.0	9.0		

Note that I and J will be indeterminate after their loops have been satisfied.

10. two

Chapter 5. Fortran: Program Organization

```
*** EXERCISE 1 ***

C      PROGRAM REFORM
C      THE OUTPUT DECK = DATA FOR EXERCISES 2-5.
       DIMENSION KX(9)
       DO 10 I = 1,16
       READ 5, KODE, KX
     5 FORMAT (A6, 4X, 9(I6, 1X))
    10 PUNCH 15, KODE, KX
    15 FORMAT (A6, 2X, 8I2, I3)
       END
*** EXERCISE 2 ***

C      PROGRAM MEAN1
       DIMENSION X(16)
       READ 5, X
     5 FORMAT (24X, F3.0)
       XM = 0.0
       DO 10 I = 1,16
    10 XM = XM + X(I)
       XM = XM / 16.0
       PRINT 15, XM
    15 FORMAT (7H MEAN =, F10.4)
       END
```

```
C      PROGRAM MEAN2
       XM = 0.0
       DO 10 I = 1,16
       READ 5, X
     5 FORMAT (24X, F3.0)
    10 XM = XM + X
       XM = XM / 16.0
       PRINT 15, XM
    15 FORMAT (7H MEAN =, F10.4)
       END
```

*** EXERCISE 3 ***

```
C      PROGRAM SUBMS1
       DIMENSION X(16,8), KODE(16)
       READ 5, (KODE(I), (X(I,J), J = 1,8), I = 1,16)
     5 FORMAT (A6, 2X, 8F2.0)
       DO 15 I = 1,16
       A = 0.0
       S = 0.0
       DO 10 J = 1,8
       A = A + X(I,J)
    10 S = S + X(I,J)**2
       A = A / 8.0
       S = SQRT(S / 8.0 - A * A)
    15 PRINT 20, KODE(I), A, S
   200 FORMAT (/ 9H SUBJECT , A6, 5X, 6HMEAN =, F10.4,
      1 5X, 7HSIGMA =, F10.4)
       END


C      PROGRAM SUBMS2
       DIMENSION X(8)
       DO 15 I = 1,16
       READ 5, KODE, X
     5 FORMAT (A6, 2X, 8F2.0)
       A = 0.0
       S = 0.0
       DO 10 J = 1,8
       A = A + X(J)
    10 S = S + X(J)**2
       A = A / 8.0
       S = SQRT(S / 8.0 - A * A)
    15 PRINT 20, KODE, A, S
   200 FORMAT (/ 9H SUBJECT , A6, 5X, 6HMEAN =, F10.4,
      1 5X, 7HSIGMA =, F10.4)
       END
```

*** EXERCISE 4 ***

```
C      PROGRAM HILO
       DIMENSION X(16), KODE(16)
       READ 5, (KODE(I), X(I), I = 1,16)
     5 FORMAT (A6, 18X, F3.0)
       KHI = 1
       KLO = 1
       DO 10 I = 2,16
       IF (X(I) .GT. X(KHI)) KHI = I
       IF (X(I) .LT. X(KLO)) KLO = I
    10 CONTINUE
       PRINT 15, X(KHI), KODE(KHI), X(KLO), KODE(KLO)
    15 FORMAT (7H HIGH =, F5.0, A7 / 7H LOW = , F5.0, A7)
       END
```

*** EXERCISE 5 ***

```
C     PROGRAM ORDER1
      DIMENSION X(16)
      READ 5, X
    5 FORMAT (24X, F3.0)
      DO 15 I = 1,16
      K = I
      DO 10 J = I,16
      IF (X(J) .GT. X(K)) K = J
   10 CONTINUE
      IF (K .EQ. I) GO TO 15
      XX = X(I)
      X(I) = X(K)
      X(K) = XX
   15 CONTINUE
      PRINT 20, X
   20 FORMAT (16F5.0)
      END

C     PROGRAM ORDER2
      DIMENSION X(16)
      READ 5, X
    5 FORMAT (24X, F3.0)
   10 K = 0
      DO 15 I = 1,15
      IF (X(I) .GE. X(I+1)) GO TO 15
      XX = X(I)
      X(I) = X(I+1)
      X(I+1) = XX
      K = 1
   15 CONTINUE
      IF (K .EQ. 1) GO TO 10
      PRINT 20, X
   20 FORMAT (16F5.0)
      END
```

Chapter 6. Fortran: Functions and Subroutines

*** EXERCISE 1 ***

```
C     PROGRAM TEN (REVISED)
C     NOTE THAT THE DIMENSIONING OF X HAS BEEN REVERSED TO SIMPLIFY
         DATA READING.
      DIMENSION X(10,50), A(10), S(10), R(10,10)
      READ 10, X
   10 FORMAT (5X, 10F2.0)
      DO 20 I = 1,10
      A(I) = SUMF(X, -I, 50, 10) / 50.0
   20 S(I) = SQRT(SUMF(X, -I, -50, 10) / 50.0 - A(I)**2)
      DO 25 I = 1,10
      DO 25 J = 1,10
   25 R(I,J) = (SCPF(X, X, -I, -J, 50, 10) / 50.0 - A(I) * A(J)) /
     1  (S(I) * S(J))
      CALL PRTS (A, 10, 1, 5HMEANS, 10)
      CALL PRTS (S, 10, 1, 6HSIGMAS, 10)
      CALL PRTS (R, 10, 10, 5HR MAT, 10)
      END
```

*** EXERCISE 2 ***

```
C     PROGRAM TWELVE (REVISED)
      DIMENSION KF(16), A(100), S(100), R(100,100)
```

```
      CALL CCDS (KF, NV, NS, I, J, K)
C
C  ALL STATEMENTS AFTER 3--WHICH IS OMITTED WITH ITS READ--REMAIN
C  THE SAME THROUGH STATEMENT 25.
C
      CALL PRTS (A, NV, 1, 5HMEANS, 100)
      CALL PRTS (S, NV, 1, 6HSIGMAS, 100)
      CALL PRTS (R, NV, NV, 5HR MAT, 100)
      END
```

*** EXERCISE 3 ***

```
C     PROGRAM SUBMS1 (REVISED)
      DIMENSION X(16,8), KODE(16)
      READ 5, (KODE(I), (X(I,J), J = 1,8), I = 1,16)
    5 FORMAT (A6, 2X, 8F2.0)
      DO 15 I = 1,16
      A = SUMF(X, -I, 8, 16) / 8.0
      S = SQRT(SUMF(X, -I, -8, 16) / 8.0 - A * A)
   15 PRINT 20, KODE(I), A, S
  200 FORMAT (/ 9H SUBJECT , A6, 5X, 6HMEAN =, F10.4,
     1 5X, 7HSIGMA =, F10.4)
      END

C     PROGRAM SUBMS2 (REVISED)
      DIMENSION X(8)
      DO 15 I = 1,16
      READ 5, KODE, X
    5 FORMAT (A6, 2X, 8F2.0)
      A = SUMF(X, 1, 8, 8) / 8.0
      S = SQRT(SUMF(X, 1, -8, 8) / 8.0 - A * A)
   15 PRINT 20, KODE, A, S
  200 FORMAT (/ 9H SUBJECT , A6, 5X, 6HMEAN =, F10.4,
     1 5X, 7HSIGMA =, F10.4)
      END
```

*** EXERCISE 4 ***

```
      FUNCTION KHIAB (X, N)
      DIMENSION X(N)
      KHIAB = 1
      DO 5 I = 2,N
      IF (ABS(X(I)) .GT. ABS(X(KHIAB))) KHIAB = I
    5 CONTINUE
      RETURN
      END
```

*** EXERCISE 5 ***

```
      SUBROUTINE CORCO (X, Y, N, XM, YM, XS, YS, R)
      DIMENSION X(N), Y(N)
      T = N
      XM = SUMF(X, 1, N, N) / T
      YM = SUMF(Y, 1, N, N) / T
      XS = SQRT(SUMF(X, 1, -N, N) / T - XM * XM)
      YS = SQRT(SUMF(Y, 1, -N, N) / T - YM * YM)
      R = (SCPF(X, Y, 1, 1, N, N) / T - XM * YM) / (XS * YS)
      RETURN
      END
```

Chapter 7. Fortran: Matrix Algebra

1. See Figure 7-5 and the text for examples.
2. Each of these terms is exemplified in the text.
3.
```
C     PROGRAM ABCDE
      DIMENSION A(2, 2), B(2, 2), C(2), D(2), X(2, 2)
      READ 5, A, B, C, D, E
    5 FORMAT (10X, 13F1.0)
      CALL AXBS (A, B, X, 2, 2, 2, 2)
      DO 10 I = 1, 2
      DO 10 J = 1, 2
   10 A(I, J) = C(I) * D(J) * E
      CALL AXBS (X, A, B, 2, 2, 2, 2)
      CALL PRTS (B, 2, 2, 5HABCDE, 2)
      END
```
DATA∆CARD∆1324233223112
The correct answer is

74	74
174	174

4.
$$\frac{N\Sigma XY - \Sigma X \Sigma Y}{\sqrt{N\Sigma X^2 - (\Sigma X)^2} \sqrt{N\Sigma Y^2 - (\Sigma Y)^2}} =$$

$$[NX_N'Y_N - U_N'X_N U_N'Y] [NX_N'X_N - (U_N'X_N)^2]^{-1/2} [NY_N'Y_N - (U_N'Y_N)^2]^{-1/2}$$

Chapter 8. Test Scoring and Distribution Statistics

1. See text.
2. Item 16 is the most difficult; the mean of .25 indicates that only 25 percent of the 16 subjects answered the item correctly. However, this item correlated *negatively* with the subjects' total scores, which suggests that there is something seriously wrong with the item itself. Item 12 had the highest correlation with the total score, but the fact that it is relatively easy is not significant, since some of the easiest items, such as item 9, had very low correlations.
3. TESTAT TITLE CARD FOR EXERCISE 3.
   ∆∆∆15∆∆1000170341
   (A5, 5X, 15I1)
   D∆KEY101010101010101
   SCALE123123123123123
4. Column 20 on the Parameter Control Card could be used for this signal (1 = print). The parameter I in the CALL statement for Subroutine CCDS would be changed to a variable name such as KO. Then, at a point in the program three statements after statement 60 — just before PRINT 65, . . . — the following statement would be inserted: IF(KO .NE. 1) GO TO 85
   This same statement would also be inserted immediately after: DO 85 I = 1, 100

5. C   PROGRAM TRANS
        DIMENSION X(9)
        DO 15 I = 1, 16
        READ 5, KODE, X
     5 FORMAT (A6, 4X, 9F7.0)
        DO 10 J = 1, 9
    10 X(J) = X(J)**2
    15 PUNCH 5, KODE, X
        END

Output from Program DISTAT, using the transformed scores, will show a reduction in the negative skewness of the distributions.

Chapter 9. Intercorrelation and Factor Analysis

*** EXERCISE 1 ***

```
C       PROGRAM CORS
        DIMENSION R(100,100), A(100), S(100), KF(16)
     5  CALL CCDS (KF, NV, NS, KP, I, J)
        T = NS
        DO 10 I = 1,NV
        A(I) = 0.0
        DO 10 J = 1,NV
    10  R(I,J) = 0.0
        DO 15 K = 1,NS
        READ KF, (S(I), I = 1,NV)
        DO 15 I = 1,NV
        A(I) = A(I) + S(I)
        DO 15 J = I,NV
    15  R(I,J) = R(I,J) + S(I) * S(J)
        DO 20 I = 1,NV
        A(I) = A(I) / T
    20  S(I) = SQRT(R(I,I) / T - A(I)**2)
        DO 30 I = 1,NV
        DO 25 J = I,NV
        IF (S(I) * S(J)) .EQ. 0.0) GO TO 25
        R(J,I) = (R(I,J) / T - A(I) * A(J)) / (S(I) * S(J))
    25  R(I,J) = R(J,I)
    30  R(I,I) = 1.0
        CALL PRTS (A, NV, 1, 5HMEANS, 100)
        CALL PRTS (S, NV, 1, 6HSIGMAS, 100)
        CALL PRTS (R, NV, NV, 5HR MAT, 100)
        IF (KP .EQ. 0) GO TO 5
        CALL PCDS (A, NV, 1, 5HMEANS, 100)
        CALL PCDS (S, NV, 1, 5HSIGMA, 100)
        CALL PTMS (R, NV, 5HR MAT, 100)
        GO TO 5
        END
```

*** EXERCISE 2 ***

```
C       PROGRAM VVP
        DIMENSION R(8,8), F(8,8), A(8), B(8), C(8), KF(16)
        READ 5, KF
     5  FORMAT (16A5)
        CALL CORS (16, 8, R, A, B, KF, 0, 8)
        CALL SEVS (8, 8, 0.0, R, F, A, B, 8)
        CALL VORS (8, 8, F, A, B, C, 8)
        CALL AXBS (F, F, R, 8, -8, 8, 8)
        CALL PRTS (R, 8, 8, 3HVVP, 8)
        END
```

3. The intercorrelation submatrix of the three factor variables will be an identity matrix, since these orthogonal factors are by definition uncorrelated. The NV by NF matrix of correlations between raw-score and factor-score variables will be the same as the matrix of rotated factor loadings, as indicated in the text.
4. No matter which matrix is entered first, the test vectors will be perfectly correlated. If the Varimax loadings are entered first, the principal-axis structure will be rotated the same way it was by Subroutine VORS. If the principal-axis loadings are entered first, the Varimax structure will be rotated back to the original principal-axis orientation.

Chapter 10. Analysis of Variance

1. FIGURE 10-1A DESIGN
△△△△1△△△△2△△△△2
(8X, F2.0)
△△△△4△GROUP△ONE
△△△△5△GROUP△TWO

FIGURE 10-1B DESIGN
△△△△1△△△△2△△△△1
(8X, F2.0)
△△△△4△GROUP△ONE
△△△△5△GROUP△TWO

FIGURE 10-1C DESIGN
△△△△1△△△△1△△△△2
(8X, F2.0)
△△△△9△ALL△SUBJECTS

2. Yes. ANOVAR problem 2: variable 2, and AVAR23 problem 1: the B main effect.
3. Zero. The scores on each of the factor variables were automatically standardized during their computation in Program FACTOR, and the means of the three variables would therefore be identical, resulting in no between-trials variance in an analysis such as that described in the question.
4. No. The statistical tests in Program DSCRIM will yield the same results, although the centroids and individual variable means will be scaled differently, as will the discriminant scores for individuals if they are computed. The correlations between original and discriminant variables will be unaffected.

Chapter 11. Regression Analysis

1. On the A side, the first canonical function is very heavily determined by variable 1 (correlation = .7784); while on the B side, variable 2(7) is almost perfectly correlated with the canonical axis. The first canonical relationship between sets A and B, therefore, may be described adequately in terms of the relationship of these two single variables.
   The root for the first canonical variate is .5530, which is the square of the first canonical correlation (.7436) between sets A and B. This root may be directly

Answers to Review Exercises   389

interpreted as the proportion (55 percent) of the total variation "explained" by the first canonical function.
2. Because the weights obtained for each side in a canonical analysis are normalized before output. Beta weights do not necessarily have this property.
3. The beta weights for variables 1, 3, and 4 in the context of all eight variables were .2308, .2432, and .2643, respectively. When only these three variables are used to predict variable 9, however, the beta weights are .2873, .5516, .3929.
4. The easiest way to accomplish this would be to insert the following statements after FORMAT number 85:

   LL = NV + 1
   W(LL) = RC

   Then the weight-punching statement — two statements later — would have to be modified as follows:

   IF (KBW .EQ. 1) CALL PCDS (W, LL, 1, KMN, ND)

   Because the regression constant (RC) is added to the end of the weight vector W, no more than 99 variables could be used if this modification was made in the program.

Chapter 12. Miscellaneous Statistical Methods

1. Because the same four numbers appear in each of the three columns (variables) of the example problem data in the text, the means and sigmas of the three variables will be identical. Prestandardization of the variables will not affect the grouping procedure in this case, although the scaling of the "error" index will be changed.
2. Insert the following sequence of statements after statement 30:

   DO 32 I = 1, NI
   V(I) = 0.0
   R(I) = 0.0
   DO 31 J = 1, NK
   X = J * NX(J, I)
   X2 = J * J * NX(J, I)
   V(I) = V(I) + X
   31 R(I) = R(I) + X2
   T = KI(I)
   V(I) = V(I)/T
   32 R(I) = SQRT(R(I) / T − V(I)**2)
   CALL PRTS (V, NI, 1, 5HMEANS, 200)
   CALL PRTS (R, NI, 1, 6HSIGMAS, 200)

3. You are the best judge of what the output means in this problem.
4. $\chi^2 = 169.258$
Expected frequencies:

	Y	N	U
D	104.0	130.0	26.0
R	54.0	67.5	13.5
I	42.0	52.5	10.5

390 ANSWERS TO REVIEW EXERCISES

Chapter 13. Compilation and Analysis of Verbal Data

```
C     PROGRAM NARAT
C
C     COMPILES LIST OF DIFFERENT WORDS IN A SAMPLE OF NARRATIVE DATA
C     PUNCHED WITH BLANK SEPARATORS BETWEEN WORDS.
C     ALL PUNCTUATION IS ASSUMED REMOVED. NO WORDS SPLIT BETWEEN CARDS.
C     COL 1-5 ON EACH CARD RESERVED FOR SAMPLE ID AND CARD NUMBER.
C     CONTROL CARD PRECEDES DATA. COL 1-5 = NUMBER OF CARDS IN SAMPLE,
C     COL 6-75 = PROBLEM TITLE, COL 76-80 = BLANK.
C     PROGRAM WILL HANDLE UP TO 1000 DIFFERENT WORDS. WORDS MAY EXCEED
C     10 CHARACTERS PER WORD, BUT ONLY FIRST 10 ARE USED.
C
      DIMENSION KT(1000,10), KF(1000), KC(75), KH(14), KW(10)
      READ 5, NC, KH, KB
    5 FORMAT (I5, 15A5)
      PRINT 5, NC, KH
      M = 0
C     BEGIN DATA INPUT. M = LENGTH OF WORD LIST.
      DO 25 N = 1,NC
      READ 10, KC
   10 FORMAT (5X, 75A1)
      J = 0
C     PROCESS ONE CARD. SEARCH AFTER EACH WORD IDENTIFIED.
      DO 20 I = 1,75
      IF (KC(I) .EQ. KB) GO TO 15
      IF (J .EQ. 10) GO TO 20
      J = J + 1
      KW(J) = KC(I)
      GO TO 20
   15 IF (J .EQ. 0) GO TO 20
      CALL SEARCH (M, J, KW, KT, KF, KB)
   20 CONTINUE
C     SEARCH IF WORD REMAINS IN KW.
      IF (J .EQ. 0) GO TO 25
      CALL SEARCH (M, J, KW, KT, KF, KB)
   25 CONTINUE
C     PRINT TABLE OF WORDS AND FREQUENCIES.
      K = M / 8
      IF (MOD(M, 8) .GT. 0) K = K + 1
      DO 30 L = 1,K
   30 PRINT 35, (KF(I), (KT(I,J), J = 1,10), I = L,M,K)
   35 FORMAT (8(I4, 1X, 10A1))
      END


      SUBROUTINE SEARCH (M, J, KW, KT, KF, KB)
C
C     LOCATE THE WORD STORED IN KW IN A ROW OF MATRIX KT, IF POSSIBLE,
C     AND RAISE COUNTER IN KF.
C     IF NO MATCH IS FOUND, RAISE M, AND ADD RESPONSE TO ROW M OF KT.
C     FILL REST OF KW WITH BLANKS IF J .LT. 10, BEFORE SEARCH.
C
      DIMENSION KT(1000,10), KF(1000), KW(10)
      IF (J .EQ. 10) GO TO 10
      DO 5 I = J,9
    5 KW(I+1) = KB
   10 J = 0
      IF (M .EQ. 0) GO TO 25
      DO 20 I = 1,M
      DO 15 K = 1,10
      IF (KT(I,K) .NE. KW(K)) GO TO 20
```

```
15 CONTINUE
   KF(I) = KF(I) + 1
   RETURN
20 CONTINUE
25 M = M + 1
   KF(M) = 1
   DO 30 K = 1,10
30 KT(M,K) = KW(K)
   RETURN
   END
```

references

Allport, G. W., "Traits Revisited," *American Psychologist,* 1966, **21** (1), 1-10.
Austin, C. J., "The Medlars System," *Datamation,* 1964, **10** (12), 28-31.
Borko, H., ed., *Computer Applications in the Behavioral Sciences,* Englewood Cliffs, N. J.: Prentice-Hall, 1962.
———, "A Factor Analytically Derived Classification System for Psychological Reports," *Perceptual and Motor Skills,* 1965, **20** (2), 393-406.
Bottenberg, R. A., and J. H. Ward, Jr., *Applied Multiple Linear Regression,* U.S. Department of Commerce Office of Technical Services, AD413128, 1963.
Bown, O. H., "The Development of a Self-Report Inventory and Its Function in a Mental Health Assessment Battery," *American Psychologist,* 1961, **16** (7), 402.
Cattell, R. B., ed., *Handbook of Multivariate Experimental Psychology,* Skokie, Ill.: Rand McNally, 1965.
Cogswell, J. F., and D. P. Estavan, *Explorations in Computer-Assisted Counseling,* System Development Corporation, TM-2582, 1965.
Cooley, W. W., and P. R. Lohnes, *Multivariate Procedures for the Behavioral Sciences,* New York: Wiley, 1962.
Corbato, F. J., *An Experimental Time-Sharing System,* Proceedings Spring Joint Computer Conference, Baltimore: Spartan, 1962.
Cronbach, L. J., "Coefficient Alpha and the Internal Structure of Tests," *Psychometrika,* 1951, **16**, 297-334.
Dimitry, D., and T. Mott, Jr., *Introduction to Fortran IV Programming,* New York: Holt, Rinehart and Winston, 1966.
Edwards, A. L., *Experimental Design in Psychological Research,* New York: Holt, Rinehart and Winston, 1960.
Feigenbaum, E. A., *The Simulation of Verbal Learning Behavior,* Proceedings of Western Joint Computer Conference, 1961, **19**, 121-132.
———, and J. Feldman, *Computers and Thought,* New York: McGraw-Hill, 1963.

Feldman, J., "Simulation of Behavior in the Binary Choice Experiment," in H. Borko, ed., *Computer Applications in the Behavioral Sciences,* Englewood Cliffs, N. J.: Prentice-Hall, 1962.
Flores, Ivan, *Computer Software,* Englewood Cliffs, N. J.: Prentice-Hall, 1965.
Fuller, L. E., *Basic Matrix Theory,* Englewood Cliffs, N. J.: Prentice-Hall, 1962.
Gerlernter, H., J. R. Hansen, and C. L. Gerberich, "A Fortran-Compiled List-Processing Language," *Journal of the Association for Computing Machinery,* 1960, **7,** 87–101.
Golden, J. T., *Fortran IV Programming and Computing,* Englewood Cliffs, N. J.: Prentice-Hall, 1965.
Green, B. F., "Attitude Measurement," in G. Lindzey, ed., *Handbook of Social Psychology,* Reading, Mass: Addison-Wesley, 1954 (1).
———, *Digital Computers in Research,* New York: McGraw-Hill, 1963.
Greenberger, M. H., and J. H. Ward, Jr., "An Iterative Technique for Multiple Correlation Analysis," *IBM Technical Newsletter,* 1956, **12,** 85–97.
Gregory, R. H., and R. L. Van Horn, *Automatic Data-Processing Systems,* Belmont, Calif.: Wadsworth, 1960.
Guttman, L., "Image Theory for the Structure of Quantitative Variates," *Psychometrika,* 1953, **18,** 277–296.
Harmon, H. H., *Modern Factor Analysis,* Chicago: University of Chicago Press, 1960.
Harris, C. W., "Some Rao-Guttman Relationships," *Psychometrika,* 1962, **27** (3), 247–263.
Hastings, C., Jr., *Approximations for Digital Computers,* Princeton: Princeton University Press, 1955.
Helm, C. E., *Simulation Models for Psychometric Theories,* Proceedings of American Federation of Information Processing Societies, Washington: Spartan, 1965, Vol. 27, Part 1.
Holsti, O. R., "An Adaptation of the General Inquirer for the Systematic Analysis of Political Documents," Stanford University, 1964 (mimeo).
Holtzman, W. H., "Statistical Models for the Study of Change in the Single Case," in C. W. Harris, ed., *Problems in Measuring Change,* Madison, Wis.: University of Wisconsin Press, 1963.
Horst, P., "Matrix Reduction and Approximation to Principal Axes," *Psychometrika,* 1962, **27** (2), 169–178.
———, *Matrix Algebra for Social Scientists,* New York: Holt, Rinehart and Winston, 1963.
———, *Factor Analysis of Data Matrices,* New York: Holt, Rinehart and Winston, 1965.
Hotelling, H., "Analysis of a Complex of Statistical Variables into Principal Components," *Journal of Educational Psychology,* 1933, **24,** 417–441, 498–520.
Hunka, S., "Program Match," Department of Educational Psychology, University of Alberta, 1965 (mimeo).
Jaspen, N., "The Calculation of Probabilities Corresponding to Values of Z, T, F, and Chi-Square," *Educational and Psychological Measurement,* 1965, **25,** 877–880.
Jennings, E., "A Subroutine System for Data Processing in the Behavioral

Sciences," Department of Educational Psychology, University of Texas, 1964 (mimeo).

Jones, K. J., "The Multivariate Statistical Analyzer," Cambridge: Harvard Cooperative Society, 1964 (mimeo).

Kaiser, H. F., "The Best Approximation of a Common-Factor Space," Berkeley: University of California Research Report 25, Contract No. AF 41(657)-76, 1958.

———, "Computer Program for Varimax Rotation in Factor Analysis," *Educational and Psychological Measurement,* 1959, **19,** 413–420.

———, "The Application of Electronic Computers to Factor Analysis," *Educational and Psychological Measurement,* 1960, **20,** 141–151.

———, *Relating Factors between Studies Based upon Different Individuals,* unpublished manuscript, University of Illinois, 1960.

———, "Formulas for Component Scores," *Psychometrika,* 1962, **27** (1), 83–87.

———, "Image Analysis," in C. W. Harris, ed., *Problems in Measuring Change,* Madison, Wis.: University of Wisconsin Press, 1963.

———, and J. Caffrey, "Alpha Factor Analysis," *Psychometrika,* 1965, **30** (1), 1–14.

Kelley, T. L., *Fundamentals of Statistics,* Cambridge: Harvard University Press, 1947, 325–331.

Kendall, M. G., *The Advanced Theory of Statistics,* London: Lippincott, 1943.

Kleinmuntz, B., "Personality Test Interpretation by Digital Computers," *Science,* 1963, **139** (3553), 416–418.

Koons, P. B., Jr., "Canonical Analysis," in H. Borko, ed., *Computer Applications in the Behavioral Sciences,* Englewood Cliffs, N. J.: Prentice-Hall, 1962.

Likert, R., "A Technique for the Measurement of Attitudes," *Archives of Psychology,* 1932, No. 140.

Loehlin, J. C., "A Computer Program that Simulates Personality," in S. S. Tomkins and S. Messick, eds., *Computer Simulation of Personality,* New York: Wiley, 1963.

McCarthy, J., "Recursive Functions of Symbolic Expressions and Their Computations by Machines," *Communications of the Association for Computing Machinery,* 1960, 3(4), 184–195.

McCracken, D. D., *Guide to Fortran IV Programming,* New York: Wiley, 1965.

———, "The Student of Tomorrow," *Datamation,* 1966, **12** (1), 25–26.

McNemar, Q., *Psychological Statistics,* New York: Wiley, 1962.

Meehl, P. E., *Clinical versus Statistical Prediction,* Minneapolis: University of Minnesota Press, 1954.

Morris, C. W., *Signs, Language, and Behavior,* Englewood Cliffs, N. J.: Prentice-Hall, 1946.

Morrissey, J. H., "The Quiktran System," *Datamation,* 1965, **11,** 42–46.

Moseley, E. C., D. R. Gorham, and Evelyn Hill, "Computer Scoring of Inkblot Perceptions," *Perceptual and Motor Skills,* 1963, **17** (2), 498.

Newell, A., J. C. Shaw, and H. A. Simon, "A General Problem-Solving Program for a Computer," *Computers and Automation,* 1959, **8** (7), 10–17.

———, ed., *Information Processing Language V Manual,* Englewood Cliffs, N. J.: Prentice-Hall, 1961.

———, and H. A. Simon, "The Simulation of Human Thought," in *Current Trends in Psychological Theory,* Pittsburgh, Pa.: University of Pittsburgh Press, 1961, 152–179.

Oettinger, A. C., "Programming a Digital Computer to Learn," *Philosophical Magazine,* 1952, **43**, 1243–1263.

Organick, E. I., *A Fortran Primer,* Reading, Mass.: Addison-Wesley, 1963.

Osgood, C. E., G. J. Suci, and P. H. Tannenbaum, *The Measurement of Meaning,* Urbana: University of Illinois Press, 1957.

Peck, R. F., and D. J. Veldman, "Computer Analysis of Personality, Research Plan and Supporting Data," Personality Research Center, University of Texas, 1962 (mimeo).

Piotrowski, Z. A., "Digital Computer Interpretation of Inkblot Test Data," *Psychiatric Quarterly,* 1964, **38** (1), 1–26.

Plumb, S. C., *Introduction to Fortran Programming,* New York: McGraw-Hill, 1961.

Purnell, R. F., "Scalval, a Program to Calculate Item Scale Values for Thurstone's Successive Interval Method," *Behavioral Science,* (in press).

Ralston, A., and H. S. Wilf, eds., *Mathematical Methods for Digital Computers,* New York: Wiley, 1960.

Rao, C. R., *Advanced Statistical Methods in Biometric Research,* New York: Wiley, 1952.

Rome, S. C., and B. K. Rome, "Computer Simulation Toward a Theory of Large Organizations," in H. Borko, ed., *Computer Applications in the Behavioral Sciences,* Englewood Cliffs, N. J.: Prentice-Hall, 1962.

Salmon, L. J., *IBM Machine Operation and Wiring,* Belmont, Calif.: Wadsworth, 1962.

Samuel, A. L., "Some Studies in Machine Learning, Using the Game of Checkers," *IBM Journal of Research and Development,* 1959, **3**, 210–230.

Sarbin, T. R., R. Taft, and D. E. Bailey, *Clinical Inference and Cognitive Theory,* New York: Holt Rinehart and Winston, 1960.

Schmidt, R. N., and W. E. Meyers, *Introduction to Computer Science and Data Processing,* New York: Holt, Rinehart and Winston, 1965.

Shannon, C. E., "A Chess-Playing Machine," in J. R. Newman, ed., *The World of Mathematics,* New York: Simon and Schuster, 1956.

Siegel, S., *Nonparametric Statistics for the Behavioral Sciences,* New York: McGraw-Hill, 1956.

Silberman, H. F., and J. E. Coulson, "Automated Teaching," in H. Borko, ed., *Computer Applications in the Behavioral Sciences,* Englewood Cliffs, N. J.: Prentice-Hall, 1962.

Sprowls, R. C., *Computers, a Programming Problem Approach,* New York: Harper & Row, 1966.

Starkweather, J. A., and B. J. Decker, "Computer Analysis of Interview Content," Western Psychological Association, April 1964, *American Psychologist,* 1964, **19** (9), 707.

———, "Computest, a Computer Language for Individual Testing, Instruction, and Interviewing," *Psychological Reports,* 1965, **17** (1), 227–237.

Sterling, T. D., and S. V. Pollack, *Computers and the Life Sciences,* New York: Columbia University Press, 1965.

Stevens, S. S., "A Metric for the Social Consensus," *Science,* 1966, **151**, 530–541.

Stone, P. J., R. F. Bales, J. Z. Namenwirth, and D. M. Ogilvie, "The General Inquirer, a Computer System for Content Analysis and Retrieval Based on the Sentence as a Unit of Information," *Behavioral Science,* 1962, **7** (4), 484–498.

Swenson, W. M., H. P. Rome, J. S. Pearson, and T. L. Brannick, "A Totally Automated Psychological Test," *Journal of American Medical Association,* 1965, **191**, 129–131.

Thurstone, L. L., and E. J. Chave, *The Measurement of Attitude,* Chicago: University of Chicago Press, 1929.

Tomkins, S., and S. Messick, eds., *Computer Simulation of Personality,* New York: Wiley, 1963.

Tryon, R. C., and D. E. Bailey, "The BC Try Computer System of Cluster and Factor Analysis," *Multivariate Behavioral Research,* 1966, **1** (1), 95–111.

Ward, J. H., Jr., "Multiple Linear Regression Models," in H. Borko, ed., *Computer Applications in the Behavioral Sciences,* Englewood Cliffs, N. J.: Prentice-Hall, 1962.

―――, "Hierarchical Grouping to Optimize an Objective Function," *American Statistical Association Journal,* 1963, **58**, 236–244.

Whyte, P. A., "The Computation of Eigenvalues and Eigenvectors of a Matrix," *Journal of the Society for Industrial and Applied Mathematics,* 1958, **6** (2), 393–437.

Winer, B. J., *Statistical Principles in Experimental Design,* New York: McGraw-Hill, 1962.

Yngve, V., "A Programming Language for Mechanical Translation," *Mechanical Translation,* 1958, **5**, 25–41.

Young, R. K., and D. J. Veldman, *Introductory Statistics for the Behavioral Sciences,* New York: Holt, Rinehart and Winston, 1965.

index

Abacus, 4
Access time, 7-8, 63
Accounting machine, 7
Accumulation loop, 99, 102
Accumulator, 18
Accuracy, 2, 34, 209
Addition, 51, 70
   matrix, 147
Aiken, Howard, 4
Aldous, 27
Algebra, 143
   matrix, 142, 210
Algol, 15, 20, 44
Algorithm, 20, 87
Alphabetic
   Interpreter, 33
   key, 360
   ordering, 353
   similarity, 347
   sorting, 40
Alpha coefficient, 173
Alphameric, 18, 49, 54, 55, 167, 341
Alternating storage in arrays, 101
Ambiguity, 318
Analysis, criterion, 371
   statistical, 23, 24
   variance, 246, 282
Argument, 80, 117, 120, 192
Arithmetic, 70
   IF statement, 73, 125
Array, 50, 51
   dimensions in subprograms, 118
   input/output, 63
   natural order, 66
   printing, 134
   punching, 135
Art and science, 368
A specification, 54-55
Assembler, 14-15
Assessment, 340, 368
   idiographic, 26
   normative, 25
Association, 327, 333
Asterisk, 51
Attitudes, 318
Autocorrelation, 200
Average (*see* Mean)
Axis,
   canonical, 282
   discriminant, 271
   orthogonal, 212
   principal, 212

Babbage, Charles, 4
Base of number system, 341
BCD, 56, 61-62, 343
Behavioral science, 23, 24, 43, 45, 206, 338
Behavioral Science, 24
Beta weights (*see* Weights)
Binary
   choice behavior, 27
   coded decimal (*see* BCD)
   digit (bit), 8, 341
   numbers, 17, 341
   program, 16
   tape statements, 63
Blank columns, 53, 54, 56
Block diagrams, 87
Buffering, 10

Calculator, 96
CALL statement, 120
Calling subprograms, 117
Canonical correlation analysis, 282
Card, 4, 5, 7, 30
   control (*see* Control card)
   data, 65
   fields and formats, 35
   Fortran, 46
   handling and storage, 33
   input/output, 59
   sorting, 38-42
Categories, 38, 319, 367, 370
Cathode-ray display, 7, 31
CDC, 15, 45, 48, 54, 55, 340, 376
   function names, 81
Cell (*see* Word)
Centroid, 272
Character, 31, 327, 341, 374
Chi-square, 272, 284, 327
   probability, 131
   program, 332
Choice responses, 338, 366
Clinical psychologist, 367
Clustering, 308
Cobol, 15, 44
Coding
   BCD systems, 343
   of data, 34

397

Collator, 34
Column
  blank (*see* Blank columns)
  printing, 348
  vector, 143
Comit, 20
Comments, 46
Common variance, 218, 281
Communality, 214, 218
Commutative operations, 147
Comparison
  of factors, 236
  paired, 318
Compilation
  termination (*see* END statement)
  of verbal responses, 347–348, 355
  See also Processing stages
Compiler, 14–15, 19, 118
  Fortran, 44, 48
Components, 283
  See also Principal axis
Composite, 281, 318
Computer, 1–3
  alphameric systems, 355
  analog-digital, 1–2
  assisted instruction (CAI), 27, 339
  history, 3
  speed and size, 5
  See also CDC; GE; IBM
Conformable matrices, 148
Confusion, 319
Conjunctive, 75
Consistency (*see* Mode)
Constant, 47–49
  as CALL argument, 120
  regression, 299
Constructed responses, 338, 366
Constructs, 206, 339
Content
  analysis, 339
  ordering, 353
Contingency table, 41, 326
Continuation, 47
CONTINUE statement, 79
Continuity correction, 333
Control card, 23, 65, 110
  group, 248, 259
  model, 295
  subroutine, 132
  transfer, 72–74, 77, 118
Conversion
  character, 343
  See also Mode
Core memory, 4, 7–8, 43, 45, 341
Correction for continuity, 333

Correlation, 101, 104, 116, 145, 237, 272
  auto- and cross-lag, 200
  canonical, 282
  multiple, 218, 281
  phi, 192
  point biserial, 173, 192
  rank-order, 192
  subroutines, 191–192
Cosine, 207, 237
Coterminous loop, 78, 105
Counter, 38, 41
Coursewriter, 28
Covariation, 190, 281
  analysis, 282, 300
  image, 218
CPI, 338
CPU, 9–10
Criterion
  external, 367
  groups, 372
  stop, 296
  variable, 281
Critical ratio, 182
Cross-lag, 200
Cross-plot (*see* Plot)
Cross-products, 127, 145
Cross-validation, 297, 368
Cumulative proportion, 321
Cyclic fluctuation, 200

Data
  card fields, 35
  deck, 132, 249
  dichotomous, 192
  missing, 195, 247, 259, 319
  narrative, 379
  natural language, 22
  nonnumeric, 38
  organization and coding, 34
  recording, 166
  transfer modes, 52
  verbal, 25, 338
De-bugging, 45
Decimal
  fractions, 53
  numbers, 341
  place, 36
  point, 48
Decision statements, 72
Deck (*see* Data)
Deflation, 208
Delta subscript, 145
Denormal vectors, 207
Dependent,

linear, 210
variable, 246
Descriptive statistical information, 181
Diagnosis
  of errors, 17, 44, 52
  psychological, 368
Diagonal matrix, 145
Diagrams, 87–88
Dichotomous data, 192, 294
Dictionary, 339, 368
DIMENSION statement, 50, 51, 64, 67, 92, 99, 118, 119, 143
Directionality reversal, 173
Disc, 8, 185
Discovery, 28
Discriminant
  analysis, 268
  scores, 271
Disjunctive relationship, 75
Display, cathode-ray, 7, 31
Distance, 199, 309
Distribution
  frequency, 41, 183, 321, 326, 345
  moments of, 182
  normal, 160
Division, 51, 70
  by zero, 112
DO statement, 76–80, 93
Double precision, 49
Driver program, 9, 23
Drum, 8
Duplication, 32

Eckert, J. P., 4
Edsac, 4, 27
Educational and Psychological Measurement, 24, 142
Edvac, 4
Efficiency, 86, 123, 125
Eigenroot (eigenvalue), 207
Eigenvector, 209, 269
Eject page, 56–57
Electrographic scoring, 32, 167
Element of vector or matrix, 143
END statement, 82
Endings of words, 378
Eniac, 4
Equal-appearing interval scale, 318–319
Equality of matrices, 144
Equation, 281
Equivalence of responses, 366
Error
  diagnosis, 17, 44, 52
  prediction, 283
  punching, 32, 368

Evaluation of expressions, 69–72
Execution
  stage, 16
  termination, 82
Expected frequency, 332
Explained variation, 218, 281
Exponentiation, 70, 99, 159
Expressions, 50, 69
  evaluation, 69–72
  relational, 75
External tape, 61–62

Factor
  analysis, 206
    parametric-statistical, 219
    transposed, 309
  in analysis of variance, 257
  comparison, 236
  image analysis, 218
  loadings, 209
  scores, 213, 215
False branch, 74
Field, 36
  card, 34
  Fortran card, 46
  identification, 35
  length, 37
  repetition, 56
  specifications, 52
Files, 34
Fixed-point (*see* Integer)
Floating-point (*see* Real mode)
Flow charts, 87–88
FLPL, 20, 22
Format
  control card, 132
  repetition, 56
  statement, 52, 89, 91
  variable, 68, 112
Formulas
  for descriptive statistics, 181
  as functions, 115
Fortran, 10, 12, 14–15, 19, 22, 43, 340
  basic, 86
  card format, 46
  compiler, 44, 48
  functions, 81–82
  integer interpretation, 353
  statement summary, 82–84
  II and IV, 43, 81
F ratio, 247, 270, 272, 297
  probability, 129
Frequency
  expected, 332

Frequency (*continued*)
  ordering, 354
  See also Distribution
F specification, 53–54
Functions, 23, 115, 121
  canonical, 285
  discriminant, 272
  formulas as, 115
  library, 80–82
  statistical, 123

Gang punch, 32
Gauss-Jordan method, 156
GE computers, 54
General Inquirer, 339
General Problem Solver, 20, 27
General-purpose program (*see* Program)
Geometric representation, 207
GO TO statements, 73
Grammatical variants, 366
Graph, 272
Group(ing)
  analysis, 308
  control card, 248, 259
  criterion, 372
  differences, 371
  membership, 294
  response, 366

Heuristic problem solving, 20
Hierarchy
  grouping, 308
  of lists, 21
  of operators, 71
Hollerith field, 60
Hollerith, Herman, 4, 30, 49, 55
Holtzman Inkblot Technique, 25, 339
H specification, 55–56

IBM, 5, 43
  computers, 5, 8, 15, 45, 48, 54, 340, 341, 376
  function names, 81
  off-line machines, 33, 35, 167
  subroutines, 162
Identification, 35, 36, 194
Identity matrix, 146
IF statements, 73, 125, 344
Image analysis, 218
Increment, 66, 78, 348
Independent
  linear, 210
  predictors, 297
  relationships, 282
  variable, 246, 283

Indexing
  DO, 76
  increment, 66, 78, 348
  matrix, 66
  nonserial, 78
  notation, 65
  variables, 65
  vectors, 64
Index Medicus, 12
Information utility, 11
Inkblots (*see* Holtzman; Rorschach)
Inner product, 149
Input, 3, 53
  of arrays, 63
  deck arrangement, 132
  devices and media, 5
  statements, 58, 63
Instruction, 9, 18
  computer-assisted (CAI), 27, 339
Integer
  constants and variables, 48, 341
  I specification, 54
  maximum, 353
Intercorrelation (*see* Correlation)
Internal
  consistency, 173
  tape, 63
Interpretation
  of canonical functions, 285
  of discriminant functions, 272
  of factors, 213
  of storage contents, 344
Interval
  measurement, 164, 181–182
  scales, 318–319
Interviews, 339
Invariance of structure, 236
Inversion of matrix, 156
IPL-V, 15, 20, 340, 360
I specification, 54
Item
  analysis, 170, 219, 318
  unanswered, 37
Iteration, 209, 295

Jacobi solution, 207
Jacquard, Joseph, 4
Jovial, 15
Judgment
  human, 370
  method, 318
Justification, 36, 55

Keyboard stations, 6
Key card, 167, 170, 319

Index   **401**

Key cells, 360
Key matrix, 361
Key punch, 31, 33
Kurtosis, 182

Labeling output, 99
Lag, 200–201
Lambda, 272
Language
  assembly, 15
  compiler, 15
  levels, 17
  list-processing, 20
  machine, 15, 17, 44
  natural, 19, 22, 46, 378
  object, 44
  programming, 10, 14, 340
  source, 44
  symbolic, 15, 18
Learning
  by computers, 27
  discovery, 28
  programmed, 27
Length of a vector, 160, 161, 211
Levels in ANOVAR, 257
Library
  functions, 81–82, 122
  matrix routines, 162
  of programs, 22–23, 45, 123
  See also Programs; Subprograms
Likert, R., 177, 319
Linear dependency, 210
Line control, 56–57
Link, 360
Lisp, 20
List
  data files, 34
  hierarchy, 21, 340
  searching, 355
  sublisting, 355
  variable, 60, 95
  vector, 50
  verbal response, 347
List-processing language, 20
Literal equivalence, 366
Load-and-go, 16
Load point, 61
Loadings, 209
Location, 8, 340–341
Locator files, 34
Logical
  errors, 17
  IF statement, 74
  operators, 74
  unit numbers, 61

Loop,
  accumulation, 99, 102
  coterminous, 78, 105
  DO, 76, 93
  interminable, 9

Machine
  accounting, 7
  language, 15, 17, 44
MAC project, 11
Magnetic
  disks, 8, 185
  drum, 8
  tape (*see* Tape)
Major product, 149
Manuals, 33, 41, 44, 72
Mark sense, 32
Masking, 375
Matrix, 50, 142
  addition, 147
  algebra, 142, 210
  asymmetric, 269, 284
  correlation (*see* Correlation)
  deflation, 208
  diagonal, 145
  equality, 144
  identity, 146
  indexing, 66
  inversion, 156
  key, 361
  multiplication, 148
  powers, 159
  printing, 134
  product, 150, 284
  punching, 135, 137
  roots and vectors, 207, 269
  scalar, 146
  signal, 327
  singular, 156, 219, 285
  size, 143
  square, 145
  subprograms, 119
  subtraction, 147
  super, 283
  symmetric, 104, 137, 145, 207
  transformation, 217, 237
  transpose, 144
Mauchly, J. W., 4
Maximum integer value, 353
Mean, 96, 97, 116
Meaning, 366
Measurement,
  attitude, 318, 319
  interval, 164, 181
  nominal, 165

402 INDEX

Measurement (*continued*)
  ordinal, 164, 166, 181
  repeated, 37, 200
Medlars, 12
Membership, 294
Memory (*see* Storage)
Minor product, 149
Mixed modes (*see* Mode consistency)
MMPI, 25, 32, 338
Mode
  agreement in subprograms, 119
  consistency, 58, 69, 71–72
  conversion, 49, 71–72, 96
  data-transfer, 52
  of names of functions, 117, 123
  in subroutines, 139
Model,
  regression, 295
  See also Simulation
Moments, 183
Monitor system, 58, 82, 117
Multiple
  choice tests, 164
  column printing, 348
  correlation, 218, 281
  discriminant analysis, 268
  regression, 281, 294
Multiplication, 51, 70
  matrix, 148
Multiprocessing and multiprogramming (*see* Time sharing)
Multivariate Behavioral Research, 142

Names
  of programs, 89
  of subprograms, 117
Napier, John, 4
Narrative data, 379
Natural array order, 66
Natural language (*see* Language)
Nested lists, 21
Nested loops, 77, 105
Nominal measurement, 165
Normal distribution, 160
Normalization, 160, 238, 284
Normative analysis, 25, 340, 368
Notation, 142
Number, 48
  binary, 17, 341
  code, 34
  identification, 35
  integer, 48, 341
  octal, 342
  real, 48, 341
  statement, 46

systems, 341–342
unit, 61
Numerals, 341
Numeric sorting, 39

Objectivity, 339, 379
Object program, 14, 44
Oblique factor structure, 237
Octal numbers, 342
Operand, 18
Operator
  arithmetic, 70
  hierarchy, 71
  logical/relational, 74–75
Optical mark scoring, 167
Optical scanning, 6
Order
  frequency and content, 352–353
  natural array, 66
  of matrix, 145, 210
  of operations, 70
  rank (*see* Rank)
  response list, 347
  serial, 360
Ordinal measurement (*see* Measurement)
Organization
  of data, 34
  of programs, 86
  of subprograms, 116
Orthogonal axes, 212, 237
Orthogonal rotation, 214
Outer product, 149
Output, 3, 53
  of arrays, 63
  devices and media, 7
  listings, 177
  statements, 58, 63

Page eject, 56–57, 177
Paired comparisons, 318
Paired variables, 327
Parameter
  control card, 132
  population, 182
Parametric factor analysis, 219
Parentheses, 56–57, 66–67, 71, 73
Pascal, Blaise, 4
Pearson product-moment (*see* Correlation)
Percentile, 181
Personality, 25, 338
  assessment, idiographic approach to, 26
Personnel, 34

Phi coefficient, 192
PL/1, 15, 20
Plot, 7, 272, 326
Point biserial, 173, 192
Population, 182
Porta-punch, 33
Postmultiplication, 148
Power
 of a matrix, 159
 of number base, 342
Pragmatic equivalence, 366
Precision, double, 49
Prediction, 281, 294, 297
Prefixes, 378
Premultiplication, 148
Prime sign, 144
Principal axis, 212–213
Print
 array, 134
 line control, 56–57
 line printer, 7
 multiple-column, 348
 statement, 60
Probability values, 129–131
Process(ing)
 cognitive, 27
 control, 3, 9–10
 methods for verbal data, 346
 model, 26
 stages, 16
Products,
 cross-, 127, 145
 matrix, 150, 284
 scalar, 127, 149
 vector, 149
Profile similarity, 198–199, 309
Program, 14
 driver, 9, 23
 game-playing, 27
 general-purpose, 110, 132, 219, 332, 346
 languages, 14
 learning, 27
 library (*see* Library)
 names, 89
 organization, 86
 system, 22
 termination, 82
 tracing, 89, 90
Program index
 ANOVAR (Groups and/or trials analysis of variance), 247
 AVAR23 (Double or triple factor analysis of variance), 257
 CANONA (Multiple canonical analysis), 286
 CHICHI (Chi-square analysis), 332
 CONTAB (Contingency tabling), 327
 DISTAT (Distribution statistics and standard scoring), 181
 DISCRIM (Multiple discriminant analysis), 273
 FACTOR (Principal axis and image analysis), 219
 HGROUP (Hierarchical grouping), 311
 LAGCOR (Auto- and cross-lag intercorrelation), 200
 LISTA (Verbal data compilation and ordering), 347
 LISTB (Verbal data compilation by sublisting), 360
 NARAT (Compilation of word usage in narratives), 390
 REGRAN (Multiple regression analysis), 295
 RELATE (Factor structure comparison), 238
 SCORE (Criterion analysis of verbal data), 369
 TESTAT (Test scoring and item analysis), 170
 TSCALE (Successive intervals scaling), 319
Proportion, 367
 cumulative, 321
Pseudovariable, 80, 116
Psychometrika, 142
Punch
 arrays, 135
 cards (*see* Card)
 machine, 31, 33
 paper tape, 5
 score vector, 139
 statement, 59
 symmetric matrix, 137
 of verbal data, 345
 zone, 30

Quantification, 338
Questionnaire, 32, 165, 318, 338
Quiktran, 11

Range of DO loop, 77
Rank
 of a matrix, 210
 order, 39, 319, 353
 correlation, 192
Rating
 scales, 165
 summated, 319

INDEX

READ statement
  BCD tape, 62
  cards, 59, 91
Real mode
  constants and variables, 48, 341
  F specification, 53
Record length, 62
Reduction to word roots, 360
Regression, 281, 294
  constant, 299
  equation, 281
Relation, conjunctive-disjunctive, 75
Reliability, 173
Remainder, 375
Remote consoles, 11–12, 17, 27
Repeated measurements, 37, 200
Repetition of field, 56
Replacement, 69
Reproducer, 32
Response
  choice, 338
  constructed, 338
  grouping, 366
  unique, 367
  verbal, 345, 347
Retrieval of documents, 12
RETURN statement, 82, 117
Reversal
  of item scales, 173
  of subscripts, 144, 195
REWIND statement, 61
Right answers, 165
Root
  canonical, 283
  of a matrix, 207, 269
  square, 99
  word, 340, 355, 366, 368, 378
Rorschach responses, 25, 338
Rotation, 213, 214, 237
Rounding, 70–71
Routines, statistical, 22, 122
Row vector, 143

Satisfaction of DO index, 78
Scalar, 143
  algebra, 143
  matrix and vector, 146
  product, 149
Scale
  equal-appearing intervals, 318, 319
  Likert, 177, 319
  of measurement (*see* Measurement)
  rating, 165
  successive intervals, 318

summated ratings, 319
  zero value, 320
Science,
  behavioral (*see* Behavioral science)
Scores
  discriminant, 271
  factor, 213, 215
  subject vector punching, 139
  T, 183
  test, 167, 170
  z (*see* z probability; z score)
  See also Measurement
Search
  list, 355
  routine, 390
Self-Report Inventory, 176, 319
Semantic equivalence, 366, 378
Semantic differential, 166, 189
Sentence completion, 338, 340
Sequence of instructions, 86
Serial order, 360
Sets of variables, 282
Sex coding, 35, 345, 369
Shape, 198–199, 309
Share, 22
Shared variation, 218, 281
Shift bit string, 355, 359, 375
Shrinkage, 300
Sight check, 40
Sigma, 97, 116
Sign, 53
  bit, 353
  column, 36
  constants, 48
  prime, 144
Signal matrix, 327
Significance, 131, 246, 272, 286, 300, 372
Similarity,
  alphabetic, 347, 353
  profile, 198–199, 309
Simple structure, 214
Simple variable, 50, 89
Simulation, 26
Singular (*see* Matrix)
Size of a matrix, 143
Skewness, 182
Slash mark
  in division, 70
  end line, 56
Sorting, 38–40, 355
Source program, 14, 44
Space, 210, 270
Spacing, 56–57
Spelling, 345

Sperry-Rand, 5
Square matrix, 145
Square root, 99, 159
SRI (*see* Self-Report Inventory)
Stability of structure, 236
Stages
 of grouping, 311
 of processing, 16
 of response compiling, 348
Standard deviation, 97, 116
Standardization, 161, 198, 311
Statement, 46
 CALL, 120
 decision, 72
 DO, 76-80
 input/output, 63
 numbers, 46
 summary, 82-84
STOP
 criterion, 296
 statement, 82
Storage, 3, 340, 343
 alternating, 101
 capacity, 45, 52
 of cards, 33
 devices and media, 7-9
 organization, 20
 reservation, 51
Structure, 211, 236
 simple, 214
Subject
 data card, 65
 identification (*see* Identification)
 score vector punching, 139
Sublisting, 355
Subprograms, 115
 functions, 121
 organization, 116
 subroutines, 120
Subprogram index
 AEVS (Roots and vectors of symmetric matrix), 269
 AXBS (Matrix multiplication), 150
 CCDS (Control card input and printing), 132
 CORD (Content ordering of verbal data), 353
 CORS (Intercorrelation), 192
 FORD (Frequency ordering of verbal data), 352
 INVS (Matrix inversion), 156
 I230 (Data conversion from IBM 1230 cards), 167
 LGTH (Count characters in word of storage), 374

MDRS (Missing-data intercorrelation), 195
PCDS (Punch output of an array), 135
PRBF (Probability of an F ratio), 129
PRTS (Print output of an array), 134
PTMS (Punch output of a symmetric matrix), 139
ROOT (Search word list for root match), 376
SCPF (Scalar product), 127
SEARCH (Search word list for exact match), 390
SEVS (Roots and vectors of a symmetric matrix), 207
SUBS (Punch subject score vector), 139
SUMF (Sum X or sum X^2 from a vector), 124
SUMF2 (Less efficient version of SUMF), 125
TDRS (Transposed-data intercorrelation), 198
VORS (Varimax rotation of factor structure), 214
Subroutine, 23, 115, 120
 correlation, 191
 statistical, 123
Subscale, 173
Subscript, 49, 50, 64, 118, 143
 delta, 145
 reversal, 144, 195
Subtraction, 51, 70
 matrix, 147
Successive intervals, 318
Sum
 of cross-products, 127
 of squares error, 282
 of X and X^2, 124
Summation notation, 142
Summated ratings, 319
Supermatrix, 283
Superscript (*see* Exponent)
Suppressor, 301
Symbol, 327
 language, 15
 manipulator, 25
Symmetric matrix (*see* Matrix)
Synonym, 366
Syntactic equivalence, 366
Syntax errors, 17
System
 monitor, 58
 number, 341-342
 programming, 22

Table, 50
  contingency, 41, 326
  indexing, 66
Tabulation, 327
Tape
  in AVAR23, 259
  in CANONA, 286
  computers without, 185
  in CONTAB, 328
  in CORS, 192
  in DISTAT, 183
  in FACTOR, 221
  magnetic, 5–8, 24, 58
  paper, 5
  statements, 61–63
TAT, 22, 338
Terminating a program, 82
Test
  multiple-choice, 164
  of hypotheses, 282, 372
  scoring, 167, 170
  vectors, 237
Time
  access (see Access time)
  sharing, 10–12, 17, 26, 27
Title control card, 132
Trace, 208, 219
Tracing
  inferences, 340
  programs, 89, 90
Transfer of control (see Control)
Transformation, 217, 237
Transpose, 144
  data matrix, 312
  factor analysis, 309
  in AXBS routine, 151
t ratio, 131, 247
Trials, 249
True branch, 74
Truncation, 70–71
T scores, 183
Typewriter, 31

Unequal N, 257
Unit
  length, 160
  vector, 146, 298
Univac-I, 5
Univariate analysis, 273

Validities, 285, 294
  cross, 297, 368
Variable, 47–49
  array, 49, 51

composite, 281, 318
criterion, 281
dependent and independent, 246
dimensioned, 50
dimensions, 51, 119
format, 68, 112
index, 65
list, 60, 63
names in subprograms, 117
sets, 282
simple, 50, 89
suppressor, 301
Variance, 99, 213
  analysis of, 246, 282
  common-shared, 218, 281
Variation, unique, 219
Varimax rotation, 214
Vector, 50, 143
  denormal, 207
  equality, 144
  indexing, 64
  of a matrix, 207, 269
  output, 134–135
  products, 149
  row and column, 143
  scalar, 146
  of scores, 139
  in subprogram, 118
  test, 237
  transpose, 144
  unit, 146, 298
Verbal data, 25, 338

Weights
  beta, 285, 294
  discriminant, 271
  factor score, 213, 217
  regression, 281
  verbal response, 368
Whirlwind I, 4
Wilk's Lambda, 272
Word
  of storage, 8, 340, 341
  root (see Root)
WRITE statement, 62–63

X specification, 52, 56

Yates correction, 333

z probability, 131
z scores, 161, 183, 198, 312, 319, 372
Zero scale values, 322
Zone punch, 30